Biology at Wor

Stephen Tomkins
Michael J. Reiss
and
Christina Morris

edited by
Stephen Tomkins

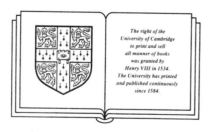

The right of the University of Cambridge to print and sell all manner of books was granted by Henry VIII in 1534. The University has printed and published continuously since 1584.

Cambridge University Press

Cambridge
New York   Port Chester
Melbourne   Sydney

Published by the Press Syndicate of the University of Cambridge
The Pitt Building, Trumpington Street, Cambridge CB2 1RP
40 West 20th Street, New York, NY 10011 - 4211, USA
10 Stamford Road, Oakleigh, Victoria 3166, Australia

First published 1992

Printed in Great Britain by Scotprint, Musselburgh, Scotland

A catalogue record for this book is available from the British Library.

ISBN 0 521 38962 3 paperback

Cover illustration by Julie Tolliday

The authors and publishers are grateful to the following for permission to reproduce photographs: 4, PBI, Cambridge Ltd; 5, Tick Ahearn; 12, 20, 104, Nigel Cattlin/Holt Studios Ltd; 13, Horticulture Research International, Wellesbourne; 19, The Independent/Paul Freestone; 26, 27, Reed Farmers Publishing Group; 34, 35, 36, Gill Harris; 48, David Thompson/Oxford Scientific Films; 51, A, B, C, D, Jenny Chapman; 55, 71, 135, Biophoto Associates; 58, Unilever Research; 61, AEA Technology; 70, Ancient Art & Architecture Collection; 73, Greene King plc; 83, from R. Scott: *Cheesemaking Practice*, Applied Science Publishers Ltd, London, 1982; 86, Societé Anonyme des Caves et Producteurs Réunis; 96*l*, Cellmark Diagnostics, Blacklands Way, Abingdon Business Park, Abingdon, Oxon; 96*r*, Dept. of Genetics, University of Leicester; 103*t*, H. Lörz; 103*b*, Date Palm Developments, subsidiary of Twyford Plant Laboratories Ltd, Glastonbury, England; 111*t*, Barry V. Charlwood, King's College London; 111*b*, 112*l*, M.W. Fowler; 126, Popperfoto; 129*t*, Jeremy Hartley/Oxfam; 139, Harlow Primate Laboratory, University of Wisconsin; 140; Tom Partridge/Chris Fairclough Colour Library; 142, Reproduced by permission of Sigmund Freud Copyrights Colchester/Freud Museum, London; 143, from D.P.H. Jones & M.G. McQuiston: *Interviewing the Sexually Abused Child* (London, Royal College of Psychiatrists, 1988); 150 © Barry Marsden; 155, Angus Dalgleish; 163, Tim Beddow/Science Photo Library; 164, Associated Press; 166, The Society of Antiquaries, London; 178, the Cystic Fibrosis Research Trust; 184*t*, The Bedfordshire and Cambridgeshire Wildlife Trust; 184*bl*, © Ian Hepburn; 184*br*, 215, E.A. Janes/Natural History Photographic Agency; 187, Eric and David Hosking; 194, Simon Fraser/Science Photo Library; 202, © T.C. Whitmore; 211, Mark Edwards/Still Pictures; 214, Zoological Society of London, © Zoo Operations Ltd; 218, Bryan & Cherry Alexander; 220, Timothy Walker/Oxford Botanic Garden; 223, High Iltis; 243, the National Rivers Authority.

Contents

Acknowledgements   iv

Preface   v

How to use this book: an introduction for
the student reader   vi

Part I Food and Food Production

1   Wheat: A Major Human Food   1

2   Integrated Pest and Weed Control   9

3   The Biology of Pig Production   18

4   The First Fast Food: The Biology of
Milk Production   25

5   At Work With the Vet   33

6   Harvesting Fish from the Sea   38

7   Bees and Honey   47

8   Cooking and Keeping Food Fresh   54

Part II Genes, Bugs and Cultures

9   Genetic Engineering   63

10   Beer and Wines   70

11   Yoghurt and Cheese   78

12   The Enzyme Revolution   87

13   DNA Fingerprinting   94

14   New Techniques in Plant Breeding   99

15   Chemicals in Culture: Using Plant Cells
for Chemical Synthesis   107

16   Recognising Self and Non-Self:
The Development of Immunotechnology   115

Part III Human Health and Hygiene

17   Clean Water for All   125

18   A Doctor's Duties   133

19   How Children Grow Up Happy   138

20   You Are What You Eat: A Review of
Human Nutrition   144

21   AIDS, HIV and the Search for a Cure   153

22   Cancer   160

23   Transplantation Today   166

24   Cystic Fibrosis: The European Disease   176

Part IV Our Environment

25   Woodland Conservation   182

26   Acid Rain   188

27   Global Greenhouse? Watching
the Carbon Cycle   197

28   Are We Making Deserts? The Ecology
of the African Drylands   205

29   Pandas, Polar Bears and Zoos   214

30   Botanic Gardens and Gene Banks   220

31   Where There's Muck There's Money   226

32   Monitoring Water Pollution   235

Matrix Charts

1   Biology Topic Index   246

2   Biology Career Index   247

Alphabetical Index   248

Acknowledgements

The authors would like to thank their families and spouses, most particularly Jenny Chapman, Mark Tester and Helga Tomkins, for their individual help, constant encouragement and, above all, their forbearance. We must also make special acknowledgement of the written contribution by Dr Mary Holt to Chapter 5, and to Dr Dick Dickinson, whose contribution to another chapter was considerable. We are also very grateful to Julie Fossitt for her support, encouragement and advice.

We would also like to thank the following professional biological scientists, researchers, consultants, university teachers and school teaching colleagues who gave of their valuable time, either in advice or in reading drafts: Mr Martin Adams, Dr Roger Austin, Ms Tara Bartley, Mr Norman Bleehan, Professor Sir Roy Calne, Dr Sally Corbet, Dr David Hanke, Professor Robert Hinde, Mr Ian Harvey, Dr David Ingram, Mr Penry Jones, Dr Colin Law, Mrs Anne Mansell, Dr C.D. Piggott, Dr Tom Ap Rees, Mr Daniel Wiedermann, Mrs Lindsey Withers, Professor Martin Wolfe and Mr Ian Woodward.

For help with library research we would like to thank Mr Richard Savage of the Botany Library, Cambridge most specifically, and also his colleagues, the librarians of the Cambridge University Departments of Applied Biology, Genetics and Zoology, the University Scientific Periodicals Library, the main University Library, the University Medical School Library at Addenbrookes Hospital, and Mr Derek Bates, the Librarian at the Fisheries Laboratory in Lowestoft.

Also for help with the provision of information, or in their support of those acknowledged above, we would like to thank the Ministry of Agriculture Fisheries and Food, the Nature Conservancy Council's Data Support for Education, the University of Cambridge School of Clinical Medicine and its Department of Clinical Oncology and Radiotherapeutics, the Cambridge University Department of Zoology, Botany, Genetics and Applied Biology, the John Innes Institute (Norwich), Plant Breeding International (Cambridge), Advanced Technologies (Cambridge) Ltd, the Science and Plants for Schools programme at Homerton College, and the Société de Roquefort.

For help with the vicissitudes of wordprocessing we are indebted to colleagues Mr John Banfield and Mr Peter Thomas. We are also grateful to the Cambridge University Press production team, particularly Lucy Harbron, Callie Kendall for her picture research, Judy Oglethorpe, Jeff Edwards for the illustrations and Chris McLeod.

Preface

The twentieth century has seen an explosion of biological knowledge. The impact of new science upon the disciplines of biochemistry, genetics, microbiology, animal and plant physiology, behaviour studies and ecology has been vast. The explosion has been echoed in a consequent revolution in biological technology. Crop science, animal husbandry, food production, medicine, nutrition, health care and environmental management have all been transformed by new understanding. For the student of biology this has meant a race to keep up to date with the applications of biology that penetrate so many areas of our lives. Now that the life sciences are so extensive how can students of biology be helped to appreciate recent developments?

This book is aimed at young scientists, particularly those in the sixth form, who need snapshots of 'biology at work' to see how their science is applied in real life. Of course, biology students learn from their own experience of doing practical science and project work. They also learn from their teachers and from radio, television and video. However, students must also develop the habit of reading extensively, for reading is the fastest means the brain has of receiving information! Good text books should enable students to gather the facts and concepts surrounding many biological ideas. But it is not possible for text books to present very full accounts of the applications of biology, nor is it their prime function. This book is a reader and is not intended to be a text book. Although good popular biology articles are regularly published in periodicals, magazines and newspapers they are not available to a class of students as a single volume. It is hoped that this book may provide such a common experience of extension-reading for a whole class at one time. Teachers know how useful this facility can be.

Biology at Work contains 32 chapters showing applied life sciences in their day-to-day context. It has been written by practising teachers. Each chapter complements some of the many different theoretical topics covered by the upper secondary biology courses. This book cannot be comprehensive, but is intended to be a complete package of the diversity of human activities in 'applied biology'.

As courses become more modular it is right that students should be able to explore across the whole field. The book has four loosely defined sections: food production, biotechnology, health and environment. The authors' aim throughout has been to stretch young minds with the ideas of science, with its excitement and its potential for good. The objectives have been to cover a broad ground, to focus on applicability, to extend experience and vocabulary, to deepen understanding and to produce a maturity of technical thought that our future citizens will need.

One further dimension of the book is to give sensitive treatment to contemporary ethical issues in farming, food production, food processing, medicine, the new genetic technology and environmental matters. Student discussion of these implications is encouraged by the 'thought questions' that go with each chapter. Some are followed by suggestions for practical activities. Follow-up study is encouraged through the 'further reading' references at the end of each chapter. Students studying on their own may be guided to a relevant chapter by means of the matrix chart at the end of the book. A second chart is designed to help in biological career choices.

S.P.T. 1991

How to use this book: an introduction for the student reader

This is not a text book in biology; it is a reader. It is written in the hope that you will sit down and go into one chapter at a time. Set aside about half an hour, read slowly and follow the story. At the end, think about some of the questions provided. Some of the key words in bold type may be useful. It may help you in your biology course if you then write a few notes on what you have remembered in particular about the chapter. Keep these notes in with your class work on the related topic. Each chapter also has some suggestions for further reading. If you find one area of particular interest you may want to follow it further by going on to read popular science paperbacks and articles in good science journals.

It is intended that this book will:

- reinforce your understanding of biology
- show you the way in which many areas of science combine together when biology is applied to everyday living
- lead you to see how biology is important to an understanding of a whole range of issues
- set you thinking more deeply about the subject and perhaps your own career.

The topic chart on page 246 is designed to help you plan your reading around your other studies. The second chart on page 247 illustrates how the chapters tie in with possible future careers in biology.

Good reading!

Stephen Tomkins
Michael Reiss
Christina Morris

1
Wheat: A Major Human Food

Both wheat and the bread that we make from it are fundamentally important to our lives; we may even take them for granted. But what is the origin of this vital plant which is now the world's major food source? How has it been selected? How is it grown to give maximum yields, and how are biologists going to direct its future? This chapter addresses these and other questions.

Wheat is important because it turns sunshine into an edible form of energy with great efficiency. It is the basic ingredient of not only bread but also biscuits, cakes, pasta and many 'cereals'. We feed it to cattle, pigs and poultry, as well as to ourselves, so it has an even wider importance in the human food chain than most of us would guess. The story of the crop goes back to the late Stone Age when hunter-gatherers first took wild grasses and applied their primitive knowledge to produce more and better food. Over centuries of both natural and artificial selection, the wheat plant has slowly been improved. In the last hundred years alone the applications of biological technology have increased wheat yields by a factor of more than four.

Origins

Wheat originated as a crop from the wild grasses of the Middle East around 8000 BC. Today, three domesticated species are recognised:

Triticum aestivum is the principal bread wheat;

Triticum durum is the hard wheat grown for pasta;

Triticum dicoccum is the ancient wheat 'emmer'.

These are **polyploids** that have arisen by **hybridisation**, the combined chromosome numbers being responsible for the development of larger and bigger grained plants. The story of wheat evolution has been put together by studying fossil remains of the seeds found in such places as the tombs of the Pharaohs. Microscopic study of the chromosomes of present-day wheat and wild grasses from the Middle East has shown that the 'emmer' wheat came from two grass species that hybridised. One variety of this evolved into the *durum* wheat, whilst another, also thousands of years ago, hybridised with a different grass to give our modern bread wheat. The ancient grass-like wheats are occasionally used today by plant breeders seeking alleles (genes) to improve or change the crop. Ancient crop varieties and wild plants are an important source of **genetic diversity**.

The plant features of wheat

A good wheat plant should germinate quickly and grow fast when planted. This makes it competitive with weeds which may otherwise smother it. If the young plant tillers well it produces several more plantlets from the base, each of which produces a leafy stalk and eventually a flowering and seeding head. A plant may produce about four or five stalks, each of which bears about six leaves up the stem. The more leaf area there is the more photosynthesis can occur. The last and highest leaf, the 'flag leaf', encloses the **flowering head**, made up of numerous **spikelets**, each of which contains several little flowers. Each of these **florets** produces a hard one-seeded fruit, the **grain**. When the mature seeding head or **ear** is ripe the grain will break off from the stalk of the head relatively easily.

The broken stalk and scales, which have been separated from the head, make up the **chaff**.

The varieties and uses of wheat

In Britain, *Triticum aestivum* wheats are classified as **feed-wheat** or **bread-wheat** according to their uses. Feed-wheats are the bulk of UK production and are fed, with little processing, straight to cattle, pigs and poultry. Much of the protein and energy value in such products as milk, meat and eggs has therefore come indirectly from feed-wheat.

Autumn-sown varieties (sown in October) are called **winter wheats**. Spring-sown varieties (sown in March) are known as **spring wheats**. The latter may follow an autumn-harvested crop, like sugar-beet, but do not yield quite so well at harvest-time. Winter wheat planted in the spring will not flower and seed the following summer, for it requires a cold winter period. This maturation process in the cold is called **vernalisation**. Commonly grown winter wheat varieties are 'Avalon' and 'Norman'. The first of these is a bread-wheat and the latter a feed-wheat.

Durum wheat, used for pasta, is grown in hotter climates than that in the UK, for example in Italy. It is richer in wheat protein (gluten) and is therefore more sticky and elastic when wet.

In making bread flour, a process of rolling the grain is followed by sieving to divide the wheat-seed embryo from the rest of the grain. This leaves the starchy **endosperm** (see Figure 1.2). The rough outer pericarp, testa and aleurone are separated as a by-product, **bran**, whilst the embryo itself is collected as the **wheatgerm**. For the finer milling of white flour the white endosperm alone is used. **Free-milling** varieties separate easily in these processes. This quality is usually found in hard wheats rather than in soft wheats where strong adhesion between starch and protein requires greater milling forces. Greater damage is done to starch grains in hard wheats during milling and this increases the water absorption of the milled flour, an important requirement in making a good dough. 'Strong' bread wheat is hard-grained and contains between 11% and 14% protein by dry weight.

1.1 Crop features of wheat

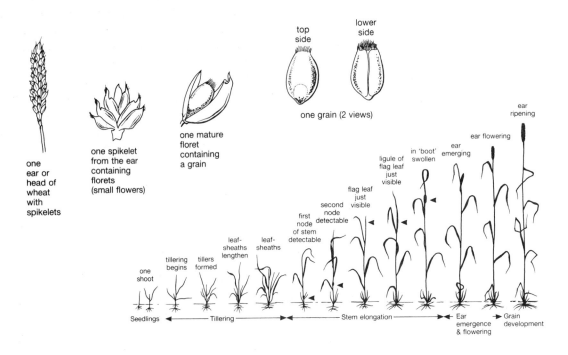

one ear or head of wheat with spikelets

one spikelet from the ear containing florets (small flowers)

one mature floret containing a grain

one grain (2 views)

top side

lower side

one shoot

tillering begins

tillers formed

leaf-sheaths lengthen

leaf-sheaths

first node of stem detectable

second node detectable

flag leaf just visible

ligule of flag leaf just visible

in 'boot' swollen

ear emerging

ear flowering

ear ripening

Seedlings — Tillering — Stem elongation — Ear emergence & flowering — Grain development

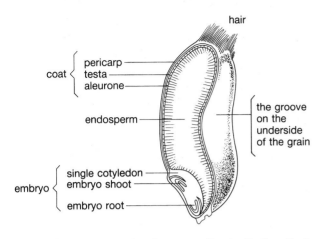

1.2 The structure of a wheatgerm (longitudinal section)

By far the most important quality in flour for bread-making is the nature, not the amount, of the protein that the wheat contains. Those proteins giving rise to 'strong' dough allow expansion in baking to produce a well aerated loaf. **Gliadins** give the dough viscosity and extensibility whilst **glutenins** give the dough elasticity. Another good bread-making quality is a low **amylase** content, for amylase breaks down the starch to sugar and can make the bread sticky to cut. **Brown** flour, for making brown bread, has some of the germ and bran returned to it. **Wholemeal** flour comes from the whole grain, milled without separation of the bran and germ. Some brown bread does not have very much fibre when compared to true whole-

meal. Wholemeal bread has a lower energy content and more fibre, protein and vitamins than the refined white breads. Most refined white breads have added vitamins and bleaching agents.

Wheat breeding

Plant breeding is carried out very largely by crossing different varieties and then selecting the progeny for particular features over a number of generations (see also Chapter 14).

The plant breeder needs to know what to look for. Fast spring growth with rapid nitrate uptake leads to more leaf, the capture of a greater amount of solar energy and hence more growth. Success in this first phase is important for it gives the young plant a maximum investment in flower formation. After pollination, when many ears have been formed, each with many grains, the filling of each grain depends largely on the success of the photosynthesis following flowering. The ear itself and the flag leaf contribute much to this second phase of growth. Drought induces ageing in the leaves, through release of the **senescence** hormone **abscisic acid (ABA)**. Growth of the grain may therefore be checked by translocation of the hormone through the phloem to the ear. Varieties which are genetically lower ABA-producers are found to be more drought tolerant.

The most successful modern wheats are 'dwarfed' because if the straw is too long the crop is

		Whole Wheat	Bran	Endosperm	Wheat Germ
Starch g/100g		66.8	23.0	73.9	28.7
Sugars g/100g		1.7	3.8	1.4	16.0
Fibre g/100g		7.0	36.4	3.1	15.6
Protein g/100g		12.6	14.1	9.4	26.7
Fat g/100g		1.8	5.5	1.3	9.2
Vitamins	B_1 mg/100g	0.31	0.89	0.10	2.01
	B_2 mg/100g	0.07	0.36	0.03	0.72
	B_3 mg/100g	4.0	29.60	0.70	4.50
Minerals	Iron mg/100g	4.0	12.9	1.8	9.7
	Calcium mg/100g	35.0	98.0	13.0	58.0
Energy kJ/100g		1377	872	1450	1276

Table 1.1 The nutritional composition of the wheat grain fractions

more likely to fall over. This is called **lodging**. Another advantage of the wheat being dwarfed is that more photosynthetic product is diverted to the grain in the ear and less is used in making the straw long. This increases grain yield. Single alleles control the production of particular gliadin and glutenin proteins.

The wheat breeder's selection criteria may therefore include:

- rapid early growth
- good response to fertilisers
- high leaf surface in the area occupied by the crop
- short straw
- large ear and flag leaf
- many grains to the ear
- tolerance of varying climatic conditions, especially drought
- pest and disease resistance
- milling and bread-making qualities
- amino acid balance in the protein.

1.3   Two different varieties of wheat in trial plots

Breeding is achieved by an initial **crop testing** for these qualities followed by the application of Mendelian genetics. Varieties with favoured features are crossed together. Sometimes **backcrossing** is employed to bring some valued feature from an old variety into the new breed. Some plant-breeding work is very advanced technically and may involve moving a particular chromosome or even alleles at one gene locus from one variety to another. From initial laboratory crosses favoured pedigree lines may be established. Very often large numbers of plants are grown in the field and subjected to **mass selection** in which undesired plants are weeded out. This is **artificial selection**, where a human agency does the selecting. The breeder may also more closely imitate the operation of **natural selection**. The crop may, for example, be infected with a disease and those plants' seeds that survive are harvested. Early maturation of a crop may be selected for by harvesting the grain when only a small fraction of it is ripe. Seed will come from plants which are more likely to have genetic characters for early ripening.

Once the breeder has a new, virtually **pure breeding variety**, homozygous at almost every gene locus, it has to be tested by an independent organisation to see that it really is a new crop variety. Plant breeders have a sort of patent on any such new **attested variety** (Plant Breeder Rights 1964). The more of a variety that farmers grow, the bigger the royalty that is paid to the breeder. Wheat produced by a plant breeder is given a variety name. 'Hobbit' is a variety that pioneered the way for the modern dwarf wheats.

Husbandry, harvests and yield

After the breeders have done their best, it is up to the farmer, by **good husbandry**, to help the plant to realise its genetic potential. How can this be done? The proportion of solar energy that is converted by photosynthesis to useful chemical energy in the wheat plant depends on **physical** and **biotic factors** during the growth period. The art of farming is largely to control as many of these factors as possible so as to optimise yields.

Choosing the right climate is important. North-west Europe is ideal for wheat, with 10–11 growing months in a year. The European Community (EC) is a net exporter of wheat. Cultivating a good seed-bed, sowing at the right time, managing the attacks of pests and diseases to minimise damage, and encouraging growth with judicious application of the right fertiliser are not easy. But at the end of the summer, when the plants have grown, flowered and set seed, the crop is ready for harvest (see also Chapter 2).

Traditionally harvesting was done late into the autumn and involved hand-reaping with a sickle, standing sheaves (bundles) in a 'stock' to dry, carting the dried crop to the farmyard, threshing the 'ears' from the straw, and winnowing the seed grain from the chaff. Mechanised reaping began in the eighteenth century with the development of a reciprocating cutter and binder, the sheaves being threshed mechanically in the farmyard. Since the middle of the twentieth century **combine(d) harvesters** have brought all these operations together in one large machine. The reaper is at the front and the thresher in the middle. The straw and chaff are ejected at the rear of the machine and the grain put into a tank before being off-loaded onto a tractor-trailer as harvesting is in progress. Winter wheat is ready for harvesting before spring wheat. It needs to have a hard grain and be as dry as

1.4 A combined harvester at work

possible before harvesting can begin.

In 1984, 512 million tonnes of wheat were produced worldwide, which is a higher seed tonnage than for any other crop. In 1983 the total UK wheat crop was 10.8 million tonnes of which 3.6 million tonnes were milled for human consumption, 4.7 million tonnes were used for animal feed, 0.4 million tonnes were used for seed and 2.1 million tonnes were exported. Wheat is close to being the perfect human food. Its amino acid spectrum (in wheat proteins) is close to the human amino acid requirement. It is only deficient in the amino acid lysine.

The breeders and the agrochemical and farm machinery manufacturers have been so successful that yields have gone up and up. From 1900 to 1940, 2 tonnes per hectare (tonnes per ha) was an average yield. By the 1960s this had doubled to 4 tonnes per ha and today it has almost doubled again to 7 tonnes per ha (the national average in the record 1984 year was 7.6 tonnes per ha). In East Anglia 8 tonnes per ha is average and 12 tonnes per ha of winter wheat is not uncommon. The yields from spring varieties (5% of the UK crop) are lower because of the shorter growing season. Straw yields are 3-4 tonnes per ha.

Catching the sunshine

We can calculate the efficiency with which wheat converts sunlight into stored chemical energy. The total harvest yield of grain is about half of the tonnage of grain, chaff and straw together; that is, the **harvest index** is 50%. The **standing crop biomass** at harvest is therefore potentially 24 tonnes per ha per annum. We must not forget the roots, however. These are about 10% of the plant and need to be added, giving a **net production** of about 26.4 tonnes per ha per annum. The wheat plant has produced more food than this, for some has been lost in respiration to enable it to stay alive and some has gone to feed its predators and parasites. Losses to respiration are likely to be 35% and to pests and diseases 2%, if the crop has been well protected. This means that the **gross produc-**

tion, from photosynthesis, is as high as about 42 tonnes per ha per annum. As yields are always expressed as inclusive of 15% moisture content, we must reduce this proportionately (42 x 85%) to 35.7 tonnes per ha dry weight. This is the **gross photosynthetic production.**

How much energy, in terms of joules does this contain? The average energy content of biomass is 1.7×10^4, kilojoules per kilogram (kJ per kg). This is the same as 1.7×10^7 kJ per tonne. The product of these two figures (35.7 tonnes per ha and 1.7×10^7 kJ per tonne) gives a **gross energy yield** of up to 6.07×10^8 kJ per hectare in one year.

We may now compare this energy production with the energy input. For a full farming year, the photosynthetically active wavelengths of light energy, in sunshine, falling on the crop is about 1.6×10^{10} kJ per ha. Dividing the energy output, in the gross photosynthetic production, by this input of usable light, we may see that the crop is making a conversion of sunlight to chemical energy of 3.8%. This is equivalent to capturing 1.9% of the total solar radiation. This is a relatively high figure for **primary production**, only exceeded by some C4 tropical grasses. If allowance is made for **photorespiration** (a light-induced respiratory loss) it approaches the theoretical maximum for photosynthesis of 8 light quanta per mole of carbon dioxide fixed. Future breeding attempts to increase yields further will probably focus on the photosynthetic mechanism, perhaps improving the efficiency of **ribulose bisphosphate carboxylase** (Rubisco) enzyme action inside the chloroplast.

Biological production and economic efficiency

It is common to think of such **biological production** as being the same as **economic production.** There is an obvious connection - the more a farmer can produce the richer he or she will become. They are not the same, however, and one must be careful to see that an expression like 'increased production' is meaningfully defined.

The plant physiologist, who studies the way the plant works, is interested in how efficiently the plant turns sunshine into plant material that can be harvested. As we have seen, this is high for wheat. But such efficiency in **primary production** is not enough; the biomass of the material produced needs to be in the form of a useful, saleable product, in this case grain. Here the plant breeder comes in to help, raising the **harvest index**, that is the proportion of the crop contributing to yield, and also the **quality** of the crop. At the outset the farmer needs to ensure that the grain is produced as cheaply as possible, for costly inputs detract from the profits. Nothing must be wasted.

The farmer's capacity to help wheat reproduce itself efficiently comes first. The amount of seed planted is about 200 kg per ha. If the yield is 7 tonnes per ha, there is a 35-fold increase in grain. Without good husbandry of the crop it is less. With good care many more plants survive, grow, flower and seed, and the yield is greater. Applied fertilisers and pesticides must pay for themselves by direct contributions to yield, for in terms of the farmers' economic survival, it is such measures of 'efficiency' that count most. At the end, harvesting must be done without loss of the vital product through problems such as lodging of the crop, spilling of grain, or loss of grain quality. Finally, the grain price is critical; a high yield is of little value if the prices crash as a result of over-production.

Biologists should not ignore agricultural economics for it is part of human ecology! In the EC, the wheat price for UK farmers has in the past been supported by an annual subsidy of up to £3.35 thousand million. Because of this, wheat prices have become inflated to over 100 per tonne, so protecting farmers from the high costs of overheads involved in high-input agricultural methods. Surplus wheat is stored to protect and maintain the market. In the EC there is a 'grain mountain' of more than 6 million tonnes. Contrary to popular supposition this represents only a few months' consumption and is therefore sensible. It has been said that it should all be shipped to Third World countries, but this would not help those countries with their own food production problems in the long term.

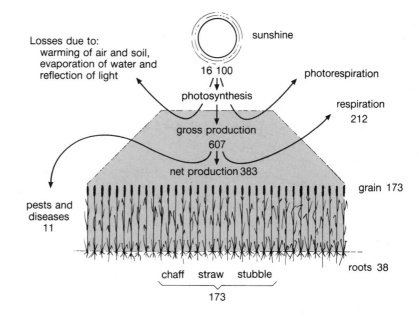

1.5 *The annual energy flow through a hectare of winter wheat. 16,000 energy units of photosynthetically active wavelength light, as sunshine, is available to the plants. Only 173 of these energy units end up in the grain (each unit on the diagram is 10,000 kilojoules)*

Straw and fuel – new ideas are needed

Farmers also have economic and production problems with straw. Biologists should be aware of the problems it causes and possibilities it offers. Long straw was traditionally used for thatching but short straw, which has also been through a combine, is quite unsuitable for this purpose. Straw is often baled for use as animal bedding, but there is little demand for all the straw produced in the East of England, where most of the wheat is grown and where there are fewer livestock. Straw may be ploughed back into the soil, but with the lower fertility levels of agrochemically treated soils, which are so dependent on fertiliser additions for nutrient enrichment, it does not rot down speedily. If extra nitrogen is added to the soil and the fertility level raised the straw does incorporate faster but this is initially expensive in fertilisers. Straw soaked with ammonia to make a fermented cattle feed is a recent development, taking a small fraction of the product.

The burning of straw has for many years been the farmers' favoured solution. The 3.5 million tonnes burned in Britain each year removes an unwanted product, at the same time destroying some economically harmful weed seeds and returning some nutrients rapidly to the soil. The argument against burning includes the damage it does to hedgerows, wild plants, birds and mammals in the fields. Burning also causes atmospheric pollution with smoke and smuts, a smoke hazard to vehicles and the loss of sunshine. The negative factors may not affect the farmer economically, but they reduce the quality of life for the community as a whole. For these reasons much field burning of straw is being phased out by legislation.

There are potential alternative uses. The cellulose in straw could in theory provide a raw material for fibreboard, plastics, absorbents, binders, thickeners and alcohol production through biotechnological processes. It is, however, bulky and hence expensive to transport. As a fuel with a low sulphur content it can be used on the farm for heating and for electricity generation.

One energy aspect of modern wheat farming that is not so impressive is the high requirement for fossil fuels (see Table 1.2). Although the fuel requirement for machinery used in the field is not very great, enormous amounts of fossil fuel energy do go into the manufacture of farm machinery and the production of chemical herbicides, pesticides and most particularly fertilisers. In energy terms, what is most wasteful is the burning of straw. The same amount of energy is lost by straw burning as is required to run the machinery employed in growing the crop in the first place. Taking the

Quantifiable inputs	10^{12} kJ	Product outputs	10^{12} kJ
All fuels	67	Harvested grain	387
Fertilisers	62	Straw (burned)	65
Other chemicals	6	Straw (baled)	105
Machinery	39		
Other	31		
Total	205	Total	557

Table 1.2 Annual energy inputs and outputs in cereal harvesting in the UK/10^{12} kJ

(from various sources including D.J. White and R.B. Austin (pers comm))

overall picture more fossil fuel energy is used in producing wheat and in then processing it into food (milling and baking) than is harvested as energy in the grain. (Table 1.2 inputs) In this sense our intensive farming system in the UK is wasteful of the earth's non-renewable (fossil fuel) resources. This waste is particularly apparent when compared with farming methods employed by very poor people in less developed countries.

Modern wheat-farming practices depend on cheap fossil fuel. For this reason, if the economic system changes, or if for environmental reasons the burning of fossil fuels is reduced, plant breeders will need to make changes accordingly to the crops. Many biologists are therefore investigating ways of breeding wheat plants that can withstand pest and disease attacks better, without the need for expensive chemical inputs. It may even be possible in the future to produce wheat plants which fix nitrogen for themselves, as leguminous plants do. This would save fossil fuel energy through making better use of sunshine, although conventional yields might need to be lower than they are today. Wheat may be bred in the future for different aims, but we are fortunate to have such a marvellous plant to work on.

Further reading

Austin, R. B. (1986) *Molecular Biology and Crop Improvement*. Cambridge University Press.
Body, R. (1982) *Agriculture: The Triumph and the Shame*. Maurice Temple Smith.
Lupton, F.G.H. (1985) Wheat. *Biologist* 32:2.
Lowe, Philip *et al.* (1986) *Countryside Conflicts*. Gower Publishing.

Thought questions

1 How would you transfer a genetic character for salt tolerance, present in a wild salt-marsh wheat grass, into a modern wheat so that the crop could be grown in a saline environment?

2 How might breeding for low amylase content in wheat grains conflict with the requirement for successful germination?

3 If wheat is such an efficient plant, why does it not grow wild in the countryside on its own?

4 In Brazil, sugar-cane is used to produce alcohol which is then used as a fuel for vehicles. What would be the crop requirements of a wheat plant grown for fuel rather than food?

Things to do

Kneading science?
Mix 25g of bread-making flour with just sufficient water to make a very stiff dough. Roll the dough until it is one entire mass. Draw the dough out until it snaps. Record its length on snapping. Roll the dough ball in your hand for five seconds then pull it out again. Record the snapping distance. Repeat the rolling, drawing out and measuring until the dough is extensible for a half a metre without snapping. Plot a graph of the number of times drawn out (x) against the distance drawn out (y). What physical change is taking place during the kneading? How could you show that this extensibility is due to wheat seed-proteins?

2
Integrated Pest and Weed Control

How can we maximise food production when the population of the world continues to rise and must be fed? This chapter looks at the ways in which we can bring about better control of the crop pests, crop diseases and competing weeds that take away the food we grow before we can even harvest it. Within the European Community, self-sufficiency in many foods has been attained and yields in excess of requirements occur, notably with cereals. This is not the case in the developing countries. In areas of rapid population increase, such as Africa, Latin America and parts of Asia, annual output is barely adequate to support the present population. Increased food production is required, particularly in these developing areas. However, much productive land is disappearing beneath buildings and roads, and marginal land is being lost through desertification. Ideally agriculture must become more productive yet its methods must also be sustainable. The level of food production per unit area of land must be increased whilst preserving declining and non-renewable resources like fossil fuels.

In farming, the natural vegetation and its animal community are removed and replaced with a single species (the crop plant). The growth of the crop is then encouraged by fertilising the soil and removing crop competitors and pests such as weeds and insects. The planting of this single species produces a monoculture. The complexity of the natural plant community is replaced with plants often of a single genotype. These artificial ecosystems are designed to channel the available energy into the crop plants efficiently. They are, however, extremely fragile as the stability of the natural ecosystem has been eliminated. In a mixed-species plant community, the spread of pathogens from host to host is restricted as the other plant species act as buffers. Many plant pathogens are species-specific or at least have a limited host range. The aggregation of plants in a monoculture therefore provides ideal conditions for the development and spread of plant pathogens. On balance, however, monocultures appear simpler to manage.

The crop yields may be improved by planting high-yielding cultivated varieties (cultivars) of crop plants which have been developed through breeding programmes. Their yield potential is often reduced by weeds. The unwanted plants compete for the raw materials of photosynthesis and so limit the productivity of the crop. Losses due to disease may be considerable. A recent estimate of global losses of crops through attack by plant pathogens is about 10–15% of potential yield.

The variety of diseases, pests and competitors

A diversity of organisms cause disease and destruction to crop plants and consequently diminish yields. They include fungi, bacteria, viruses, nematodes and insects. The following will serve as examples of each of these classes.

Fungal pathogens are of particular importance in cereal crops. The most frequent and often severe disease of spring and autumn-sown cereals in the UK, particularly of barley, is powdery mildew which is caused by *Erysiphe graminis*.

Rice is susceptible to brown leaf spot caused by the fungus *Helminthosporium oryzae*. Also, epidemics of the destructive disease rice blast (caused by the fungus *Piricularia oryzae*) have occurred in Asia when large regions have been planted with a single rice cultivar.

Bacterial pathogens of crop plants are few in

the UK, although subspecies of *Erwinia carotovora* may cause potato blackleg and soft rots of various plants, including potato.

Virus diseases reduce the yield of vital food crops. For example, black streak dwarf virus of rice was particularly severe in China from 1970 to 1972. The disease then disappeared abruptly; this coincided with the appearance of strains of its vector, the plant-hopper, in which the efficiency of transmission of the virus was markedly reduced.

A potentially serious virus disease of sugar beet was first reported in the UK in 1987; 'Rhizomania' virus is spread by the highly motile zoospores of the fungus *Polymyxa beta*. The virus causes reduction in growth of the main tap root and a proliferation of the lateral roots resulting in a tiny, 'bearded' beet.

The devastation which may be caused to crops by **invertebrate pests** was demonstrated in the USA during the late nineteenth century. The Colorado beetle (*Leptinotarsa decemlineata*) spread rapidly across the continent, destroying potato crops and seriously threatening food production and the national economy.

Nematodes cause direct damage to crops and may also spread fungal pathogens within the soil. For example, *Heterodera avenae* is recognised as an important pest of oats, barley, wheat and rye in northern Europe. Other cereal pests include wireworms and leather jackets, the larvae of the cranefly. Army worms are very serious pests of wheat in African countries.

Several species of aphid feed and breed on a variety of crop plants including cereals, potatoes and brassicas. The aphids cause damage directly by sucking sap from the phloem of the plant tissues, or indirectly by acting as vectors of plant viruses.

Weeds also diminish yields. Unwanted plants compete with the crop and may at the same time be reservoirs of disease infection. For example, several viruses and the take-all pathogen of cereals (*Gaeumannomyces graminis*) frequently survive in weedy species of grass such as couch grass (*Agropyron repens*).

The control of weeds, pests and diseases

Various control measures have been adopted in an

Table 2.1 Major diseases of cereals in the UK

Causal agent	Disease	Symptoms
Erysiphe graminis	Powdery mildew	Buff-coloured pustules on leaves.
Gaeumannomyces graminis	Take-all	Blackened root system. Poorly filled ears (whiteheads).
Pyrenophora teres	Net blotch	Brown stripes or irregular blotches on leaves.
Septoria tritici	Leaf spot/stripe	Short, brown stripes on leaves. Pinhead-size black spore cases (pycnidia).
Septoria nodorum	Leaf spot/stripe and glume blotch	Irregular brown lesions with yellow margins. Occasionally very small brown pycnidia.
Rhynchosporium secalis	Scald	Grey lesions with dark brown margins.
Pseudocercosporella herpotrichoides	Eyespot	Dark brown, often eye-shaped, lesions below the first node.
Puccinia striiformis	Yellow rust	Yellow pustules on leaves, usually in stripes.
Puccinia hordei	Brown rust	Brown pustules with pale haloes.
Ustilago hordei	Loose smut	Grain replaced by a mass of black spores.
Barley yellow dwarf virus		Bright yellow leaf discoloration extending from tip to base. Stunting.

From Carlile, W.R. (1988) Control of Crop Diseases. *Edward Arnold.*

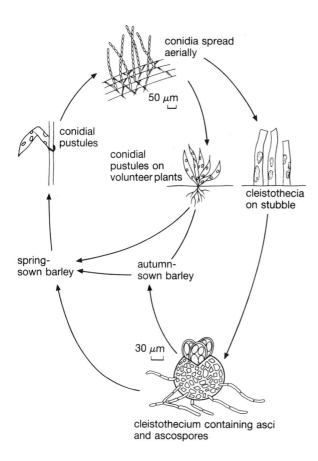

conidia spread
aerially

50 μm

conidial
pustules

conidial
pustules on
volunteer plants

cleistothecia
on stubble

spring-
sown barley

autumn-
sown barley

30 μm

cleistothecium containing asci
and ascospores

2.1 Life cycle of Erysiphe graminis hordei *(powdery mildew of barley)*

attempt to reduce crop losses and increase yields. These are: cultural practices, plant breeding, chemical control and biological control.

Cultural practices

Techniques of **crop husbandry** aim to allow the control of weeds, pests and diseases. The complete elimination of crop pathogens is difficult to achieve under field conditions. However, the removal or destruction of soil- or debris-borne inoculum will restrict the establishment and spread of disease. For example, the burning of cereal stubble, although polluting to the atmosphere, is effective in destroying many fungal pathogens. Alternative hosts such as weeds or other plant matter left after harvesting ought to be destroyed. Similarly, 'roguing' - the removal of individual infected plants - can be carried out. However, this is only economic for high-value crops, such as potatoes grown for seed tubers. The eradication of vectors such as aphids and nematodes is most effective in the control of many viral diseases. Also, plant tissue can now be assayed (tested quantitatively) for the presence of virus particles and then virus-free plants can be produced by tissue culture.

Cultivation practices such as minimal cultivation are quick and labour-efficient, but debris-borne pathogens are left on the soil surface to infect emerging seedlings.

Crop rotation has the effect of destroying species-specific pathogens by removing the host plants. Rotation has become progressively less common on arable farms in the United Kingdom, with a consequent increase in the incidence of fungal disease. Many farmers do, however, grow a 'break-crop' (for example, oil-seed rape every 4–5 years). Sugar-beet is rarely grown in the same field in consecutive years due to the risk of severe nematode attack.

The sowing of 'clean' seed is vital. Barley seed crops in the United Kingdom are routinely inspected for the fungus *Ustilago hordei* which causes loose smut. If more than 0.5% contamination by the fungus is found, then the crop may not be offered for sale as seed. Various certification schemes exist for seed and plant stock; also, there are legislative measures such as quarantine regulations and restrictions on the growing of susceptible varieties within a particular region.

Plant breeding

Since plants were first domesticated, the art of plant improvement has been practised. Seed from the best individual plants at harvest would have been selected and planted on for the next season's crop. Plant breeding today involves far more than simple selection. Usually, the breeding is 'artificial': self-pollinating plants may be deliberately crossed with pollen from another plant and difficult crosses may be achieved by genetic manipulation of embryos *in vitro*. Chemicals or irradiation may be

2.2 Sugar beet uninfected and infected with 'Rhizomania' virus. The infected root has a reduced growth and is 'bearded' with lateral roots

2.3 Grain aphids on barley ears

2.4 African Army worm caterpillars on damaged maize/corn leaf

used to induce genetic mutations (see also Chapters 9 and 14).

The principal aims of the plant breeder are to improve the quality and the yielding of the crop plant. Also important is **disease resistance** as this will directly affect both yield and quality at harvest.

Disease resistance genes have been discovered in the wild relatives and in land races (locally developed and propagated populations) of several crop plants. For example, resistance genes to late blight of potato have been found in wild species of *Solanum*, the potato genus. The preservation of these plants is very important in order that there is a wide diversity of genetic stock from which to breed. Resistance to a particular race of pathogen may be conferred by the presence of one or a few genes. The incorporation into new cultivars of the **specific resistance** to viral diseases is relatively easily achieved. For example, *Phaseolus* bean cultivars, which are resistant to common mosaic virus, have been successfully bred.

Many crop cultivars also display **nonspecific resistance** to all races of a particular pathogen. This form of resistance commonly involves the combined action of several different genes and is thus difficult to characterise and to incorporate into new cultivars.

An unfortunate consequence of the wide-scale planting of new cultivars which possess specific resistance genes is that selection pressure will be exerted on the pathogen. New races of the pathogen may arise against which the cultivar has no resistance. The potential for mutant pathogens to develop and become established as new races is high. The risk of breakdown of the specific resistance in the crop is correspondingly high.

The development of new cultivars involves the execution of carefully designed and managed **breeding programmes**, often over a period as long as 12–15 years. As shown in Figure 2.6, disease resistance may be introduced by backcross breeding. This involves the crossing of the susceptible (P_2) cultivar with a resistant cultivar, land race or wild relative, then backcrossing over several generations with the P_2 to stabilise the resistance. After each backcross, selection for disease resistance and good agronomic characteristics is carried out. Any new, genetically stable cultivar with characteristics distinct from those of all other such cultivars may then be classified within a Plant Variety

2.5 Phaseolus *bean plants both innoculated with mosaic virus; the one on the left has a specific gene resistant to the effects of the virus*

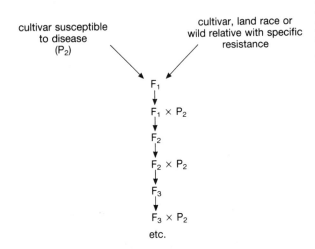

cultivar susceptible
to disease
(P_2)

cultivar, land race or
wild relative with specific
resistance

F_1

$F_1 \times P_2$

F_2

$F_2 \times P_2$

F_3

$F_3 \times P_2$

etc.

2.6 Backcross breeding programme. Selection for disease resistance and agronomic acceptability is practised after each cross

Protection scheme, and marketed. This places a sort of 'patent' on the plant variety from which royalties go to the breeder.

A simple and inexpensive means of restricting the establishment and spread of disease in crops is to grow a **mixture of cultivars**. The component cultivars are genetically different and so possess different resistance genes. The spatial density of plants susceptible to a particular pathogen is reduced and a barrier effect is provided by the resistant plants. This practice is routinely carried out for winter wheat crops grown in the USSR.

Mixtures have been found to yield as well as single cultivars and have led to large reductions in levels of disease. For example, reductions of up to 80% of powdery mildew infection in spring barley have been recorded. However, cereal cultivars may well vary in characteristics other than resistance and, consequently, harvested grain will not be uniform. For this reason, single cultivars are preferred for processing and brewing.

An alternative is the planting of **multilines**, in which the component cultivars differ only in the specific resistance genes they possess. In all other respects, the cultivars are identical and so acceptable to industry. Crop losses due to disease will be lessened as for variety mixtures, but acceptability to processors will be greater due to the uniformity of the grain. Unfortunately, the development of multilines has not been widely adopted by cereal breeders and growers as it involves complex and expensive breeding programmes.

Chemical control

As early as AD 500 the Chinese were using arsenic as a **pesticide**. However, it is since the 1950s that there has been a rapid development in this field.

The function of pesticides (herbicides, insecticides and fungicides) is to improve crop quality and prevent losses. Consequently a greater proportion of crops grown can be harvested, this being particularly important in the tropics where losses may be as high as two-thirds of the crop grown. The average increase in financial return to farmers in the UK is estimated to be £5 for every £1 spent on pesticides. The use of chemicals, particularly herbicides, also serves as a substitute for human and mechanical labour.

Many traditional **herbicides** were non-selective inorganic compounds based on arsenic which were highly toxic to animals. These have been largely superseded by various organic compounds which may be highly specific in their effects. For example, a high degree of specificity is exhibited by the auxin-like herbicides which are based on the naturally occurring hormone **indoleacetic acid (IAA)** (see Figure 2.7). These compounds are cheap to manufacture and are very effective at low concentrations. Cereals, which are monocotyledons, are unaffected by the concentrations of herbicide used, but broad-leaved weeds (dicotyledons) are caused to 'overgrow' and destroy themselves.

Early **insecticides** included both inorganic arsenicals and organic compounds, such as nicotine, which have been used in this manner since the seventeenth century. Of the wide range of synthetic organic insecticides now available, the organophosphorous compounds form a large and important group. These compounds, of which the most widely used is parathion, exhibit a range of toxicity to mammals. All have the effect of inhibit-

2.7 The structure of the naturally occurring plant hormone indole-3-acetic acid (IAA) and two synthetic compounds with similar structures (2,4-D and MCPA) which are used as weed killers

ing the enzyme cholinesterase. This causes the insect to die as a result of prolonged and unco-ordinated muscle contractions. The chlorinated hydrocarbons, such as DDT, dieldrin and aldrin, are also important insecticides. They are effective at low concentrations and are cheap to produce.

Fungicides are able to protect the plant surface (protectant fungicides) or to enter the plant (systemic fungicides) and kill fungi in the tissues. **Protectant fungicides** are effective only at the site of application and are non-specific in their action. They include many metal-based compounds, such as the copper-based Bordeaux mixture which has been used for over a hundred years to control powdery mildew.

Systemic fungicides are specific in that they inhibit a particular biochemical process. For example, benomyl forms an active compound (MBC) in the plant which inhibits the growth of powdery mildew on barley; phenylamide compounds inhibit RNA synthesis in potato blight fungi.

Major problems have arisen through the uncontrolled use of pesticides; one of these is the development of **resistance**, which arises by natural selection. For example, leaf-miner flies have become a serious potato pest in South America as they are now resistant to all main classes of insecticide. Similar problems have been encountered for the brown plant-hopper, the worst rice pest in Indonesia: the use of large quantities of insecticide killed many predatory insects and also resulted in the development of pesticide resistance in the plant-hopper. The resistance of fungi, particularly to

systemic chemicals, is also common and often develops quickly.

Various measures can be taken to avoid the development of resistance. For example, the judicious and rotational use of a variety of fungicides or of a fungicide mixture is important; also, chemicals ought to be used sparingly, according to the disease risk.

There are problems associated with the **persistence** and **toxicity** of pesticides. For example, tin- and mercury-based fungicides may shortly be withdrawn from the market in view of their toxicity to mammals. Adverse effects on non-target organisms are a major cause for concern. For example, MBC-generating fungicides affect annelids and severely deplete earthworm populations. The deleterious effects of DDT on the environment have been well documented. DDT accumulates in the adipose tissues of higher animals which are near the top of food webs. It affects the central nervous system of small mammals and the metabolism of calcium in carnivorous birds (see also Chapter 32 on pollution).

It is clear that pesticides are useful agricultural tools. However, as they are potentially dangerous chemicals it can be argued that their use should be minimised and be subject to stringent regulatory controls.

Biological control

The term **biological control** may be defined as 'the action of parasites, predators or pathogens in maintaining another organism's population density at a lower average level than would occur in their absence'. Unlike chemical control, biological control aims to reduce pest numbers without eradicating the pest entirely.

Biological controls were being used as early as the seventeenth century when fresh cow dung and urine were applied to apple trees to control canker disease!

The first successful transfer of a natural enemy from one country to another was the introduction of the mynah bird from India to Mauritius in 1762 to control the red locust. A more recent example is the importation from France to Australia of a leaf-mining moth to control the weed Salvation Jane (*Echium plantagineum*). The weed both poisons livestock and drastically reduces the production of farmland.

Biological control may therefore involve introduced antagonistic species. Alternatively, the resident flora of many soils appears to be antagonistic to many potential pathogens. The recognition and use of such 'suppressive soils' has proved useful in the control of pea wilt caused by the fungus *Fusarium*.

The treatment of seeds, bulbs and corms with microbes such as the bacterium *Bacillus* and the fungus *Penicillium* has been shown to be very effective in reducing disease levels. However, to date there has only been one commercial exploitation of the microbial control of pathogens: the surfaces of pine stumps are routinely inoculated with *Peniophera gigantea*, a microbe which is antagonistic to woodrotting fungi such as *Heterobasidion annosum*.

Soil-borne pathogens such as nematodes have

successfully been controlled by both 'trap plants' and fungi. The legume *Crotalaria spectibilis* has the effect of trapping nematodes in its roots and can be grown alongside potatoes. Nematodes are also preyed upon and trapped by over a hundred species of fungus, some of which, as shown in Figure 2.8, have constricting hyphal rings. Other fungi produce paralysing toxins.

Pheromones (volatile hormones) have been used to attract potato tuber moths away from stored potatoes; similarly, in Pakistan, plastic twist-ties have been attached to cotton plants to protect them against the cotton bollworm. The high concentration of pheromone which is released into the air by the twist-ties prevents the male bollworm from locating the female for mating. Consequently, bollworm populations are maintained at very low levels and crop losses are minimised.

Various **biological preparations** have been developed for the control of crop pests and pathogens. For example, powdered *Eucalyptus* leaves provide a simple but effective pesticide for potato crops. Extracts from the neem tree (*Azadirachta indica*) act as a natural insecticide and have been incorporated into a broad-spectrum insecticide. The first commercial pesticide based on a live, genetically engineered organism was recently produced in Australia: 'NoGall' controls crown gall disease and contains a genetically altered benign strain of the very bacterium which causes the disease, *Agrobacterium tumefaciens*. The benign strain produces an antibiotic which is lethal to its pathogenic relative.

Biological control is often slow, unpredictable and not without failures. Also, the development of

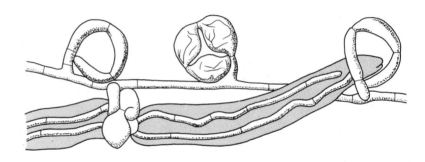

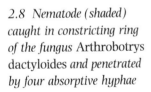

2.8 Nematode (shaded) caught in constricting ring of the fungus Arthrobotrys dactyloides *and penetrated by four absorptive hyphae*

'biocontrol' products may be difficult and expensive. However, such measures are long-term, sustainable and environmentally desirable.

Integrated control

In many cases, the use of a single control measure such as chemicals or biological control alone has failed to reduce crop losses. It is becoming increasingly clear that a stable solution to the problem of crop disease will come through the continuing balanced application of a range of disease control measures: **integrated pest management (IPM).**

An early success for IPM was the control of cotton pests in the Cañete Valley, an important cotton-growing region in Peru. Following the introduction in the late 1940s of organochlorine insecticides, the cotton yields of the valley initially increased but then proceeded to drop progressively year by year. By the mid-1950s the Cañete farmers were spending about 30% of their production costs on insecticides. Two main problems arose from the use of the chemicals. First, the pests began to develop resistance to the insecticides which meant that more and more insecticide had to be applied to the crops. Also, the chemicals killed not only the pests but other insects too, many of which were the natural predators of the pest species. The result was that in 1956, pests destroyed 70% of the cotton crop in the Cañete Valley.

This ineffective and expensive blanket application of insecticides was replaced with an IPM programme which involved a combination of control strategies. The valley was repopulated with beneficial insects and spraying was carried out only once or twice a year, using selective pesticides. Strict regulations governing cultivation practices, such as the time of planting and harvesting, were introduced. Regular checks of fields to estimate the levels of pests and beneficial insects were reinstituted. After only two years of the IPM programme the yields of cotton in the Cañete Valley were approaching normal, acceptable levels.

Initially the expression 'integrated control' referred simply to a combination of chemical and biological control. The concept has now been broadened and the main components of an IPM programme may include cultivation control, host resistance, biological control, **autocidal insect control** (the release of sterile or genetically altered insects) and the use of chemicals such as pheromones. IPM cannot replace pesticides completely, but it makes possible the use of slower-acting, less tenacious chemicals.

No two control programmes are likely to be identical. Before control measures are applied, detailed field studies are required to identify and count the numbers of key pests and predators in order to estimate the **economic threshold**. This threshold is the density of a pest population below which the cost of measures to control it exceeds the losses caused by it.

Integrated control programmes provide a sustainable means of controlling crop losses and so increasing yields. However, such programmes are inherently complex and their effects are often long-term and subtle. It is likely that chemicals and cultivars with specific resistance will continue to be important. If integrated control is to be implemented widely, then government agricultural departments, industry and farmers must become committed to its principles.

Further reading

Carlile, W.R. (1988) *Control of Crop Diseases*. New Studies in Biology, Edward Arnold.
van Embden, H.F. (1974) *Pest Control and its Ecology*. Studies in Biology, Edward Arnold.

Thought questions

1 Produce a table which lists the advantages and disadvantages of each of the control measures outlined in the text.

2 Which form of pest control would you advocate, and why?

3 How does an organic farmer distinguish an organic pest control method from an agrochemical one? Is there a real difference?

3
The Biology of Pig Production

The pig is a wonderful mammal; it grows very fast, reaching sexual maturity when six months old; it is efficient in its food conversion and is the source of a great variety of animal and meat products. The domestic pig is biologically quite similar to us in its digestive machinery, bone structure, blood circulation and skin. Like us, pigs are unquestionably sensitive to their physical and social environment, for they are quite intelligent; they even make exciting pets. However, in some human cultures they are reviled as unclean animals and the word 'pig' is commonly used as a term of abuse. But something about a pig often arouses human affection and in other cultures it is a highly valued and respected domestic animal. There are 9 million pigs in Britain. For most of them life is short, breeding stock alone being kept alive beyond their first year. On our farms, the pig's style of life and the manner of its death, both of which we control, raise important ethical issues for pig-meat eaters and indeed for all concerned about animal welfare.

Nomenclature

Taxonomically the pig is classified in the mammalian Order Artiodactyla, the hoofed mammals with an even number of toes. Unlike deer, sheep and cattle, however, it is not a ruminant and is closest in evolutionary kinship to the hippopotamus. The domestic pig is recently descended from the **wild boar** Sus scrofa, with which it is fully interfertile. Pigs have a complex nomenclature. An adult male pig is known as a **boar** and is distinguished from a castrated male which is called a **hog** (**castration** is the practice of removing the testicles from a male, so suppressing the action of the male sex hormone on development). An adult female is a **gilt** until she has reared her first **piglets**, after which she is termed a **sow**. Pigs are also known as **swine**. Pig meat is eaten as **pork** joints and chops or as cured **bacon** or **ham**. Any characteristic attribute of a pig may be described as **porcine**.

History and natural history

Wild boar are fierce forest animals with large canine tusks. Before their extinction from much of Europe they were feared and respected. They have **omnivorous** feeding habits. Besides eating plant matter such as roots, tubers, fruits, leaves and nuts, they ingest a great deal of soil and may also kill and eat small animals up to the size of a lamb. They associate naturally in large **family groups** in which a **territorial male** defends a small number of females and their nests. Before giving birth the female will root out a moulded hollow for herself. She then lines the nest with leaves and grass and covers it over with large branches before entering the nest to give birth, which she does lying down.

The wild boar was hunted extensively in prehistory. During the Neolithic period it gradually became a **domesticated species**, for pig bones on archaeological sites show a gradual transition to the modern form. Pigs were domesticated from about 7000 BC in Europe and perhaps even earlier in Eastern Asia. Wild piglets today may be readily tamed. Once domesticated the swine became shorter in stature, less tusky, longer, fatter, faster growing, less bristly and more docile. Although the pig is not a ruminant, and is therefore unable to digest cellulose, it can recycle much food waste from around human habitations, producing a

3.1 Domesticated wild boar

succulent meat, much lard (fat) used for cooking and as lighting oil, hides (skin) and bristles for brushes.

Pigs have their highest status in Western Asia, particularly in China and in Papua New Guinea. For Jews, Arabs and Ethiopian Christians the pig is 'unclean'. It may be that there was a biological reason for this taboo. Pigs and humans share some serious **worm parasites**. Pigs scavenge for human faeces and can become infected by *Taenia solium*, the pork tapeworm, and *Trichinella spiralis*, an intra-muscular nematode. People can be infected by both of these by eating uncooked pork.

At one time swine were kept in large herds of small free-ranging animals, particularly in woodlands to which they are well adapted. Pigs may easily be trained to come to the sound of a horn for food, and require little shepherding. In a way they behave more like dogs than sheep. Pigs kept close to the homestead were traditionally reared to be large and fat and were kept confined in a sty. Pigs are voracious feeders and will eat almost anything nutritious put before them.

The science behind pig farming

Modern pig farming has a good **scientific re-**

search foundation. Each of the following factors has a biological basis and contributes to economically successful pig farming.

- Viewed from the standpoint of ecological energetics the efficiency of a pig is measured in terms of how much of the food it is fed is converted into pig. For the first six months of life this figure is about 20%.
- This conversion is achieved most successfully if the animals are healthy, well housed and well cared for.
- Food costs are 80% of the running costs on a pig farm, so, from the farmer's point of view, the pigs should have good but cheap food, and should not waste their assimilated food energy by running around or on keeping warm.
- Ideally they should breed as fast as possible to maximise economic throughput: every piglet reared is another pig for the market.
- They should grow quickly to increase the economic turnover.
- They should produce the best quality carcase to get the highest grade price at market.
- They should be sent for slaughter before they begin to use their food wastefully (this will be when they pass puberty and no longer put on so much weight for the same amount of food fed).

Improving pig production through higher fertility

On average a wild boar sow rears about four to five piglets in a single litter in the spring. By contrast, a good farm sow may give birth at any season and averages 2.3 litters per annum. Good farm pigs will give birth to a mean of 11 piglets per litter and may therefore raise, on average, about 25 offspring a year. This is a five- to six-fold increase on the fertility of their wild ancestors. How is it achieved?

For centuries the Chinese had been selecting for **prolific pigs** (having many piglets per litter). There was an early importation of these high-yielding varieties to Britain from China in the eighteenth century, before the present pig varieties were established as breeds. This introduced **prolificacy** is

3.2 Young Large White sow and four-day-old piglets

apparently due to increased embryonic survival and not to increased ovulation. There is still interest in some modern prolific Chinese varieties. The Mei-shan sow, for example, produces 15 piglets on average and has one more pair of teats than the typical seven pairs (i.e. 16 teats instead of 14). There is a finite limit to how many piglets a sow can feed, for when numbers are high piglets compete for teats and may fight for the ownership of one position. The losers become the **runts** of the litter.

After being mated with a boar, a gilt or sow has a **gestation** (pregnancy) of 114-116 days' duration (easily remembered as 3 months, 3 weeks and 3 days). **Parturition** (the moment of birth) is known as **farrowing**. After birth the sow's **lactation**, or giving of milk, begins. Unless separated from them, the gilt or sow will suckle her piglets until they are fully able to feed themselves at eight weeks old. They are then said to be **weaned**. For production reasons weaning is brought forward as explained below.

The domestic sow has lost all seasonality in her **reproductive cycles**, but once weaning is complete her reproductive cycles will immediately start again. A sow will therefore not come back into **oestrus** (sexual receptivity to the boar) until she has completely finished weaning the piglets.

Oestrous cycles occur every three weeks. If producing the greatest number of litters per annum is to be the farmer's aim, the shorter the lactation period the better. It is therefore common practice to give piglets a supplement of milk powder pellets from the end of their first week of life so that they are encouraged to take less milk from the sow and are weaned off her milk in three weeks. Following this practice the sow will come 'into season' again about forty days after giving birth. She will by then have been taken away from her piglets, and will now be mated and start her next pregnancy. The weaned piglets of one litter are commonly joined with those of another into a large **social group**. This forms a group of animals that soon know each other intimately - greeting each other nose-to-nose and recognising each other by smell. Males will be castrated at 14 days if they are to become hogs.

Improving pig production through faster growth

The essence of fast growth is a **high nutrient input**. Proteins form a high percentage of the feed initially, but the percentage declines as the animals reach marketable size (see Table 3.1). **Proteins** in milk, fish and soya have a higher value for the animals in growth than the low-grade protein in cereals. Pigs are fed cooked animal waste from slaughter-houses (offal), but the digestibility of animal proteins declines with cooking so offal and bonemeals are second-class proteins. Some cereals, like barley, are rough and may cause scouring (diarrhoea) if given to very young pigs. All pigs are given **iron** and **vitamin** supplements.

Intensively reared pigs are given disease-free conditions that would be the envy of some people. But even under these conditions **virus diseases** like foot-and-mouth, Aujeszky's disease and meningitis are threats to health. Many farms operate quarantine arrangements for it is often human visitors who bring diseases in (see also Chapter 5).

A feeding regime such as that outlined in Table 3.1 is followed in the intensive production of pigs for pork and bacon. Figure 3.3 gives the biological basis behind this feeding regime whilst Figures 3.4 and 3.5 give the experimental evidence for the feed

Stage	Age of pigs *weeks*	Duration of stage *weeks*	Type of feed	Energy in feed *10³kJ per kg*	Protein in feed %	Biological value of protein *Highest =1.0*	Feed ration fed	Lower critical temperature °C	Notes
Sucking and creep feeding	0 – 3	3	Sow's milk, milk powder pellets	18	22%	0.85	Unlimited	34° at birth 28°	Mineral injections given
Weaning	3 – 6	3	Milk powder, soya and maize	15	20%	0.75	Unlimited	21°	Antibiotic given
Fattening	6 – 16	10	Soya, maize and barley	13	18%	0.65	Unlimited	19°	Vaccination
Finishing	16 – 24	8	Soya and barley	11	15%	0.60	Restricted to 2.5kg/ pig/day	18°	Energy intake is reduced to slow fat deposition

Table 3.1 A typical pig management regime

management system and food ration reduction from 16 weeks.

Figure 3.3 shows the **differential growth rate** of the tissues in the body of any mammal. You can apply it to yourself! Initially nervous tissue grows the fastest (mostly in early childhood), then the skeleton (in your early teens), then muscle (late teens), and then fat. Pigs are grown principally for the **muscle** (meat) and are therefore usually slaughtered before they reach puberty at 25 weeks. At this age they are still relatively lean but are beginning to increase their proportion of **body fat** (see Figure 3.4).

Figure 3.5, McMeekan's experiment, shows the effect of four different nutritional regimes. On low-level rations throughout (low-low) pigs grow

very slowly. If the low rations are increased from 16 weeks (low-high), initially rapid growth has been held back for too long for any significant recovery to be made. If fed on high-level rations throughout (high-high), pigs are often too fat to reach optimal market prices for pork and bacon. However, if switched at 16 weeks to a lower level of rations (high-low) pigs are forced to reduce their proportion of body fat to match the deficit in energy supply. This is the reason for the **finishing period**;

3.3 Differential growth rate of tissues

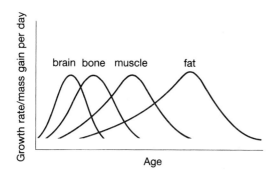

3.4 Absolute growth in mass of pig tissues

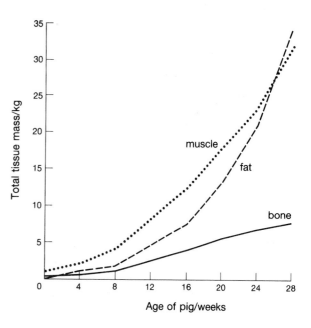

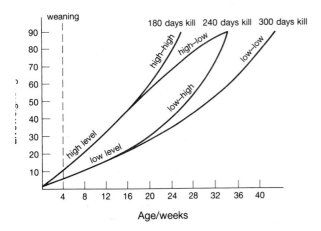

3.5 McMeekan's Experiment (see text p 21)

pigs are essentially put on a 'slimming' diet. During this time they are under some stress, being more aggressive and irritable (as you might be!), and appear to be very hungry when they are fed. Once a pig reaches 60 kg live weight its daily increment of lean meat is at a maximum, about 0.5 kg per day. This is maintained for many weeks and only begins to decline once the pig is fully mature at 120 kg. However, from the twentieth week, unless the pig is on a restricted diet its body mass of fat will increase faster than the body mass increment of lean meat (see Figure 3.4).

The following market **size-classes** of pig are recognised:

Class	Weight/kg	Typical use
Weaners	25–27	Sucking pig
Porkers	55–68	Roast joint
Cutters	70–75	Chops
Baconers	75–80	Bacon
Heavy pigs	80+	Ham

It is obviously in the farmer's interests for the pig to grow quickly to a marketable size. The longer it takes a pig to grow to a particular size-class the greater the proportion of its diet which is used for maintenance and respiration, for the extra days spent growing. A cold pig will eat more food, as a high proportion of its energy intake is directed towards **thermogenesis**, that is keeping it warm. However, if the pig is too warm it will eat less and

may grow less if it is uncomfortably hot. Pigs have a very limited capacity to **thermoregulate** by sweating. Keeping the pigs comfortably warm in their houses, above a **lower critical temperature** (LCT) below which they would eat more to keep warm, is therefore important (see back to Table 3.1). This is done by controlling heating and ventilation, and in a large pig unit this may be under computer control.

Numerous studies have shown that abnormally high levels of **heavy metals** in the body reduce the respiratory pathway to thermogenesis in the pig's liver. Adding **copper sulphate** to the pig's food at levels of between 125 and 250 parts per million therefore increases growth rate. Most of the copper ions are excreted and not passed on into the human food chain, but the practice has serious environmental consequences. **Slurry** from pig units is a major **pollutant** of streams, even without the threat of heavy metal toxins (see Chapter 32).

A comfortable and unstressed pig grows faster. Much more attention is therefore now paid to **housing** conditions and to reducing **stress** during early growth than was at one time the case. Recent experiments in Holland have shown that confined and tethered sows have almost double the glucocorticoid hormone levels of untethered sows which are free to roam in a small pen. Glucoorticoid is a good stress indicator. Stress reduces growth rates and depresses mothering ability.

Improvement in carcase quality

Pigs were selected for their fatness during much of their early history, but a changed preference for a leaner cut of meat has grown during the twentieth century, and may well continue. As consumers have become more insistent on leaner pig meat, **pig breeders** have been working hard at the genetic base of the pig population to improve the conversion of pig-food to lean meat. They have been very successful. For example, in the decade 1971–1981 the Meat and Livestock Commission monitored a mean decrease in **back fat** on marketed bacon pigs of nearly 30%. Although part of this reduction was due to the method of 'finishing', by reducing rations before slaughter, a substantial part of the reduction of back fat, perhaps 20%, has been achieved by genetic selection for a leaner pig.

It is certain that selection has produced huge changes over time. It is also true that physical and behavioural traits can be modified by breeding. For example, **porcine stress syndrome** (PSS) is known to be controlled by a single gene, and is expressed in the homozygous recessive condition. This can be detected by a test involving halothane gas inhalation. Pigs that go rigid under these test circumstances are more prone to suffer the condition and produce an inferior **pale soft exudative meat** (PSE) that reduces carcase quality. This kind of defect in our pig herds can be eliminated.

However, there may be problems surrounding selection programmes. Pigs have recently been selected for higher efficiency in converting limited feed into **live weight gain**. The selection process for pigs that grew best on the least food resulted in some improved **conversion efficiency**. However, it was subsequently found that the selected animals had smaller appetites! Thus when allowed to eat as much as they wanted they ate less than the unselected (control) group and grew more slowly! In another trial, selection was practised to produce maximum lean meat gain whilst the pigs were allowed to eat as much as they wanted. After the processes of selection these pigs ate a great deal more than those in the control group, and produced more lean meat, but did not produce any less fat in proportion to the food fed.

Hormones influence the proportion of lean meat laid down (see Chapter 4). Growing pigs produce a **growth hormone** called **porcine somatotrophin** (PST). Synthetic PST may be implanted to promote growth; this is banned under current European Community law, but allowed in the USA. Young boars that have not been castrated grow with less fat on them. Unfortunately older intact (uncastrated) boars are reputed to have an unpleasant musky taste and smell to their flesh which is known as **boar taint**. However, it should be said that many people cannot detect boar taint at all. Castrated hogs are more docile and have flesh that is fatty, tender and sweet. Today most

male piglets grown for bacon are spared the trauma of castration and left intact.

What every pig-meat eater should know

Pigs going to **slaughter** suffer from the stress of travel, unfamiliar company and, prior to being killed, the stress of the smells and noise of the abattoir. Much **lactic acid** is released from the glycogen reserves in muscle before slaughter, especially if the animal is at all badly treated. This may detract markedly from the curing quality of hams and bacon. Quite apart from this commercial consideration the 13 million pigs killed in Britain each year deserve better treatment than they may sometimes get. Research into more **humane methods of killing** is important and there is at present good co-operation between animal welfare groups and veterinary authorities.

In an abattoir about two hundred animals are slaughtered per hour. The pigs are electrically

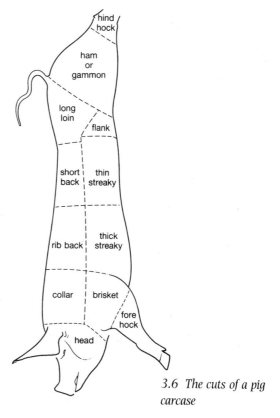

3.6 *The cuts of a pig carcase*

stunned with a 100 volt shock across the head, and then hoisted head-down on to a conveyor system. The totally unconscious animal is then 'stuck', a process of draining blood from the neck. The dead animal is then scalded in boiling water, scrubbed of its hair and other dirt, and left to hang. Later when cold the carcase is gutted, the head is removed and the body divided into two 'sides'. These pass straight to butchers' shops or bacon factories, where the further processing of meat takes place. Uncured pig meat is used for pork joints and pork chops. Hind-leg muscles cured by smoking become ham; smoke-cured 'sides' are bacon. Waste meat scraps are used to make sausages. Pig fat is rendered down to lard. Some is used to make ice-cream, described as containing 'non-milk fat'!

One alternative

Not everybody is happy with **intensive** pig production. On a farm in Oxfordshire about 100 gilts and sows are kept in a **semi-extensive** system. They are fed on cereals and bean feed grown on the farm. Each one-acre paddock has 24 gilts or sows. The animals root around and eat a large amount of soil and rough grass. Paddocks are ploughed after one year and spend the next three years under cereals. The pigs are selected for their **hardiness** in living out of doors, and they certainly use more of their food intake for keeping warm. The farrowing paddocks are supplied with huts and ample straw for the sows to give birth in. The huts are un-heated, but feed is provided for piglets. The sows come and go, in and out of the houses as they please, and make their own nests. Despite being out in all weathers the average sow rears 20 piglets a year, compared with 24 indoors. The piglets are still weaned at three weeks, and are then housed together intensively. After weaning the sows go back to a fresh grass paddock for mating with the boar and for their next pregnancy. The young pigs have minimal heating early in life. Although feed costs are more, housing and heating costs are much less compared with a fully intensive system. The pigs are sold as 60 kg porkers without the stress of 'finishing'; some selected gilts go out of doors to become the mothers of the next genera-tion. This semi-extensive system is only slightly less profitable; there are fewer capital costs (like build-ings) and the farmer, who also has to work outside in all weathers, is happier with the enterprise.

Reading and references

Hammond, J. jnr, Bowman, J.C. and Robinson, T.J. (1983) *Hammond's Farm Animals*. Edward Arnold.
King, J.W.B. (1983) Exploited Animals - Pigs. *The Biologist* 30:5.
Tudge, C. (1986) *The History of the British Pig*. Duckworth.
Whittemore, C.P. (1987) *Elements of Pig Science*. Longman

Thought questions

1 Having read this chapter, have you changed your views on eating pig-meat products? Does our culture protect us from the truth?

2 What is the ideal pig? How would you widen the genetic base for selecting the animal that you would most like to see?

3 How would you design a pig production unit so that the pigs could choose how they lived? Would it make a profit?

4
The First Fast Food:
The Biology of Milk Production

Milk is the first food you ever had and many of us have not given it up yet; we start life with our mother's milk and later drink that which comes from cows. So dependent are we on milk, cream, butter, cheese and yoghurt that we tend to forget where they come from.

Humans and cattle have been associated for at least seven thousand years. Today domesticated cattle provide us with meat, milk, hides (for leather) and, traditionally, animal power for ox-drawn ploughs and carts. In return we have provided them with care, food and protection from their natural predators and diseases.

> The friendly cow, all red and white
> I love with all my heart.
> She gives me cream with all her might
> To eat with apple tart.
>
> *Robert Louis Stevenson*

The selection of cattle breeds for milk production

The wild ox or **auroch** (*Bos primigenius*) was a fearsome animal once found in ancient Europe and the Middle East. These beasts were long-horned, the bulls standing 6 feet at the shoulder. They roamed the woodlands of Europe and temperate Asia, and were hunted until historic times. The last auroch died in Poland in 1627, making the ancestral species **extinct**. The wild oxen domesticated some seven thousand years ago became the ancestors of the 1200 million cattle alive today. The new species (*Bos taurus*) has evolved and diversified enormously. The earliest prehistoric forms were smaller than their wild ancestor, selected no doubt also for their docility and the ease with which they could be held and herded. From Roman times onwards larger **breeds** were selected. Across Europe, Africa and Asia locally adapted forms have evolved, either for draught, or for their meat or milk.

Artificial and **natural selection** have made each form better adapted to its locality and very often more specialised to beef or dairy use. Table 4.1 lists the principal breeds classed as either specialist beef producers, milk-yielding dairy varieties or dual-purpose animals. Britain has exported many of its breeds, such as the Hereford, to other parts of the world. The **dairy breeds** most famous for their high butterfat, like the Jersey, come from the Channel Islands. The champion milk-volume producers are the very large Friesians (originally from Holland) and the Holsteins (from Germany). Being meaty they were dual-purpose beef and dairy animals. There are numerous breeds worldwide, but being all one species, *Bos taurus*, all are interfertile.

This chapter is concerned with milk production and will therefore focus on the biology of the milk-yielding varieties. These are animals that have been selected for the following criteria:
- Docility and tractability (easily led)
- Ease of hand- or (today) machine-milking
- High milk volume
- High butterfat (the lipid that makes cream)

4.1 A suckler herd of Hereford-cross cows

- High conversion ratio (of feed into milk)
- Sustained yield of milk (through oestrus and on during the next pregnancy).

The wild auroch cow probably produced a maximum of 5 litres per day for a single calf. By contrast a typical dairy cow can produce 20 litres of milk a day for much of the year and peak yields of 30 litres are common for short periods. A good dairy cow will therefore produce 6000 litres of milk in one year and perhaps 50 tonnes of milk in her lifetime.

During the twentieth century there has been selection for both higher **butterfat** content to the milk and increased **milk volume**. Jersey cattle produce a mean of 5.5% butterfat and Friesians 4.0%. The percentage of butterfat produced is

partially under genetic control, for hybrids between breeds demonstrate a **polygenic inheritance** pattern. The genetic control is also demonstrated by the fact that selection over the past century has been effective in raising the Friesian milk butterfat from a lower mean of 3.4%. Milk volume is also under genetic control, though diet is all-important. The milk yield potential has a hormonal basis that is discussed later.

The ideal dairy cow has a wedge-shaped body, in three planes, tapering from posterior to anterior and dorsal to ventral (see Figure 4.2). She therefore has a huge pelvis from which her udders are suspended – a wonderful machine for converting grass into milk for people.

Our co-evolution with the cow

In the **symbiosis** between cattle and humans there has been **co-evolution**. It is obvious how the cow must have changed, but, perhaps surprisingly, humans have changed in one small biological way as well. All mammals drink milk in early life and can digest its rich carbohydrate energy stores of **lactose** sugar. But nearly all mammals, between infancy and adulthood, rapidly lose the ability to produce the enzyme **lactase** which digests lactose. The one exception is the human species. Western and northern Europeans and many Africans (with their centre of origin in the Nile basin) are avid fresh-milk drinkers. In these areas, where cattle-keeping evolved, the human capacity to go on

Table 4.1 *The principal breeds of cattle in domestication in northern Europe*

Beef breeds	Dual-purpose breeds	Dairy breeds
Aberdeen Angus	Dairy Shorthorn	Brown Swiss
Beef Shorthorn	Dexter	Friesian–Holstein
Charolais	Friesian–Holstein	Guernsey
Devon	Redpoll	Jersey
Galloway		
Hereford		
Highland		
Welsh Black		

4.2 The three wedge shapes of the ideal dairy cow

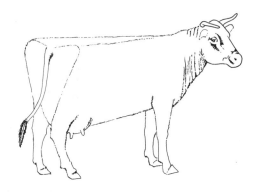

digesting lactose for longer in life has apparently been selected for. It is very common for other peoples, such as West Africans and East and South-East Asians, to find milk much less digestible, the undigested lactose inducing colic and diarrhoea. It seems that the cattle-keepers have retained their infant enzyme secretions for longer in life. Adult Europeans often lose their lactose-digesting capacity once past middle age. All people, including adults with **lactose intolerance**, can digest milk easily if it is fermented. The fermentation of milk into **yoghurt** (when the lactose forms lactic acid) is common practice in much of Eastern Europe and the whole of Asia (see also Chapter 11).

How milk is produced by the cow

All mammals, by definition, produce **milk**. The infant cry 'Mamma' is most probably the origin of the Latin word *mamma* for breast. **Mammary glands** are present in both sexes; their development is brought about by the female s**ex hormones**. The glands, each of which has one teat (nipple), are either placed anteriorly on the thorax (as in elephants and people) or posteriorly (as in cows and goats) or in both positions (as in pigs and rats). The dairy cow has four mammary glands, united in one udder, each served by a separate blood supply. The udder is suspended by tendons and ligaments from the pelvis and has a large blood supply. Four hundred litres of blood flow through the organ for each litre of milk produced. The size of the efferent

4.3 The prominent milk vein of a Jersey cow

blood vessel, the '**milk vein**', on the flank of the dairy cow is a good indicator of her milking capacity (see Figure 4.3). Each teat has two **sphincter muscles**, one at the top and another at the base. Inside the teat is a **cistern** from which milk is expelled at each suck. This is recharged from the udder **sinus** above it. Ducts lead from the sinus back to the milk-secreting **lobules**, each one of which has about two hundred smaller 'alveoli'. Each **alveolus** is surrounded by muscular tissue and lined with the **secretory cells** that produce the milk itself. Secretion is achieved by detachment of a whole part of the cell, furthest from the nucleus and basement membrane (see Figure 4.4).

Lactation is the period during which a cow gives milk. Secretion of milk in the udder is a continuous process under the influence of many hormones. **Oestrogen**, the primary female hormone, stimulates the growth of the duct system, whilst **progesterone** develops the lobules and alveoli. Both these hormone levels are high in pregnancy. Oestrogen also stimulates the production of **prolactin** and it is this hormone that promotes the cellular synthetic and secretory activity. At least two other hormones are involved in lactation, oxytocin (see next paragraph) and growth hormone (see next section).

Milk **let-down** is a voluntary process; the cow must *want* to be milked. Milk is stored mostly in the alveoli and ducts but also in the udder sinus. When the necessary stimulus of a calf (or a milking-machine and familiar human) is present, the touch, sight, smell and sound are received by the brain. The hormone **oxytocin** is then released by the posterior pituitary into the bloodstream. This surge only lasts for four to six minutes, but causes powerful contractions of the udder muscle tissue and ducts. A sucking calf, or the intermittent suction of a milking-machine, allows sufficient stimulation to the teats to allow the sphincter muscles to relax and the milk under pressure to be forcibly expressed. A frightened cow will produce **adrenalin**. This immediately arrests the release of milk.

Milk is produced continuously by the secretory cells, not just at milking. It takes three hours to

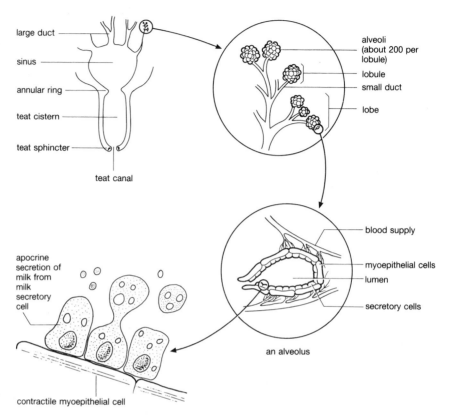

4.4 The structure of the bovine mammary gland. There are four glands in an udder each with a teat. The numerous lobules of the gland are each composed of about 200 alveoli. Each alveolus contains many milk secretory cells. Parts of these cells break away to form milk (apocrine secretion)

refill the udder sinus and a further eight hours to fill the ducts from the lobules. Milk pressure rises exponentially during the intervals between milking, and discomfort occurs if the interval is prolonged to 15 hours. Sucking has a reflex **positive-feedback** effect on prolactin secretion; retained high milk pressure has a **negative feedback**. This means that reduced frequency of sucking and draining of the udder will slowly 'dry off' the cow. Figure 4.5 shows a typical lactation curve for one cow. Once she is past her milk-yielding peak she will be mated again and only 'dried off' for eight weeks before calving and the start of the next lactation. Cows will perform well for many years on this routine if carefully tended.

Hormones natural and artificial

We have already seen that prolactin, the milk-inducing hormone, plays a vital role in the physiol-ogy of the dairy cow. However, it is another hormone that today fuels a controversy over milk production. This is **bovine somatotropin (BST)**. There is suspicion in the public mind about 'hormones in the milk' and to some extent some scientists have been party to the deception by insisting on the name BST and not a description that includes the word 'hormone'. **Growth hormone (GH)** is also known as somatotropin (ST) and that produced by cattle is therefore called bovine somatotropin. Growth hormone is produced by all mammals when they are growing and to some extent secretion continues throughout life. This hormone comes from the anterior pituitary, at the base of the brain, and is produced in pulses, flowing in response to feeding and sleeping rhythms. Human growth hormone, for example, flows more at night than by day. GH acts on most body tissues to produce a second wave of insulin-like growth factors (IGF). These seem to affect cell

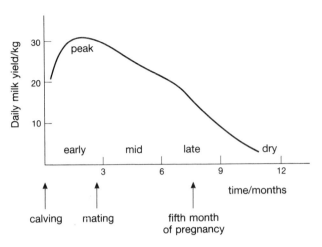

4.5 The milk yield of a cow over one lactation

membranes directly to stimulate mitosis, and generally increase body size. Both GH/ST and IGF are polypeptides.

Different mammals produce different amounts of hormones. For example, breeds of large dogs like Great Danes have much more GH than dachshunds: after all, in evolutionary terms, one is a selected giant and the other a selected dwarf. The selected dairy breeds have higher levels of GH than beef breeds. Could it be that GH is the power behind 'growing' more milk?

In 1937 it was discovered that **pituitary hormones** could increase milk yields when injected into cows. Some scientists even hoped to increase milk yields by this means in the Second World War. In 1947, Sir Frank Young demonstrated that the active ingredient was a polypeptide growth hormone. Because protein synthesis by **biotechnology** was then unthought of, nobody could obtain very much of it except from the pituitary glands of slaughtered animals. However, in 1982 Baumann used **recombinant DNA** technology to produce cow growth hormone using a bacterial culture. It was quickly discovered that when injected this synthetic hormone increased milk yields. If a Friesian cow is injected with 77 mg per day of synthetic BST, its cardiac output (blood output from the heart) increases by 10%, and the percentage of the cardiac output going to the udder

increases from 14.4% to 18.7%. As a result there is an immediate 21% increase in milk yield, with some recorded increases as high as 40%. Long-term studies have so far shown no major adverse effects on the health of animals, although they need milking more frequently and may find it harder to walk; their discomfort grows unless they are milked more than twice a day. There is apparently little increase in the cow's live weight, but an increase in appetite does take place to match the increased milk yield. The mammary tissue certainly grows but the actual cells are *no more efficient*, still producing 1.9 cm^3 milk per gram of mammary tissue per day. The udder merely get bigger, works harder and develops a better blood supply.

The injection of BST is controversial. Some trials have suggested that it increases the chances of udder infection, decreases fertility and stresses cows. Other trials do not show these side-effects. The use of BST is allowed in the United States at present but not in the EC. Small amounts of growth hormone are present in milk from untreated cows (9 mg per dm^3). In theory it should be digested in the human stomach. The use of BST might add another 5 mg dm^{-3} of growth hormone to the milk we drink. Following the legal criteria for permitting changes in veterinary practice it is certainly a 'chemically pure, safe and efficacious' additive. However, can it be argued to be 'necessary'? Most dairy farmers would welcome the freedom to use BST if they could. Governments commonly operate a **quota system** on dairy-farming production: maximum levels of production are set. Use of BST is therefore not seen as a way of producing a greater total amount of milk, but of producing more milk without having so many cows. This of course saves money.

The composition of milk

Milk is a fluid mixture of emulsified fats, soluble and sparsely soluble proteins, lactose sugar, vitamins and minerals (see Table 4.2). Once left to settle for a few hours the larger **butterfat** globules rise to the surface and form a layer of cream. This is the 'single cream' of the supermarket or 'top of

	Human	Cow
Water/%	87.2	87.1
Total solids/%	12.9	12.8
Fat/%	4.5	3.7
Lactose/%	7.0	4.9
Proteins/%		
casein	0.4	2.8
whey proteins	0.6	0.6
Minerals/mg per dm^3		
calcium	340	1170
phosphorus	140	920
magnesium	40	120
iron	0.5	0.5
Vitamins/per dm^3		
A/IU	1898	1025
B1/µg	160	440
B2/µg	360	1750
B3/µg	1470	940
B12/µg	0.3	4
C/mg	43	11
D/IU	22	14
E/mg	1.8	0.4

Table 4.2 The composition of human and cows' milk

the milk', whose fat content may be increased by centrifugation to yield 'double cream'. The **emulsion** of the lipid in water can be made more stable by breaking up the larger globules mechanically into minute ones which are then unable to rise: such milk is said to be 'homogenised'. If the cream is removed altogether the milk is known as 'skimmed'.

The milk first produced after the birth of a calf is thick with protein, is highly digestible and contains relatively more Vitamin A than later milk. It is called **colostrum** and unlike the milk produced later is rich in antibodies. Rightly, colostrum is fed directly to the calves for whom it is vital. The **antibodies** are absorbed through the gut into the bloodstream and confer a natural acquired immunity. The milk produced later is more uniform but

varies somewhat in composition. During a given milking the butterfat content of the milk increases towards the end; it is also higher at the evening milking than the morning one. Increasing the frequency of milkings, from two to three per day, increases both yield and butterfat content.

To a very large extent the volume and richness of the milk are affected by the quality of food fed to the cow. Being a **ruminant** the cow can utilise nitrogen in the form of urea or ammonia to synthesise amino acids through bacterial fermentation. The products of cellulose digestion are used directly for the formation of volatile **fatty acids** (acetic, propionic and butyric acid). It is from these that the butterfat (lipid) is synthesised in the alveoli; a higher cellulose content in the diet produces more butterfat. High-volume milkers, like Friesians, have a lower percentage of butterfat.

Cows' milk has a different composition to **human milk**. The latter is richer in lactose, has less casein (protein) and has a different spectrum of vitamins and minerals. Human milk has more lactose than the milk of any other mammal on record. **Lactose** is particularly important for the synthesis of galactolipids, which form nervous tissue and hence contribute to optimal brain development. Cows' milk is low in specific fatty acids needed for nervous tissue. Human milk contains the enzyme **lipase**, and cows' milk does not. Consequently the buttermilk in cows' milk must take longer to digest. Two of the other important differences are in the spectrum of **amino acids** that the two milks contain (see Figure 4.6). The amino acid **cystine,** for example, is an essential amino acid for the newborn human but is present only in small amounts in cows' milk; whilst the large amounts of **tyrosine** in cows' milk can poison a premature baby. It is the special composition of human milk that nourishes human bodies correctly. Cows' milk has evolved as nourishment for calves, not human infants, and it is wrong that industrial **powdered milk** producers have used their commercial power, through advertising and inducements, to persuade women to give to their infants cows' milk products rather than natural breast milk.

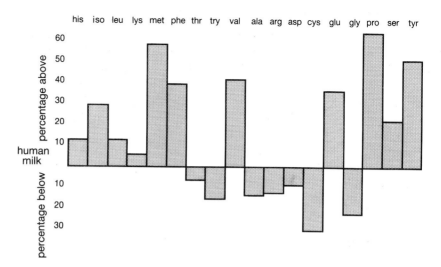

4.6 Amino acid differences between human and cows' milk

The production of milk through the parlour

The milking parlour is a highly specialised area designed to produce clean, healthy milk in a bulk-liquid form, taken from the cows with minimal human labour and minimal distress to the animals. From what has been said about 'let-down' it will be clear why the cows should be contented. Modern **dairy milking** proceeds as follows. Each cow is individually identified and goes into a stall. She is then fed an amount of concentrated feed to balance her milk yield output. It is common to 'strip' a little milk from the teat by hand to look for signs of **mastitis**. This is a bacterial infection of the udder (see also Chapter 5). If untreated, mastitis can be very dangerous to the animal and may also contaminate the bulk milk. The cows' teats are then washed with mild disinfectant. In machine-milking, sterile rubber-lined teat-cups are fitted to the teats (hand-milking is very hard work). Milking should be over in a few minutes, when suction is released and the teat-cups removed. Individual **milk yield** is recorded by mass and the cow is released from her stall. Teat-cups must be disinfected after milking each cow.

Milk is a perfect medium for bacterial growth and every effort must be made to avoid **bacterial contamination**. All piping systems are therefore washed through after milking with cold water (preventing milk-protein coagulation) and then with detergent, disinfectant and hot water (at a temperature greater than 60°C). The milk is cooled to 4°C in a refrigerator, and is kept cool and stirred in a bulk tank while awaiting daily collection by a milk-tank lorry.

Considerable interest is currently being expressed in robotic milking systems. These fully automated machines would allow the cows to choose when they are milked. They would have teat-cups which fitted comfortably to their individual teat shapes and adapted to individual teat flow rates. Milk would be tested automatically at each milking for tell-tale changes in pH and conductivity. This last measure would discover mastitis earlier than the visible test and would enable prompt **antibiotic** treatment by the dairy farmer. Robotic milking is a real possibility. There is evidence that it would stress the cows less than conventional milking parlours, and milk yields could be higher: cows would naturally choose to be milked more than twice a day.

Milk from transgenic animals

One of the advantages of **biotechnology** that promises to be of increasing importance is the production of proteins in milk that have not been programmed for by the animal's own DNA but by an **implanted gene**. For example, there are now sheep on research stations producing hormones such as **insulin** in their milk in considerable amount. This can be extracted, purified and used to treat diabetics. Using plasmids and the techniques of recombinant DNA, the genes for such proteins can be inserted into the zygote prior to the animal's development. Because the genes from one species are inserted into another, the transformed animal is described as **transgenic**. As a result of the gene implant the lactating animal will have alveolar secretory cells that *may* make the desired protein, even if it is only in small amounts (see Chapter 9).

Experiments with mice have already shown the possibility of **gene transfers** into cows, the protein products of which would confer disease resistance against bacteria in the udder. So far, a recombinant antibacterial protein, lysostaphin, has been induced to destroy *Staphylococcus* bacteria in the mammary gland of a mouse! As yet scientists are hesitant to produce a **transgenic dairy cow**. Would it be wise? The possibility is certainly there.

Further reading

Blake, P. (1985) *Livestock Production*. Heinemann.
Clutton-Brock, J. (1989) *A Natural History of Domesticated Animals*. Cambridge University Press.
Palmer, G. (1988) *The Politics of Breastfeeding*. Pandora.

Thought questions

1 'If a cow were discontented after injection with BST she would produce less milk.' Discuss this statement.

2 It has been suggested that unimproved low-yielding dairy cattle in some Third World countries should be given BST to boost their milk production. Would you support such a programme?

3 If a cow could be engineered transgenically to produce only human milk would it be a good idea?

Things to do

Dairy techniques

1. Make a microscopic examination of full-cream milk and skimmed milk. Record your observations. Place samples of each in a centrifuge and spin them for five minutes. Explain the results of the centrifugation.
2. Incubate 100 parts of cows' milk with one part of rennet enzyme for ten minutes at 40°C. What milk component gives junket its structure? (See also Chapter 11.)

5
At Work With the Vet

Wanting to become a vet (veterinary surgeon) is a popular ambition among young biologists. Whether a veterinary career is your ideal or not, this chapter will give you more of an idea of the profession. It contains a personal account of veterinary career options and is specially written for this book by a vet, Mary Holt.

At the moment there are six universities in the United Kingdom where you can study for a veterinary degree, which is what you need in order to be a veterinary surgeon. The courses at Bristol, Edinburgh, Glasgow, Liverpool and London last for five years; the one at Cambridge takes six years.

Most people starting to study for a veterinary degree either go to University immediately after doing 'A' levels or take a year off first. Generally speaking, the entry requirements are much the same as those for medicine. The competition for places is extremely severe. Excellent 'A' level grades – As or Bs – are needed in three subjects. 'A' level Chemistry is essential, and most candidates also do Biology and Physics or Mathematics. Application is made through UCCA (Universities Central Council on Admissions) in the same way as for any other university course.

Careers with a veterinary degree
by Mary Holt, MRCVS, PhD

The jobs that are available for people with veterinary degrees are many and varied. Many of us are familiar with the role of vets in general practice, either through having consulted them about our own animals, or through programmes on television. There are also exciting opportunities for vets in many fields of research and in industry.

General practice can be conveniently divided into two types: large- or farm-animals practice, and small- or companion-animal practice. In **small-animal practice**, the vet is important not only in caring for the animal, but also in providing support and reassurance to the owner. The routine of a small-animal vet involves a mixture of consulting, operating and house visits. In consulting, owners bring their animals to the surgery for advice. Home visits are necessary when either the animal is too ill or the owner is unable to get to the surgery. Generally, it is better if the animal is able to come to the surgery for two reasons: first, because all the

facilities for diagnosis and treatment are available there, and second, because it is usually much easier to examine an animal away from its home territory. Most animals will submit to a clinical examination on neutral ground as shown in Figure 5.1. In its own territory, however, an animal may resent even having its temperature taken. On a day-to-day basis, small-animal practice is very varied. You never know whether your next patient will be a dog, a cat or a guinea-pig, or even a parrot or snake. It certainly keeps you on your toes! The job has also become more challenging as medical science has advanced. More techniques are now available for diagnosis and treatment. For instance, many conditions caused by hormone imbalance that were incurable in the past, such as diabetes and thyroid hormone imbalance, can now be successfully treated.

In **large-animal practice**, most of the vet's time is spent visiting farms as shown in Figure 5.2. Frequently this is for 'fire brigade' work. These are emergency cases to examine and treat an individual animal with a problem, such as difficulty in

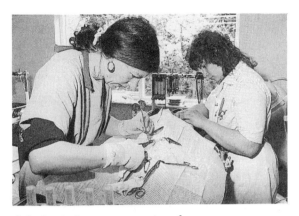

5.1 A veterinary surgeon at work

calving or lambing, 'milk fever' in cows, or some infection. These cases can easily be identified in the 'James Herriot' stories! However, an increasing part of the large-animal vet's time is spent in **preventative medicine**. With a veterinary training you are uniquely placed to appreciate all aspects of animal production, not only in relation to prevention and control of disease, but also in relation to housing, nutrition and reproduction. For example, one of the major problems in dairy practice is **mastitis**. This is an infection in the udder of a cow, caused by a bacterium. However, there is usually an underlying problem which allows the bacteria to establish in the udder, sometimes due to a combination of various factors. Such a combination could be: badly regulated milking machines which are exerting too much pressure on the tissue of the udder; bruising of the cows' teats on hard, rough concrete; and then, if the ground is also very dirty, bacteria that normally cause no problems may be able to invade and multiply. It is clear that simply identifying the bacteria will not solve the problem. To do that you must discover the underlying causes and correct them (see also Chapter 4).

Large-animal vets can often help farmers ensure that their animals' diets are adequate. Cows, for example, can collapse and die from **staggers** or **milk fever.** Staggers is caused by a lack of magnesium in the diet; milk fever by inadequate calcium. These diet-induced conditions are easy for a vet to diagnose and remedy, if he or she is called in time. Other dietary imbalances, such as a marginal

shortage of copper or excess of molybdenum, may have less obvious consequences: for example, a slight loss of fertility or reduction in milk yield. To detect such dietary imbalance requires a good working knowledge both of the farm and of how the farmer looks after the cows. Diagnosis is easier if the vet visits the farm throughout the year to monitor the behaviour and performance of the animals on a regular basis. This side of large-animal practice involves repeated meetings with the farmer to talk about the animals, walks round the farm and planning for the future. In the short term such work may appear less satisfying than the 'fire brigade' work. In the longer term, though, such work is very satisfying as you develop a detailed knowledge of the working of each individual farm, and can see problems eradicated and animals in better condition.

It is often an interest in preventative medicine that leads a vet into research. Indeed, the boundary between practice and research is frequently rather blurred, as quite a lot of research in veterinary science is done by vets in practice, recording and analysing their results. Because of the breadth of veterinary training, a vet is able to contribute to any field of research that includes a study of the biology of animals. A great deal of veterinary research is stimulated by problems encountered in the field, and may therefore involve investigations in reproductive physiology, housing, nutrition, welfare or disease.

In order to conduct research into such areas as housing, diet or disease, however, it is necessary to have a good understanding of how the animal 'works' in the first place. For example, to develop a vaccine against disease it is essential to have a thorough knowledge of the immune system. It is then possible to begin to determine which part of the immune system is most important in protecting the animal from that particular disease. Vaccines can then be developed which ensure that the relevant part of the immune system is stimulated to produce the maximum response.

Another area of research to which vets contribute is wildlife biology and ecology, particularly as the importance of conservation is increasingly

5.2 Oral medical dosing of a restrained bullock

realised. One area of conservation where veterinary knowledge is useful is in trying to understand the role of disease in regulating animal populations. This may be done by veterinary examination of animals that have died. For example, a great deal of veterinary research was carried out on the epidemic of rinderpest that killed many of the wildebeest and buffalo in East Africa in the 1970s. Sometimes useful data can also be obtained from animals that have been shot. Samples of faeces (droppings) may provide useful data on internal parasites; their occurrence is often revealed by the presence of eggs in faeces. Blood samples can sometimes be taken from animals that have been anaesthetised using an anaesthetic fired from a dart gun. Each of these techniques can help to build up a picture of the health of a population of wild animals. From a conservation perspective it may be important to know whether, for instance, a disease is affecting all the individuals in a population, or whether some sectors are unaffected. If the susceptibility of an individual animal to a particular disease is affected by genetic factors, then the environment will select for disease resistance through survival of the fittest.

An example of how practice and research can complement each other is provided by a project

Table 5.1 Working with animals

Job title	Qualifications needed	Training
Pet shop assistant	Depends on employer	Correspondence course for pet trade diploma
RSPCA: hospital assistant	Age 18+; good GCSEs	6 months on full pay
RSPCA: inspector	Age 22–35: good general education; clean driving licence; physical fitness	7 months, residential
Guide dogs:		
kennel staff	Age 17+; 3 GCSEs	6 months at kennels
trainer	Age 18–25; 5 GCSEs, depending on experience	6 months at kennels followed by on-the-job work as trainer
Groom/stablehand	Age 18+; at least 18 months' full-time work experience with horses	Diploma
British Horse Society:		
instructor	Age 22+; assistant and intermediate instructor certificates	Instructor examination
Stockman/manager	Depends on level	Varies from non-advanced courses to degree courses
Laboratory animal technician	Usually GCSEs in English, mathematics and science	BTEC 2 level examination or IAT 3 level examination. Each takes at least 5 years
Zoo keeper	Depends on zoo; usually GCSEs in English and mathematics	Usually on the job: City and Guilds Certificate in Zoo Management

that I have been working on. In the late 1970s and early 1980s a new disease of pigs was observed. The disease affected young pigs reared in intensive pig farms. It usually occurred just after weaning and could be recognised by the combination of a high temperature and the presence of hot and swollen joints which made the pigs lame. In some cases **meningitis** – infection of the meninges (membranes) enveloping the brain and spinal cord – was also found. Many of the affected pigs died. So, from the observations of farmers and vets in large-animal practice, the clinical symptoms, the age and type of animal affected, and the nature of the **husbandry system** in which the disease was found were all known. However, to understand more about the disease, research was needed to isolate and identify the **causative organism**.

Post-mortem examination of samples taken from infected pigs led to the isolation of a streptococcal bacterium subsequently given the name *Strepto-*

5.3 A veterinary nurse with an anaesthetised Siamese cat

coccus suis type 2. Having isolated this bacterium, it was then necessary to carry out experiments to ensure that the correct organism had been found, and to investigate how it caused the disease. Was the bacterium alone responsible for the disease, or were other factors important? How did the disease spread between pigs and between farms? How could the disease be treated? The overall aims of this research were to develop accurate tests to detect the disease-causing organism, to design practical management procedures to prevent the spread of the disease and to develop a protective vaccine. In the short term, research like this can often be frustrating and rather unrewarding; experiments may not lead anywhere or they may produce results which are difficult to interpret. However, it can be very rewarding to design and carry out careful experiments which can turn an initial hunch into a testable hypothesis. If the results of the study do lead you to understand a little more of the problem and its likely solution, then the work becomes extremely exciting and all the previous frustration appears worthwhile. In the long term, it is extremely satisfying to feel that you are helping to prevent a disease as unpleasant as meningitis.

In Britain, most veterinary research is done either in universities, where the people who do the research are usually also involved in teaching veterinary students, or in research institutes. Funding for veterinary research comes from a number of sources. The government pays for some research, largely through the Ministry of Agriculture, Fisheries and Food and the Agricultural and Food Research Council. Some research money comes from private sources, such as the Wellcome Trust or the Horse Race Betting Levy Board. Research is also carried out in industry, especially when it is intended to lead to the development of a product to be marketed by the company, such as a new drug.

Most people who qualify as vets spend some time in practice after qualifying, even if they subsequently go into research. Many researchers enjoy maintaining close contact with practice, either by doing 'locums' – replacing vets in practice who are ill or on holiday – or by acting as consultants in their research specialities. So, whether you remain in practice or go into research, it is usually possible for a vet to maintain and enjoy both the breadth and the depth of the training received during a veterinary degree course.

Veterinary nursing

A veterinary nurse works alongside veterinary surgeons in much the same way in which nurses work alongside doctors. After all, non-humans need nursing just as humans do. A veterinary nurse does not do any surgery, but carries out veterinary work under the direct supervision of a vet. The work involves everything from handling and restraining animals to feeding them and carrying out first-aid as shown in Figure 5.3.

The minimum qualifications to begin training as a veterinary nurse are four GCSEs (grades C or above), which must include English and either mathematics or a science. You must be at least 17 years old, so some students studying to be veterinary nurses have done 'A' levels too. Training is done on the job. You have to have a full-time job (at least 35 hours per week) at an approved establishment such as a veterinary practice. Then you have to register with the Royal College of Veterinary Surgeons (RCVS). As well as learning 'on the job', you attend formal lectures at a college and take a number of written, oral and practical examinations. It takes at least two years to complete the necessary training. At the end, if you pass all the examinations, your name is placed on a list of veterinary nurses kept by the RCVS and you are entitled to call yourself a veterinary nurse.

Other careers with animals

There are many other ways of working with animals apart from being a veterinary surgeon or nurse. A selection of these is given in Table 5.1. A fuller list can be found in the leaflet *Careers with Animals* produced by the Universities Federation for Animal Welfare (whose address is listed below under 'Useful organisations').

Useful organisations

Royal College of Veterinary Surgeons, 32 Belgrave Square, London SW1X 8QP. Produces a number of very helpful booklets including *A Career as a Veterinary Surgeon* (1988), fifth edn, £3.00 incl. p&p; and *Veterinary Nursing: A Guide for Persons Wishing to Train as Veterinary Nurses* (1986), twelfth edn, £2.00 incl. p&p. Universities Federation for Animal Welfare, 8 Hamilton Close, South Mimms, Potters Bar, Herts EN6 3QD. Tel: 0707 58202.

> ### Thought questions
>
> 1 Why do you think it requires better 'A' level grades to read veterinary science than to read medicine?
>
> 2 Do you think large-animal vets suffer a conflict of interest, having to balance the interests of the animals and farmers?
>
> 3 Should there be a National Health Service for animals as well as for humans?

6
Harvesting Fish from the Sea

This chapter is concerned with how we harvest fish from the sea. Attempts by people to manage fisheries contain some important lessons in applied ecology. These are particularly well illustrated by the history of fisheries around the British Isles. **Marine ecology** and **fisheries research** are expanding and highly technical subjects.

The fish species of the North Sea are household names. Herring, cod, mackerel, plaice, haddock, sole, whiting, pilchards and sprats make up much of the one million tonnes landed each year in the UK. Although this harvest is rich, it was once much richer. Today the resource is extremely badly managed; the best **food species** have been overfished. Perhaps worst of all, the shallow sea-bed where many fish live, feed and spawn is used as a dumping ground for much of Europe's industrial waste and is fouled with sewage and toxic substances from its rivers.

History of North Sea herring fisheries

The edge of Europe's continental shelf dips below the surface of the sea so that the British Isles and the European coastline of the north-east Atlantic are surrounded by shallow water. In these shallow waters nutrient-rich sediments are stirred up by storms and currents; as a result, algal productivity from photosynthesis is high during the long summer days. Zooplankton grow rapidly on the phytoplankton; there is high productivity and the sea supports a wealth of fish.

Since the end of the last Ice Age (15 000 years before present) the fishery of the North Sea has been exploited by coastal people. Herring, which are perhaps the easiest fish to net, have been harvested for many hundreds of years. Autumn is still the principal season. Long lines of nets are set. The amount of fish caught in a single night often much too great for people to be able to consume immediately. From this surplus was evolved the practice of salting or smoking fish to prevent it from rotting. 'The Statute of Herrings' in 1347 was an early Act of Parliament concerned with food hygiene; it set out conditions for the sale of fresh fish, and the packaging and transport of salted fish from East Anglian ports to London. Salted herring were exported all over Europe from this time. The 'red-herring' and 'Yarmouth bloater' are ungutted, lightly salted and smoked herring. The smoking process dries the fish flesh whilst the tannins in the smoke inhibit bacterial growth. The gutted, opened and smoked herring is a 'kipper'. This more recent nineteenth-century invention is one of the most celebrated British foods, and was a major dietary item until recent years. Many present-day kippers are chemically treated with annato, a vegetable dye, and are not the true product.

Herring have been a major food in the past. In the seventeenth century the Anglo-Dutch Wars were fought over the possession of North Sea fishing grounds. The technological change from sail to steam and then to diesel-powered boats has changed fisheries immensely, extending the range and seasons of the catch. Herring have been caught further away from the traditional ports and exploited repeatedly until populations of fish have been reduced to extremely low levels. More recently storage of the catch on board has been revolutionised by freezing.

Mechanised trawling of the bottom of the sea switched attention from the herring to flat-fish: haddock, plaice and sole. Populations of North Sea plaice and now haddock have been consistently overfished this century and trawlermen have moved on to distant waters, to the north of the USSR and south of Morocco, to satisfy the market demand. As one fish species declines in numbers, fishing effort shifts to other species. In the wake of this consumer preferences have inevitably changed.

Fish and fisheries

Two types of fish can be distinguished – pelagic and demersal. **Pelagic** fish spend much of their time in open waters. These fish are best caught by drift nets or purse-seine nets and are typified by herring, sprats and mackerel. **Demersal** fish are predominantly bottom-living. They are caught in trawls along the sea-bed; examples are cod, whiting, plaice and sole. The distinction is not absolute for some deep-water bottom-feeding, high-order carnivores such as cod may be netted in the upper ocean.

The type of net used depends on the behaviour of the fish. **Drift nets** are traditionally used for herring and are still used by small herring-fishing fleets. The nets are buoyed at the surface and weighted at the bottom, hanging like a curtain some 10 metres beneath the surface. When the fish migrate vertically to the surface at night in pursuit of zooplankton they are unable to see the net and become caught by their gills. The extensive nets are left out for four to six hours and are hauled in before dawn.

Purse-seine nets are long nets which hang vertically as drift nets do, but are used to surround entire fish shoals, detected by sonar. The net in this case is hauled from both ends and the fish are literally bagged in the 'purse' end. Tuna are caught by this method in the Pacific. Because fish predators such as dolphins are caught in the purse, the carnage of these predators may be considerable. About twenty purse-seiners, each with a small crew, may operate in a fleet. These centre on one mother factory-ship which sorts, processes and packs fish. In the 1970s three such fleets depleted

6.1 Drifter with drift net and trawler with a bottom trawl

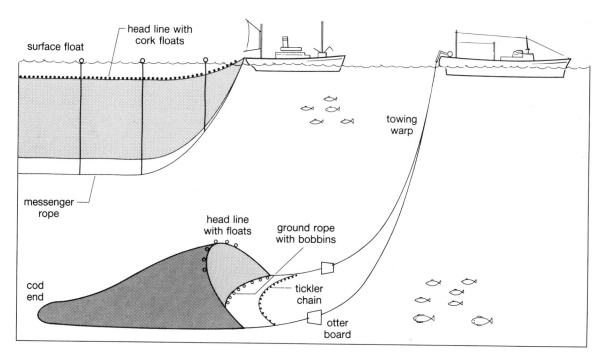

the herring fishery of the west coast of Scotland. Competition between fleets and the high level of industrialisation have been the principal cause of pelagic overfishing. Besides purse-seine nets, pelagic fish may also be caught at night by the use of lights and suction-pumping devices. Other methods include electrical stunning.

Trawling, with one or two trawls per boat, captures fish living on or near the bottom. The bottom trawl consists of a wide net bag with a tickler chain that causes fish to swim up and be caught as they are overtaken by the net following behind. Trawls may damage the sea-bed ecosystem, killing bivalve molluscs and altering the food web. Many of the shallow demersal fishery beds in the North Sea were overfished of haddock by bottom trawling in the 1980s.

Mid-water trawls have been used increasingly in recent years. Here the depth and location of the fish shoal are established by sonar, and the depth of the net mouth is adjusted by the speed of the boat and length of its wires to the net. Fine-mesh trawls

can remove very large numbers of small fish fry. Many of these smaller fish are sent for 'reduction' to make fish-meal for animal feed.

Fisheries research

There are five major fisheries research stations bordering the North Sea, at Aberdeen, Bergen, Hamburg, Ijmuiden and Lowestoft. One of the problems facing the fisheries scientist is that fish are very hard to see; it is difficult to work out food preferences, food webs, patterns of growth, breeding behaviour, shoaling behaviour and seasonal patterns of migration. Nevertheless we know more about the North Atlantic populations than any other fishery.

The **food web** of the **North Atlantic herring** was first worked out by Sir Alister Hardy (1924), whose two-volume book *The Open Sea* is a classic work in marine biology. Fine plankton nets were used to trawl through seas where herring were found. Analyses were made of the gut contents of

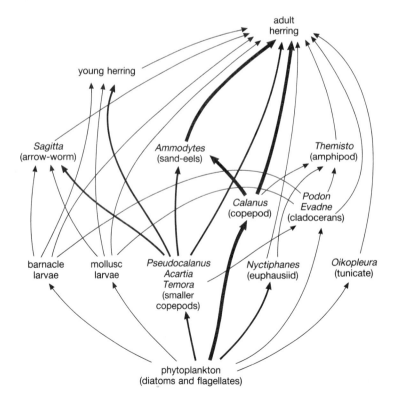

6.2 *The food web of the North Atlantic herring based on the pioneering fishery studies of Sir Alastair Hardy (see text)*

herring of all ages, and also of their prey. The young herring, known as whitebait, has a diet of very small planktonic animals; as it grows it gradually shifts to larger prey such as sand-eels (see Figure 6.2). Its ability to feed on *Calanus* rather than on the sand-eel *Ammodytes* is a valuable adaptation for it shortens the food chain and increases the transfer of energy to herring when sand-eels are scarce, as they were in the 1980s.

Most fish can be aged by counting the **annual rings** on the otoliths of the inner ear or more easily by counting annual rings on fish scales. These rings, like those of trees, are produced by unequal growth during different seasons. If the size of fish and their ring-count age are taken together, growth rates may be computed. Figure 6.3 shows that in some years herring have a very successful recruitment of individuals to the population and this age class can be followed in the population for a long as twenty years before it disappears. Quite why these successful years occur is not certain.

During the 1950s and 1960s the Norwegians used the **mark-release-recapture** research method with tagged herring to obtain estimates of

6.3 In some years, larger numbers of herrings are spawned or seem to survive

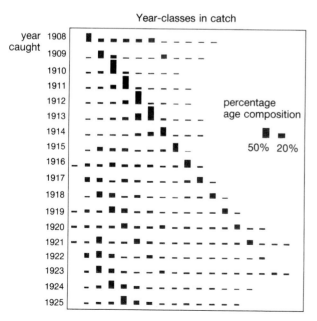

Year-classes in catch

percentage age composition

50% 20%

population change. To mark fish, a small disc is pinned through the base of the dorsal fin. Months or years later some of the marked fish may be recaptured. Today, in the UK, micro-tags are more commonly used. These are made of short lengths of fine wire coded with numbers, as transverse notches, injected into the fish's nasal cartilage. They are only 1 mm in length and may be fitted in very small fish. A research worker can micro-tag 5000 fish a day. Micro-tagged fish are marked, for future identification as fish carrying a micro-tag, by the removal of a small (adipose) fin between the main dorsal fin and the tail.

Echo-sounding (sonar) may be used in rough quantitative population surveys; if surveys are correlated with the biomass (tonnage of fish) harvested in each area, then sonar surveys alone may subsequently be used to find out how many fish there are without the use of nets. For the North Sea herring the patterns of **spawning** and **migration** have been worked out with sonar and by the painstaking analysis of the ages of tagged fish at different times of year in different areas (see Figure 6.4).

New techniques of fisheries investigation are being developed that allow individual fish to be followed all the time. A high-frequency sonic 'pinger' has been developed, weighing only 1.16 g and measuring only 17 mm by 7 mm, which can be implanted into a fish. Sonic signals emitted by the pinger in the 30–300 kHz range can be picked up by hydrophones attached to buoys. The buoys can transmit radio signals to a receiver on a ship or on land. Using such equipment A.D. Hawkins has recently tracked salmon out at sea and in the estuary of the River Fowey in Cornwall. Over a period of 266 days the fish were recorded repeatedly entering and leaving the estuary, apparently sensing the outflow of fresh water. When flood conditions occurred the 'run' up to the spawning grounds began.

Population and population dynamics

Fish production is influenced by two sets of factors – population dynamics and trophic factors. The

6.4 *The home-range of the North Sea herring. Planktonic herring larvae drift from their U.K. coastal spawning grounds (1,2 and 3) to shallow water off the Continental mainland (4). Here the larvae metamorphose into whitebait and migrate to nursery grounds (5). Once grown bigger the young herrings migrate again from their nursery grounds to the North Sea adult feeding grounds (6). Sexually mature adults return annually to the spawning grounds*

factors influencing **population dynamics** are **birth rate** (spawning), **death rate** (predation and fishing), and rates of **immigration** and **emigration**. It is hard to define a 'population' in an open system like the sea, but to a large extent each race of each species follows similar patterns of migratory movements within a defined area.

The rate of change in a whole population is the sum of the different contributory rates. Over a period of time, like one year, the rate of change in numbers of fish in a population may be expressed by the equation:

$$\Delta N = Rn + In - Mn - En - Fn$$

where ΔN equals the rate of change in the total number of fish, and where n is the rate of change in the number which are either recruited into the population by reproduction (R) and immigration (I) or are lost due to natural mortality (M), emigration (E) and fishing (F).

Understanding the dynamics of a fish stock involves not only numbers of fish, but also their biomass and rates of growth. We shall therefore return to the equation in a different form, below.

The **trophic** aspects (to do with food) are clearly important in governing the success of recruitment to the population for well-fed fish will spawn better. Vast numbers of fry are hatched at each spawning and well-fed fish fry will survive better as well. Predation (natural mortality) also affects survivorship. The critical nature of **survivorship** for such a fast reproducing species is illustrated by an example. It is not unusual for a fish to produce 100,000 eggs. If 99.8% or 99.9% die in the first year, through predation or from lack of food, we should not be surprised. But there is a very significant difference between these two percentage figures, for in the first case there will be 200 survivors at the end of the year and in the second only 100. This may make a big difference to the population later on (see Figure 6.3 again).

The intensity of predation may clearly make a huge difference. It is believed, for example, that cod eat young herring. So if fishermen are catching more cod this will lower predation pressure on herring and so increase the supply of food available to other fish in the sea.

In a fishery, because food supply controls growth rate it is better to look at the population dynamics not from a number viewpoint (N and n) but from a **biomass** viewpoint (B and b). If the population equation is expressed as a rate of change in biomass, that is tonnes of fish rather than numbers, then a growth component (G) needs to be added to the formula. The fish stock is changing in mass because of births, deaths and migration but also very largely because the fish are growing.

$$\Delta B = Rb + Gb + Ib - Mb - Eb - Fb$$

In this second equation ΔB is the rate of change in biomass, whilst b is the rate of change in biomass for each of the component factors.

How can we use these ideas of population dynamics? From the viewpoint of human predation the optimum use of the fishery means obtaining the greatest catch of fish from the population (F). It is best to catch the fish before they are so old that their rate of growth (G) is low, but not before at least some of the fish are old enough to reproduce (R). Clearly if *too many* of the fish capable of reproduction are caught very few new young fish will be added to the population. On the other hand, if many larger fish which are surplus to this basic breeding requirement are caught, and so removed from the population, the growth rate of young fish may be faster for there will now be more for them to eat. Figure 6.5 summarises this crucial dilemma.

Overfishing

Throughout the twentieth century North Sea stocks of herring, plaice and cod have been consistently overfished: more adult fish have been taken than was advisable to ensure adequate recruitment of young fish. Fisheries scientists had long suspected this, and first had their view confirmed by two unplanned experiments in the North Sea caused by the First and Second World Wars. During the wars hostilities at sea kept fishermen in their home ports. By 1919 and 1945, after fishing had been considerably curtailed for a few years, the fish stocks had had time to recover. Many more and larger fish were easily caught. In the 1950s and 1960s fisheries scientists fully understood the problem but were still helpless to stop the over-exploitation.

Figure 6.6 shows the relationship between the North Sea herring biomass, the fish stock, and the

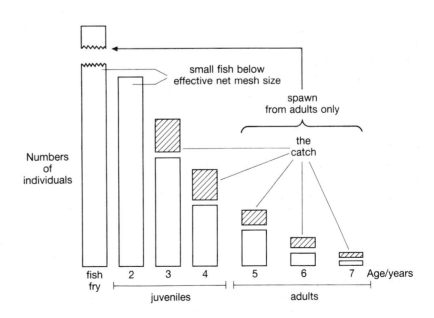

6.5 *If the catch of adults is too great there will be insufficient spawn to produce a large population of fish fry. If mesh size is reduced the catch of juveniles may deplete the population of future adults*

43

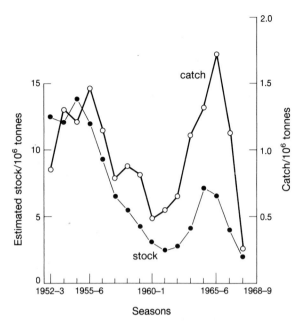

6.6   The relationship between the North Sea herring stock (biomass) and the total herring catch between 1952 and 1968 (see text)

actual landed catch for the period 1952 to 1967. Clearly the stock was steadily declining until 1961. The catch declined correspondingly and fishing became barely worthwhile. In this brief recession fewer boats went after herring and the stock slowly began to recover. However, further population growth was prevented because the increased fishing activity, in response to the rise in herring numbers, resulted in too many breeding adults being taken and the stock collapsed even further. By the end of the 1960s the herring population had totally collapsed.

The reason for the seemingly high catch in the mid 1960s was an increased fishing activity, one measure of which is called 'fishing effort'. **Fishing effort** is the amount of time spent fishing for the amount of fish caught. In the 1960s this was very high. For a constant fishing effort the fish population will equilibrate to allow a **sustained yield**, i.e. one that would not change from year to year. But if the effort is very high the sustained catch will forever be low. The relationship between fishing

effort and this level of sustainable yield is expressed in Figure 6.7. Between the two extremes of **under-fishing**, where the sustained yield can be increased with little increased effort, and **over-fishing** is an **optimal fishing intensity**. The tragedy of the fishing industry is that the competitive nature of boats, fleets and nations drives the fishing effort up to give ever-diminishing returns. If less fishing were done and stocks allowed to recover, very much more fish could be caught for less wasted effort. The population level for a **maximum sustainable yield** is thought to be at about half the population that the fish would reach if they were not fished at all.

Calling a halt to overfishing is difficult. Many fishing nations subscribe to the International Council for the Exploration of the Sea (ICES) in the hope of settling some disputes and gaining international co-operation. ICES has an Advisory Committee on Fishery Management made up of fisheries scientists who report factually on the state of fish stocks to such bodies as the North East Atlantic Fishery Commission. This is an international

6.7 The relationship between increasing the sustained yield (biomass of fish regularly caught, each year over many years) and increasing the fish effort (biomass of fish caught per time spent fishing, each year over many years). At the optimal fishing intensity there will be the greatest yield of fish

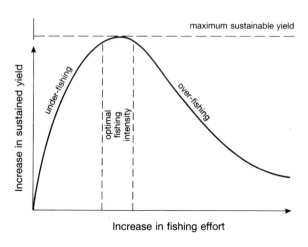

commission for the European countries bordering the North Sea. It sets annual quotas that should limit the exploitation of fish. The following methods of fishery regulation are practised:

- setting a minimum **mesh size** so that young fish go free, allowing enough of them to become adult and breed
- setting minimum legal sizes of particular fish species that may be landed
- limiting the number of fishing vessels from a port or country
- limiting the total annual catch for each type of fish
- confining fishing to a particular season to avoid the times when shoals are about to spawn
- disallowing fishing in certain areas where spawning occurs.

Many of these methods are enforced by the countries that fish the North Sea and to some extent they are successful. However, they are open to abuse and the fish, the fishermen and the consumer are the losers. Politicians who represent fishing constituencies often push for representation on the decision-making bodies. As a result, scientific advice to stop fishing for a while is ignored, or pressured against, to protect the livelihoods of the fishermen. When a stock is overfished, the use of a small mesh size will quickly bring in larger numbers of smaller fish. In the short term yields will rise, but this will eventually damage the stock further. In recent years the biologists' consistent advice for cod fisheries has been for a 150 mm trawl mesh size, allowing only 8- to 10-year-old fish to be caught for the first time (the younger ones getting away). However, the legal limit has been set, under pressure from the fishermen's lobby, at the smaller mesh size of 120 mm. Furthermore, analysis of the size of fish actually landed reveals that mesh sizes have not been adhered to strictly. The 'effective mesh size' for UK-landed cod is 113 mm, on the basis of the fish that come ashore. Somebody is cheating!

As in many other examples of environmental controls, resultant fines to fishermen are small in comparison to potential profits and the risk of being detected. As the quotas are set for fish *landed* and not for fish actually *caught*, extra fishing goes on at sea to find the more marketable fish. The unwanted remainder are discarded dead back into the sea, in order not to incur a landing penalty.

If there is any good news in this whole sorry business it is that the fish stocks are amazingly resilient. There was a total ban on herring fishing in the North Sea between 1977 and 1983. Surveys of herring larvae on their breeding grounds and acoustic surveying of the adult fish spawning off Robin Hood's Bay showed an increase in the adult population from 12 000 to 200 000 in five years from 1979 to 1984. The herring is back on the market but meanwhile our food preferences have changed!

Hunting or farming

The American ecologist Garrett Hardin pointed out in 1968 that fisheries of this kind express the **tragedy of the commons**. On many land-tenure systems where there is commonland grazing, individuals build up their stock numbers in the hope that their gains will be greater than those of their neighbours. This results in a temporary marginal gain for the herder, but also in degradation of the pasture by overgrazing (see also Chapter 28). As a result the competing parties all become poorer. In the same way the race between fishing fleets of different nations to loot the world's oceans of fish, as the European nations have done in the North Sea, is now on. British ships are today fishing further afield; some nations, like the USSR, Peru, Japan and Norway, have huge fleets. For this reason, in 1982, the United Nations put into operation a Law of the Sea giving coastal nations 200-mile exclusive fishing limits. Today the pattern of agreed exploitation of an area like the North Sea is very complex. For a start, fish movements are not bound by lines on a map: no nation owns the fish. Second, any nation that establishes an unfished reserve (and there are now several) will inevitably be restocking the fishery resources of any over-exploitive neighbours.

Pollution and politics

The North Sea is polluted from several sources: the dumping of **toxic wastes**, the burning of waste chemicals at sea; and on a large scale, the incessant inflow of **pollutants from rivers**. The Rhine and Elbe are now the worst offenders. Demersal fish seem to suffer most. Research in 1990 revealed that over half the whiting fish embryos in the German Bight had growth deformities. The same study showed that between 5% and 20% of the demersal sole, cod, flounder and plaice embryos were fatally deformed. Many had **chromosomal aberrations**. The damage was highest where dumping of industrial waste had occurred over a period of twenty years or more.

In March 1990 Britain was criticised at a North Sea Protection conference for being slow to improve its North Sea pollution record. However, the position is now getting better, thanks in no small part to the 'green lobby'. **Heavy metal** discharge will be cut to 70% of 1985 levels by 1995. Britain will stop marine dumping of toxic waste by 1992 and has led the way in producing legislation to destroy all polychlorinated biphenyls (**PCBs**). These are toxic chemicals which derive largely from discarded electrical transformers: they do not degrade but accumulate in food chains and are a serious threat to the fertility and immune systems of top-order carnivores such as dolphins and seals. The North Sea has sustained us with good fish in the past. With good biological monitoring and heeded scientific advice it should regain its value.

Further reading

Hardy, A.C. (1959) *The Open Sea, Fish and Fisheries*. Collins.
Meadows, P.S. and Campbell, J.I. (1987) *An Introduction to Marine Science*. Blackie.
Wheeler, A. (1969) *The Fishes of the British Isles and North West Europe*. Macmillan.

Thought questions

1 What fish species do you most like to eat? What factors govern the fish that people most want to buy?

2 What is biomass? Why is biomass a better indicator of production in a fishery than the numbers of fish?

Things to do

How to cook, dissect and eat a kipper.
Many people who have tried to eat kippers are ignorant of both how to cook them and how to avoid the bones. The herring, when originally kippered, is gutted and split by a long ventral incision to open it into two longitudinal halves. It is then smoked to preserve it. All the skin is thus on one side. Kippers should be cooked by light grilling (both sides) or by steaming for five minutes. They should not be boiled.
When brought to the table the kipper should be placed skin-side uppermost with the head towards you. If right-handed, remove the skin from right to left by running the point of a knife down the edge of the fish. Remove the rows of muscle blocks (the fillets) lengthwise from the bones that lie below. After the first half has been consumed, rotate the plate through 180° so that the fish's tail is towards you. Now remove the skin, again to the left, and remove the flesh by lifting it up from the bones below. All that will be left on the plate is the skin and ordered rows of bones instead of a mess of bones and fish which for most people marks the end of a somewhat unequal struggle.

7
Bees and Honey

Bees have fascinated people for thousands of years. Figure 7.1 shows a Stone-Age rock painting from Spain of people collecting honey, dated at 7000 BC. Most early civilisations prized honey very highly and in many parts of the world 'honey-hunting' was superseded by beekeeping. The craft of beekeeping remained almost unchanged for thousands of years, until the nineteenth century when major developments were made. These developments enabled honey to become an international commodity. Nowadays honey is transported around the world.

Honey is produced in quantity by only one species, the honeybee *Apis mellifera*, which evolved over twenty million years ago. However, there are 250 species of 'bees' in Britain alone. All bees are insects and belong to the order Hymenoptera. The 250 British species are classified into almost thirty genera, of which the two best known are *Apis*, the honeybee, which is not native to Britain, and *Bombus*, which contains the bumble (or humble) bees. Although bumblebees do not produce honey in sufficient amounts for us to collect, they are important pollinators, along with honeybees. Without them, many wild flowers and certain crops would be unable to set seed.

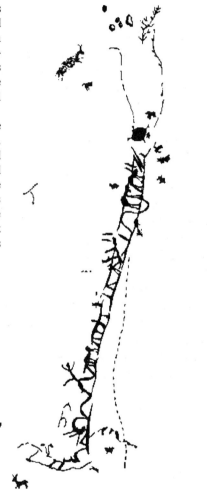

7.1 Rock painting at Barranc Fondo, Castellón, Spain, showing the collection of honey from a bees' nest, reached by a ladder. Bees can be seen flying around. There are human figures on a ladder reaching up to the nest, and what appears to be a group of people waiting to share the honey. This painting is believed to date from about 7000 BC. Drawing approximately one quarter of actual size

Life in a honeybee colony

At its peak in summer, a healthy colony of honeybees typically contains 50 000 **workers**, a few hundred **drones** (males), a single **queen** and a number of combs containing eggs, larvae, pupae, honey and pollen as shown in Figure 7.2. The eggs, larvae and pupae are kept in an area of the hive known as a brood nest which is surrounded by pollen. Honey is stored above and around the pollen. In 1845 a Polish beekeeper, the Rev.

47

7.2 Honeybee workers at the edge of the brood nest. Here the cells are packed with pollen

Johann Dzierzon, put forward his now famous theory to explain the development of the three kinds of adult bees found in a colony. Dzierzon suggested that when a queen has mated and returns to her colony, she can lay two kinds of eggs. These two types of eggs differ in only one respect: one is fertilised and the other is not. Dzierzon suggested that drones develop from unfertilised eggs, and workers and queens from fertilised ones.

Dzierzon's theory that **parthenogenesis**, or virgin birth, is responsible for the production of males was hotly disputed, but is now fully accepted. When a queen mates, she receives spermatozoa from a drone which she stores in her **spermatheca**. The sperm may be stored here for years. As the queen is able to control the release of sperm from her spermatheca prior to each egg being laid, she can determine whether an egg will develop into a haploid male or a diploid female.

The vast majority of fertilised eggs develop into workers. However, a few fertilised eggs are laid in special **queen cells**. These hang vertically from the comb and are larger than the horizontal worker cells. For the first three days, queen larvae and worker larvae appear to be treated by the workers in exactly the same way, being fed on **royal jelly** – a highly nutritious food secreted by the hypopharyngeal and mandibular glands of the worker honeybees. After the first three days worker larvae are switched from royal jelly to a mixture of pollen and nectar, or dilute honey; the larvae destined to develop into queens continue to be fed on royal jelly.

New queens are produced, often at the height of the breeding season, should the existing queen die or become old, diseased or injured. Typically several queens are reared and these fight so that only one survives. When she is about ten days old the surviving virgin queen will go on a **nuptial flight**. During the flight she attracts drones from other colonies, and mates with several of them.

After mating the young queen returns to her hive and continues to be fed by the workers. She grows larger and after a few days begins to lay eggs. Each year she will lay up to two hundred thousand eggs – her own weight in eggs every day!

The queen is the only female within the colony to reproduce; the workers do not normally lay eggs. They are altruistic in that they reduce their opportunities for reproduction by helping another individual, the queen. This puzzled Charles Darwin. How, he wondered, could such **altruism** evolve? He reasoned that the drones and new queens are related to the workers. From the point of view of a worker, each drone is her brother, and each new queen is her sister. Although a worker forgoes her own reproductive opportunities, copies of her genes are carried in the queen (her mother). In a sense, therefore, although workers do not themselves reproduce they reproduce via the queen. The evolutionary process that allows such a surrender of an organism's reproductive potential to its relatives is called **kin selection**. It must be added that some scientists paint a less rosy picture of life in a honeybee colony. They suggest that the queen manipulates the workers into rearing her offspring, through the production of **pheromones**, rather than reproducing for themselves.

Most workers live about six weeks, though those that emerge in autumn may survive until spring. Workers perform a variety of tasks. They clean out brood cells from which bees have recently emerged; assist in thermoregulation of the hive by fanning their wings; feed the larvae; build combs; forage for water, pollen and nectar and sometimes help guard the colony. The tasks performed by a worker depend on her age. When she has only recently emerged she is most likely to stay in the hive cleaning out brood cells or helping to incubate the developing larvae. Towards the end of her life she is more likely to perform the dangerous job of foraging outside the hive.

Worker honeybees can communicate with each other using what may be the most sophisticated communication system of any animal species except ourselves. This is an impressive feat, considering their brains are a thousand million times lighter than ours!

Communication in honeybees

More than 2000 years ago Aristotle found that although a rich source of food might remain undiscovered by honeybees for hours or even days, once a single bee had located the food, many new bees soon appeared. The way in which honeybees communicate about food sources was discovered by the great Austrian ethologist Karl von Frisch in a series of classic experiments early this century.

Distance communication

When a worker collects high-quality food within about 80 metres of the hive, she performs a **round dance** on her return to the hive as illustrated in Figure 7.3. This dance is performed in the dark on a vertical comb. The other workers follow the dancing bee about on the comb and sense the vibrations she produces. After this, some of the workers may fly out of the hive and search for the food source. They search only within about 80 metres, but have no information about the direction of the food. They are helped by the fact that they pick up odour cues from the body of the dancing bee, and may taste regurgitated nectar. The round dance does contain information about the richness of the food source. The richer it is, the more often the returning forager changes the direction of her dance.

If a worker finds a rich source of food more than about 80 metres from the hive, she performs a

7.3 The round dance of the honeybee. This is performed when the food source is within about 80 metres of the hive. The dance contains no information about the direction of the food

waggle dance on her return as illustrated in Figure 7.4. The waggle dance conveys information about the precise distance of the food source from the hive, in the range of 80–1000 m. The information is conveyed in three ways:

- the greater the distance to the food, the longer it takes for the returning forager to complete each dance circuit
- the greater the distance to the food, the fewer abdominal waggles are given during the central straight-run portion of the dance
- the greater the distance to the food, the lower the frequency with which the dancing bee produces vibrations while dancing.

Direction communication

The waggle dance also conveys information about the direction of the food source as indicated in Figure 7.4. In the dark hive, the angle which the straight-run portion of the dance makes with the vertical is the same as the angle of the food source (clockwise) from the sun.

Honey

The surplus honey that a beekeeper can harvest without harm to a colony may be between 5 and 50 kg in any one year, with a mean of about 15 kg. Today, with the availability of sucrose (cane and beet sugar), honey is no longer as important to us as a sweetener as it once was; until the sixteenth century there was no sugar producing crop in Europe.

About 40% of a honey is **fructose**, 30% is **glucose**, 10% consists of various disaccharides including **sucrose** and **maltose**, and only 17% is water. The remaining 3% or so consists of amino acids, minerals, vitamins and various acids. No two honeys are identical. Most honeys are best eaten within two or three years. After that time the honey does not go bad, but it loses its characteristic flavour and simply tastes sweet.

Nectars usually contain more water than honeys do. A larger proportion of the sugar in nectars is disaccharide than in honeys. The conversion of nectar into honey can be brought about only by the action of certain enzymes present in glandular secretions of the hypopharyngeal glands of bees. **Sucrase** converts the sucrose from the nectar into glucose and fructose. Another important enzyme produced by the bees' hypopharyngeal glands is **glucose oxidase**. This oxidises glucose to **gluconic acid** and is therefore responsible for the low pH of honey (on average about 3.9). Gluconic acid inhibits bacterial growth and in Ancient Egypt and medieval times honey was an important ingredient of many medicines. More recently honey has occasionally been used in hospitals as a surgical dressing for open wounds. A further enzyme produced by bees is amylase which breaks down starch to maltose and may be involved in the bees' digestion of pollen.

Pollen is collected by bees, and is carried to the hive on their hind legs as shown in Figure 7.5. Pollen is rich in amino acids and is used to feed the larvae. Although it is stored in different cells from honey, some pollen inevitably gets into the honey. The pollen grains from different plant genera or even species can be distinguished under a microscope by their size and shape, and surface patterns such as furrows, pores and spines (see Figure 7.6). The study of pollen is known as **palynology**, and palynological investigation of pollen present in honey enables the floral sources of a honey to be identified.

Life in a bumblebee colony

A honeybee colony may last for many years, and its queen does no foraging. Within a colony, hundreds or thousands of the workers overwinter with the queen. With bumblebees, however, only the queen survives the winter, buried in the soil. In spring she emerges from hibernation and forages actively. After a few weeks she looks for somewhere

7.4 The waggle dance of the honeybee. (a) The directional information contained in the dance is most easy to see when the dance is performed outside the hive on a horizontal surface. In this case the bee runs directly at the food source in the central part of her dance. (b) Inside the dark hive the dance is performed on a vertical comb. Here the dance is oriented with respect to gravity

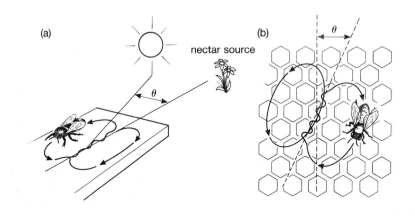

to establish her nest. Often she takes over an old bumblebee nest or the deserted nest of a small mammal or bird. Having formed a suitable nesting chamber the queen lays her first eggs. Within a month or so the first workers emerge, and soon begin foraging and helping the queen to tend the other eggs and larvae. Once there are sufficient workers to do all the foraging the queen remains within the nest.

When the colony is mature some unfertilised eggs are laid which develop into males, and some fertilised eggs are reared as new queens. As in honeybees, males do little except try to reproduce with young queens from other colonies, though male bumblebees may occasionally help in colony defence. The life cycle of a typical bumblebee is shown in Figure 7.7.

7.5 *Honeybees collecting pollen from willow catkins* (Salix caprea). *The bee on the left is removing pollen from the anthers with her mandibles. The bee in flight is transferring honey from her tongue to the pollen, enabling her to pack it on her 'pollen baskets' on her hind legs. The bee hanging by a foreleg is shaping her pollen loads with her middle legs*

7.6 *Pollen grains of different plant species have characteristically different shapes and sizes. A. yellow loosestrife, B. white water-lilly, C. bluebell, D. meadowsweet. All to scale and magnified 1250 x*

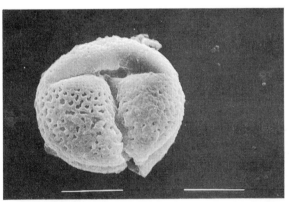

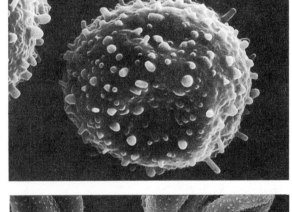

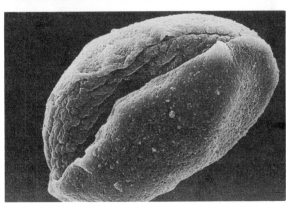

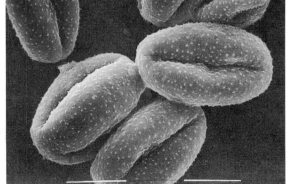

Bees as pollinators

The flowering plants (**angiosperms**) first evolved about a hundred and twenty million years ago during the Cretaceous period. At this time there were already many species of insects in existence – thrips, cockroaches, hemipteran bugs, beetles and the more primitive flies are all known from the fossil record of that time. The origin and early evolution of the angiosperms is still not understood – in a private letter Darwin once referred to the origin of the angiosperms as an 'abominable mystery'. Nevertheless, it is clear that there has been a long period of insect-plant co-evolution which continues to this day. Many insects rely on plants to supply them with nectar and pollen; many plants rely on insects for their pollination.

The relationship is typically **mutualistic**, both partners benefiting from the association. It may be that the origin of the angiosperms in the Cretaceous period helped the insects to undergo an explosive **adaptive radiation**, leading to the evolution of many new species of insects. This in turn may have fuelled the evolution of new species of flowering plants.

We are familiar with the idea that many wild plants rely on insects for their pollination. It is not so often realised that many crops depend on bees for their pollination and hence seed set. The Cambridge ecologist Sally Corbet has pointed out that even in crops traditionally thought of as self-fertilising, cross-fertilisation by bees may increase the number and quality of seeds. Occasional episodes of cross-fertilisation may lead to **hybrid**

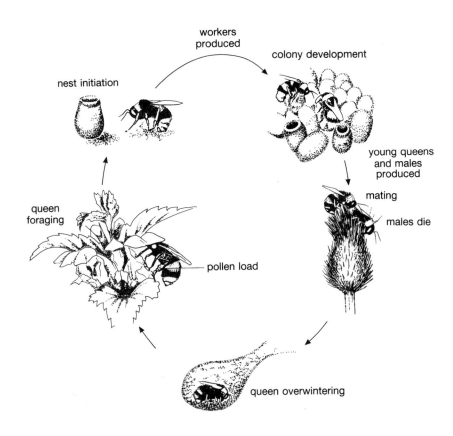

7.7 Life cycle of a typical Bombus, *bumblebee, in a temperate region. Only queens overwinter*

vigour as new alleles are introduced into the genome, leading to more loci being heterozygous.

In Britain, few farmers and agriculturalists imagine that they can manipulate pollination to increase the yield of their crops, yet in Canada yields of alfalfa crops have increased dramatically since farmers introduced the alfalfa leafcutter bee *Megachile rotundata*. Fruit growers sometimes have apiaries in the hope that the honeybees will assist in pollination and thus enable the trees to set more fruit. It is possible, though, that bumblebees would be more effective pollinators. Bumblebees might be encouraged by providing nest sites and allowing wild herbs to grow between the trees.

Different bee species pollinate different flowers. Honeybees, for instance, have short tongues and find it difficult to reach nectar in the relatively deep flowers of red clover *Trifolium pratense*. This means that some crops require longer-tongued bees for their pollination, such as species of bumblebees. During the last 30 years most species of bumblebee have declined in Britain as natural habitats have been destroyed. These habitats, including old meadows, saltmarshes, sand dunes and shingle, are rich in bumblebee nest sites and contain many biennial and perennial plants that provide food for bumblebees throughout the year. It is known that before 1960, a total of 15 different species of bumblebee occurred in central and eastern England. By 1976, eight of these had disappeared from the most intensively farmed part of the region. It is even possible that the decrease in bumblebee populations is partly responsible for the shift from insect-pollinated to wind-pollinated crops in much of England. Crops such as seed clover and field beans which require bumblebee pollination became less attractive to farmers, partly due to their reputation for irregular seeding. The irregular seeding will have been partly due to the loss of many of our bumblebees.

Further reading

Crane, E. (1980) *A Book of Honey*. Oxford University Press.

Gould, J.L. and Gould, C.G. (1988) *The Honey Bee*. W.H. Freeman & Co.

Heinrich, B. (1979) *Bumblebee Economics*, Harvard University Press.

Thought questions

1 What advantages do honeybees gain from living in large colonies?

2 How might the commercial importance of bumblebee pollination be investigated?

3 Honeybees have been kept by people for thousands of years. Suggest what effects this may have had on their behaviour and ecology.

Things to do

1. A great deal of valuable information on honeybees can be gathered simply by recording their behaviour at different times of year and under different weather conditions. See how the numbers of bees and their activity depend on temperature, windspeed and cloud cover. Try to describe the different techniques the workers use for collecting pollen and nectar from different plant species.

2. If you want to make a delicious and refreshing sweet drink using honey, here is a receipt for 'instant lemon refresher' taken from Eva Crane's *A Book of Honey* (1980), Oxford University Press.

   Take one lemon, 50 g of honey, six ice cubes and 800 ml water. Cut the lemon into a dozen chunks. Place in an electric blender and switch to maximum speed for a few seconds. Add the ice cubes and water, and switch to maximum speed for 20 seconds. Strain. Return to the blender. Add the honey and switch on for a final 15 seconds.

3. *Bumblebees* by O.E. Prys-Jones and S.A. Corbet (1987), Cambridge University Press, contains lots of suggestions for projects on bumblebees, and also has a key to the different species in Britain.

8
Cooking and Keeping Food Fresh

Foods are chemical substances. When eaten, digested and absorbed by the body they produce energy and provide for the growth and repair of tissues.

The human diet worldwide encompasses a vast array of different food types, many of which are routinely prepared for consumption by the application of heat: in other words they are **cooked**. There is archaeological evidence to show that experiments in domestic cooking began far back in prehistory; Paleolithic firehearths are well known, certainly in Europe, dating back to almost one million years ago. This chapter examines the biology of cooking and looks at other ways in which we keep food fresh.

Why do we cook food?

Cooking may have been carried out by primitive man as a ritual or symbolic act, 'a piece of magic' to render the food clean and safe. Cooking played a part in promoting restraint in early man. Rather than devouring raw game at the kill, the meat was taken back to be eaten by members of the group around the hearth.

Cooking may also be used to improve the flavour, texture, colour, smell and hence **palatability** of food, although palatability is a matter of opinion and often of tradition. Raw fish may be perfectly palatable to a Japanese but is conspicuously absent from the English diet. Certainly salad and fruit are appetising to a European, but imagine a diet composed entirely of raw food! Cooking may also increase the **digestibility** of food. Milk, for example, is more easily digested once boiled; tough meat may be made more tender if cooked by an appropriate method.

To understand the changes which cooking causes in food, we need to consider the effects of heat on the cells and chemicals it contains.

Proteins are present in the form of enzymes and as major structural molecules. They are particularly sensitive to heat; at temperatures above about 40°C protein is denatured, its molecular structure breaks down and **coagulation** occurs. This tends to make the proteins more easily attacked by digestive proteolytic enzymes, although prolonged heating renders proteins hard and indigestible.

Meat, pastry and bread typically develop a pleasing brown coloration during cooking; this is due to the production of various **browning pigments**. For example, reducing sugars combine chemically with amino acids, peptides and proteins under the influence of heat to give a distinctive colour.

Intercellular **pectin**, which cements cells together in vegetable matter, becomes more soluble on heating and enters the cooking water. As a result vegetables become softer on cooking, although the desirability of this change is a matter of personal opinion.

Starch is insoluble, being a large carbohydrate molecule. During bread-making, starch granules in the dough are heated and become increasingly soluble and viscous; the resultant gelatinised starch is much more easily hydrolysed by amylase in the human alimentary canal.

In contrast to these desirable effects of cooking, the heating of food may result in some loss of flavour through volatile chemicals being driven off; soluble materials including certain **vitamins** may be lost in the cooking water. Additionally, vitamin C and those in the vitamin B group are destroyed by heat. The cooking of foods may well lead to a decrease in their nutritive value.

Food spoilage: native enzymes and microbes

A vital outcome of the process of cooking is the **preservation** of food. It must have become apparent even to primitive people that cooking food enabled it to be kept for a longer time.

Why does cooking help to preserve food? Any food remains palatable and safe to eat only for a limited time, after which it shows obvious signs of spoilage or deterioration. For example, when wheat grain is kept at 10°–15°C in dry conditions it typically lasts well for several years, whereas raw meat or soft fruit only keeps for a couple of days.

In active living tissue, complex enzyme-catalysed biochemical reactions take place, carefully controlled by the cell. In raw, unpreserved food, however, the cellular structure breaks down and the reactions become uncontrolled. Hydrolytic enzymes are released from **lysosomes** ('suicide bags'). The enzymes digest the molecules of the cells which leads to undesirable changes in food. For instance, in bruised plant tissue the breakdown of carbohydrates under anaerobic conditions yields ethanol or acetaldehyde, both of which taste unpleasant. Breakdown of structural pectin also occurs which causes plant tissue to become progressively softer, until the tissue collapses altogether. The enzyme-controlled reactions leading to this breakdown are those which occur naturally as fruit ripens. When they cause food tissue to change beyond the stage at which it is best for eating, they are undesirable.

Unrefined fats and oils often contain lipases as contaminants. In time, these enzymes cause the fat or oil to go rancid by oxidising them to their constituent glycerol and fatty acids. Similarly, oxidation of phenols rapidly turns the surfaces of apple slices brown. Physical changes such as desiccation tend to play only a small part in the spoilage of food.

The above changes are caused by the action of **native enzymes** naturally present within food. Much deterioration, however, is caused by **microbes** – various fungi and bacteria. Such microbes make no distinction between 'food for humans' and 'valuable available nutrients'. Microbes are ubiquitous; they readily contaminate any food source and reproduce rapidly. In breaking down the foodstuffs to obtain nutrients, the microbes bring about changes which cause different forms of decay.

Fungal moulds such as *Aspergillus*, *Mucor* and *Rhizopus* can grow on most food types, but grow particularly well on sugary or starchy foods stored in damp conditions. Airborne spores settle on the

8.1 *Types of food spoilage microbes*
i) *Fungus*, Aspergillus flavus
ii) *Yeast*, Saccharomyces cerevisiae
iii) *Bacterium*, Salmonella typhimurium

(i)

× 160

(ii)

× 670

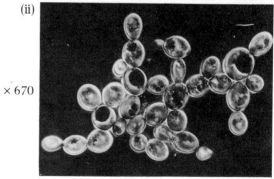

(iii)

× 1000

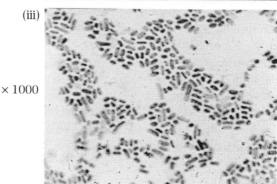

food and germinate; a visible mycelial mat then grows over the surface of the food. Yeasts are another group of fungi which cause food spoilage, by fermenting sugars to alcohol and gaseous carbon dioxide.

Of the **bacteria**, many affect the palatability of food and reduce its nutritive value. One example is the *Lactobacillus* genus of bacteria, which produce lactic acid and cause sourness in milk. Others not only cause spoilage but are also pathogenic. Foodstuffs such as fish, meat and poultry provide moist, low-acid, nutrient-rich conditions ideal for the growth of such bacteria. These pathogens may cause illness when they are taken into the body with food and multiply there, setting up an infection. *Salmonella*, for example, may cause enteritis or typhoid. Other pathogenic bacteria, such as *Staphylococcus aureus*, produce toxins as they grow. It is these **toxins** rather than the organism itself that cause illness when consumed. The most serious form of food-poisoning is caused by a neurotoxin produced by the bacterium *Clostridium botulinum*. Such poisoning is usually fatal. Fortunately the toxin is readily destroyed by heating and the incidence of botulism is rare.

It should be noted that even those changes which result in food eventually becoming unacceptable, and indeed positively dangerous, may be considered desirable in their early stages. Certain changes caused by microbes, such as the **fermentation** of grape sugars by yeasts, are put to good use in the production of wine. Blue cheeses such as Roquefort and Stilton owe their characteristic flavour to the presence of the mould *Penicillium roqueforti* (see Chapters 10 and 11). Cheese-making provides a good example of the possible beneficial effects of bacteria. Likewise, certain biochemical changes render food more acceptable. Game meat matures because of a lack of oxygen in the muscle tissue, becoming more tender and stronger-tasting as it is hung. Similarly, much fruit attains its optimum ripeness after picking. However, the degree to which food may change as a result of biochemical or microbial action and still remain acceptable is a matter of opinion. Such opinion varies between differing human cultures and

between individuals within a culture. Some people prefer meat with a strong flavour and their milk sour. In certain parts of East Asia a 'good' egg is partly decomposed.

Why preserve food?

Whatever individual tastes may be, it is necessary at some point to arrest the deterioration of food which will occur through the action of microbes and native food enzymes.

Inevitably, time will elapse between harvesting or slaughter and the consumption of food. Areas of food production are often far from the main centres of population and food must be transported between the two. Many staple foods such as vegetables are seasonal, but demand for them is perennial and they need to be stored for consumption during the following months. Food also spends time in the shop and pantry.

Preservation and storage of food has now advanced beyond the bounds of necessity into the realms of convenience. For example, demand in the temperate world for tropical fruits such as pineapple or mango, and the desire for a fresh fig in February, can and is being met.

Food therefore needs to be able to withstand storage and transportation without deterioration in quality. To this end, various methods of food preservation have been developed.

The theory and practice of food preservation

The overall aim of **food preservation** is to prolong the length of time for which the food retains its quality and acceptability. Such preservation has been carried out for thousands of years in attempts to improve food supplies. The Egyptians used vinegar or salt to preserve fish and meat; the Romans mixed straw with snow and packed this around perishable foods. Sun-drying, smoke-curing, immersion in oil and cooking have been used for centuries as means of preservation.

For all these methods, in addition to others more

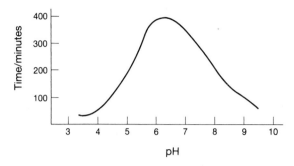

8.2 *The maximum time that the heat resistant spores of* Clostridium botulinum *can survive, after heating to a temperature of 100°C, under different pH conditions.*

recently developed, the underlying principle is the same. The food is protected from decay or deterioration by arresting natural changes within the food itself, or by preventing or destroying sources of contamination.

Whether spoilage is caused by biochemical or microbial factors, the enzymic reactions responsible for it are essentially the same. The reactions must be stopped or inhibited if food preservation is to be successful. The rates of such reactions can be reduced by the following methods:
- lowering the temperature
- removing or excluding a reactant
- removing or inactivating the enzyme(s) or microbes
- altering the reaction system.

All methods of food preservation, several of which are employed routinely in industry, apply the basic principle of controlling rates of reactions. We will now consider the main features of the individual methods.

Cooking

At temperatures above 70–80°C, the heat of cooking destroys bacterial toxins and enzymes both native to the food and introduced by microbes. Although the majority of microbes are killed when heated to 100°C, certain bacterial spores and toxins, such as those of *Clostridium botulinum* and *Staphylococcus aureus* respectively, are particularly resistant to heat. They require extended periods of cooking at very high temperatures in order to be rendered harmless.

The **sterilisation** of milk involves heating it to a temperature of 63°C under pressure, and then filtering and sealing it in bottles which are further heated for 30 minutes at about 100°C. This process effectively kills the majority of microbes, but causes changes in the composition and flavour of milk, with a loss of up to 50% of the vitamin C and vitamin B content.

A less severe method of heat preservation is that of **pasteurisation**, traditionally done by heating milk to 65°C for 30 minutes before cooling it. In the faster flash process milk is heated to 72°C for just 15 seconds then rapidly cooled to 10°C. This

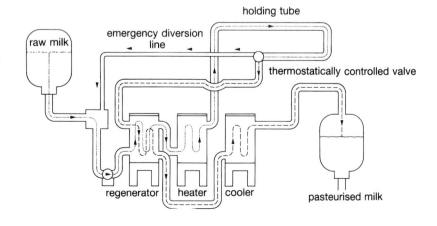

8.3 *A simplified diagram of a flash-pasteurizing plant. Milk is heated in two stages to 72°C and held at a high temperature for a few seconds before giving up some of its heat to incoming milk and then finally being cooled further to 10°C.*

process destroys pathogenic microbes but leaves unaffected many others which will in time cause souring and clotting of milk. The spoiling reactions of the remaining microbes are slowed by refrigerating the milk.

Fruit and vegetable juices are also preserved by pasteurisation. The high acidity of these juices discourages the growth of microbes and protects the vitamin C they contain.

Canning

Canning involves heat sterilisation of food accompanied by **hermetic** (that is, making it air-tight) **sealing**. In this way, all microbes and enzymes are destroyed and a potential reactant, oxygen, is removed.

Vegetables in particular may be preserved prior to canning by **blanching**: heating to 90–100°C for 1–5 minutes. This destroys enzymes which could be sufficiently active to cause discoloration of the food before they are denatured by the high temperature of the sterilisation process during canning.

Prepared food is placed in cans which are swept out with nitrogen or evacuated to exclude air. The cans are then sealed while still under vacuum.

x 2

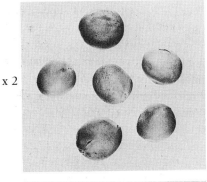
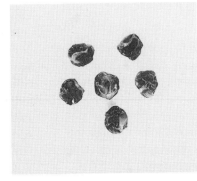

x 10

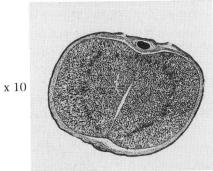
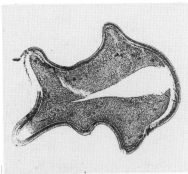

x 800

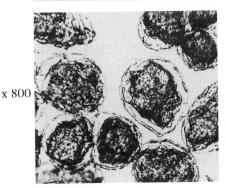
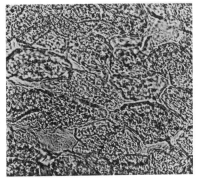

8.4 A comparison of air-dried and freeze-dried peas

(i) Freeze-dried peas (x 1.5). These largely retain their original shape, although cracks develop in their skins

(ii) Air-dried peas (x 1.5). These show a shrivelled appearance due to contraction on drying

(iii) Section of freeze-dried pea (x 7.5). This shows retention of much of the original cellular structure

(iv) Section of air-dried pea (x 7.5). This shows the contraction and compaction of the cells

(v) Section of freeze-dried pea (x 600). This shows cells still capable of separation

(vi) Section of air-dried pea (x 600). This shows a dense structure of collapsed and adhering cells.

(From Nuffield Advanced Science (1974) - "Food Science")

Sterilisation by heat follows, the temperature and duration of which depends upon the contents of the can. Some foods require more time to attain sterility than is necessary for optimum palatability, in which case canning may be an inappropriate method of preservation for them.

Vacuum/gas packing

Hermetic sealing is used as a means of preservation in **vacuum** or **gas packing**. Food is placed in a plastic or aluminium foil packet which is flushed

8.5 How temperature and a common preservative, sodium chloride, together protect against the growth of salmonellae on food such as meat. The two diagrams, based upon the rate of growth of bacteria in a laboratory medium, show the computer's prediction of how long it takes for the bacteria to double in number at given concentrations of salt and degrees of temperature at two different levels of acidity

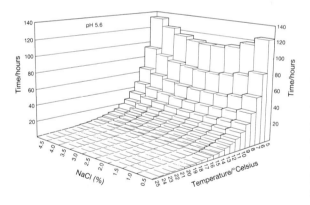

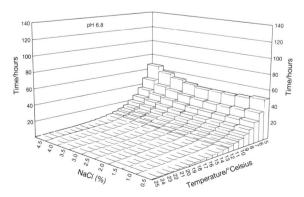

out with nitrogen or evacuated, and then sealed. This method prevents the growth of **aerobic microbes**, but **anaerobic microbes** and enzymes naturally present within the food remain active. Rigorous standards of hygiene are therefore necessary in the preparing and packaging of the food; the method is most appropriate for dried or salty foods which are poor media for microbial growth.

Dehydration

Removal of water is the oldest form of food preservation. Records of **dehydration** of meat and fish date back to 4000 BC, and sun-drying remains a routine procedure in many countries. Dehydration is effective in preventing or inhibiting the spoiling action of microbes as it reduces the amount of water in which microbial (or food) enzymes can carry out their reactions.

Modern methods of drying include air- and freeze-drying. **Air-drying** involves the use of temperatures of 40–100°C in air. Although food so preserved is very resistant to penetration by oxygen, there are disadvantages. The heat treatment may cause discoloration and, as a result of denaturation of structural proteins, the tissue cannot regain its original form and texture on rehydration.

Freeze-drying involves freezing of food, and then applying a high vacuum which causes the ice in the food to change directly from the solid state to the gaseous water vapour state. In this process, volatile compounds and hence delicate flavours are preserved. Freeze-dried tissue has a porous, open structure which rehydrates readily to produce a quite acceptable texture. However, freeze-drying does provide a large inner surface area for oxidation.

Chilling and freezing

Chilling inhibits the activity of enzymes and so slows the process of spoilage by all microbes except psychrophilic (cold-tolerant) bacteria. Chilling is suitable only for short-term storage. In the case of apples and potatoes, chilling may be combined with a modification of the atmosphere of the store-room, when part of the atmospheric oxygen is replaced with carbon dioxide. This slows both the respiratory activity and ripening process of the plant tissue. An alternative method, only very recently developed, is to combine chilling with the use of the spray 'Nutri-save' which is a derivative of chitin. The spray forms a semipermeable coating on fruit such as apples, pears and peaches which restricts the flow of oxygen to the fruit tissues and so slows the ripening process.

In **freezing**, very low temperatures prevent the action of most enzymes, and water is immobilised as ice, so preventing it from acting as a solvent for spoilage reactions. Food begins to freeze between about -1°C and -3°C. The normal temperature for commercial deep freezing is around -20°C, at which point most microbes are killed. Rapid freezing techniques are employed as this results in the formation of only tiny ice crystals, too small to cause major structural damage to the cells of the food tissue. Some foods with a very high water content, such as strawberries, cannot be successfully preserved by freezing as they suffer such a marked deterioration in texture on thawing.

Once thawed, food should be eaten without delay as any microbes or enzymes which survive the freezing process will become active and multiply rapidly.

Chemical additives

Many familiar chemicals are employed in the preservation of food. Sodium chloride, **common salt**, has long been used in the 'curing' of meat. Its effect is to reduce the availability of water in the food by increasing the ionic concentration, so inhibiting microbial growth. A curing solution also contains **nitrates** which certain salt-tolerant microbes convert to nitrites. These nitrites combine with haemoglobin to form nitrosohaemoglobin

Dye (British List)	EC No.	Australia	Canada	EC countries	Finland	Japan	Norway*	Spain	Sweden	Switzerland	South Africa	United States
Ponceau 4R	E124	+		+	+	+		+	+	+	+	
Carmoisine	E122	+		+				+		+	+	
Amaranth	E123	+	+	+	+	+		+	+	+		
Erythrosine BS	E127	+	+	+	+	+		+	+	+	+	+
Red 2G	–										+	
Tartrazine	E102	+	+	+	+	+		+	+	+	+	+
Yellow ZG	–	+										
Sunset yellow FCP	E110	+	+	+	+	+		+	+	+	+	+
Quinoline yellow	E104			+	+			+	+	+	+	
Green S	E142	+		+					+	+	+	
Indigo carmine	E132	+	+	+	+	+		+	+	+	+	+
Brilliant blue FCF	–		+	+	+	+					+	+
Patent blue V	E131			+				+	+	+	+	
Brown FK	–		+	+						+		
Chocolate brown	–		+	+						+		
Black PN	E151	+	+	+				+	+	+	+	

*No artificial colours permitted

From: Pyke, M. (1981) *Food Science & Technology.* John Murray.

Table 8.1 Permitted food colours. These colours are generally permitted. Local regulations may change from time to time and not all foods may be coloured

Absorbed dose	Application	
Low: less than 1 kilogray	To kill parasites such as *Trichinella spiralis* and *Taenia saginata* in raw meat	
	To kill insects in cereal grains, fruit, cocoa beans and other crops	
	To inhibit sprouting or germination in certain crops, for example, onions and potatoes	
	To control ripening, for example, tropical fruits	
Medium: 1–10 kilograys	To reduce microflora that spoil meat, fish, fruits and vegetables	
	To kill live food-poisoning bacteria, particularly *Salmonella* and *Campylobacter* in raw poultry, prawns and shellfish	
High: greater than 10 kilograys	To reduce bacterial contamination of herbs and spices	

Table 8.2 The use of irradiation in food preservation.

(from J. C. Platt Inside Science New Scientist 15th May 1988)

which is responsible for the characteristic pink colour of cured meat

In the Dutch cheese industry, sodium nitrite has traditionally been used to prevent undesirable changes in flavour as a result of the growth of *Clostridium* spp. There is now some concern that high levels of nitrates and nitrites may be carcinogenic (see also Chapter 17).

The preservation of food by **pickling** in vinegar is very effective because the solution (acetic acid) has a pH which is too low for most enzyme activity and all microbial growth. Concentrated sugar solutions also osmotically inhibit the growth of microbes by effectively dehydrating them, and fruits are often preserved in this way as jams.

Many less familiar chemicals are also added to food but their use is strictly controlled by law. A list of officially permitted chemical additives is available. **Antioxidants** may be added to butter, oils and fats; sulphur dioxide is sometimes added to blanching solutions to enhance colour retention by vegetables; the antibiotic nisin, which does not have a medical use, is added to canned food and some cheeses. A variety of synthetic diazo compounds is employed as **food colours** although their use is controversial. Certain additives have been linked with

hyperactivity in children and have been reported to be carcinogenic in experimental animals. The identification of all additives to food, the **E compounds**, is required by law.

Irradiation

Short-wave ionising **radiation** from electrons, gamma- or X-rays destroys microbes as it passes through food. It neither cooks the food nor signifi-

8.6 *Comparison of the storage properties of irradiated and non-irradiated strawberries*

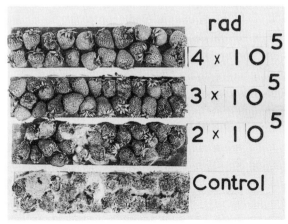

cantly increases its natural level of radioactivity. Medium doses (0.1–1.0 Mrad) of radiation effectively 'pasteurise' foods such as raw chicken, and low doses (8000 rad) are used commercially to prevent sprouting in potatoes. However, the level of radiation required to 'sterilise' foods as thoroughly as is achieved in canning (5 Mrad) results in the development of unpleasant flavours and would not normally destroy any bacterial toxins present in the food.

The future of food preservation

Many of the current methods of food preservation result in a deterioration in one or several of the factors which go to make up its quality, that is colour, flavour, texture, appearance or palatability. The aim of the food scientist and technologist is to improve present preservation techniques and to develop new ones which will prolong the life of food without detracting from its overall quality.

Further reading

Pyke, M. (1981) *Food Science and Technology*. John Murray.
Platt, J.C. (1988) The Food We Eat. *New Scientist*, May 1988, p. 3.

Thought questions

1 List the advantages and disadvantages of food preservation.

2 Explain why irradiation is a controversial means of preserving food.

Things to do

Make your own Christmas pudding.

A good Christmas pudding is steam-cooked beneath a pudding cloth. It is thus preserved by heat sterilisation; subsequent microbial decomposition is further prevented osmotically, by the ingredients' high sugar content. Enclosed in its bowl it will keep for many months or years and improve markedly in flavour with keeping (this is complex biochemistry!).

Ingredients

250 g self-raising flour
juice and grated rind of an orange
375 g fresh white breadcrumbs
1 teaspoon mixed spice
500 g currants
half a nutmeg grated
500 g sultanas
1 teaspoon salt
500 g stoned raisins
6 eggs beaten to froth
375 g finely chopped suet
120 cm^3 brown ale
125 g chopped candied peel
500 g brown sugar
65 g shredded almonds
1 grated apple

Mix all the ingredients together. Empty into a greased bowl. Cover with greased paper and then a flour-covered cloth, well tied down. Steam for 6 hours. Leave to cool. Store in a dry place; no refrigeration is needed. Steam again for 3 hours before serving.

9
Genetic Engineering

Until recently the only way in which people could alter the genetic make-up of organisms was by the slow process of artificial selection. Within the last 15 years, though, **genetic engineering** has opened up prospects for people to control the DNA of organisms. Genes can already be moved quite easily from one species to another. In a very real sense scientists can now create and manipulate life itself. The next couple of decades will see whether we use or abuse this power.

The principles of genetic engineering

Genetic engineering is also known as **recombinant DNA technology** and it is with DNA and gene splicing that we must begin. As you will know, the Watson-Crick model of the structure of genetic material first proposed in 1953 is still held to be fundamentally correct. The genetic information within cells is determined by the order of the four different **organic bases** which are found in the **nucleotides** of **deoxyribonucleic acid (DNA)**. During the stage of the **cell cycle** known as **interphase**, when the cell is neither dividing nor preparing for division, genes are **transcribed** into **messenger RNA** by **complementary base pairing**. This messenger RNA leaves the nucleus of eukaryotes via the **nuclear pores** and is then **translated** into polypeptide chains on **ribosomes** which may either be free in the **cytosol** or attached to **rough endoplasmic reticulum**.

The most common type of genetic engineering is that in which a gene is removed from one species and inserted into the DNA of another. We will first look at how this is done, and then consider the potential uses of the technology.

The basic tool of recombinant DNA technology consists of enzymes called **restriction enzymes**. The natural function of these enzymes is to protect the cells in which they are found against attack by other organisms such as viruses. They cut up foreign DNA by breaking the bonds between adjacent nucleotides. For this reason they are called **restriction endonucleases**. Restriction endonucleases are very specific and can only act on DNA at points with particular nucleotide sequences. One of the most widely used restriction enzymes is EcoRI, so called because it is produced by a gene on an R plasmid in the colon bacillus *Escherichia coli*.

9.1 The restriction endonuclease EcoRI recognizes the DNA sequence GAATTC and cuts the DNA between the G and A nucleotides

Eco RI recognition sites

"sticky" end

A **plasmid** is a circular, relatively small piece of DNA separate from the main DNA. EcoRI recognises the base sequence GAATTC and cuts between the G and the A as shown in Figure 9.1.

Most restriction enzymes cut DNA in such a way that one strand ends up with a few more nucleotides than the other, as is the case for EcoRI. The result is that the double-stranded DNA has a short single-stranded **sticky end**. Sticky ends can form hydrogen bonds with complementary single-stranded sticky ends on other DNA molecules. This property turns out to be extremely useful in genetic engineering. It means that if the same restriction enzyme used to obtain a piece of DNA from one species is then used on the DNA of another species, the same sticky ends are produced. It is then a relatively easy matter to insert the DNA removed from the first species into the second. For example, a human gene can be removed from human DNA and then inserted into a bacterium such as *E. coli* by means of the same restriction endonuclease, as demonstrated in Figure 9.2. The enzyme **DNA ligase** is then used to join up the sticky ends. Once the foreign DNA is in the bacterium, the bacterium

can be allowed to multiply asexually. Transcription and translation then result in large amounts of the protein coded for by the foreign gene being made by the cell machinery of the bacterium. A cell that has had its genetic material altered by the uptake of foreign DNA is said to have been **transformed**.

It is important to note that restriction enzymes cut DNA only at **palindromic sequences**. (A palindrome is a sequence of letters that reads the same backwards or forwards e.g. the name 'Hannah', or the phrase 'Madam I'm Adam'.) You can see from Figures 9.1 and 9.2 that it is only because restriction enzymes always cut DNA at specific palindromic sequences that they can be used to insert foreign DNA.

Difficulties with genetic engineering

Unfortunately for the genetic engineer, genetic engineering is not as easy as the account above may imply. One problem is that the messenger RNA made by eukaryotic DNA frequently includes long regions that do not code for any amino acids in the final polypeptide. The regions in the DNA

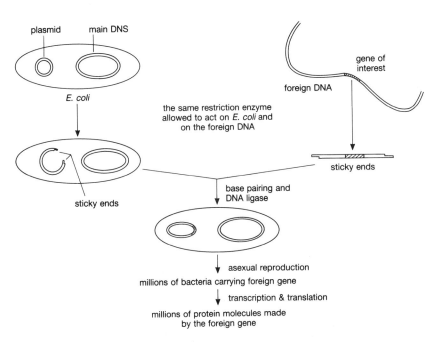

9.2 The fundamental principles of recombinant DNA technology. A restriction enzyme is used to cut the foreign gene one wants to multiply from its DNA. The same enzyme is then used to produce the appropriate sticky ends in the recipient cell that carries a plasmid, such as is found in E. coli. After insertion of the foreign DNA into the recipient cell, the cell is placed in the appropriate environmental conditions to allow rapid multiplication. Finally, messenger RNA synthesis followed by protein synthesis result in synthesis of the foreign protein

that correspond to these regions are known as **introns** because they intrude into the gene. Their discovery in 1977 came as a complete surprise and it is still not known for certain why they are there. There is some evidence that they function in gene regulation. Another possibility is that they are parasitic or selfish stretches of DNA, serving no function other than to replicate themselves.

Whether or not introns serve a function, their presence complicates DNA recombinant technology. In the eukaryotic cell such introns are transcribed into messenger RNA along with the useful regions, known as **exons**. However, before the messenger RNA leaves the nucleus, the introns are removed by special enzymes to leave a shorter piece of messenger RNA which is then translated into the desired polypeptide on the ribosomes as summarised in Figure 9.3. However, if the whole gene is inserted into a bacterial plasmid, the bacterium has no way of knowing which bits are introns and which are exons. The result is that the entire length of messenger RNA is translated into protein – introns and exons. Consequently the protein which is made has a completely different structure from the intended one.

A way round this problem is to obtain messenger RNA from eukaryotic cytoplasm and make **complementary DNA** from it in the laboratory.

Complementary DNA can be made using the enzyme **reverse transcriptase** which makes DNA from messenger RNA by base-pairing in much the same way that messenger RNA is made from ordinary DNA. Since the messenger RNA used is obtained from the cytoplasm, it has already been processed by the cell to remove the regions that correspond to the introns. Accordingly, the complementary DNA made contains all the bases necessary for the synthesis of the desired protein. When this complementary DNA is inserted into a bacterial plasmid, the polypeptide that eventually results has the desired sequence of amino acids.

A quite separate problem with DNA recombinant technology is obtaining the right gene in the first place. Humans, for instance, have between 30 000 and 100 000 genes. How can a molecular biologist find the right one? A variety of techniques is used. One of the most powerful involves the use of **genetic probes**.

Suppose that you want to use bacteria to make large quantities of tropomyosin – one of the proteins involved in muscle contraction. The first thing to do is to obtain the primary sequence of the protein – that is, the sequence of amino acids in the protein. There was a time when such an exercise might involve a team of researchers in full-time work for several years. Nowadays, though, such a

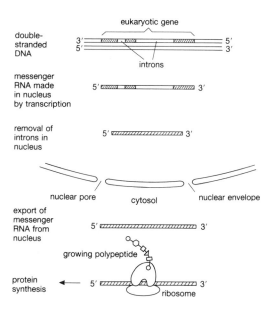

9.3 In eukaryotes messenger RNA is processed in the nucleus by the removal of those sections that correspond to the introns in the DNA. The processed messenger RNA is then exported from the nucleus for translation

task is comparatively routine, and can be done almost automatically by computer-controlled equipment. Once the primary sequence is known, the next stage involves guessing the sequences of bases in the messenger RNA that codes for the protein. Some guessing is involved because most amino acids are coded for by several **codons**, triplets of bases. For instance, phenylalanine is coded for by both UUU and UUC. Having worked out the possible order of bases in the messenger RNA, the next step is to synthesise some single-stranded RNA with this sequence of bases. Such a procedure is completely automatic nowadays and can be done within hours.

Meanwhile, restriction enzymes are used to break up the entire human **genome** into thousands of bits. These bits are then randomly incorporated into bacteria so that no one bacterium contains more than a few bits of human DNA. These bacteria are allowed to grow on agar plates and then the colonies are treated so as to break open the cells and expose the DNA on the plates. Finally, the RNA that was made with the sequence of bases corresponding more or less to the sequence of bases in the messenger RNA that codes for tropomyosin is poured over the agar plates. Hopefully some of the artificially made RNA **hybridises** (i.e. base pairs) with the DNA that codes for tropomyosin. The great majority of the RNA fails to base pair with any of the bacterial DNA. This single-strained RNA can easily be separated from any of the RNA that has hybridised with the bacterial DNA. Hybridised bacterial DNA must contain the gene for tropomyosin. It is then a relatively straightforward job to separate this DNA from the RNA bound to it, clone it up and sequence the gene in question.

The uses of genetic engineering

We are still in the early days of recombinant DNA technology. However, a number of its uses have already been explored. Some have been proven and are now being exploited. Others remain at the research stage.

Synthesis of insulin and human growth hormone

Insulin was one of the first human proteins to be made by genetic engineering. Before this, **diabetics**, who typically produce little or no insulin of their own, had to rely mainly on porcine or bovine insulin obtained as a by-product of the slaughter of pigs and cattle respectively for meat. By the autumn of 1989 at least three-quarters of the 200 000 diabetic patients taking insulin in Britain used human insulin obtained either by recombinant DNA technology or by the enzymatic conversion of porcine insulin into human insulin, known as **semisynthesis**. By contrast, in 1985–6, genetically engineered human insulin was not available and only about 6% of the insulin used in Britain was obtained by semisynthesis.

One advantage of human insulin is that allergies to it are rare, whereas some diabetics develop allergies to porcine or bovine insulin. However, when the British Diabetic Association sent out questionnaires asking about people's experiences on changing to human insulin, about half of those who replied thought they were worse off, mostly because of **hypoglycaemia** which occurs when blood-sugar levels drop dangerously low. The switch to human insulin seems to be accompanied by a change in the symptoms experienced by a patient about to suffer from hypoglycaemia. Instead of the characteristic symptoms of sweating, tremors and palpitations, incipient hypoglycaemia was now associated with an inability to concentrate, speech disturbances and headaches.

It is not yet clear whether it may be advisable for large numbers of diabetics to switch back to porcine or bovine insulin. However, this episode helps to caution against the notion that the use of materials produced by genetic engineering will always be a universal blessing.

Although insulin can be obtained from pigs and cows and given to humans, this is not the case with growth hormone. Growth hormones are more species-specific than insulins, and growth hormones obtained from other species are generally ineffective if given to people. Because of this, the only way of obtaining growth hormone for use in people who fail to produce enough of it, and are therefore significantly shorter in height than normal, used to be from the pituitary glands of people who had died. As you may imagine, this was an extremely time-consuming and expensive procedure, as each pituitary gland at the moment of death contains only a minute amount of growth hormone. Accordingly, gram for gram, human growth hormone used to be far more expensive than gold. However, the substance has now been made by genetic engineering and seems extremely effective.

Genetic engineering in plants

So far it has proved surprisingly difficult to move genes from some species of plant to another. Part of the problem is the difficulty of finding a suitable vector to carry the genes. However, it has recently been found, somewhat to everyone's surprise, that literally firing foreign DNA at a plant with an air gun works quite well! The DNA is mixed with small tungsten particles, approximately 1 μm in diameter, to which it sticks. When fired into a plant, some of the host cells take up the foreign DNA and integrate it into their cells (see Chapter 14). These cells can subsequently be identified and **cell culture** techniques used to generate entire plants from such single cells (see Figure 14.2).

One recent example where genetic engineering has been accomplished in plants is in the tobacco plant. This species, in common with several others, is susceptible to infection by cucumber mosaic virus, a virus with RNA for its genetic material. Researchers at Plant Breeding International in Cambridge have managed to breed tobacco plants resistant to this virus. The strategy developed from the chance observation that some varieties of cucumber mosaic virus contain, in addition to their main RNA molecule, a small extra molecule of RNA known as **satellite RNA**. This satellite RNA is dependent on the virus for its replication and is, in essence, a parasite of the virus. Interestingly, plants infected with cucumber mosaic viruses that bear this satellite RNA produce milder symptoms of the disease than do plants infected with the satellite-free virus.

The procedure followed by the researchers was to manufacture tobacco plants so that they had DNA complementary to this satellite RNA incorporated into their own DNA. These tobacco plants can therefore make the satellite RNA by normal transcription. When infected with satellite-free cucumber mosaic virus the plants show far fewer of the symptoms normally associated with the virus. To all intents and purposes the plants are resistant.

Another instance where genetic engineering has been used to reduce the susceptibility of a plant to infection is in the control of crown gall disease which is discussed in Chapter 2.

A very different use of genetic engineering in plants is the use of nucleic acid hybridisation to allow rapid identification of plant viruses. Plant viruses may cause considerable crop damage. Before they can be treated they generally need to be identified. Conventional methods of virus identification are time-consuming and difficult. Nucleic acid hybridisation is faster and easier. The technique is based on the fact that complementary strands of nucleic acid will bind to one another, as we saw earlier. All that is needed is for a set of representative probes to be made. These probes contain DNA or RNA complementary to candidate viruses. By seeing which probe binds to the virus infecting the crop, the virus attacking the crop can be identified.

Such probes are now becoming widespread in medicine too. They allow doctors to identify rapidly which virus is infecting a person. It may soon be a thing of the past to be told by a doctor that you have 'a virus infection' – your doctor may be able to tell you exactly which virus has attacked you, and you will therefore have a much better idea of what the likely symptoms will be and how long recovery will take

Genetic engineering in industry

Recombinant DNA technology is already beginning to make significant contributions in the food, chemical and pharmaceutical industries. It may also provide solutions to some sorts of pollution.

In brewing, it is possible that yeasts may be genetically engineered to make more alcohol, or to produce compounds which will be toxic to the organisms that can infect and spoil beer and wines. In the chemical industry, genetically engineered organisms may become capable of making certain chemicals from cheap sources. After all, that is what autotrophs such as plants do all the time. They start with compounds such as carbon dioxide, water, oxygen, nitrates and minerals, and make carbohydrates, proteins, fats and vitamins. Advantages to an industrial chemist of using genetically engineered organisms in preference to inorganic catalysts include the greater specificity of biological catalysts, and the low temperature and near-neutral pH at which they work. Organisms genetically engineered to break down complex hydrocarbons into soluble sugars might prove invaluable in dealing with oil slicks.

Transgenic animals

Transgenic animals are animals which carry the genes of other animals. Imagine a cow that could produce human milk, or a sheep that could grow angora wool (currently produced only by certain goats) or synthesise factor VIII (needed by haemophiliacs). All of these possibilities are likely to be realities within the next few years. Such research should cause us to examine our attitudes to animals. Do we want this sort of work to be done?

Mapping the human genome

Recombinant DNA technology has allowed scientists to start on what is the most ambitious biological research programme ever undertaken – the **mapping of the human genome**. By working out the sequence of bases in the entire human DNA, all 3000 million of them, we will know the sequence of every human gene. It is hoped that such knowledge will allow **gene therapy** to become a realistic possibility. Gene therapy would involve correcting the genetic faults responsible in humans for such conditions as haemophilia, sickle-cell anaemia and cystic fibrosis (see Chapter 24).

Other possibilities

With the techniques of recombinant DNA technology there is almost no limit to what can be done. In Chapter 13 we will look at one very specific use of DNA technology which is already proving invaluable in a number of fields – namely genetic fingerprinting.

As a final note, very little legislation has been passed by governments to regulate genetic engineering, with the exception of laws governing the release of genetically engineered organisms into the wild. By and large the assumption seems to be that it is best to let scientists carry on and police themselves. One hopes the years ahead will not show that such trust is misplaced.

Further reading

Nossal, G. and Coppel, R. (1990) *Reshaping Life.* second edn, Cambridge University Press.
Primrose, S.B. (1987) *Modern Biotechnology.* Blackwell.
Sharpe, P. (1990) Transgenics – Animals with Changed Genomes. *Biological Sciences Review* 2, pp.5–6.
Wymer, P.E.O. (1988) *Genetic Engineering.* Hobsons.

Thought questions

1 Explain how you might attempt to increase the tolerance of wheat plants to salt by a combination of conventional plant breeding and recombinant DNA technology.

2 Genetically engineered animals and other organisms may be patented. Is this right?

3 Do you feel controls should be placed on the extent to which molecular biologists are allowed to transfer genes from one species to another? Defend your answer.

Things to do

1. Modelling recombinant DNA.

Using rolled out modelling clay (Plasticene) of about six different colours, model the series of genetic engineering events that would be required to transfer a eukaryotic gene into a functional form in *E. coli.*

1. Length of DNA eukaryotic gene with promoter and containing introns
2. RNA transcript of the DNA containing the introns
3. Natural excision of introns to form mRNA
4. Reverse transcription back to a length of cDNA
5. Use of enzymes to ligate ends on to the gene
6. Use of the same enzyme to open a plasmid with matching ends
7. Reformation of the plasmid with the cDNA gene enclosed (see Primrose 1987)

2. Philip Harris produce a bacteriophage kit which allows the culture of *E. coli* and a bacteriophage, and a plant tumour kit which allows the bacterium *Agrobacterium tumefaciens* to infect sunflower seedlings resulting in the release of a plasmid which gives rise to a tumour. Either pack would make the basis of a good 'A' level investigation.

10
Beer and Wine

The production of alcoholic beverages has been practised for many centuries. Archaeological evidence reveals that as far back as 6000 BC, the Egyptians were using **yeast** to produce a type of acid beer called 'boozah' (see Figure 10.1). However, little was known of how yeast helped to make alcohol until the work of Pasteur in the late nineteenth century. He showed that living yeast cells cause *fermentation* in the absence of air, converting sugar (glucose) to ethanol and carbon dioxide. Subsequent work revealed that the fermentation results from the action of substances contained within the yeast cells, now known to be enzymes. (The word enzyme literally means 'in yeast'.) This chapter will introduce you to the biology and technology that lie behind beer- and wine-making.

10.1 Model figures from the tombs of the pharoahs (XIth Dynasty) preparing beer and kneading bread

Metabolism of yeast

During aerobic growth on low levels of glucose, yeast metabolises the sugar to carbon dioxide and water by the normal respiratory pathways (glycolysis and the Krebs cycle). When yeast is grown in aerobic conditions on high levels of glucose or else in anaerobic conditions, the glucose is metabolised via the Embden-Meyerhof-Parnas (EMP) pathway to pyruvate. This molecule is decarboxylated to acetaldehyde which in turn is reduced to ethanol using $NADH_2$ generated in glycolysis (see Figure 10.3).

The production of most alcoholic beverages involves the fermentation of a sugar-containing material using species of the yeast *Saccharomyces*, notably strains of *S. cerevisiae* or *S. carlsbergensis*.

The presence of free sugar is essential for alcoholic fermentation by *Saccharomyces* as these yeasts are not capable of initially hydrolysing polysaccharides to simple sugars.

Yeast plays various roles in the production of an alcoholic beverage. It is responsible for the production of both ethanol and a wide variety of organoleptic compounds. These compounds, which are present only in trace amounts, include acids, esters, aldehydes, ketones and sulphur compounds. They contribute to the aroma and flavour of the drink although other factors, such as the quality of grapes for wine or the addition of hops for beer, are of critical importance. In addition, as yeast ferments sugar to ethanol, carbon dioxide is given off. The gas is allowed to escape during wine production but is important in making beer fizzy.

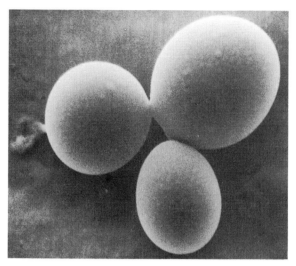

10.2 Cells of the yeast Saccharomyces cerevisiae *as imaged by the scanning electron microscope at 4000 x magnification*

10.3 *The anaerobic production of ethanol from glucose, by the EMP metabolic pathway*

The history of beer

Although the date remains obscure, it was discovered in early times that starchy grains such as barley, wheat and maize could be made to ferment. A sixteenth-century writer, Girolamo Benzoni, reported the preparation of *chicha* in Peru. He observed women chewing ground maize before putting it into water to ferment. The chewing would have resulted in the hydrolysis of stored starch to fermentable sugars by salivary amylase. Not surprisingly, this technique for the conversion of cereal starch is very rare! The method normally used today, which was employed as early as 3000 BC in Egypt and Babylon, is malting. The grain is moistened and then allowed to germinate for several days, during which time starch-digesting amylase is synthesised within the grain itself.

Wherever both beer and wine have been available, beer has tended to be the drink of the ordinary people and wine the drink of the rich, mainly because grain is cheaper than grapes. It is clear that the Greeks and Romans regarded beer as an imitation wine produced by barbarians: Pliny described it as 'a cunning if unnatural invention'!

Beer became established as an important bever-age in much of Europe. By the ninth century alehouses were common in England. Considering the likely contamination of many water sources by human and other wastes, it was probably the healthiest liquid to drink. Strictly, the beverage produced in England until the sixteenth century was 'ale'; true beer was produced when the resinous flowers of the hop vine *(Humulus lupus)* were added.

The economic value of beer in England was recognised by Charles I who, in 1643, imposed the first beer duty as a source of tax revenue! Beer remains an important beverage in many countries around the world, for example in much of northern Europe, Australia and the United States.

Brewing processes

Beer is made today much as it was in ancient times, but technological developments have greatly improved the uniformity, quality and stability of the product.

Variations in procedures, raw materials and

71

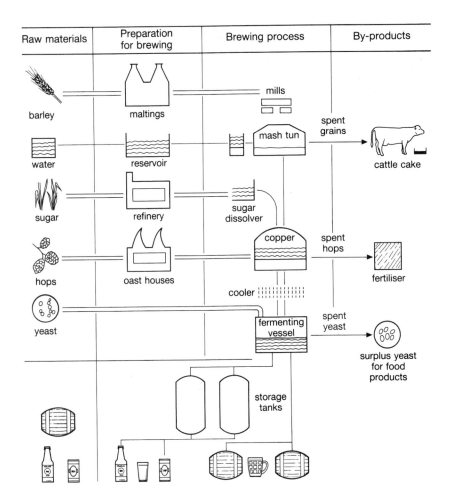

10.4 *The stages in the brewing of beer*

yeast types result in products with different characteristics. For example, top- or bottom-fermenting yeasts may be used, the former rising to the top of the tank and the latter settling to the bottom during active fermentation. *Saccharomyces carlsbergensis* is a bottom-fermenting yeast which is used for the production of lager.

There are several stages in the brewing process.

Malting

Malted barley is the major component of beer. Cleaned barley is soaked in water at 15–20°C and then transferred to aerated chambers where its temperature and moisture are controlled to encourage uniform and maximum germination of the seeds. During germination, various hydrolytic enzymes such as amylases are activated. The malt is then kiln-dried for future use as a source of amylase, proteases and various nutrients.

Mashing

Crushed malt and other starchy materials (adjuncts) such as rice, wheat or sucrose are mashed with water at controlled temperatures of up to 67°C. The mashing process allows the native enzymes in the malted barley to hydrolyse the starch and protein present in the grains. The separation of the clear amber liquid, the **wort**, by filtration from the insoluble spent grain and settled

10.5 From the top, coppers, in the Greene King brewhouse, a large fermentation unit and, below, the racking line where beer is put into barrels

proteins completes this process. The insoluble materials are rich in nutrients and so are used as cattle feed.

Addition of hops

The wort is boiled with hops in large copper or stainless steel brew kettles for 30–60 minutes. Hops aid the formation of foam, inhibit the growth of certain bacteria and contribute to flavour. To produce a beer of known alcohol content, the wort is adjusted to an appropriate specific gravity. This is dependent upon the sugars available for fermentation. As the concentration of alcohol in the wort increases, specific gravity decreases.

The wort is gradually cooled and pumped into primary fermentation tanks.

Fermentation

Liquid yeast is added to the wort and the solution is incubated for 12–24 hours. During this time dead yeast cells, precipitated proteins and hop resins settle out. The wort is then held for 8–12 days at 3–15°C in a second fermenter, according to the preferences of the brewer.

During fermentation the pH falls from about 5.5 to 4.2. The final alcohol content, which is controlled by the amount of sugar available for fermentation, varies from about 3.3–5.5%.

Finishing and polishing

After appropriate fermentation, the beer is held for several weeks in rush (storage) tanks at about 0°C. The low temperature encourages settling of the yeast cells. The beer is pumped from the ageing tanks through a filter to the **finishing** tank where the carbon dioxide level is adjusted. The beer then receives a final **polishing** (filtration) and is transferred to the last holding tank.

Pasteurisation at 55–60°C for 15–30 minutes then follows for beer which is to be bottled or canned; keg beer is not pasteurised and so has a limited storage life.

10.6 The regions of the world with the soil and climatic conditions favourable to the growing of grapes

The history of wine

The grape vine *Vitis vinifera* originated in Central Asia and spread throughout the Middle East. It was used for the production of wine in the earliest civilisations of Mesopotamia and Egypt. By about 700 BC wine was the commonest everyday drink in Ancient Greece, and vine growing soon became established in Italy where it flourished. The Greeks referred to southern Italy as Oenotria, which means 'land of the grape'.

The Romans advanced the art of wine-making considerably. They were sufficiently aware of the tendency of wine to sour that they mastered the ageing of wine. Although they generally used earthenware pots *(amphorae)*, the Romans were the first to introduce wooden storage casks. It was only later that the value of such casks was realised. They are crucial to the development of fine wines as they permit a controlled, limited contact with air.

It was the vineyards of France which developed into the pre-eminent source of wine in Europe. Together, France and Italy produce about half the world's supply of wine. However, many regions in the world have soils and climates which are ideal for the production of grapes for fermentation (Figure 10.6). Nearly all wine is made from some 5000 varieties of the grapevine *Vitis vinifera*, but other species such as the muscadine grape *V. rotundifolia* and the native American grape *V. labrusca* are also used.

Wine-making

Wine is produced when yeasts ferment the sugars contained in grape **must**, that is, the juice released by the crushing of fresh, whole grapes. Grape must is a perfect medium for wine production because of three factors: its high sugar concentration, a natural acidity which inhibits undesirable microbial growth, and the tendency to produce pleasant flavours and aromas. It is often necessary, however, to adjust the balance of sugars and acids. For this, sucrose, calcium carbonate and tartaric acid may be used.

Red wines are produced by allowing all or part of the fermentation of black grapes to take place in the presence of the skins. The alcohol formed dissolves out anthocyanin pigments and other flavouring materials from the skins. If the skins are removed at an early stage of the fermentation, rosé wines result.

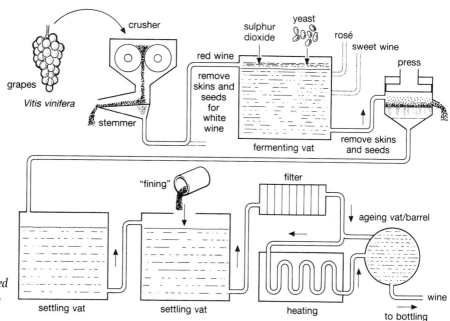

10.7 The sequence of industrial processes involved in the making of wine (see text)

White wines are usually made by fermenting white grapes with little or no skin contact.

Traditionally, sweet or semi-sweet wines are made from grape must with a higher than normal sugar content. Some special fine wines, such as Sauternes, are produced from grapes which have been infected by the fungus *Botrytis cinerea*. The fungus causes dehydration of the grapes, resulting in an increase in the sugar concentration, often up to 30–40%.

There are many different ways of making wine. However, the basic stages involved are fairly constant, and are described below.

Harvesting

The annual grape harvest and the wine made from those grapes is the **vintage**. Although a 'vintage year' strictly means simply the year in which a wine was produced, a popular interpretation of the term is 'a good year'. Certainly, wines produced during a year when conditions are optimum would be of high quality and would not be blended with other wines.

Grapes are harvested when the sugar/acid

(mainly malic and tartaric acids) balance is judged to be ideal. They are gathered as quickly as possible to prevent deterioration, most grapes being gathered by hand but some by machines which shake the grapes from the vines. Care is taken to break as few grapes as possible at this stage; undesirable microbes develop rapidly in the juice released from broken grapes.

Crushing

Rotten grapes, especially those infected with the fungi *Aspergillus* or *Penicillium*, are eliminated prior to the extraction of the must as these microbes would affect the final flavour of the product. Crushing is vigorous enough just to break the skins but not to crush the pips as these would release undesirable flavouring materials.

The must, which consists of about 85–95% juice, 5–12% skins and 0–4% pips, is treated with sulphur dioxide to prevent excessive contamination by wild yeasts and bacteria which might sour the wine to vinegar. At this stage the sugar/acid balance is also adjusted.

For white wine the skins and pips are then separated from the grape juice and discarded.

Fermentation

Until recently, wine-makers relied on yeasts which occur naturally on grapes to carry out the fermentation process. However, there are disadvantages to this. For example, the microbe population may be so low that fermentation is delayed; also, some strains produce undesirable levels of hydrogen sulphide. Consequently, the inoculation of musts with starter cultures, pure strains of particular species of yeast, is now typical. Strains of the species *Saccharomyces cerevisiae* are frequently used as they are strong fermenters and will dominate the fermentation.

Two factors critical to the fermentation process are aeration and temperature. At first the must is aerated to allow the yeast to become established; subsequently, contact with air is limited so that the yeast produces ethanol by anaerobic respiration.

Ethanol produced by the yeast will inhibit the growth and division of the cells, the degree of inhibition increasing as the temperature rises. The lower the temperature, the higher is the yield of alcohol because fermentation is more complete. More volatile aromatic molecules are produced by the yeast cells at lower temperatures. These molecules influence the flavour of the wine.

With red wines, the skins are removed from the fermentation tanks when sufficient pigment molecules and tannins have been extracted. Tannins are astringent. They are polyphenols which stabilise the red pigments and help to clear the wine of large suspended molecules.

The resultant new wine is generally cloudy, contains only small amounts of sugar and has an alcohol content ranging from 10–14%. Also present are traces of methanol and various higher alcohols, synthesised by the yeast cells from amino acids. These are known as congeners and in wine they may contribute to hangover as well as to bouquet! The wine also contains a variety of other molecules including glycerol and aromatic compounds, all of which contribute to the eventual character of the wine.

Racking and fining

The new wine is **racked** in cool tanks, during which process the yeast and other large particles settle to the bottom of the tanks and are known as 'lees'. Three or four times in the first year and twice a year subsequently, the young wine is drawn off and transferred to other tanks leaving the lees behind. Any carbon dioxide produced during the fermentation of remaining sugar is allowed to escape, great care being taken to prevent aeration of the wine.

Late in the racking procedure, sulphur dioxide may be added and the wine is **fined**. Fining is an important part of the clearing process. Materials such as gelatin, isinglass (fish collagen), casein or synthetic substances are added to the wine. As the material settles to the bottom of the tank, it attracts and takes with it suspended particles. Any particles remaining in the wine are removed by a fine filter before bottling (for wines to be drunk young and fresh, such as Beaujolais) or else whilst ageing in wooden barrels or stainless steel vats.

For some wines, the growth of acid-producing bacteria in the barrels prior to bottling is encouraged. Grapes grown in relatively cool climates with a short season, such as in the Burgundy region of France, are generally picked with a high malic acid content. Species such as *Lactobacillus* convert the malic acid ($HOOC-CH_2-CHOH-COOH$) to lactic acid ($CH_3-CHOH-COOH$), giving off carbon dioxide. Lactic acid has only one carboxyl group (-COOH) whereas malic acid has two. Consequently, the proportion of the wine's total acidity resulting from malic acid is reduced to half its former amount.

Ageing

During the ageing of wine a wide variety of chemical reactions takes place. Of major importance is the oxidation of various molecules. Pasteur in 1863 concluded that 'it is oxygen which modifies the harsh principles of new wine and makes the bad taste disappear'.

Wooden barrels, traditionally made from oakwood *(Quercus robur* and *Q. sessilis)*, allow a slow aeration of the wine. The control of oxidation is a complex process. It is vital, however, as excessive aeration spoils wine.

During ageing in wood, a 'barrel aroma' is developed, this being due mainly to tannins and vanillin which leak out from the oak. Generally, white wines are aged in the barrel for six months to a year, and red wine for a year or two. Often the wines are then filtered before being bottled.

Although it is greatly reduced, oxidation does continue in the bottle. Air is picked up by the wine during bottling and the bottle is always sealed with a small space between wine and cork. It is important that bottled wine be stored on its side so that the cork stays moist and does not shrink to allow in more air.

White wines and rosés benefit from about a year of ageing in the bottle, during which the aroma develops. Ordinary red wines improve greatly after one to two years and those made from quality Cabernet Sauvignon grapes, for example, may continue to mature favourably for five to ten years or more.

Further reading

Berry, D.R. (1982) *The Biology of Yeast*. Studies in Biology No. 140, Edward Arnold.
McGee, H. (1984) *On Food and Cooking*. Allen & Unwin.

Thought questions

1 What conditions and ingredients of the brewing and wine-making procedures do you think will discourage the growth of contaminating microbes?

2 Explain the physiology of the hangover (see McGee, pp. 493–8).

11
Yoghurt and Cheese

Milk is a highly nutritious foodstuff. It is composed of the milk-sugar lactose, several soluble proteins including casein, lipids and a variety of vitamins and minerals. Unfortunately milk is very susceptible to microbial infection and consequently sours easily. However, the action of certain **lactic bacteria** allows milk to be preserved in the form of **fermented** milk products such as **yoghurt** and **cheese**. The bacteria convert (ferment) lactose into lactic acid which in turn causes the breakdown and coagulation of casein molecules. If you examine milk microscopically the fat droplets are visible; if the milk is curdled, the coagulated proteins can also be seen. This chapter will introduce you to the biology and technology behind yoghurt- and cheese-making.

Yoghurt

The history of yoghurt

Persian tradition held that Abraham owed his fecundity and longevity to yoghurt; indeed, belief in the beneficial influence of yoghurt on human health has existed in many civilisations for centuries.

It is probable that yoghurt (from the Turkish work *'jugurt'*) was made originally by the nomadic tribes of the Middle East who kept cows, sheep, goats and camels. This area has a sub-tropical climate with summer temperatures as high as 40°C. In such a climate milk readily sours and coagulates through the action of various microbes. The primitive milking conditions would have resulted in a high likelihood of contamination by microbes from the air, from the animal and from the milker. The action of lactic acid bacteria produces a pleasant fermented product, 'sour milk', which became known as yoghurt. However, it would have been apparent even at an early stage that the souring of milk is not a uniform process: fermentation by non-lactic acid bacteria gives rise to an unpalatable, insipid, lumpy mess.

Over time it was established that pre-heating the milk on a fire before putting it into animal-skin containers encouraged the formation of the desired fermentation product. Increasing the temperature has several effects including the eradication of any pathogenic microbes in the milk, such as those causing tuberculosis, and the slight concentration of the milk so as to increase the viscosity of the final coagulum. The practice would also have encouraged fermentation to take place at a higher temperature during cooling, so selecting for thermophilic (heat-loving) strains of lactic acid bacteria.

The yoghurt so produced would have lasted only a few days. However, it was found that yoghurt left for any length of time in the skin containers altered greatly. The liquid portion *(whey)* seeped through the skin and evaporated. The end result was a condensed or concentrated yoghurt with a high solids content and acidity which was relatively resistant to spoilage. Essentially, this was a simple lactic cheese.

Today, in the Lebanon, such condensed yoghurt is salted and then rolled into balls which are placed in the sun to dry. The yoghurt balls are then covered with olive oil and stored in earthenware jars to be eaten as 'winter yoghurt'.

'Kishk' is a form of yoghurt produced in Turkey, Lebanon, Iran and Iraq with almost indefinite

keeping qualities. Wheat flour is rubbed into yoghurt and then flattened rolls of the mixture are left in the sun to dry. The product may then be ground into a flour, mixed with water and simmered gently to produce a kind of porridge.

Refrigeration has led to a general decline in the use of traditional methods of preservation, and to an increase in the widescale production of yoghurt. In the UK, the market for yoghurt extended considerably in the 1950s and 1960s as a result of the addition of sugar and various fruits, nuts and flavours to the basic product. Sales figures for yoghurt in Britain during the late 1980s were about £150 million per annum and production continues to rise.

Yoghurt-making

The way in which yoghurt is made has changed little over the years. There are two popular methods for large-scale production. One is the stirred yoghurt method (Figure 11.1), which involves the fermentation of the yoghurt in bulk before it is poured into containers. Alternatively, in the set yoghurt method, fermentation is allowed to take

place once the yoghurt has been poured into the cartons in which it is to be sold.

Slight modifications have been made to the traditional process. For example, reliable, pure cultures of the lactose-fermenting cultures can now be obtained; the temperature of incubation can be controlled accurately so that the processing time is known in advance; the acidity of the yoghurt can readily be measured and the desired level attained through rapid cooling.

The essential steps in the production of yoghurt (Figure 11.2) are as follows:

- standardisation of fat and protein content
- homogenisation
- pasteurisation
- fermentation with a starter culture
- stirring and cooling
- putting in additives
- packaging for retail.

The cream content of milk varies. The yoghurt's **fat content** is standardised by removing part of the fat or by adding cream. In Britain the standard levels average 1.5% fat for 'medium-fat' and 0.5% for 'low-fat' yoghurt. The level of non-fat solids (protein) is also standardised. The 'fortification' of milk may be achieved by the addition of either the milk **protein** casein or buttermilk powder, or by evaporation. Traditionally, boiling was carried out to reduce the volume of the milk, but this process also caused a number of undesirable changes in the physical and chemical properties of the milk.

Very large fat globules are broken up into smaller ones by a mechanical process. This **homogenisation** of the milk is carried out in order to prevent the fat fraction from separating and rising to the surface during standing.

The **pasteurisation** process (named after Louis Pasteur, 1822–95) has various effects (Table 11.1). Of note is the destruction of microbes in the milk, some of which are pathogenic. All milk comes from the udder of an animal which has bacteria already in it. Unless destroyed, these native milk microbes would provide unwanted competition for the bacteria in the yoghurt starter culture.

Yoghurt starter cultures usually comprise two

11.1 The manufacture of stirred yoghurt

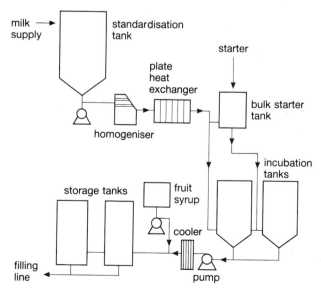

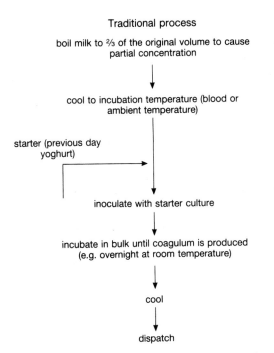

Traditional process

boil milk to ⅔ of the original volume to cause
partial concentration

↓

cool to incubation temperature (blood or
ambient temperature)

starter (previous day
yoghurt)

↓

inoculate with starter culture

↓

incubate in bulk until coagulum is produced
(e.g. overnight at room temperature)

↓

cool

↓

dispatch

Improved process

preliminary treatment of milk (standardisation
of fat, fortification of milk solids, addition
of additives e.g. sugar, stabilisers or preservatives)

↓

homogenisation

↓

heat treatment of the milk

↓

starter
culture   cool to incubation temperature
propagation

↓

inoculate with starter culture

↓

produce set or stirred yoghurt

11.2 Differences in method between the traditional and improved processes for the manufacture of yoghurt

Table 11.1 Chemical and physical effects of heat treatment of milk and their relevance in yoghurt manufacture

bacterial species, *Streptococcus thermophilus* and *Lactobacillus bulgaricus*. These organisms are used as a mixed-strain culture, as the rate of acid production is found to be greater than with either of the strains on its own (Figure 11.3). The association between the organisms has been found to be mutualistic, *L. bulgaricus* supplying the essential

Milk constituent	Heat-induced changes	Consequences for yoghurt
Whey proteins	Denaturation and aggregation, inactivation of immunoglobulins	Reduction in creaming ability
	Active SH group production	Formation of antioxidant properties
	Casein interaction	Minimises separation, increases micelle size, stabilises gel
Enzymes	Inactivation	Minimises rancid and bitter off-flavours
Other	Decomposition of amino acids to flavour compounds	Contributes to flavour
Lactose	Decomposition to form organic acids	Reduces pH and contributes to flavour
Fat	Formation of lactones, methyl ketones and other volatile ketones	Contributes to flavour
Vitamins	Destruction of some water-soluble vitamins	Reduction in nutritive value
Micro-organisms	Destruction	Ensures public safety and minimises quality defects

From Tamine, A.Y. and Robinson, R.K. (1985) *Yoghurt, Science and Technology*. Pergamon Press

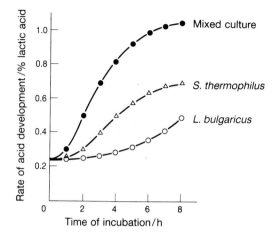

11.3 *The difference between the two single strain yoghurt cultures and a mixed culture of both strains to illustrate the symbiotic relationship between* Streptococcus thermophilus *and* Lactobacillus bulgaricus *(in autoclaved skimmed milk at 40° Celsius)*

amino acids for *S. thermophilus* and the latter producing a formic acid-like compound which promotes the growth of *L. bulgaricus*. The activity and growth of both yoghurt bacteria may be inhibited by the presence of various chemicals. For example, the antibiotic penicillin is frequently found as a contaminant in milk. Penicillin is used as a treatment for cows with infected udders (mastitis). Consequently, the enzyme penicillinase may be added to milk with the starter culture to remove the harmful effects of the penicillin.

The breakdown (catabolism) of lactose by *S. thermophilus* and *L. bulgaricus* results mainly in the production of lactic acid:

Lactose + water → lactic acid
$$C_{12}H_{22}O_{11} + H_2O \rightarrow 4C_3H_6O_3$$

Lactic acid is important during the manufacture of yoghurt as it causes the progressive breakdown of casein molecules until the casein coagulates at a pH of about 4.6–4.7, so forming the yoghurt gel. It is the lactic acid that gives yoghurt its distinctive and characteristic sharp and acidic taste. Enzymes from the starter bacteria also break down various milk components and help produce substances such as ketones and esters which are responsible for the flavour and smell of the fermented product. The optimum temperature for yoghurt culture is 46°C.

During the fermentation process, both *L. bulgaricus* and *S. thermophilus* actively synthesise the vitamins niacin (B_3) and folic acid.

Once the desired acidity is achieved (around pH 4.6), the coagulum is cooled rapidly to about 5°C in order to inhibit the activity of the bacteria.

Fruit or fruit pulp may be added at this stage. Stabilisers such as natural or synthetic gums may also be added to enhance and maintain the texture and appearance of the final product.

The yoghurt is then poured into retail containers and packed into cases. Once packaged and refrigerated at 4°C, the yoghurt has a shelf life of about two weeks.

Cheese

The history of cheese

It was a short step for the early tribes of the Middle East to progress from producing fermented milks to cheese. Condensed yoghurt, which is formed by draining off liquid whey, is essentially curds or lactic cheese. Archaeologists have found perforated earthenware bowls and reed baskets, probably used for curd drainage, in several locations in Europe and Asia. Possible evidence of cheese-making is provided by an early Sumerian frieze which depicts milking and the curdling of milk. Remnants of food material from the tomb of Hories-Aha (around 3000 BC) have been identified as cheese.

Early cheeses would have been made from the milk of local domesticated animals. For example in hilly terrain there would have been sheep and goats, and on fertile plains, cows. With invasions and migrations of populations, the craft of cheese-making no doubt spread widely. Subtle modifications to the process, and the use of milk from other animals including yak, ass, reindeer and even camel, led to the emergence of new varieties of cheese. Early European varieties included Gorgonzola, first noted in AD 879, Roquefort in AD 1070 and Cheddar in AD 1500.

Cheese type	Water in fat free substance/%	Fat in dry matter/%	Descriptive class
Extra hard	<51	>60	High fat cheese
Hard	49–55	>45–<60	Whole milk cheese
Half fat	53–63	>25–<45	Half fat cheese
Semi-soft	61–68	>10–<25	Low fat cheese
Soft	>61	>10	Skimmed milk cheese

Table 11.2a Classification of cheese by composition

The cheese-making process was not studied scientifically until the late 1880s. Traditional methods had by then already been translated into factory practice in the United States. The first cheese factory in England was established at Derby in 1870. Mass production of many cheese varieties is now carried out using a combination of traditional craft and applied scientific knowledge.

Almost two thousand names have been given to different cheeses and new varieties continue to be announced. International agreements exist concerning nomenclature, including protection for names such as 'Roquefort Appellation d'Origine'. This name can be applied only to cheese made in the Aveyron Département of France and ripened in the Roquefort Caves.

Cheeses may be classified according to composition (Table 11.2a) or ripening characteristics (Table 11.2b). Within the range of recipes available for varieties of cheese certain operations occur repeatedly.

Cheese-making

The different stages in cheese-making are listed below.
- Standardisation of fat and protein content
- Homogenisation
- Pasteurisation
- Fermentation with a starter culture
- Putting in additives
- Rennet addition and coagulation
- Cutting the curd
- Salting
- Pressing
- Coating and wrapping
- Ripening and maturing

The first three stages are carried out as for the production of yoghurt.

Until 1880, most cheese-making relied on the natural souring of milk for acid development. Nowadays various **starter cultures** are available, the choice of culture depending upon the type of cheese to be produced (Table 11.3). *Streptococcus lactis*, for example, produces acid quickly, but some strains of the bacterium produce the antibiotic nisin which may cause bitter flavours in cheese.

A number of additives are used in the preparation of cheese milks and cheese curds. Calcium salts may be added to replace those destroyed by the heat treatment of the milk. Sodium nitrate, an oxidising agent, is used in less acid cheeses such as Gouda to inhibit the growth of gas-producing *Aerogenes* bacteria which cause 'blown' cheese (Figure 11.4). The natural yellow or orange milk

Table 11.2b Some examples of classification of cheese by ripening characteristics

Class of cheese	Example of the class by cheese variety
Very hard	Parmesan
Hard (with no gas holes)	Cheddar
Hard (with eyeholes)	Emmenthal
Semi-hard	Port du Salut
Soft (ripened)	Coulommier
Surface smear ripened	Limburg
Surface mould ripened	Camembert
Internal mould ripened	Roquefort
Acid coagulated	Cottage cheese
High fat (cream)	Cream cheese

From: Scott, R. (1986) *Cheesemaking Practice*. Elsevier.

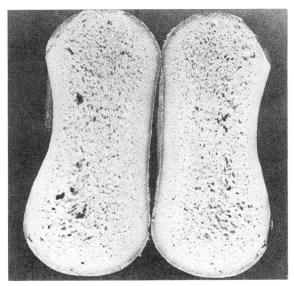

11.4 A blown cheese made from highly contaminated milk

pigments, riboflavin and carotenoids that colour cheeses are often enhanced using saffron, annatto (pigment extracted from the seeds of *Bixa orellana*) or chlorophyll. Benzoyl peroxide may be used as a bleach. The use of additives is generally under strict legal control.

Rennet is a crude extract of coagulant enzymes which may be animal, plant or microbial in origin. The most important rennet for cheese-making is prepared from the fourth stomach of young calves; it contains the proteolytic enzymes **chymosin** (or 'rennin') (88-94%) and **pepsin** (6-12%). The enzymes ensure that the young animals' milk diet is more readily retained in the stomach and digested. The slightly acid conditions produced by the starter bacteria and a temperature of around 40°C are necessary for the enzymes to act on the milk protein casein. The proteins link up to form an insoluble coagulum which encloses the remainder of the components of milk. This is the cheesemakers' 'soft curd' which may also be eaten as junket.

Rennets are also prepared from the stomachs of piglets, kids, lambs and water-buffalo calves. Rennet from the latter is routinely used in the Philippines for Kesong Puti cheese. Amongst the earliest rennets are vegetable coagulants including the latex of the fig tree *Ficus carica*. As shown in Table 11.4, many vegetable extracts will coagulate milk.

A wide range of microbes produces enzymes like chymosin but many attack casein too indiscriminately and result in bitter-tasting cheese. Several species of *Mucor* (the bread mould) produce useful

Table 11.3 Some micro-organisms used in cheese as starters or by subsequent inoculation

Streptococcus lactis	Many strains but avoiding nisin producers	M
Streptococcus lactis var. *hollandicus*	Edam, Gouda types of cheese	M
Streptococcus cremoris	Flavour forming	M
Streptococcus thermophilus	Withstands higher temperatures	T
Streptococcus faecalis	Sometimes used for its flavour production and higher temperature growth	T
Streptococcus citrovorus	Flavour production	M
Lactobacillus casei	Used in high scald cheese	T
Lactobacillus lactis	Used in high scald cheese	T
Lactobacillus bulgaricus	Used in high scald cheese	T
Lactobacillus helveticum	Used in high scald cheese	T
Propionibacterium shermani	Used for gas and flavour in some cheese	T
Penicillium roqueforti	Blue mould growth (internal)	M
Penicillium glaucum	Blue mould growth (internal)	M
Penicillium camemberti	White mould (surface growth)	M

M = Mesophilic;   T = Thermophilic
These cultures may be in liquid form, grown in the milk or sprayed on the cheese.

From: Scott, R. (1986) *Cheesemaking Practice*. Elsevier.

83

Burdock	*Arctium minus*
Bittersweet	*Solanum dulcamara*
Mallow	*Malva sylvestris*
Thistle	*Cirsium and Carlina* spp.
Fig tree	*Ficus carica*
Hogweed	*Heracleum sphondylium*
Knapweeds	*Centaurea* spp.
Lady's bedstraw	*Galium verum*
Ragwort	*Senecio jacobaea*
Spearworts	*Ranunculus* spp.
Nettle	*Urtica dioica*
Teasel	*Dipsacus fullonum*
Yarrow	*Achillea millefolium*
Spurge	*Euphorbia lathyrus*

From: Scott, R. (1986) *Cheesemaking Practice.* Elsevier

Table 11.4 Plants giving extracts for milk coagulation

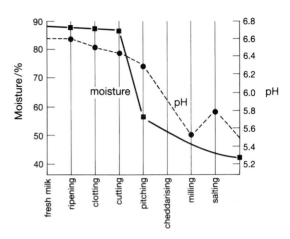

Stages in making cheddar cheese

11.5 pH and moisture changes in cheddar cheese making

substitutes for chymosin. Recently, the gene for calf chymosin has been cloned into a food-grade yeast which now produces a ready supply of chymosin in commercial quantities. This is an important bio-technological advance which avoids the routine slaughter of calves for rennet.

After a period of between 25 minutes and 2 hours, the 'soft curd' coagulum is ready to be cut. The size of the curds is defined in the recipe. In the production of soft cheese, Camembert for instance, the cut curds are moulded for drainage. The curds shrink but retain the shape of the mould as the whey drains away. This may result in a large overall loss of moisture; for example, a fall in water content from 87% in milk to less than 40% in mature Cheddar cheese is common (Figure 11.5). The rate of loss of whey depends upon temperature, pH and the way in which the curd is cut; in practice these factors are controlled so as to give rapid loss of whey. Subsequently the reduced water content increases the resistance of the finished cheeses to microbial attack.

Salting of cheeses may be carried out by direct immersion in brine or by rubbing dry salt onto the outside of the cheese after pressing. Different cheeses vary considerably in the amount of salt they contain.

Cottage cheese	0.25–1.0%
Cheddar	1.75–1.95%
Gorgonzola	3.5–5.5%

The rate at which salt is added to the curd and the pH of the curd are controlling factors in the further ripening of the cheese, as they affect the activity of the resident bacteria. Generally, the higher the acidity and the greater the amount of salt added, the lower the activity of the microbes.

The main aim of pressing is to expel any re-maining free whey and to form the loose curd particles into a shape which is compact enough to be handled.

Softer cheeses acquire a rind during ripening, often as a result of the growth of moulds and bacteria. Evaporation of moisture hardens the rind.

Various coatings are used. For example, after drying the rind, grape must or marc is used on Tomme de Marc cheese; coloured wax is usually reserved for sweeter cheeses such as Edam or Danbo; Gorgonzola has been coated with plaster of Paris as a protective layer inside a woven basket; early cheese-makers used whey butter and lard to coat the rinds of cheese but these tended to give the cheeses a rancid smell. Smoking a cheese helps to preserve it, due to phenolic compounds from the smoke.

Cheeses such as Emmenthal require a 'pre-ripening' period for the growth of 'eye-holes' in the curd. These pockets are formed by carbon dioxide released into the curd by the bacterium *Proprionobacterium ghermanii*.

The **ripening** of cheese is generally brought about through enzymes produced by bacteria which have grown on or are growing in the curd. Ripening is typically a slow, controlled process of decomposition in which proteins and fats in the cheese are enzymically converted to flavour and aroma compounds. Proteins are progressively hydrolysed to amino acids, particularly in soft-cheese varieties where intense protein digestion results in the ripe cheese being almost liquid internally. In hard cheese a large amount of native protein may remain intact. Fats are hydrolysed to glycerol and fatty acids, such as butyric acid. These fatty acids are volatile and strong-smelling and contribute to the flavour of cheese.

Amines, aldehydes, ketones and ammonia yielded by the hydrolysis of amino acids and fatty acids cause an increase in the pH of the cheese and also contribute to flavour. Although a large number of different breakdown compounds are involved in flavour and aroma production, a considerable amount of fat and up to two-thirds of the protein in cheese may remain intact.

The activity of microbes on moist, sheltered areas of human skin produces molecules very similar to those produced during the ripening of cheese. The similarity between the smells of cheese and feet is often remarked upon – the French poet Léon-Paul Fargue is said to have named Camem-bert 'les pieds de Dieu' ('the feet of God')!

Ripening may also be influenced by the action of specific internal and surface moulds and bacteria. For example, following an initial ripening period of 18–25 days, Roquefort cheese is transferred to the Roquefort Caves (cellars) for 'blueing' and final ripening. The cellars are built around natural limestone cliffs. Air currents at a constant temperature of 8°C and 95% humidity circulate through cracks ('fleurines') into the cellars (Figure 11.6), so regulating the environmental conditions of the cellars. The spores of the fungus *Penicillium*

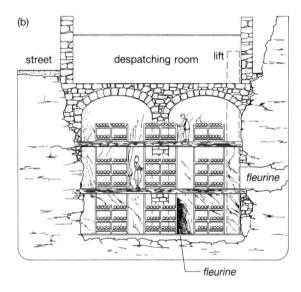

11.6b Roquefort cheeses, impregnated with Penicillium, *ripen over a period of months in the constant environmental conditions of the cellar (see text)*

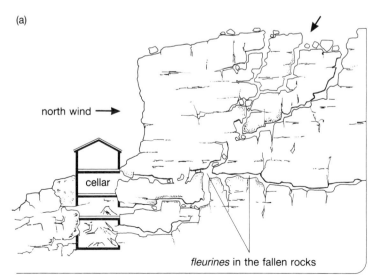

11.6a Air of constant temperature and humidity moves through cracks in the rock leading to the Roquefort cellars

85

roqueforti are added to ewes' milk prior to coagulation. Under the conditions prevailing in the cellars, the fungus develops within the cheese to produce the characteristic blue-veined appearance and flavour of Roquefort. After 3–4 days the cheeses are wrapped in pewter foil (an alloy of tin and lead) to deprive the fungus of oxygen and so slow its growth. Ripening continues slowly for a further three months (Figure 11.7).

The ripening of cheese is typically a slow process. Obviously the cheese industry has a strong incentive to shorten the time which cheese spends in the store. Advances have been made in the acceleration of the ripening process, particularly for hard and semi-hard cheeses such as Cheddar and Gouda. Ripening enzymes have been produced but the high production costs set against savings in storage cost– a gain of only £20 per tonne per month for Cheddar – have limited their commercial exploitation.

11.7 In the Roquefort cellars whole ripening cheeses are laid on their sides, on oak benches, to allow the air to circulate around them

Enzymes can be added to cheeses during normal dry salting. However, for those cheeses which are salted by immersion in brine, such as Feta cheese, an alternative method has been devised. The enzymes are encapsulated in phospholipid spheres, 'liposomes', and added via the milk. The liposomes immobilise the ripening enzymes but, within days of manufacture of the curd, the liposomes are ruptured by the action of enzymes present in the cheese. In this way the ripening enzymes are released into the cheese and begin catalysis.

The manufacture of yoghurt and cheese is an ancient art. Modern biotechnology promises to improve and extend the range and availability of such fermented milk products.

Further reading

Tamine, E.Y. and Robinson, R.K. (1985) *Yoghurt, Science and Technology*. Pergamon Press.
Scott R. (1986) *Cheesemaking Practice*. Elsevier.

Thought questions

1 Why is UHT milk used for home yoghurt making?

2 Why is the milk/yoghurt mixture heated to such a high incubation temperature?

Things to do

Make your own yoghurt.
Take 600 cm^3 (or 1 litre) of UHT milk. Warm it to 48°C exactly.
Add a teaspoon of live plain yoghurt and stir. Pour it into a thermos flask and cover only – do not screw on the lid. It should then slowly cool to 40°C.
After 8 hours shake out the yoghurt. Whisk it and refrigerate.
Reculture every few days. It is best to reserve a small volume that has been kept away from oxygen in a sealed pot in the refrigerator.

12

The Enzyme Revolution

Enzymes are a class of proteins whose function is to speed up the many reactions of metabolism; without enzymes, metabolism would proceed at a rate too slow to sustain life. The digestion of a meal – which involves enzymic hydrolysis – is completed in 3–6 hours; it has been estimated that without enzymes the process would take 30 years or more! Today enzymes are being put to work in industry, medicine and the home to an increasing extent. Biotechnology is in part an 'enzyme revolution'.

The properties of enzymes

- Enzymes are globular proteins which may have other associated molecules.
- Enzymes can only speed up reactions that would occur slowly in their absence.
- Enzymes are neither altered nor consumed during a reaction and so may be used many times.
- Enzymes catalyse reactions towards a state of equilibrium. In doing so, they can catalyse reversible reactions in both directions, providing it is energetically feasible.
- Enzymes are specific to the particular substrate molecules they alter in a reaction. The degree of specificity varies from fairly wide to absolute.

The high catalytic power and specificity of enzymes may be explained in terms of the mechanism of their action. A particular region on the surface of the enzyme molecule known as the **active site** is designed to accept **specific substrate molecules**. The active site is often a small cleft which exposes certain specific amino acid residues. The substrate molecules fit precisely into the active site, non-covalent interactions occurring between the amino-acid residues and regions on the substrate molecule to form an **enzyme-substrate complex**. The reaction takes place and the **product** is formed; it then detaches from the active site. The process is referred to as the 'lock and key' mechanism (Figure 12.1).

The degree of **specificity** of an enzyme depends upon the requirements of the active site. For an

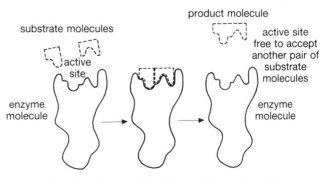

12.1 The mechanism of enzyme action

enzyme + substrate   enzyme substrate complex   enzyme + product

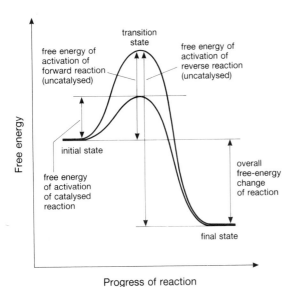

12.2 Enzyme catalysed reactions lower the energy barrier so making chemical change happen more readily

enzyme with absolute specificity, the requirements are met only by one particular substrate molecule.

Enzymes are sensitive to heavy metals and to extremes of temperature and pH. These factors may cause bonds to break with consequent irreversible change in structural conformation of the vital active site. The enzyme thus loses its powers of catalysis and is said to be **denatured.**

The energy required to make and break chemical bonds constitutes an **energy barrier** (Figure 12.2) which must be overcome if a reaction is to occur. As a result of precise molecular interactions which take place at the active site, enzymes are particularly effective in reducing this energy and so facilitating reactions.

How enzymes work in different preparations

Whole cell preparations

The human domestic use of enzymes, in the most elementary types of biotechnology, began thousands of years ago in processes such as cheese-making, bread-making and brewing (see Chapters 10 and 11). This exploitation of the enzymes synthesised by bacterial and fungal cells was unrecognised at that time. Today, such microbial cells are seen as highly versatile biocatalysts.

Catalysis by **whole cells** is not very efficient, however, as much of the substrate in the fermentation 'broth' is converted by the microbes into new growth and unwanted by-products. Also, the optimum conditions for the growth of the microbes may be different from those required for maximal formation of the product. Finally, at the end of the process, the isolation and purification of the product from the microbes and broth may be difficult.

This raises the question of whether enzymes may be used on their own.

Isolated enzymes

Until recently, almost all biological catalysis in industrial processes was achieved using whole cells or tissues, as in the fermentation industry. However, enzymes which have been isolated from cells retain their catalytic powers *in vitro*. The advantages of using such **cell-free preparations** include greater efficiency of substrate conversion, higher yields and uniformity of product.

An early example of the use of isolated enzymes is 'takadiastase'. This was marketed in Europe from 1876 and was a rather crude mixture of hydrolytic enzymes prepared by growing the fungus *Aspergillus oryzae* on wheat bran. Today crude enzyme preparations are commonly used in clarifying (removing the cloudiness) of wine. There is now an increasing range of purified enzyme preparations with diverse uses and potential benefits in medicine and industry. Most of the enzymes used on a wide scale are extracellular in their action, in particular hydrolases which are water-soluble and readily extracted from microbes. Some are intracellular in their natural action, such as glucose oxidase which is used in food preparation. Although many useful enzymes are derived from plant and animal sources, it is likely that microbial sources will become increasingly popular (Figure 12.3).

The isolation and purification of enzymes is expensive, often costing hundreds of pounds per

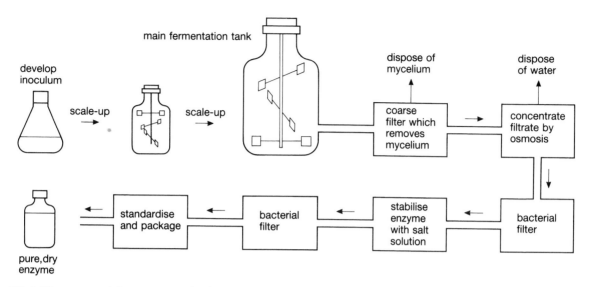

12.3 The commercial preparation of isolated enzymes from microbial sources

gram compared with pounds per kilogram for crude enzymes. Another drawback is that purified soluble enzymes tend to have poor stability: they tend to change shape easily. In addition it is difficult to recover isolated enzymes at the end of a process for re-use.

Immobilised enzymes

A new technique which makes more efficient use of isolated enzymes involves their **immobilisation**. This restricts the free movement of the soluble molecules. As shown in Figure 12.4, the enzyme is attached to or located within an insoluble support by one of four methods:

- adsorption on to an insoluble matrix, for example porous glass or Sephadex
- covalent binding to a solid support, for example ceramics, cellulose or nylon
- entrapment within a gel, for example poly-acrylamide or collagen
- encapsulation behind a selectively permeable membrane, for example nylon or cellulose nitrate.

Immobilised enzymes have several advantages. First, the method can increase stability, many

enzymes becoming less heat-sensitive when immobilised. Second, enzymes so treated can be recovered easily and re-used, this being of great economic benefit. Third, the final product is free of enzyme and so can be readily collected. Fourth, immobilisation can alter the catalytic properties of an enzyme favourably, so extending the range of possible reaction conditions. For example, immobilised glucose isomerase, which is employed in the production of high-fructose syrups, can be used continuously for over a thousand hours at temperatures of between 60° and 65°C.

The use of immobilised enzymes has increased rapidly in medical and analytical applications. Although employed in several industrial processes, the initial costs of installing an immobilised enzyme system may mean that it will be some years before the full potential of the technique is realised in large-scale industrial processes.

How enzymes are put to work

Medical applications

Analytical tools
Enzymes are highly specific to their substrates and can catalyse reactions at very low levels of substrate concentration. These inherent characteris-

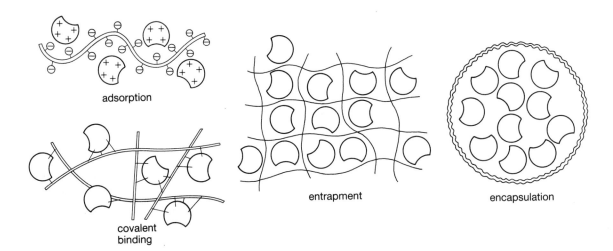

adsorption

entrapment

encapsulation

covalent binding

12.4 Methods for the immobilisation of enzymes

tics, combined with the wide range of enzymes available, mean that enzymes are highly suitable as tools in biochemical analyses. For example, **enzyme electrodes** may be made for substrate-specific detection. An enzyme electrode consists of a combination of a thin layer of appropriate enzyme with a suitable electrochemical electrode sensor. These **biosensors** are highly sensitive and versatile, being used, for example, to detect a person's blood cholesterol level, or the presence of monoamines in meats – an indicator of the meat's freshness.

Immobilised enzymes are employed in a wide range of 'dip-and-read' diagnostic test strips, such as that used to test for the presence of glucose in urine (Figure 12.5). The device consists of a thin strip of plastic with a small pad at one end. The pad is coated with an ethyl cellulose membrane, and contains colour reagents and the enzymes glucose oxidase and glucose peroxidase which are immobilised on the cellulose mat. Within 15 seconds of being dipped in a urine sample containing glucose, the pad responds with a colour change. The colour can be matched against a chart in order to obtain a semi-quantitative estimate of the glucose concentration.

Breakdown of protein
Protein degradation (proteolysis) is catalysed by

protease enzymes. These molecules, which are derived from various sources and show differing degrees of specificity, are employed in a variety of medical treatments (Table 12.11).

Proteases have long been used in the **treatment of wounds**. Early surgeons extracted proteolytic saliva from the mouthparts of maggots, whilst the Indians of the Caribbean are reported to have applied pineapple flesh containing the protease enzyme bromelain directly on to wounds. In surgical practice dead (necrotic) tissue is enzymically removed from a wound to allow proper healing. This process, called **debridement**, is also carried out prior to skin grafting in cases of severe burns, when trypsin and chymotrypsin are used.

Various proteases with fairly narrow specificities such as trypsin, bromelain and streptokinase are used in combination with anticoagulants in the treatment of **thromboses**. In a blood clot (thrombus), the long protein chains of **fibrin** may be hydrolysed by the catalytic action of these protease enzymes on the arginine and lysine amino acid carbonyl group endings. The clot is dissolved away, enabling the circulation to recover.

Gastro-intestinal disorders, for example dyspepsia, may be treated with proteases such as papain, bromelain and pepsin which act as digestive aids.

Enzyme replacement
Various medical disorders such as haemophilia (due

pad
impregnated with
enzyme + chromogen

colour chart

12.5 Application of a diagnostic test strip reagent for semi-quantitative analysis

to lack of Factor VIII) or acatalasaemia (catalase deficiency) are due to the absence or ineffectiveness of a particular enzyme. The aim of **replacement therapy** is to supply the required enzyme, often by intravenous injection. The technique is not straightforward as the defence mechanisms of the body may inactivate the enzyme or produce antibodies against it. Encapsulation of the enzyme within a selectively permeable membrane overcomes these problems in some cases. For example, considerable success has been achieved, at the research stage, using catalase encapsulated in liposomes in the treatment of acatalasaemic mice. The results of tests which employ this technique for the treatment of people also appear encouraging.

Industrial applications

The potential for application of enzymes as catalysts in both large- and small-scale industrial processes is considerable. Enzymes are currently used in a variety of biochemical processes in the food industry, such as cheese manufacture (see Chapter 11), and brewing and wine production (see Chapter 10). They are also used in the textile and chemical industries, although for economic reasons the latter continues to use mainly inorganic catalysts.

Detergents

Protease enzymes derived primarily from *Bacillus* bacteria are routinely added to the so-called **biological washing powders**. These enzymes are used as they are stable in the alkaline conditions

Table 12.1 Some proteolytic enzymes used in medicine

Enzyme	Source	Purpose
Trypsin	Mammalian pancreas	Clearing of tissue prior to skin graft; treatment of thromboses
Chymotrypsin	Mammalian pancreas	Clearing of tissue prior to skin graft; treatment of thromboses
Bromelains	Pineapple juice	Treatment of thromboses
Plasmin	Blood	Treatment of thromboses
Papain	*Carica papaya* plant latex	Treatment of gastro-intestinal disorders
Pepsin	Mammalian stomach	Treatment of gastro-intestinal disorders
Urokinase	Urine	Activation of plasminogen molecules – treatment of coronary thromboses
Streptokinase	*Streptococcus* bacteria	Activation of plasminogen molecules – treatment of coronary thromboses

After: Bickerstaff, G.F. (1987) Enzymes in Industry and Medicine. Edward Arnold.

required for the action of detergent, they are compatible with the many additives used in detergents and they can catalyse substrate breakdown at temperatures up to 65°C for as long as two hours. The proteases break down resistant protein-based stains, such as bloodstains, without requiring high washing temperatures or risking dye loss or shrinkage of fabrics. One initial problem with biological detergents was that the enzymes induced skin **allergies** in some people. Enzymes, being proteins, can cause an **allergic reaction**. This problem was overcome by encapsulating the proteases in granules which swell and rupture when in contact with water. Obviously you should not immerse your hands in biological detergent solutions. Clothes washed in them should be rinsed very thoroughly to remove the enzymes.

Lipase enzymes, which break down fats, have recently been incorporated into clothes-washing powders. **Amylase** enzymes are used in detergents for machine dish-washing to remove resistant starch residues.

Textiles

Starch is commonly used as an adhesive or 'size' on the threads of certain fabrics to prevent damage during weaving. Traditionally, strong chemicals were used to desize the fabrics. Bacterial amylases, which can withstand working temperatures of 105–110°C, now represent a more efficient desizing agent.

Leather

In the **tanning industry** proteases derived from *Bacillus licheniformis* are now used to dehair hides in place of traditional chemical processes which resulted in the production of polluting toxic wastes.

Traditionally cow, horse, dog or pigeon dung was applied to leather to render it more pliable and workable. The active ingredients in the dung were the proteases trypsin and chymotrypsin, which degraded various protein components within the leather. This process of 'bating' has now been made less offensive, the dung being replaced by enzymes extracted directly from the pancreas of slaughtered cattle or pigs.

Tenderisation of meat

Beef carcases are routinely kept in cold storage for 10–12 days after slaughter to allow natural **autolysis** to begin (autolysis is the self-digestion of tissues upon death, brought about by the rupture of lysosomes). Most important are the proteases released from the lysosomes which catalyse the

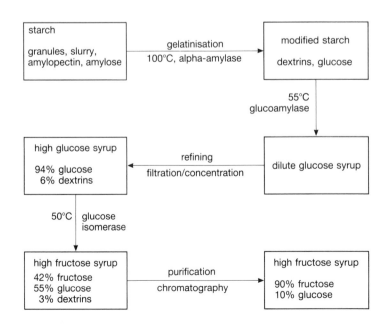

12.6 The production of fructose sugar syrup from starch

breakdown of fibrous proteins in the connective tissue, so increasing the tenderness of the meat.

The protease **papain**, which is derived from the latex of the paw-paw *Carica papaya*, can be injected into the bloodstream of cattle prior to slaughter, or else added post-slaughter, to achieve tenderisation. *This first practice is not carried out in the UK.* Papain is sold commercially for home application, but much **tenderisation** of meat is achieved during cooking before the protease enzymes are inactivated at around 90°C.

Baking

In the production of white bread, dough is bleached through the action of lipo-oxygenase enzymes present in the soy flour which is often used to supplement wheat flour. Fungal ∝-amylase enzymes are also added as they catalyse the breakdown of flour starch to glucose. The glucose can then be metabolised by yeast cells in the dough.

Proteases derived from the fungus *Aspergillus oryzae* are added to doughs used in biscuit manufacture. The enzymes reduce the gluten protein content of the dough, which reduces its elastic properties. Extensibility and strength increase, allowing the dough to be rolled out thinly.

Sugar production

The sugar industry is a major consumer of enzymes, where they are used in the hydrolysis of starch as shown in Figure 12.6.

The starch is first gelatinised, and then partially hydrolysed by ∝-amylase from *Bacillus licheniformis* to dextrins which are used as thickening agents and stabilisers. The dextrins are converted to glucose using glucoamylase from *Aspergillus* fungi. After refining and concentration, the glucose syrup is used in an extensive range of products. The glucose may be converted to fructose syrup which has enhanced sweetening properties and, for its sweetness, a lower calorific value. This final conversion is achieved using microbial glucose isomerase, an intracellular enzyme which is effectively immobilised inside a dead cell mass. Refining of the product follows to yield a high fructose syrup which is the principal sweetener in soft drinks and sweets. An estimated 3 million tonnes of high fructose syrup are produced in Europe and the United States each year.

The application of enzyme technology to existing medical and industrial processes has enormous potential and there is clearly scope for new developments in a wide range of industries in the future.

Further reading

Bickerstaff, G.F. (1987) *Enzymes in Industry and Medicine.* Edward Arnold.
Smith J.E. (1988) *Biotechnology.* Edward Arnold.

Thought questions

1 Why are food products not labelled to show what enzymes they contain?

2 If enzymes are not used up in reactions, how are they eventually degraded?

3 When do you think the costs involved in the isolation and purification of enzymes are justified?

Things to do

A procedure for the immobilisation of yeast cells and investigations which can then be carried out are given in:

Ingle, M.R. (1986) *Microbes and Biotechnology.* Blackwell, p. 69.

13
DNA Fingerprinting

In Chapter 9 we looked at the basic techniques of recombinant DNA technology, concentrating on the transfer of genes from one species to another. In this chapter we will look at another aspect of DNA technology, one that does not involve the transfer of genes between species. **DNA fingerprinting** (also called **genetic fingerprinting**) is a powerful method for identifying individuals and determining genetic relationships within a species. We will concentrate on its uses for identifying humans, but the years ahead are likely to see a considerable extension of its application to other species.

Lying behind the principle of DNA fingerprinting in humans is the fact that the genetic material of each human cell contains approximately three thousand million DNA nucleotide pairs arranged on the chromosomes in linear sequences. The resulting molecules are exceptionally long and quite delicate. They are protected by accompanying **histone** proteins and are tightly coiled to form the characteristically shaped chromosomes that can be seen under the light microscope at cell division.

How is genetic fingerprinting done?

In order to understand how genetic fingerprinting is done, one must first appreciate that the DNA of most organisms is unique to the individual, just as finger and thumb prints are. Obviously the genetic material of one species differs from another, even when those species are closely related. However, within a species most individuals have their own unique genetic material. The exceptions to this generalisation are individuals that result from some form of asexual or vegetative reproduction. A case in point in our own species is that of identical twins. Unless such individuals differ by virtue of **somatic mutations** (associated with mitosis), they will be genetically the same in every way. The genetic uniqueness of each individual is the result of **mutations**, the **independent assortment** of chromosomes, their **crossing-over** at meiosis and the **fusion** of genetically distinct gametes at fertilisation.

In most species, and certainly in all species of mammals including ourselves, there are countless thousands of genetic differences between each of us (identical twins excepted). Part of the reason for this is that a surprisingly large percentage of our DNA appears to have no function. In these regions mutations accumulate and individuals differ greatly from one another in the order of their organic bases. The net result is that if you compare two humans at random (so long as they are not closely related) on average their DNA differs about once every 100 base pairs. This may not sound very much, but as we have approximately three thousand million base pairs in our DNA, any two people have about 30 million differences between them in the order of their bases.

The genetic uniqueness of the individual lies at the heart of DNA fingerprinting. Consider what happens when human DNA is placed in the presence of a mixture of **restriction endonucleases**, enzymes that split DNA at specific sequences. The result is that each person's DNA produces a unique set of fragments. These fragments are called **restriction fragment length polymorphisms** or **RFLPs**, pronounced 'riflips' (see Figure 13.1).

Before we get on to the use of RFLPs in DNA fingerprinting it is worth mentioning their use in the diagnosis of genetic disorders. If it can be

```
5' ... T G G | C C A T A C G T G G | C C C T A T G C T T T C G G | C C A C ...
3' ... A C C | G G T A T G C A C C | G G G A T A C G A A A G C C | G G T G ...


5' ... T G C | C C A T A C G T G G C A C T A T G C T T T C G C | C C A C ...
3' ... A C G | G G T A T G C A C C G T G A T A C G A A A G C C | G G T G ...
```

13.1 The action of the restriction enzyme HaeIII which splits DNA whenever the nucleotide sequence GGCC is found running in the 5' to 3' direction. The upper piece of DNA is split in three places. However, the lower piece of DNA differs from the upper in its base sequence at one base pair. This is sufficient to cause HaeIII to split it at only two points

shown that a particular RFLP is closely linked to the locus of a serious genetic disorder, then this can be used to tell whether an unborn child will show the genetic abnormality once it is born. Suppose, for instance, that the disorder in question is due to an autosomal dominant mutation, as is the case with Huntington's chorea, and that one parent is heterozygous (*Hh*) and the other is homozygous recessive (*hh*). If a few cells can be obtained from the foetus, whether by **foetoscopy, chorionic villus sampling** or **amniocentesis**, cutting up the DNA from these cells with the appropriate restriction enzyme will enable testing to see whether the foetus has inherited the normal (*h*) or the mutant allele (*H*) from the heterozygous parent. RFLPs are now being extensively used in this way in cases where it is feared that foetuses may have inherited

conditions such as sickle-cell anaemia, Huntington's chorea and ß-thalassaemia, each of which is due to a single abnormal allele.

Returning to genetic fingerprinting, the basic procedure followed is summarised in Figure 13.2. Once the DNA has been broken down into shorter pieces by the restriction enzyme, the fragments are separated by **gel electrophoresis** which distinguishes molecules on the basis of their size and charge. This means that larger DNA fragments move more slowly. A variety of methods can be used to show up the bands that result from electrophoresis. Typically the DNA is allowed to react with a radioactive probe which enables **autoradiography** to be used to obtain a permanent DNA fingerprint. The end result is a characteristic pattern unique to each individual as shown in Figure 13.3

Genetic fingerprinting was developed by Alec Jeffreys, a geneticist at Leicester University, in the 1980s (Figure 13.4). In 1986 ICI bought the world rights to this technology from the medical charity that funded the work. ICI then set up two laboratories to develop it on a commercial basis, one at Abingdon near Oxford and the other in Washington. Already a variety of uses for the process has been found.

13.2 The essential steps involved in DNA fingerprinting. The final result is a DNA fingerprint which consists of bands that correspond to DNA sections of different sizes produced by the action of restriction endonucleases on the DNA

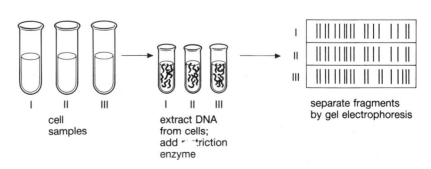

cell samples

extract DNA from cells; add restriction enzyme

separate fragments by gel electrophoresis

95

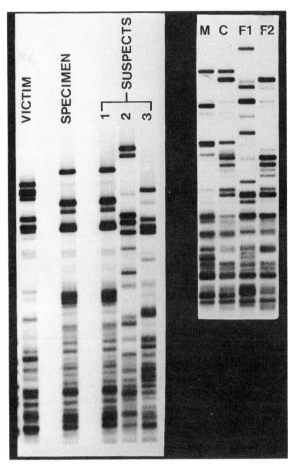

13.4 *Professor Alec Jeffreys*

13.3 *At left, the DNA fingerprint of a victim and a specimen from their assailant is compared to three samples from suspects. In a separate investigation, at right, the DNA fingerprint of a mother and her child are compared to those of two possible fathers F1 and F2. The fingerprint bands of the child must be common to one or the other parent*

The uses of genetic fingerprinting in humans

One of the earliest uses of genetic fingerprinting was to trap a rapist in Bristol. Robert Melias was well known to the Avon and Somerset Police as a petty burglar. One day he was arrested on a tip-off that he had in his possession a microwave oven that belonged to a woman who had been raped. On being questioned by the police he admitted to stealing the microwave, but denied the charge of rape. The police decided they would use the new technique of genetic fingerprinting. They took a blood sample from him and it was sent to be compared, by genetic fingerprinting, with a sample of semen found as a stain on the victim's clothes. The two patterns were absolutely identical. It is relatively straightforward to calculate the probability of this happening by chance alone – the probability usually works out at much less than one in a million. In this particular case when the suspect was confronted with the results of the genetic fingerprinting, he changed his story and pleaded guilty on 13 November 1987 in Bristol Crown Court.

The case made legal history. Since then the technique has been used many times in **forensic science**, where the aim is usually to work out who has committed a crime. The particular attractions of the technique are that its results are so conclusive and that only minute amounts of DNA are required. A single hair root gives enough DNA, as does 0.001 µl of blood or an even smaller quantity of semen. This is because techniques now exist which allow large amounts of DNA to be copied from a very few DNA molecules.

It is clear that DNA fingerprinting can be used in rape cases. More generally, if traces of a person's blood or one or more hair roots are left at the scene of a crime, potential suspects can be checked out. It is worth emphasising that genetic fingerprinting can prove a person's innocence as much as his or her guilt. One case, widely publicised in the media a few years ago, concerned the rape and murder of two 15-year-old girls in Leicestershire. A 17-year-old youth had confessed to the second of these crimes. However, Jeffreys was able to show that both girls had been raped by the same man, and that he was definitely not the 17-year-old. Regretfully the police had to let him go, despite his confession. The police then formed the hypothesis that the person responsible lived locally, since although the two cases had happened three years apart, they had taken place within 500 metres of each other. Eventually the police took blood samples from every man within the 16–34 year age range who lived in the three villages nearest the crime, and carried out genetic fingerprinting. Only two people refused to be tested. One was a Jehovah's Witness who refused on religious grounds (Jehovah's Witnesses believe that the taking of blood for any reason is wrong); the other was the man who was eventually found to be guilty. However, it took some time to catch him because he persuaded a workmate to go in his place to give the blood sample. It was only when his friend got drunk in a pub and happened to mention the story to someone that the deception was realised. The conversation was overheard and reported to the police who arrested both men at 5.30 a.m. the next day. Genetic fingerprinting showed that the man who had avoided giving a blood sample was indeed the rapist. He is now in prison, having been sentenced to life imprisonment.

The other major use of DNA fingerprinting has been in **paternity cases**. During 1987 ICI Cellmark Diagnostics were asked by the Home Office and the Foreign Office to do a pilot DNA study on people who had applied to immigrate to the United Kingdom on the grounds that they had close relatives there already. The pilot study showed the reliability of the technique and genetic fingerprinting is now routinely used to determine genetic relationships in such immigration cases. For instance, one case involved a boy who wished to enter Britain to be with a woman whom he claimed to be his mother. However, the immigration authorities were not convinced of the relationship. Even though the father was not available for testing, genetic fingerprinting was able to show that the probability that the boy was unrelated to the woman was 2×10^{15}. For comparison, the current world human population size is about 6×10^9. The boy was allowed to enter the country.

Genetic fingerprinting of non-humans

Although most of the applications of genetic fingerprinting have so far been in humans, zoologists and even some botanists have been quick to see its potential in evolutionary and ecological studies too. Remember that **reproductive success** or **fitness**, usually measured as the number of offspring an individual produces during its lifetime, is the cornerstone of Darwin's theory of natural selection. To a population geneticist, fitness is not just a concept that can be applied to individuals, it can also be applied to particular alleles. For example, we can talk about the fitness of the allele responsible for sickle-cell anaemia relative to the fitness of the allele that makes the normal sort of haemoglobin. When a population is in equilibrium, the fitness of alternative alleles is equal. When a population is evolving under the influence of natural selection, however, some alleles are fitter than others.

Until the advent of genetic fingerprinting it was very difficult to measure the fitness of individuals. Usually the best that could be done was to observe the individuals patiently and measure their mating success. This technique has been adopted with red deer, for example. Being large animals which only mate at a particular time of the year – the autumn rut – it is fairly easy to obtain quite good measures of reproductive success by direct observation. But what does one do about less conspicuous species? This is where genetic fingerprinting comes into play.

One example where genetic fingerprinting has been used to investigate the reproductive success of non-humans is a study of the hedge sparrow, or dunnock, by Nick Davies and others at Cambridge University. Dunnocks have a remarkably complicated mating system. **Polyandry**, in which one female mates with two or more males, is observed more often than any other type of mating behaviour. However, **monogamy**, in which a female and a male each mate only with each other, and **polygyny**, in which a single male mates with two or more females, are also found. When polyandry occurs, one male, the ∝ male, is clearly dominant to the other, the ß male. However, before DNA fingerprinting there was no way of determining with any accuracy whether both males fathered the young or just the ∝ male. Using the new technique, Davies was able to show that ß males often do father some of the offspring. Not only that, but they clearly know they do! In cases where genetic fingerprinting subsequently showed that a ß male had fathered an unusually high percentage of the offspring of the female, Davies found that the same male also undertook much more feeding of the brood than normal.

Future advances in genetic fingerprinting

It is worth remembering that genetic fingerprinting only arrived on the scene in 1984! Already, however, there have been a large number of refinements to the technique. Indeed, some authors restrict the term DNA fingerprinting to a new technique in which particular regions of the DNA known as 'minisatellites' or 'hypervariable regions' are studied. For the moment, however, most people seem still happy to use the terms genetic finger-

printing and DNA fingerprinting interchangeably. The next few years are likely to see advances on several fronts: the techniques will need even less DNA; the final fingerprints will be sharper and easier to interpret; computer analysis of the results will become routine rather than visual analysis; massive DNA fingerprint databases will be set up; and the whole process will become increasingly automated. There is also every reason to imagine that the technique will become cheaper and more widespread, and no doubt new uses will be found for the technology.

Further reading

Cadogan, A. (ed.) (1989) *Biotechnology Topics – For A-level*. Maths Science and Technology Centre, Avon.

Thought questions

1 Imagine that you are a defence lawyer. Your client has been accused of burglary at an exclusive hotel 180 miles from where he lives. DNA fingerprinting points to the presence of drops of your client's blood on a broken window pane at the hotel. What questions might you want to ask your client so as to prepare his defence?

2 In Vietnam there are thousands of children – now young adults – fathered by American GIs stationed there during the Vietnam War. Presumably extensive DNA fingerprinting of these people, and those American GIs still living who were there during the war, could establish paternity in many cases. Would you approve of this?

3 If details of the DNA fingerprints of every male in the country were stored in a central computer, it would mean that the identity of most rapists could be determined with almost complete certainty. Would you consider this desirable, or an infringement of civil liberties?

14
New Techniques in Plant Breeding

This chapter examines the ways in which recent developments in molecular biology and tissue culture are influencing the ways we breed plants. Many new and exciting processes are involved, and new thinking is taking place. Some of the plant breeders' techniques can be approached, or modelled, in the school and college laboratory. Many opportunities exist for young biologists to take up careers in the new plant biotechnologies.

How plant breeding started

To a very large extent the crops and ornamental plants around us have been modified by people over the course of our history. Some tens of thousands of years ago the earliest Neolithic farmers started to cultivate wild plants, rather than just gathering seeds, fruits, leaves and roots from plants in their native environment. What started as merely looking after a wild plant became a process of selecting the best seed and keeping it for planting in the future. Little by little, crops became less like their wild ancestors and closer to an ideal. Gardeners have similarly always selected what has taken their fancy, for mutation, crossing over and the independent assortment of chromosomes, continuously produces new varieties. Since the start of the twentieth century **artificial selection** has been made more powerful by our understanding of genetics and its application in breeding technologies.

Believing in genes

The **concept of the gene** as a particle controlling some aspect of plant behaviour has always been fundamental to scientific plant breeding. We know that a large proportion of genes can exist in more than one form, as **alleles**, at the same locus on a chromosome. The alleles in the **genotype** of a plant are what are expressed, in translation, as the **phenotype** or appearance of the plant. Although the influence of environment is important as well, the plant breeder is confident that behind the phenotype lies a developmental process controlled principally by genes that can be captured and used to better effect.

In order to bring a crop closer to a perceived ideal a breeder looks for a combination of the most desired characteristics in the pool of variability of the plant species concerned. Often the starting point is a cross between the best parental plants available. Amongst the offspring will be chance combinations which are even better than the parental plants; they may lead to the selection of a new variety. Breeders may search beyond the existing population to find valuable genes. Then by breeding and cross-breeding from the variant, the desirable alleles are captured into the main stock. One of the oldest ways of doing this is by achieving a polyploid hybrid (allopolyploidy) between two different species.

Today the breeder is invariably aiming to find out how many genes are involved in a particular trait, where exactly these genes are on the chromosomes, and what their precise action is on the whole plant.

Classical plant breeding

The aim of crop-plant breeding is to improve the **yield** and **quality** of the harvested crop. In this many influences interact, but the focus of directed breeding must always be rigorous and precise. Plant shape and size often govern yield; a rapid expanse of green leaf feeds the products of photosynthesis back into growth. Pest and disease resistance are selected for because without some resistance the yield and quality will fall (see Chapter 2). Plants with good pest and disease resistance also produce financial savings on economic inputs, reducing spending on items such as fungicides and insecticides, and lessening the environmental impact of these chemical controls. Breeding for stress tolerance may be important; drought or flooding, for example, may induce ageing and poor growth in a plant. The proportion of crop biomass channelled into the harvested product, and ease of harvesting, are both crucial in determining the yield at the end of the growing season (see Chapter 1). All these qualities are important to the breeder.

The type of breeding programme employed in classical breeding depends on whether the plant is naturally an **inbreeder** or an **outbreeder**. A selected crop species that is self-pollinating (for example, wheat or tomatoes) requires a different programme from a cross-pollinating one (for example, fruit trees or oil-seed rape). The methods of improvement may be complex, but they include the following:

- **single plant selection**: lines containing the most desirable characters are produced by self-crossing and selection
- **mass selection**: there are many lines or intercrosses and the inferior variants are strongly selected against to leave the favoured forms
- **pedigree breeding**: an original cross produces a new variety that is then intercrossed repeatedly in successive generations
- **bulk population breeding**: an initial cross produces an F_1 generation and then larger F_2 generation upon which artificial and natural selection are practised for several generations

- **backcross breeding**: a good variety lacking a desirable character such as disease resistance (called the recurrent parent) is crossed with an otherwise less good variety possessing the disease resistance (called the donor). The resistance-carrying hybrids are then repeatedly crossed back to the good variety (recurrent parent) line and selection is made for resistance in each generation (see Figure 2.6).

These are all skilled technical practices, often requiring extensive field trials, much labour, intensive selection of plants in the field, carefully controlled crosses and long waits for new generations to develop. Classical breeding is undoubtedly an art as well as a science. Little can be done in a hurry. Although the whole process may take as long as 12 years for an annual crop like wheat, the methods are tried and successful, and most of them will continue well into the future.

The impact of molecular biology on plant breeding

Since the 1960s an understanding of the molecular biology of the gene has begun to influence methods of plant breeding. First, new techniques centring on **recombinant DNA technology** have become increasingly important (see Chapter 9). Second, there have been exciting developments in **tissue culture** that promise, with other cytogenetical and biochemical procedures, to help classical breeding advance by several steps. Four broadly new approaches to plant breeding are now being practised.

Importing alien genes

In classical breeding it is possible to bring in an allele only from a source that is interfertile with the plant to be improved. For example, in wheat genetic variety can only be obtained either from other wheat plants or from the ancestral grasses that have contributed to the evolution of the crop. Such **wide crosses** between distantly related plants often produce embryos that do not survive well. Techniques of increasing the rate of genetic exchange by **crossing over** during early embryonic stages now make possible the selection of embryos with genes from more distantly related plants. Other plants, like beans, do not outbreed at all easily; it is hard even to make crosses with quite closely related plants. Prospects for improving them have therefore depended, in the past, on waiting for a mutation to generate the variety. Molecular biology techniques of **gene insertion** now make possible the introduction of **alien** or **foreign genes** from other species, whether they are closely or distantly related (see below for methods). Any plant containing foreign genes is said to be **transformed**.

Improving the precision and speed of selection

In the past, finding the required variation always involved physically looking for it in the adult plant, or testing parts of the plant chemically. Today the biotechnological use of such techniques as **fluorescent antibodies** may show up a protein gene product, or, if the actual allele **DNA sequence** that produces the phenotype is known, then the allele can be found with a labelled **DNA probe**. A **marker gene** may be attached to the gene of interest that is being transferred so that cells or tissues with the marker will show whether insertion of the new gene has been successful. In such a case, very large numbers of cells or tiny embryos in a culture may be screened, and the transformed plants selected.

Changing the breeding system

Self-pollinating plants have the advantage of being increasingly pure-breeding the longer they are self-pollinated. Pure lines of plants with genetic uniformity and complete homozygosity are advantageous as crops, because all the gene products are totally predictable; the crop and its offspring will breed true. This capacity to self-pollinate and produce viable seed is still not present in some important crops, for example oil-seed rape. The pollen of a given flower is not able to germinate on the stigma of the same flower. It is known that this **self-incompatibility** mechanism has a complex genetic basis, no doubt evolved to prevent inbreed-

ing. Overcoming this self-incompatibility will most probably be achieved by molecular techniques of gene transfer, once the many independent genes are known.

Decreasing the generation time

Progress in plant breeding has often been severely limited by the time it takes to breed from one generation to the next. Using artificial environments with special culture conditions of light, daylength and temperature it is now possible to speed up developmental stages, shorten the generation time and hence increase the rate of the selection process. For example, 3–4 generations of spring wheat and 2–3 generations of winter wheat can now be grown and tested in just one year. Even apples, which used to take 10 years from seed to new apple variety, can now complete their seed-to-seed cycle in less than three years. The prize for the fastest cycles must go to the **rapid-cycling brassicas**. These are cultivars of the species to which cabbage, kale, sprouts, broccoli, chinese leaves, turnips and mustard belong. The most speedy is *Brassica campestris (rapa)*; this little plant can complete its life cycle in just 36 days, from seed to seed, so achieving up to ten cycles in one year. These 'fast plants' are grown under continuous fluorescent lighting. They are important in brassica crop breeding for their speeding up of processes of selection and gene transfer. Recently they have begun to be used in schools and colleges as experiments on them can be completed so quickly (see 'Things to do' at the end of this chapter).

Manipulating cells and tissues

It is not possible to review here all the techniques involved in modern plant breeding. Treatment has been limited to those that are easier to describe, or easier to understand.

The general method of plant **cell and tissue culture** now commonly practised is set out below (based on Dodds, 1985, with *Solanum* and *Nicotiana*. See also the full account in Chapter 15). Tissue culture is already widely exploited commercially for

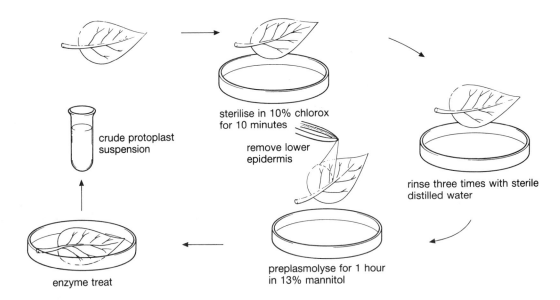

crude protoplast
suspension

sterilise in 10% chlorox
for 10 minutes

remove lower
epidermis

rinse three times with sterile
distilled water

preplasmolyse for 1 hour
in 13% mannitol

enzyme treat

14.1   *The preparation of a naked protoplast suspension from a whole leaf*

vegetative propagation and has potential for plant breeding. It is also a most elegant demonstration of the **totipotency** of plant cells, for from one mesophyll cell of a leaf, a whole new plant may be regenerated.

Figures 14.1 and 14.2 show the typical processes of tissue culture. A young leaf is selected from the parent plant, surface sterilised, washed and then dipped into a 13% solution of mannitol to plasmolyse the cells slightly. Plasmolysis removes wall pressure, so that when naked and without a wall the **protoplast** (naked plant cell) will not burst. After one hour the lower epidermis is carefully teased away. The whole leaf is then subjected to enzymic hydrolysis of the mesophyll cellulose walls using **cellulase**, hemicellulase and pectinase enzymes. It is important that the enzyme mix be lipase-free to avoid any membrane damage. Gentle agitation for a few hours releases the protoplasts as small spherical cells into the suspension (see Figure 14.2).

The protoplasts are next washed with a sterile and osmotically balanced **nutritive medium**. Under the right conditions the cells begin to rebuild their walls within hours; they divide by mitosis

within a few days. Daughter cells adhere to each other in small clumps of cells that form a **callus** colony (see Figure 14.3). By manipulating the concentration of **cytokinin** and **IAA** in an agar medium, callus tissue may be induced to form shoots and then roots. These **regenerated plantlets** can be transferred to larger culture containers and later transplanted into sterile soil. The *in vitro* plantlets have little cuticle and the humidity must be reduced gradually so as to allow the plantlets to grow to complete independence. Finally they may be planted out altogether.

Employing tissue culture in plant breeding

The uses of tissue culture are numerous. Each cell is capable of giving rise to one new plant. Tissue culture may therefore be a method of **vegetative cloning**, and the potential for multiplication is clearly enormous. Garden centres now sell many exotic plants such as orchids and carnivorous plants propagated by these means, and tissue culture is an important means of plant conservation (see Chapter 30). Tissue culture is also employed in the propagation of selected virus-free stocks of such plants such as strawberries.

One important future development of the cell

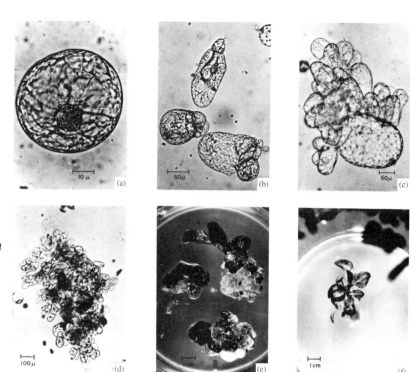

14.2 Whole plant regeneration from a single isolated protoplast: (a) freshly isolated protoplast; (b) cell division; (c) small clumps of cells formed; (d) formation of small callus colonies; (e) shoot formation; (f) plantlet. (Courtesy H.Lörz)

techniques may be to use the culture medium to select for stress-tolerant lines. This is analogous to the way in which plants with a tolerance to heavy metals have been looked for by selecting from trays of seedlings grown in a heavy metal medium. If the selection is made from many thousands of protoplasts in a culture then survival of the few medium-tolerant cell mutants can quickly be seen. Clearly there must be variation among the protoplasts for this to be successful.

One way in which new variability has been generated is by inducing the **fusion of protoplasts** of different species: for example, potato and tomato plants. In this case nuclear fusion occurs but, sadly, the hybrid plant has neither good tubers nor edible fruits! Advantages of successful hybrids are likely to be due to cytoplasmic organelles combining from both parent cells, or to some chromosome material from one cell joining the nucleus of the other. Higher plant cells will not tolerate having two nuclei. Hybrid embryos often shed chromosomes from their cells until they reach a stable state. Some **sterile triploids** have been successfully produced. These cannot reproduce because of their odd

number of chromosomes. Some sterile triploid plants are commercially very important: for example, seedless tangerines.

At present one commercial use of large-scale tissue culture is the production of **cloned** oil palms and date palms. Palm trees show great variation in the quality of their fruits. They also have a long life-cycle from seed to seed and cannot be tested for quality until mature. This makes conventional breeding difficult. Palms do not branch and therefore have little **meristematic tissue** other than

14.3 Cloned date palms, being grown for planting out

that in the crown of the tree. This tissue grows well in culture. From hormonally treated palm callus tissue come **embryoids** (vegetative embryos with plumule, radicle and cotyledon) that can be grown into **plantlets**. This **somatic embryogenesis** is being practised commercially by 'Date Palm Developments'. They have cloned 15 'elite genotypes' of the date palm that were initially selected for their fruit quality. Date palms are very important crops in North Africa and the Middle East, two million tonnes of dates being harvested each year. DPD now export 40 000 palm seedlings each year from Britain to the Arab world.

Perhaps the most exciting recent development in this field is **anther** and **microspore culture**. When given the right kind of shock treatment in the culture medium, the haploid post-meiotic cells in an anther (the microspores that develop into pollen grains) can grow into **haploid embryos**. These grow rather weakly and are of course sterile. However, they occasionally undergo a doubling mutation to produce **double haploids**, a form of diploid, in which all the alleles are in homozygous pairs. A plant produced by this method is of course absolutely pure-breeding, forming an **isogenic line**. The potential for this technique is still largely unexplored, because of the problems in some plants of self-incompatibility.

Gene transfer

Introducing entirely new genes to a plant requires some means of inserting them. This may be done by *Agrobacterium* transformation or by ballistic transformation.

Agrobacterium tumefaciens is a soil bacterium that has become part of the plant breeder's tool kit. It has been known for many years that the callus-like cancerous growths of dicotyledonous plants, known as **crown galls**, are due to infections by this bacterium. The crown gall tumour grows easily in culture without any hormonal assistance and produces nutrients to nourish the bacteria. The latter do not need to be present once an infection has taken place; as discovered in 1977, the cause of

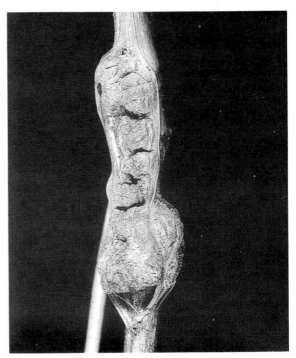

14.4 *A crown gall formed on a loganberry stem. The tumour is induced by* Agrobacterium tumefaciens

the crown gall is a **tumour inducing (Ti) plasmid**. A **plasmid** is a length of DNA of only a few kilobases, joined in a circular chromosome. The Ti plasmid comes initially from the bacterial cytoplasm and is subsequently incorporated into the host plant's tumour cell chromosomes. In 1980 it was discovered that a Ti mutant could be produced that did not have the capacity to form a tumour but was none the less present and functioning in the plant cell after infection. Here lay an opportunity of using *Agrobacterium*, with the mutant plasmid, to introduce foreign DNA into a plant without causing a tumour. However, the challenge was then to put a foreign gene into the Ti plasmid.

Using **restriction enzymes** (see also Chapter 9) a gap was opened in the plasmid into which the gene for an antibiotic-destroying enzyme was then inserted. When tobacco cells were subsequently infected with *Agrobacterium* carrying the new plasmid, the tobacco cells were able to produce the functional antibiotic-destroying protein. This was in 1983. A year later it was shown that whole tobacco plants, grown from the tissue culture, were able to express this gene taken from any part of the plant. Such a plant that has had foreign DNA incorporated into its genome is said to be **transformed**. Several transformations of experimental dicotyledonous plants have now been made using foreign dicotyledon genes rather than bacterial ones. Tobacco, potato and carrots were transformed initially, some of them with herbicide-resistant genes. The great hope for the future is that alien gene implants will be increasingly possible. Specific genes for fungal resistance or for a particularly valuable seed protein might be taken from one plant, cloned, inserted in Ti plasmids and incorporated into a plant in the main breeding stock. The cultivation of transgenic plants is governed by legal controls, because of public concern about the release of **genetically engineered organisms**. The first research plots to study gene dispersal were set up at the John Innes Centre for Plant Science Research in Norwich in 1990.

Although we can exploit the system of gene insertion that *Agrobacterium* has evolved with many dicotyledonous plants, it does not work with monocotyledons. Some of these, like the cereals, are our most important crops. Here, therefore, other techniques are being tried. One of the most surprising is shooting cloned DNA plasmids into cells directly with a **particle gun**! This was first done in 1988 and is called **ballistic transformation** (See also Chapter 9). Originally a 0.22 calibre pistol was used to shoot hundreds of 1 μm tungsten particles, coated in DNA plasmids, through a partial vacuum

14.5 Three varieties of wheat showing, from left to right, decreasing quantities of bread wheat protein

into plant meristems. This is now done with a **Biolistics particle accelerator**. Colour **marker genes** can be used to enable identification of cells cultured from the meristem and successfully transformed. It is usual to insert a marker gene with all plasmids, such as one for herbicide resistance, so that cells in a culture may be selected on the basis of whether they have received the plasmid or not, when the culture is treated with that herbicide.

The plant breeding prospective

It is easy to confuse the potential of ideas with hard results. Up until now, biotechnology has produced no miracles in plant breeding, and not a few disappointments (it would have been so nice to have a plant with tomatoes on top and potatoes on the bottom)! Nevertheless there are many creatively exciting ideas around. So, what may be possible in the future?

An example of what could be done in **wheat plants** will serve to show what a programme of molecular cytogenetic improvement is already achieving. Analysis of wheat seed proteins, collectively called gluten, shows that there are more than fifty proteins or polypeptides present, only some of which are important for giving bread dough its elastic nature and hence ability to rise in the oven. The proteins may be separated by two-way electrophoresis, counted up, classified and even sequenced. It has been shown that superior bread wheats have quite specific **gliadin** and **glutenin** proteins. By using **reverse transcriptase** on the messenger RNA in the seed it has been possible to produce complementary DNA from the cells' RNA. This **cDNA** may be cloned up in bacteria to make many copies. By using labelled **DNA hybridisation** techniques it has already proved possible to find the actual genes. It seems that there are only two or three loci for each of the most important breadmaking proteins. Wheat might therefore be improved if it had either more such gene sites (loci) or better alleles at them. Better proteins, more suited to requirement, could be designed. Looking for the right genes is not easy, but one method is to use the patterns produced by DNA restriction fragments on an electrophoretic gel. In wheats resistance to the 'eye spot' fungus disease is linked to a genetic marker for a particular enzyme in the seed. Looking for the few plants with this 'fingerprint' will therefore find those with the resistance.

Oil-seed rape *(Brassica napus)* is a crop of great potential. It has quite good protein in its seed-cake and a valuable vegetable oil, called canola, that can be crushed out of it in processing. Crushed rape-seed is used for feeding cattle and its oil for making margarine. However, the oil has a minor toxic component, erucic acid, that may damage heart muscle. This is still present in some rape-seed varieties, whilst the bitter glucosinolates in the seed-cake are disliked by cattle. The crop is being improved by their removal and by the insertion of genes for the synthesis of a better spectrum of long-chain **polyunsaturated fatty acids** more suited to human dietary requirements (see Chapter 20).

Recombinant DNA technology allows, in theory, for the transfer of genes from any one life-form into another. One intriguing idea is to take a butterfly gene and insert it into oil-seed rape. The female cabbage-white butterfly will lay eggs on oil-seed rape unless the crop has been protectively sprayed with insecticide. As she lays her eggs the butterfly leaves behind a **pheromone** which deters other females from laying on the same plant. If the plant could produce the butterfly pheromone, by having the gene for synthesis of this chemical inserted in it, then the pest might be deterred, damage by the cabbage-white caterpillar might be reduced, so there might be no need to spray many thousand of hectares of the crop with so much insecticide.

One of the most important objectives and difficult ambitions of breeders is to introduce into crop plants the alleles for **nitrogen fixation** found in bacteria such as *Rhizobium* and *Azotobacter* and in cyanobacteria such as *Anabaena*. At present only leguminous crops like peas and beans, and plants like the water fern *Azolla* have the symbiotic association that allows them to receive fixed nitrogen from their microbial partners. Analysis of the *Rhizobium*–bean association in the root nodules has been most promising so far. There appear to be a considerable number of bacterial genes for fixation. Of these the key set are in 17 separate DNA sections, coding for the enzyme **nitrogenase**; there seem to be an even greater number for nodule management in the host plant! However, if a crop like wheat could be persuaded to fix nitrogen on its own it would be a huge saving on the future need for nitrate fertiliser, not to mention the fossil fuels required to make them. If you can sort this one out you might even be awarded a Nobel prize!

Further reading

Austin, R.B. (1986) *Molecular Biology and Crop Improvement*. Cambridge University Press.
Dodds, J.H. (1985) *Plant Genetic Engineering*. Cambridge University Press.
Shaw, C.L. (1988) *Plant Molecular Biology: A Practical Approach*. Oxford University Press

Thought questions

1 Only 14% of the sugar-beet tap root (the sucrose) is useful to us. Thousands of tonnes of pulped root produced annually in Britain is waste. It contains lipids and proteins as well as cellulose. How could you engineer sugar-beet to produce something else useful as a by-product of sugar?

2 There are blue flowers in your garden, yet nobody has yet bred a blue rose. Why not? How might you breed one? (A prize at the Chelsea Flower Show for this one!)

Things to do

1. MacIntyre (Mottingham Garden Centre, Mottingham Lane, London SE12 9AW) retail a 'fast plants' kit, with rapid cycling *Brassica campestris (rapa)* seed and growing instructions. These plants provide an excellent introduction to the material and techniques used in plant breeding.
2. Tissue culture kits are marketed by several firms including Philip Harris Ltd. Meristem culture is perhaps the easiest. Help and advice is also available from 'Science and Plants for Schools', Homerton College, Cambridge CB2 2PH.

15

Chemicals in Culture: Using Plant Cells for Chemical Synthesis

Much of our food, clothing and materials come from plants. In addition the plant kingdom has for many centuries been a major source of chemicals for human use. This chapter explores what these chemicals are, how the plant cells that produce them may now be grown in culture, and what the prospects are for this new branch of technology. Using **plant cell biotechnology** biologists may be able to use tissue culture to produce sophisticated chemicals, not *in vitro* (in the test-tube) but *in vivo* – employing the enzyme machinery of the living cell.

Chemicals from the green plant

Besides the primary metabolic reactions taking place in plant cells, some chemical reactions lead to the formation of compounds which are unique to a few species or even to a single cultivated variety (cultivar) of one species of plant. These compounds are known as **secondary metabolites** and include alkaloids, resins, volatile oils, tannins and cardiac glycosides. For us, they may be important drugs, food additives or perfumes. For the plant, these secondary metabolites often play significant physiological and ecological roles. For example, many such compounds are important in the protection of plants from fungal or insect attack.

Since secondary metabolites are of considerable economic importance, they have been increasingly developed as products in a wide range of industries. (see Table 15.1).

Pharmaceuticals are a major group of important products obtained from plants, particularly in terms of their monetary value; some 25% of prescribed drugs are derived from the plant kingdom. Plant poisons, some of which are classified by pharmaceutical chemists as **medicinals**, are often

Table 15.1 *Natural products from plants and their associated industries*

Industry	Plant species	Plant product	Uses
Pharmaceutical	*Papaver somniferum*	Codeine (alkaloid)	Analgesic (pain killer)
	Dioscorea deltoidea	Diosgenin (steroid)	Anti-fertility agents
	Cinchona ledgeriana	Quinine (alkaloid)	Antimalarial
	Digitalis lanata	Digoxin (cardiac glycoside)	Heart regulation
	Datura stramonium	Scopolamine (alkaloid)	Lowers blood pressure
	Catharanthus roseus	Vincristine (alkaloid)	Antileukaemic
Agrochemical	*Tanacetum cinerariifolium*	Pyrethrin	Insecticide
Food and drink	*Cinchona ledgeriana*	Quinine (alkaloid)	Bittering agent
	Thaumatococcus danielli	Thaumatin (chalcone)	Non-nutritive sweetener
Cosmetics	*Jasminum* sp.	Jasmine	Perfume

From: Fowler, M.W. (1983) in Mantell and Smith (eds) (1983) Plant Biotechnology. *Cambridge University Press.*

potent **neurotoxins**. For example, **curare** from the plant *Strychnos toxifera* is used by many African and South American tribes for hunting wild animals. The drug is smeared on to a dart or arrow head, and wounded animals are quickly paralysed. **Ricin**, produced by the castor-oil plant *Ricinus communis*, may one day be developed as a **biocide** for killing unwanted forms of life. Similarly, the flowers of the perfume daisy *Tanacetum cinerariifolium* produce **pyrethroids** which are potent insecticides and have direct application in farming and horticulture.

Many other secondary metabolites are used as perfumes, flavours, colorants and food materials. These products range considerably in cost and market volume. For example, the fat **cocoa butter**, a basic constituent of chocolate, costs about £2500 per tonne with a market volume of about 20000 tones per annum; the perfume jasmine costs around £3,750 per kilogram with a market volume of perhaps only 20–30 kg per annum. Products range from single components like **quinine**, the anti-malarial drug, to complex mixtures such as the monoterpene oils which form the basis of the perfume industry.

Where products consist of a single secondary compound, attempts have often been made to produce them through chemical synthesis from much simpler starting compounds, with varying degrees of success. Despite advances in the field of organic chemistry, the constraints of high costs, low yields and difficult chemical conversions and purifications from complex mixtures have often made this too difficult. In such cases, the intact plant itself remains the only effective means of synthesis, but this is by no means easy.

First, there are technical and economic problems inherent in the cultivation of plants as a source of secondary metabolites. In most cases, the plants have not been subjected to intensive genetic breeding programmes for the optimum production of a particular compound. Second, when grown in large plantations, usually located in the tropics or sub-tropics, the plants are subjected to seasonal environmental factors including climate and pests. Third, the political instability of some developing nations in which medicinal plants are grown means that the supply of crude plant material for processing in industrialised countries cannot be guaranteed.

Some of these difficulties may be overcome by the advent of **plant cell biotechnology**. This involves the large-scale culture of isolated plant cells. Given appropriate conditions, the cells synthesise the desirable substances characteristic of the parent plant. The chemical product is formed in cells and generally passed into the culture medium.

Plant cell culture offers several advantages over traditional cultivation of plants as a method of producing secondary metabolites:

- no expensive breeding of highly selected crop varieties necessary
- independence from environmental and geographical factors
- defined production system, with more consistent product quality and yield
- reduction in land requirement.

Consequently, much research is being devoted to the investigation of plant cell culture as an effective means of exploiting the chemicals produced in the plant kingdom. In addition to being an alternative route to natural product synthesis, cell culture may be of value when a new desirable substance has been identified in a plant which proves particularly difficult to grow. An example of this is the poppy *Papaver bracteatum* from which the narcotic alkaloid **thebaine** is derived; thebaine is the commercial source of the pain-killer codeine.

The products from large-scale culture of isolated plant cells may not be easily obtainable from the intact plant. First, cell culture may allow the expression of 'silent genes', that is, genes which are not normally expressed in the intact plant. Thus potentially useful compounds may be obtained from cell cultures which are not synthesised in the parent plant. One example is the pigment **lucidin** from cultures of the hedge burnet *Galium mollugo*. Second, plant enzyme systems may be isolated from cell cultures. These groups of enzymes are capable of catalysing changes in molecules which are either impossible or are too difficult or too costly to make economically viable through the traditional techniques of organic chemistry. The commercial synthesis of **digoxin**, a cardiac drug, involves such a **biotransformation** using an enzyme system isolated from cell cultures of the foxglove *Digitalis lantana*.

A clear idea of how plant cell culture is going to become more important in plant biotechnology is set out in the rest of this chapter; the ways in which cells are cultured and products collected are also explained.

Plant cell cultures

An early success in **cell culture** technology was achieved by Haberlandt in 1878 when he cultured single cells isolated from different parts of various plants in simple nutrient solutions. It was not until the late 1930s, however, that growth and **cell**

division was reported in such cultures. Progressively, the requirements for successful culture became recognised; an important development was the regeneration of whole plants from cultured cells. Undeveloped plant cells are **totipotent**, that is, they have the ability to give rise to an exact genetic copy of the parent plant. Consequently, in the presence of the required balance of nutrients and plant growth regulators it is possible to regenerate whole plants from cells taken from plant parts such as roots, stems, leaves, seeds and anthers (see Figure 15.1). This potential for regeneration is of great importance in horticulture and agriculture. For example, it is well known that plants can be grown from cuttings, tubers and bulbs.

15.1 The alternative pathways of regeneration of a whole new plant from tissue explants derived from various parts of a carrot plant

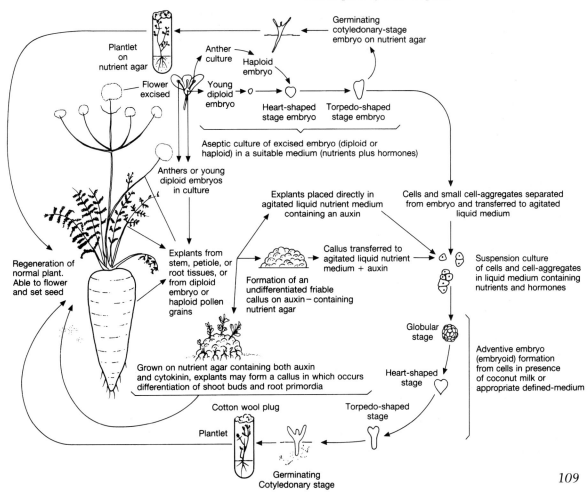

Plant cell cultures are initiated through the formation of **callus**. This is a mass of undifferentiated cells which looks like disorganised green parenchyma. The callus is obtained by placing a seed or a piece of tissue, an 'explant', from the parent plant onto nutrient agar. The tissue is generally selected from plants with the highest yields of the desired product as these tend to give high-yielding cultures. Present within the agar are various **plant growth regulators**, a source of carbon which is usually sucrose, a source of nitrogen which is typically nitrate or ammonia, and inorganic macro- and micro-nutrients.

Early growth media were unsophisticated, relying heavily on the addition of complex mixtures such as coconut milk to achieve cell growth and division. These media have now been superseded by a variety of clearly defined media (see Table 15.2).

Aseptic (completely sterile) conditions are vital for the successful establishment of a cell culture. The nutrient agar provides an excellent environment for bacteria and fungi which would, if unchecked, compete with and rapidly outgrow the plant cells. Before being transferred to the agar, the explant tissue is therefore carefully surface-sterilised in, for example, 5% sodium hypochlorite. The sterilising solution is then removed by repeated washing of the tissue in sterile distilled water.

The sterilised tissue explant is placed on nutrient agar in a flask with a cover. This is gas-permeable but excludes bacterial and fungal spores. The flask is placed in an incubator, sometimes with light for photosynthesis, at an optimum temperature of about 25°C.

After about 1–2 weeks, depending upon a variety of factors such as the source of the tissue and the nutrients supplied, the cells proliferate to form a callus. When the callus is about 2–4 cm in diameter, it is transferred to fresh nutrient agar on which it continues to grow. It becomes more friable: that is, it readily breaks up when placed in a liquid (see Figure 15.2).

The callus is typically slow-growing and heterogeneous, and is not suitable as a production system. For this reason the friable callus is transferred to a liquid medium in a rotating flask. The swirling motion of the liquid disperses the cells producing a **suspension culture** composed of a mixture of free cells and small aggregates of cells (see Figure 15.3). In suspension cultures, more cells are in direct contact with the nutrients which means that growth is more rapid and the culture is more uniform than in callus culture.

Suspension cultures are generally grown in the same way as microbial cells: they are maintained at temperatures of about 25–27°C on orbital shakers at rotational speeds of about 120 rpm. However, the design of plant-cell culture vessels must take account of such factors as the large size of plant cells; a lower oxygen demand than microbial cells; variation in the tendency for cell clumps to form; and the susceptibility of the cellulose cell wall to shearing forces set up by stirring blades. Mixing

Table 15.2 Examples of media recipes for the growth of plant cells

Component	Formulation and component concentration/mg per litre	
	Murashige & Skoog (1962)	Gamborg et al. (1968)
$(NH_4)_2SO_4$	—	134.0
$CaCl_2.2H_2O$	440.0	150.0
$NaH_2PO_4.2H_2O$	—	169.6
KH_2PO_4	170.0	—
NH_4NO_3	1650.0	—
KNO_3	1900.0	3000.0
$MgSO_4.7H_2O$	370.0	250.0
$CoCl_2.6H_2O$	0.025	0.025
$NaMoO_4.2H_2O$	0.25	0.25
$CuSO_4.5H_2O$	0.025	0.025
KI	0.83	0.75
H_3BO_3	6.20	10.0
$MnSO_4.7H_2O$	22.30	13.20
FeNaEDTA	36.70	40.00
$ZnSO_4.7H_2O$	8.6	2.0
Meso inositol	100.0	100.0
Nicotinic acid	0.5	1.0
Thiamine HCl	0.1	10.0
Pyridoxine HCl	0.5	1.0
Glycine	2.0	—
Sucrose	20 000.0	20 000.0
pH	5.8	5.8

Fowler, M.W. (1987) in Bu'lock and Christiansen (eds) Basic Biotechnology. Academic Press

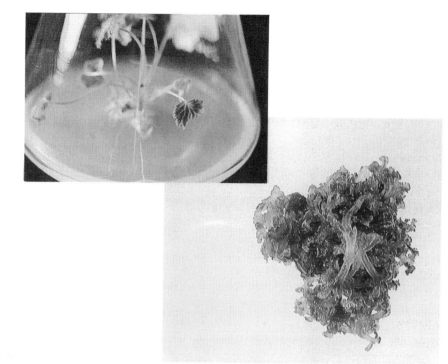

15.2 A friable (easily broken up) callus from a scented leaf Pelargonium, with a regenerated plantlet

and aeration are two basic requirements for mass growth and these have been achieved for plant cell culture in a variety of vessels, notably the **airlift loop vessel** (see Figure 15.4).

15.3 Cells from a high alkaloid yielding suspension culture of Catharanthus roseus

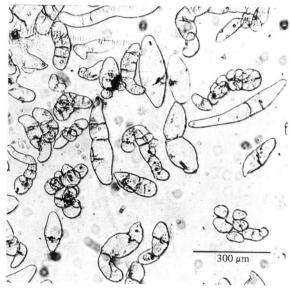

300 μm

In some systems, for example the high-nicotine yielding *Nicotiana tabacum*, little cell **differentiation** is needed before the desired metabolite is produced. The cells here are quite unspecialised. On the other hand, suspension cultures of the poppy *Papaver somniferum* produce substantial yields of **opiate alkaloids** only when high numbers of specialised **lactiferous cells** have developed.

The pattern of growth of cultured plant cells is similar to that of microbial cells (Figure 15.5) but is invariably much slower. The doubling time for many microbes is in the order of minutes or hours, whereas for plants it is usually measured in hours or days.

Two-stage production systems are often employed. The first stage is a form of **continuous culture** during which conditions are adjusted to permit optimum growth of the culture (production of biomass). The cells are then transferred to a second vessel, for **production culture**, with the appropriate nutrient supply for high production of the desired product. Alternatively, instead of being free in solution, the culture may be of **immobilised cells** for the second stage of synthesis. Plant cells

111

15.4a An airlift loop bioreactor

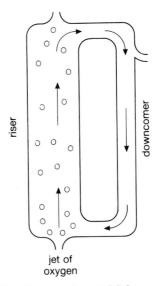

15.4b Outline diagram of an airlift loop vessel

ums). Pelargonium cells have been entrapped in polyurethane foam, which allows secreted monoterpenes to be washed away from the immobilised culture with a continuous flow of fresh medium. This is important as, when free, monoterpenes are highly toxic to plant cells; in the intact plant they are stored in specialised glandular hairs. Such **end-product toxicity** is not uncommon and immobilisation of cells provides a way of overcoming this.

There are problems inherent in the immobilisation of cells, however. They include the difficulty of ensuring an adequate transfer of gases through the

15.5 *The growth curve of a cell suspension culture of* Catharanthus roseus

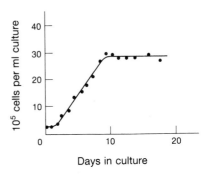

have been successfully immobilised on a variety of supports including polyacrylamide, starch and agarose. Typically, cells remain viable for more than 150 days and continue active synthesis. This is true of the cells of pelargoniums (these plants are commonly and erroneously referred to as gerani-

Natural product	Species	Cell culture yield	Whole plant
Anthraquinones	*Morinda citrifolia*	900 nmol per g dry weight	110 nmol per g dry weight, root
Anthraquinones	*Cassia tora*	0.334% fresh weight	0.209% dry weight, seed
Diosgenin	*Dioscorea deltoidea*	26 mg per g dry weight	20 mg per g dry weight, tuber
Ginseng saponins	*Panax ginseng*	0.38% fresh weight	0.3–3.3% fresh weight
Nicotine	*Nicotiana tabacum*	3–4% dry weight	2–5% dry weight
Serpentine	*Catharanthus roseus*	1.3% dry weight	0.26% dry weight
Thebaine	*Papaver bracteatum*	130 mg per g dry weight	1400 mg per g dry weight, leaf and 3000 mg per g dry weight, root
Ubiquinone	*Nicotiana tabacum*	0.5 mg per g dry weight	16 mg per g dry weight, leaf

From: Fowler, M.W. (1987) in Bu'lock and Christiansen (eds) Basic Biotechnology. Academic Press.

Table 15.3 Natural product yields from cell cultures and whole plants

inert support; the prevention of cell growth and division; and promotion of the development of sufficiently 'leaky' cells which allow the release of the desired product into the bathing medium for its subsequent recovery.

Products from plant cell cultures

A wide variety of secondary metabolites has been isolated from plant cell cultures. For many of these products the yield obtained compares very favourably with that from the intact plant (see Table 15.3). However, relatively few products are as yet considered to be economically viable for production on a large scale. A notable exception is the red pigment **shikonin** derived from *Lithospermum erythrorhizon*. Shikonin, which is used as an anti-inflammatory drug, has been produced in Japan on an industrial scale since 1982. Other metabolites which are promising targets for commercialisation through plant cell culture are the alkaloids **agmalacine** and **serpentine**. These substances are obtained from cell cultures of the periwinkle *Catharanthus roseus*, often at levels higher than in the intact plant. The drugs act as agents for treating irregular heartbeat. The antileukaemic alkaloids **vinblastine** and **vincrystine** are also produced by the periwinkle but so far have not been synthesised in cell culture. Considering their medicinal importance in treating cancer patients, these chemicals represent an obvious target for

further research. Various other natural products are receiving similar attention; one is the cardiac glycoside digoxin which has been demonstrated in cell cultures of the foxglove *Digitalis lantana*. **Diosgenin**, a steroid synthesised by cells of the yam *Dioscorea deltoidea*, is used in the production of oral contraceptives. The painkilling alkaloids **codeine** and **morphine** are obtained from cultures of the opium poppy *Papaver somniferum*.

In addition to medical and pharmaceutical applications, many natural plant products are of potential importance in the food, cosmetic and agrochemical industries. A variety of natural colours has been obtained from cell culture, the majority being red. One problem is that the molecules of these substances are generally most stable in acid conditions, while most foods are neutral or slightly alkaline. The alkaloid **quinine**, important as an anti-malarial drug and also used as a bittering agent in foods and soft drinks, has successfully been isolated from cell cultures of *Cinchona ledgeriana*; the anti-malarial drug was first obtained from the bark of this South American tree.

Aromatic oils are readily obtained from cell cultures of several species including geraniums (*Pelargonium* spp.) These oils are rich in **geraniol** and **citronellol**; they are widely used in perfumes, cosmetics and soap and are also used in cooking to impart a delicate flavour to food.

Of interest to the agrochemical industry is that various antimicrobial and particularly antifungal substances have been isolated from many different plant cell cultures. With an increase in yield of product, culture techniques may allow the commercial exploitation of these natural products. Such a development might transform our present agrochemical industry.

Future prospects

Recent developments in plant biotechnology indicate that certain aspects may well have direct industrial application. These include the synthesis in cell culture of a variety of high-value secondary metabolites, for which yield of product is of vital importance; and biotransformations using either extracted plant enzymes or immobilised cells. Much further research and great patience are necessary, but it appears that plant cell culture is proving to be a realistic alternative technology.

Further reading

Fowler, M.W. Products from Plant Cells in Bu'lock, J. and Kristiansen, B (eds) (1987) *Basic Biotechnology.* Academic Press.
Dixon, R.A. (1985) *Plant Cell Culture – A Practical Approach.* IRL Press.

Thought questions

1 Do you think that plant cell culture may be regarded as 'unnatural' and, as such, undesirable? Is plant cell culture a half-way development between completely synthetic drugs and herbal remedies?

2 Many different plant products which are applicable to a range of industries (such as food, pharmaceutical and agrochemical industries) have been detected in culture although they are not yet produced in yields which are high enough for commercialisation. All are potentially useful. Given that funds for research are inevitably limited, do you think that priority should be given to the development of any particular group of natural plant products?

Things to do

Investigating plant glandular tissues
Many plants produce glandular secretions from their leaves, stems, fruits or flowers. Remarkably few have been thoroughly investigated.

1. Make a microscopic investigation of the glandular hairs of the stinging nettle *Urtica dioica*. Make a study of the hairs that sting. How is the bulbous end fractured? Why is the hair so brittle? At what point does the needle-end form? When a nettle hair is fractured it releases acetylcholine and histamine (the sting and the itch respectively).

2. *Pelargonium* plants (commonly misnamed geraniums) secrete monoterpenes from cells on to the surface of the leaf. When brushed they smell very strongly. What change to the leaf surface causes this release? Why do different *Pelargonium* varieties smell distinctively? Can these odours be collected in a solvent?

3. Where on a rose petal is the scent coming from? What petal surface features are associated with a good scent? Do freshly collected herbs, which are sweet-smelling, retain their scent when dried? Find out which do and which do not. Why are glandular secretions from plants often so strong on young buds and flowers? For any plant secretion that you investigate make an hypothesis about its role in nature. How can you test your hypothesis?

4. Feed a Venus fly-trap (*Dionaea* sp.) with a fly-sized piece of developed photographic film (print negative or slide positive). After two days remove the 'prey'. Study the gelatin surface microscopically. What is the glandular hair secreting?

16
Recognising Self and Non-self – The Development of Immunotechnology

A multicellular animal is able to recognise 'self' and 'non-self', that is, to discriminate between its own molecules and those of foreign, invading microbes. This sensitive recognition mechanism forms the basis of the **immune system**.

In the past 30 years our understanding of how the immune system works has increased dramatically – to such an extent that

monoclonal antibodies have become some of the most sophisticated tools in use in modern biology and medicine. This chapter explains how the immune system works, how diseases have been combated by vaccination, and how monoclonal antibodies are now being employed against more than simple disease organisms.

Natural immunity

In lower animals, natural immunity operates through phagocytic leucocytes (white blood cells) whose function is to engulf and then digest foreign material. As early as the 1880s the Russian biologist Metchnikoff discovered that small splinters, when implanted into invertebrates such as molluscs, were surrounded and engulfed by wandering amoeboid cells.

As any phagocytic cell has the potential to recognise and to respond to any foreign material, this form of immunity is referred to as **non-specific** or **natural immunity**. In mammals, non-specific immunity is provided by two main categories of **phagocytic cells**. They both arise from **pluripotent stem cells** (cells capable of differentiating into any of the different cellular components of blood) in the bone marrow. The first group comprises motile amoeboid **monocytes** which are transported in the blood and **macrophages** which are resident in organs such as the liver, spleen and lungs. These cells are the body's first line of defence, and attack invaders that have entered through the lungs and gut. The lung alveolar macrophages are

free to move about but those of the liver, the Kupffer cells, are fixed. Together, the macrophages form a network system lining these internal surfaces and hence are described as the **reticuloendothelial system (RES)**.

The second category of phagocyte comprises the most numerous type of white blood cell, the **granulocytes**, or polymorphonuclear leucocytes. They play a major role in the body's defence

16.1 The different types of leucocyte (white blood cell) involved in the immune mechanisms of mammals. Some red blood cells are given for comparison

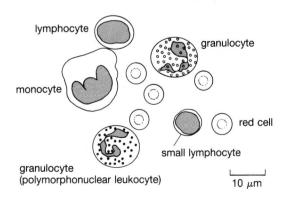

against acute infection. Transported throughout the body in the blood, they can adhere to blood vessels and can also migrate out of them, into the tissues where they actively engulf pathogens.

Phagocytes are the first cells to come into action during the initial period of any infection. They also clear any dead cells remaining after an immune response, and digest old or damaged cells.

The complement system

Another non-specific defence of vertebrates is the **complement system**. This consists of a series of about twenty blood serum proteins which are activated in turn in a cascading pathway. One molecule causes the activation of several of the next molecules in the sequence. This is much like the blood clotting cascade. The key function of the complement system is the coating or **opsonisation** of microbes; microbes coated with serum protein complement are more easily recognised by macrophages and more easily engulfed by phagocytosis.

Around an infection there is swelling and reddening; many of the complement molecules

contribute to this **inflammatory response**. Some increase the permeability of blood capillaries whilst others cause the **chemotaxis** (movement up a chemical gradient) of macrophages towards a site of infection. The entire sequence of complement activation can also lead to the lysis (bursting) of whole microbes as a result of certain complement proteins causing major damage to the microbial membranes. The complement system, therefore, is of great importance in its own right and also in augmenting the action of phagocytes.

Acquired immunity

Vertebrates also display **acquired** or **specific immunity**. The presence in the body of a foreign molecule **(antigen)** can elicit the production of a counteracting molecule **(antibody)** which is highly specific to that particular antigen.

Antigens

Antigens, by definition, are able to provoke an immune response and to react with its products, antibodies. Antigens are proteins, glycoproteins or polysaccharides and may be free molecules or may be present on the surface of an invading microbe. Only parts of the antigen molecule, the **antigenic determinant sites** or **epitopes**, are actually involved in the reaction with the antibody. A particular antigen may have several epitopes, each of which can cause the production of a specific antibody molecule. Generally, therefore, an immune response involves the production by the immune system of a mixture of antibodies.

It is important to understand that antigenic molecules are present on all cells, not just those of microbes. For example, all human cells have cell-surface glycoproteins which are referred to as **human histocompatibility antigens (HLA antigens)**. These are genetically determined, so unrelated individuals possess different HLA antigens. Similarly, **blood groups** are determined by the presence of particular mucopolysaccharide molecules on the membranes of the red blood cells. If tissue type matching is inadequate prior to trans-

16.2   The basic structural organisation of an immunoglobulin molecule

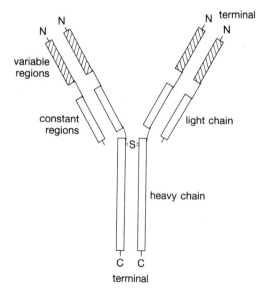

plantation, these cell surface molecules provoke very vigorous immune reactions (see Chapter 23).

Cell-surface antigens therefore act as recognition factors, and they only elicit an immune response if they are foreign.

Antibodies

All antibodies are proteins with similar structures and are known collectively as **immunoglobulins (Ig)**. There are five classes of antibody (IgA, IgD, IgE, IgG, IgM) each with a specific role in immunity.

The antibody molecule has a four-chain structure: two identical heavy chains (H) which determine the class of immunoglobulin, and two identical light chains (L). Each light chain is made up of about 110 amino acids, held together in a loop by a disulphide bond.

Comparisons of the amino acid sequences of the chains show that both the H and L chains can be divided into constant (C) and variable (V) regions. The amino acid sequence is very similar for all antibody molecules. In the variable region at the N-terminal end of each chain, however, the amino acid sequence varies between different antibody molecules and is unique to an antibody of any one specificity. The variable region of each antibody molecule has a specific three-dimensional structure which provides a unique **antigen-binding site**.

Structurally, the different classes of Ig are similar although they show differences in function (see Table 16.1).

Lymphocytes

Antibodies are produced by **lymphocytes** which are small leucocytes typically with little cytoplasm. There are two main categories of lymphocyte, **B-cells** and **T-cells**, both of which originate from stem cells in the bone marrow. B-cells mature in the bone marrow but T-cells must migrate to the **thymus** for a period of maturation and differentiation. The thymus and bone marrow are known as primary lymphoid organs. Once mature, the lymphocytes circulate in a definite pattern through the secondary lymphoid tissues (which include the spleen, lymph nodes, adenoids and tonsils), the lymphatic vessels and the bloodstream.

Both B-cells and T-cells are initially activated by the combination of an antigen with antigen-specific receptors on the cell surface. In contrast to phagocytes, lymphocytes are highly specific in that each T- and B-cell can be activated by one particular antigen only.

B-lymphocytes
On the surface of each B-cell is an Ig molecule which acts as its antigen-binding site. Each B-cell is

Table 16.1 Immunoglobulin classes and their functions

Antibody class	IgG	IgM	IgA	IgD	IgE
Molecular weight (D)	150 000	900 000	160 000	180 000	200 000
Configuration*	Monomeric	Pentameric	Dimeric	Monomeric	Monomeric
Serum concentration (mg per 100 ml)	700–1500	60–170	150–400	3.0	0.01–0.03
Antigen-binding sites	2	5(10)	2	?	2
Placental passage	†	–	–	–	–
Functions	Fixes complement; opsonisation for macrophages	Produced early in antibody response, fixes complement; efficient lysin and agglutinin	Neutralisation at mucosal surfaces – predominant in body secretions	Receptor on lymphocyte membrane	Binds to mast cells† in the tissues; responsible for allergies such as hay fever

*number of basic subunits   †mast cells are cells in connective tissue which release histamines

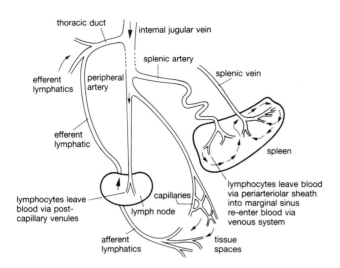

16.3   A schematic view of the main pathways of lymphocyte circulation

genetically precommitted to make an antibody of one specificity. Many, many thousands of different cells are made by the body in preparation for invasion. Contact with an antigen stimulates a B-cell to divide and differentiate, generating many antibody-producing **plasma cells**. The surface Ig

16.4   A summary of the humoral response (Simpkins J and Williams J. I. Advanced Human Biology, *Unwin Hyman (1987))*

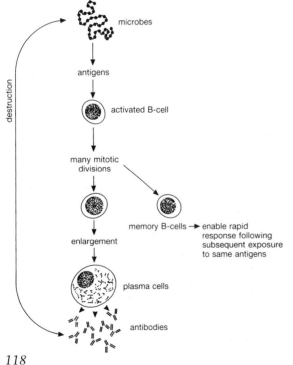

and secreted immunoglobulin are identical. All its descendant plasma cells synthesise the same antibody. Simultaneously, a population of **memory cells** is produced from the originally activated B-cell, each of which has the same surface Ig receptor. These memory cells retain the ability to recognise the specific antigen which caused their production, and allow a rapid immune response following subsequent exposure to the same antigen (secondary response). Memory cells may live for many years.

The production by B-lymphocytes of antibody following stimulation with an antigen is referred to as **humoral immunity**. The alternative form of acquired immunity is **cell-mediated immunity**. This involves lymphocytes and responses which, although specific, may not include the production of antibodies: for example, the killing by direct contact of graft cells by T-lymphocytes.

T-lymphocytes

T-cells are also activated by the combination of an antigen with a specific receptor. The 'sensitised' T-cell undergoes many mitotic divisions to produce a clone which includes T-cells with various functions:

Helper T-cells   Plasma cells derived from B-lymphocytes will not respond directly to most antigens. They require a second signal, possibly in the form of secreted soluble factors, from T-cells before they will synthesise antibody.

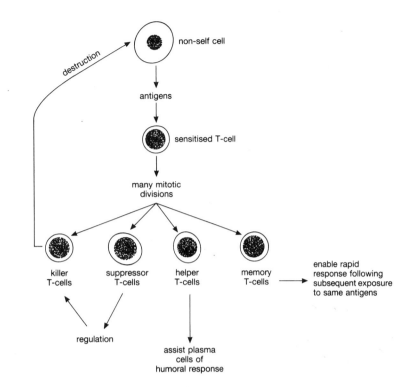

16.5   A summary of the cell-mediated response (Simpkins J and Williams J. I. Advanced Human Biology, Unwin Hyman (1987))

Suppressor T-cells   These suppress the activity of killer T-cells and B-cells. Regulation of the immune response is achieved through interactions between suppressor T- and killer T-cells.

16.6 Primary and secondary response to an initial and then subsequent identical dose of antigen (from Green, N.P.O. et. al. (1990) Biological Science, Cambridge University Press.)

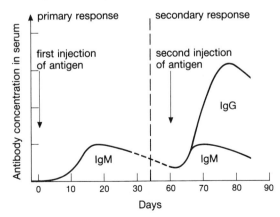

Killer T-cells   These cells have various functions:
- cause lysis of cells infected with virus particles
- attract macrophages
- activate phagocytosis
- release molecules called **lymphokines**.

Lymphokines include **interferon** which prevents viral replication, and other molecules which direct the inflammatory response.

Immunological memory

A characteristic feature of specific immunity (both humoral and cell-mediated) is the generation of **immunological memory**. Once an animal has responded to an antigen it is said to be primed. On subsequent encounters with the same antigen, a secondary response is observed. Typically, secondary antibody responses show a shorter time-lag before the appearance of antibody, and a peak production of antibody which may be ten to fifty times higher than that of the primary response. This is due to the presence in the primed animal of small amounts of preformed antibody and of circulating memory cells, capable of rapid production of antibody. Immunological memory forms the basis of all immunisation procedures.

Vaccines

Immunity may be acquired **naturally** in two ways: **passively**, through the transfer to a child before birth of antibodies across the placenta and from the mother after birth in the colostrum (first mammary secretion) and breast milk, and **actively**, as a result of exposure to an antigen which triggers an immune response in the host such as during a natural infection.

Alternatively, immunisation may be **artificially induced**. This may be done **passively**, through injection of an individual with antibody preformed in other individual or animals. For example, antibodies against diphtheria and tetanus may be cultured in horses. The antibodies are extracted and purified from the blood serum. This form of immunity is short-lived because the antibodies are gradually broken down as the patient's immune system recognises them as foreign. Alternatively, artificially induced immunisation may be induced **actively**. This involves the deliberate administration

of antigenic materials in the form of a **vaccine**.

Immunisation with vaccines is accepted as an effective way of controlling the spread of infectious diseases. For example, notification of diphtheria in Scotland before 1940 averaged about 10 000 cases annually. Widespread immunisation was instituted in 1940. The incidence of diphtheria then declined and, with the exception of six cases in 1968, the disease is virtually eliminated. Vaccines have similarly led to the virtual elimination of polio from the western world and to the total eradication of smallpox. However, for many diseases including malaria, syphilis and AIDS, no effective vaccine has yet been produced.

Every vaccine has the potential to produce unwanted side-effects in some people. For example, complications such as encephalitis (brain inflammation) after vaccination against smallpox have been reported; similarly, vaccination against rabies has led to cases of nervous damage. During the 1970s there was a significant fall in the percentage of mothers bringing their children for whooping cough immunisation: from 80% in 1974, it decreased to 31% in 1978. This followed adverse publicity about the possible risks of severe damage to the nervous system. As a consequence the incidence of whooping cough, which is a serious and highly infectious disease, increased dramatically. Over 110 000 cases were notified between 1977 and 1979; during this period 26 children

Table 16.2 Current recommended immunisation schedule

Age	Vaccine and timing	
3–12 months	Diphtheria/tetanus/pertussis/whooping cough(DTP) + oral polio vaccine (first dose)	
		← Interval 6–8 weeks
	Diphtheria/tetanus/pertussis + oral polio vaccine (second dose)	
		← Interval 4–6 months
	Diphtheria/tetanus/pertussis + oral polio vaccine (third dose)	
1–2 years	Measles/mumps/rubella (MMR)	
5–6 years (school entry)	Diphtheria/tetanus + oral polio (booster doses)	
10–13 years	Bacillus Calmette–Guérin (BCG)	
		← Interval of at least 3 weeks
11–13 years (girls)	Rubella (German measles)	
15–19 years (school leaving)	Tetanus + oral polio vaccine (booster doses)	

died from the disease while a similar number suffered permanent brain damage. In contrast, the risk of serious brain damage attributable to immunisation is about 1 in 100 000 children. During the 1980s, the acceptance rate for vaccination steadily increased.

Much consideration is given to the safety of vaccines and, although no vaccine can be 100% safe under all circumstances, the benefits of immunisation for a child, and for society, clearly outweigh the risks.

Routine immunisation

A schedule for immunisation is recommended by the Department of Health in the United Kingdom. In the absence of any medical complications, vaccination is a standard procedure for all children.

Recommendations for vaccination are similar in most other western countries.

Production of vaccines: old methods and new

Vaccines are prepared so as to be as antigenic as possible, but not pathogenic (disease-causing). Three main types of vaccine have traditionally been produced:

Living vaccines
These comprise attenuated (weakened) organisms which remain antigenic but are no longer pathogenic. **Attenuation** may be achieved by culturing the organism at high temperatures or by the addition of chemicals to the culture medium. Obviously the attenuation procedure and the growth of the pathogens for live **vaccines** must be rigorously controlled. Examples of living vaccines include BCG (Bacillus Calmette-Guérin) for tuberculosis, and live virus vaccines for polio, rubella, mumps and measles.

Toxoids
These are the soluble exotoxins secreted from bacteria such as diphtheria and tetanus bacilli which have been detoxified by gentle heating or the addition of formaldehyde. **Detoxified exotoxins**

may be injected in solution and provide many useful years of immunity.

Killed vaccines
Organisms may be killed by heat or chemical treatment or by ultra-violet radiation. The dead pathogens are then injected. Protection against cholera, whooping cough and typhoid can be achieved using such **killed vaccines**.

In general, live vaccines are more successful than inactivated vaccines (killed organisms or toxoids). Characteristically, they induce a strong, long-lasting immune response because the organism multiplies and remains antigenic over a number of days. Booster doses may not be required for these vaccines.

The advent of genetic engineering technology has allowed the development of new methods of vaccine production. If the antigenic protein molecule can be mass-produced, without being pathogenic, then this will perform as a vaccine. The production of **subunit vaccines** depends upon the correct identification of component protein molecules of the pathogen which are capable of acting antigenically. The gene coding for the protein may be isolated from the organism and transferred into a bacterium such as *Escherichia coli*. This multiplies rapidly in culture and allows large-scale production of the antigenic protein for use as a vaccine.

Only limited success has been achieved with this **recombinant DNA method** for several reasons (see Chapter 13). First, single protein molecules tend to produce weak immune responses and, unlike the whole organism, cannot multiply in the body. Second, to be effective it appears that subunit vaccines must be injected along with a booster chemical such as aluminium hydroxide. Also, many surface antigens are proteins with sugar or lipid side-chains. Bacteria cannot synthesise these often highly antigenic side-chains and so the immune response elicited by the subunit vaccine is only short-lived and weak. However, the use of yeast, which can add sugar side-chains, has allowed the production of a near-marketable subunit vaccine for hepatitis B virus, and research work continues on the development of vaccines against viruses such as those causing influenza, polio and herpes.

A second new method with potential for vaccine production is the chemical synthesis of short fragments (peptides) of surface antigens. When injected into the body these peptides can stimulate an immune response, but only if linked to a large carrier molecule. This requirement for both a booster chemical and a carrier molecule to be injected along with the antigenic peptides is presently limiting the progress of the new method.

The most exciting method of conferring passive artificial immunity is undoubtedly the use of B-cells. This has become more attractive with the development by Kohler and Millstein of monoclonal antibodies.

Monoclonal antibodies

The injection of an antigen into an animal elicits the formation of a **polyclonal** mixture of antibody molecules, each of which recognises the triggering antigen. (Polyclonal means belonging to many clones.) The advantage of **monoclonal** antibodies (those belonging to a single clone) is that they are far more specific and reproducible, and consequently lend themselves to many diagnostic and therapeutic uses. (See Figure 16.7)

Production of monoclonal antibodies

Initially a mouse (or rabbit) is injected with an antigen. The **spleen**, which contains antibody-producing B-lymphocytes, is then removed and individual spleen cells are isolated. B-cells are capable of growth on artificial media only for a few days. In contrast, myeloma (bone marrow cancer) cells are capable of continuous growth in tissue culture. Individual **myeloma cells** are selected to lack a certain enzyme which is necessary for the synthesis of DNA and, hence, for growth. Consequently, these selected cells can grow only on certain special media, a characteristic which is useful for the identification of the cells at a later stage in the preparation of monoclonal antibodies.

Spleen cells are mixed with the selected myeloma cells in a solution containing the chemical polyethylene glycol (PEG). The PEG destroys the surface tension forces which normally cause cells to repel each other in solution. As a result about 10% of the original spleen cells fuse with myeloma cells to produce 'immortal' antibody-secreting **hybridomas** (hybrid cells).

The cell suspension resulting from the fusion stage is plated out onto a culture medium. On this medium, due to their lack of enzyme, any unfused

16.7 The formation of antibody producing hybridomas

Stage 1. Myeloma cells and antibody producing cells (derived from an immunized animal or person) are incubated in a special medium containing polyethylene glycol which enhances fusion

Stage 2. The myeloma spleen hybridoma cells are selected out and cultured in closed agar dishes

Stage 3. The specific antibody producing hybridoma are selected and propogated in culture vessels (in vitro) or in animals (in vivo) and monoclonal antibodies harvested

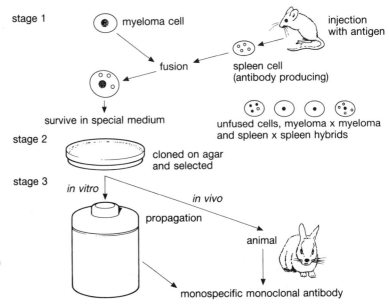

myeloma cells cannot grow, and unfused B-cells die after a few days. Only the hybridoma cells grow successfully – the genes necessary for the production of the required enzymes are provided by their B-cell 'half', and their myeloma 'half' enables continuous growth.

If all the hybridoma cells that occurred after a fusion were grown up together, then a mixture of antibodies would be released, similar to those found in the serum of the whole animal. Single hybridoma cells must be isolated and allowed to grow up as a **clone** in which each cell is a replica of the others. In this way only one antibody will be secreted by a particular clone: that is, a monoclonal antibody.

Prior to cloning, each hybridoma cell is screened to establish which antibody it produces. Various screening techniques are available, the most simple depending upon the ability of a monoclonal antibody to bind to its antigen. The **antibody-antigen complex** may then be detected using a second antibody which reacts specifically with the monoclonal antibody. The detector antibody is labelled with a radioactive isotope or, as in enzyme-linked immunosorbent assays (ELISA), with an enzyme. In the presence of the appropriate substrates, such as the monoclonal antibody-antigen complex, the enzyme will cause a measurable colour change. (See Figure 16.8)

If it produces the desired antibody, then a particular hybridoma will be frozen for later use or will be propagated into a large population of genetically identical cells either in culture vessels or

16.8 The technique for screening of hybridoma cells for the production of a specific antibody (see text)

in animals. Each population produces an antibody of a single specificity. Using this technique, large quantities of antibody of one particular specificity can be obtained.

Applications of monoclonal antibodies

Each monoclonal antibody is specific to one particular antigen and has the capacity to seek out that antigen. Monoclonal antibodies have gained wide application in various techniques which require a high degree of specificity.

Passive immunisation
Monoclonal antibodies against an antigen of a particular pathogenic organism may be used as an inoculum. The antibodies will 'home in' specifically on the pathogen and destroy it. This form of treatment avoids the possibility of injecting antibodies which may attack the tissues of the patient, as may be the case with polyclonal inocula.

Purification of compounds
Any antigenic compound may be purified from a mixture by passing the solution down a column which contains monoclonal antibodies specific to that compound. The antibodies are immobilised on an inert support, such as Sepharose. The desired compound binds specifically to the antibodies and can subsequently be recovered; the remainder of the solution passes on through the column.

Diagnosis
The urine of pregnant women contains the hormone **human chorionic gonadotrophin (HCG)**, which is secreted by the placenta. The use of

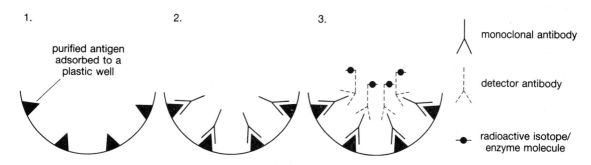

1.

purified antigen
adsorbed to a
plastic well

2.

3.

monoclonal antibody

detector antibody

radioactive isotope/
enzyme molecule

monoclonal antibodies to test for the hormone now permits the ready diagnosis of pregnancy as early as a week or two after conception. Similarly elegant and reliable are monoclonal antibody tests for diabetes and specific blood groups.

Identification of the causal agent of gonorrhoea is also facilitated by monoclonal antibodies. The disease can be caused by either of two different organisms, which require different treatments. Previous tests took 2–3 days; the use of monoclonal antibodies has reduced this time to 15–20 minutes.

Monoclonal antibodies may be used as **marker molecules**, if they are linked to a chemical which is detectable. Such chemicals may be radioactive, fluorescent or luminescent, or may be colour-producing enzymes. In this way, monoclonal antibodies are used to 'image' (locate) cancerous cells which possess surface antigens different from those of most other normal cells. Also, testing for compatibility between donors and recipients of grafted organs can be carried out using monoclonal antibodies which recognise specific HLA antigens.

Other uses include the detection of undesirable trace molecules in the food industry.

Treatment

Monoclonal antibodies may be used not only to detect cancerous cells but also to treat them. Initially, the antibodies alone were used in cancer therapy. More effective, however, is the linking of the antibodies to toxins or radioactive isotopes, so producing **magic bullets** which can deliver cytotoxic (cell poisoning) molecules specifically to target cells. A recent method involves the injection of monoclonal antibodies bound to an enzyme. The antibodies dock on to cancer cells and then an injection of an inactive 'pro-drug' is given. On encountering the enzyme, the drug is activated and so a high dose of cytotoxic drug is delivered close to the cancer.

The specificity of monoclonal antibodies in cancer treatment is not absolute, unfortunately, as the antigens they recognise are not completely restricted to cancer cells. Also, side effects such as nausea, fever and chills have been experienced by patients, although these have been relatively mild.

To prevent **rejection of foreign tissue**, kidney transplant patients are routinely given drugs to suppress the activity of their immune system. The use of monoclonal antibodies specifically to suppress the activity of T-lymphocytes alone (they mediate the rejection process), and to leave the other aspects of the immune system functional, results in patients being less open to infectious diseases. Monoclonal antibodies have proved to be more effective than conventional drugs in preventing kidney rejection and may also be less prone to side-effects.

Early work suggests that monoclonal antibodies may provide a new form of treatment for **auto-immune diseases**, such as certain forms of arthritis. Here, the body regards its own tissues as foreign and mounts an immune response against them. The monoclonal antibodies would be directed against the immune cell components thought to be responsible for triggering the diseases. This work is still in its early phases but results appear to be encouraging.

Further reading

Antebi, E. and Fishlock, D. (1986) *Biotechnology, Strategies for Life*. MIT Press.
Inchley, C.J. (1981) *Immunobiology*. Studies in Biology, Arnold.

Thought questions

1 Do you consider that the benefits of using vaccines outweigh the risks?

2 Is the use of mice and rats to make monoclonal antibodies justified?

17
Clean Water for All

This chapter describes how clean water-supplies have developed through the centuries, how water-borne diseases are an ever-present danger to people, and why obtaining pure drinking water is often so difficult to achieve.

The importance of water

All organisms depend upon water and humans are no exception. The earliest known living sites of humans, 1.5 million years ago, were on lakesides in Africa. Our ancestors must have drunk water from the lakes and water-holes, for they lived in the tropical savannah and hunted large animals in the warm climate. Perhaps it was then that humans developed their enormously efficient sweat-cooling system; a man may sweat up to 1.5 litres an hour and not overheat, even when running in a hot climate. Present-day hunter-gatherers like the Kung of the Kalahari collect their water in the dry season from hand-dug wells in river beds, and may carry that water with them in ostrich shells.

From the earliest times good water sources have had special importance for human communities. Five thousand years ago the earliest civilisation sprang up alongside the ancient rivers of the Middle East. Here the rivers were revered as the bringers of vital water for drinking, cooking, washing, sewage disposal and irrigation. Wells were dug to obtain microbially pure water. A good understanding of methods of obtaining more healthy water supplies existed long before the discovery of microbes. The early Greek scientist Aristotle described the use of porous pot filters in 350 BC and, even earlier, Sanskrit writings showed that people practised water filtration through charcoal. Early European populations must have valued clear water coming from springs in the ground. Settlements often developed around such good water sources. Their importance to people is shown by historical references to 'sacred springs', 'holy wells', and spas with 'medicinal waters'.

The water cycle

Figure 17.1 illustrates the **water cycle**. Although the waters of the world's oceans provide us with fresh water through evaporation they are too salty to drink directly, as the Ancient Mariner discovered to his cost: "Water, water, every where,/Nor any drop to drink". The human kidney is not powerful enough to correct the sodium imbalance that results from a person drinking sea-water; human urine has a lower salt concentration than sea-water. Marine mammals manage higher levels of sodium excretion.

Less than 1% of the world's surface water is fresh; it all comes from **precipitation**. Rain is naturally acidified by atmospheric gases, but is bland and tasteless if very pure. Water that has infiltrated the ground and percolated through rocks picks up many useful soluble minerals; it is these that give water its subtle and regionally character-istic taste. Water-soluble fertilisers, pesticides, land-fill chemicals and industrial pollutants may also easily join **ground-water** sources. Much rain-

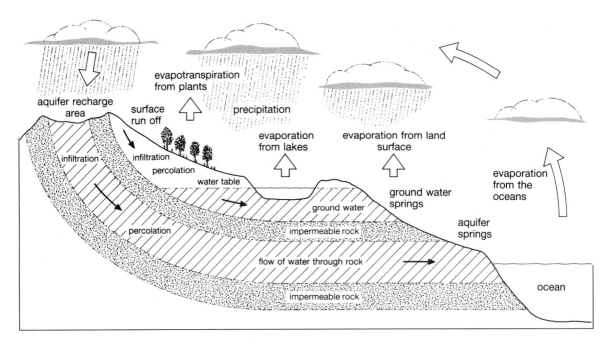

17.1   The water cycle

water collects into surface run-off streams. Some may join ground water, returning to the surface later in springs. Streams converge into larger streams or lakes and rivers. Such **surface waters** are easily contaminated and are therefore not such good water sources as the deeper ones.

Good, clean drinking water supplies depend on adequate rainfall and protection of water sources. In many parts of the world rainfall is very low, infrequent or unreliable. Alternatively, it may fall torrentially and so not be easily managed to provide clean water supplies.

Water-borne diseases

Access to fresh drinking water is not always easy. It may be as hard as it was for the Ancient Mariner, even in certain wet situations. Figure 17.2 shows a **water relief operation** in Dhaka, Bangladesh. Relief workers are giving out chlorinated drinking water. Two days previously the Brahmaputra River had burst its banks; 95% of the city went underwater and became an open sewer. Water backed up through the sewerage system into the streets, and

garbage and excrement floated into homes. In these floods 25 million people became homeless and 1 500 died. Most of those who died were children and elderly people, who suffered from diarrhoea and not from drowning.

Britain too has had many **water-borne diseases**

17.2 Clean water relief in Dhaka floods (see text)

even in the twentieth century. In 1937 a workman, unknowingly infected with typhoid, was employed to repair a deep well in Croydon. Whilst below ground he defecated in the borehole. Due to a subsequent misunderstanding the well water was channelled into the mains water supply of the town without chlorination. In a short space of time there were 341 typhoid victims in Croydon, of whom 34 are known to have died.

Understanding the nature of water-borne diseases helps greatly in their control. **Cholera** is perhaps the most feared. Prior to the nineteenth century it was confined to India. Pilgrims to Benares, the Holy City on the Ganges River, probably contributed to the spread of the disease to other river basins. In 1817 cholera spread from the Indian sub-continent, reaching the Middle East; there was a pandemic from Arabia to Russia in 1826 that spread into Western Europe in 1829 and on to Britain in 1831. In the Crimean War, 1854–56, many more died from cholera than in the actual battles. Cholera still takes millions of lives each year in Asia and Africa.

Vibrio cholerae, the causative agent of cholera, is a comma-shaped motile bacterium. In the intestine it multiplies rapidly and produces an enterotoxin that stimulates adenyl cyclase enzyme, and hence the rate of cell secretion. As a result the intestinal epithelium pours out water and valuable ions, resulting in a profuse and watery diarrhoea. (The term diarrhoea comes from Greek, meaning 'through-flowing stream'.) The diarrhoea of a cholera victim, descriptively known as 'rice water stools', is little more than a rich culture of the bacterium and is highly infective to other people. Once infected, rapid dehydration as a result of the diarrhoea is the principal threat to life; hence a rapidly administered oral rehydration treatment of salts and glucose in solution works wonders. This **oral rehydration therapy** saves many lives, even without an antibiotic, like tetracyclin, to kill the bacteria.

Typhoid, also a bacterial disease, spreads through infected food and water from carriers who harbour it. Carriers are a small percentage of those that have survived infection; the causative bacterium *Salmonella typhii* lives in their gall bladder or kidneys. The typhoid bacillus does not multiply outside its human host, but minute traces of faeces or urine may be highly infective. (*Salmonella typhii*, the typhoid bacillus, should not be confused with *Salmonella enteritidis*, which causes severe food poisoning.) The insanitary behaviour of just one person may cause many deaths, as the 1937 Croydon outbreak indicates. The most infamous carrier was undoubtedly 'Typhoid Mary', a cook in New York who caused eight separate outbreaks of typhoid between 1901 and 1907, one of which involved 1300 people. The disease is characterised by a gradually mounting fever, headache and malaise, followed in the second week by a rash and severe diarrhoea. Today typhoid is easily treated with amoxycillin, which both arrests the disease and destroys the dormant infection in carriers.

Poliomyelitis (polio) is an extremely widespread viral disease which is commonly waterborne and transmitted by faecal contamination of water supplies (it is an RNA virus). Interestingly, it does not cause outbreaks of epidemic proportions in communities with low standards of hygiene. In such populations everybody is infected. Mothers therefore transfer antibodies to their foetuses and infants (by natural passive immunity) so that when children are first naturally infected by the virus they already have a residual immunity that saves them. By building up their own antibodies they then gain life-long resistance. As with typhoid, some of those infected continue as carriers. In communities with higher standards of water hygiene, the lack of maternal resistance results in higher rates of polio amongst children.

If the polio virus enters the nervous system it may attack motor neurones in the spinal cord, leading to severe or fatal paralysis of skeletal muscles. In Britain, polio became a disease of significance after other water-borne diseases were virtually eliminated. With the coming of the live Sabin vaccine in the 1960s (artificial active immunity) the disease is now very rare. In the United Kingdom almost every child is vaccinated; there are very few cases of the disease, no deaths and few cases of paralysis.

How Britain cleaned up its drinking water

The experience of such dreadful diseases was a spur to the development of better drinking water in Britain in the nineteenth century. It is important to understand that at the start of the nineteenth century there was no germ theory of disease, and only the haziest notion of transmission. Nevertheless, in the early 1800s the Scots had already experimented with deep sand filter beds to clean up their water, first at Paisley and then at Greenock and Glasgow. In 1829 this method of purifying public water-supplies was introduced from Scotland to Chelsea in London by James Simpson. The Chelsea Water Company passed polluted water from the River Thames very slowly through a deep sand filter and then on to customers. Such sand filter beds are still used in water treatment today. They depend on bacteria being scavenged by protozoa in the wet sand, as well as being physically filtered out of the water. In 1831 cholera struck London for the first time. It was noted that those served by the Chelsea Water Company escaped, though quite why they did so was not understood.

In 1854 during a further cholera outbreak a London physician Dr John Snow noted that the inhabitants of Broad Street, Westminster, were particularly affected. Six hundred and sixteen deaths had occurred locally and Snow firmly suspected the water. It so happened that a lady from Islington, some way away, 'with a predilection for the waters of Broad Street', regularly had water collected from the Broad Street water pump. She and a niece both died of cholera. Snow had the pump removed from the street, and the epidemic ceased. Great improvements were made to London's water supplies after 1854.

It was not until 1861 that Pasteur, in France, proposed the **Germ Theory of Disease**. In 1876 Koch, in Germany, demonstrated that bacteria were the cause of many water-borne diseases. In 1884 Escherich identified the colon bacillus, universally found as a commensal in the human gut: **Escherichia coli** is present in thousands of millions in human faeces. Early in the twentieth century a test for **coliform bacteria** was devised (see below). The presence of faecal bacteria at any level in a water supply indicates potential contamination by much more harmful species. The nineteenth century saw tremendous advances in the development of water supply systems and sewerage systems. These were of immense importance in improving health. Such engineering enterprises have saved more lives in urban environments than any other medical development.

Chlorination

The nineteenth-century work of Pasteur and Koch on micro-organisms and that of Lister on antiseptics opened a new era in biology and public health. The processes of sterilisation by heat and by bactericidal chemicals (antiseptics and disinfectants) became understood. It was recognised that filtration followed by chemical sterilisation of water would give the greatest security against bacteria in water supplies. The earliest chlorination of a water supply using hypochlorite was at Maidstone in 1903. An outbreak of cholera in a mental hospital outside Cambridge in 1905 raised fears for the safety of the university and town's water supplies. At the well near the asylum the first commercial chlorination plant was built.

Chlorine is a powerful oxidising agent, the oxidation of bacterial enzymes being the basis of its bactericidal action. In a modern water-treatment works water is super-chlorinated in a tank for 30 minutes by the addition of 0.5 mg of chlorine per litre of water (0.5 mg dm^{-3}); this is 0.5 parts per million (ppm) by weight. After 30 minutes all the bacteria will have been killed. The water is then dechlorinated to 0.1 ppm, the remaining chlorine inhibiting bacterial growth in the piped water distribution and storage. At this level the taste of chlorine is acceptable to most people.

The coliform test

The effectiveness of any chlorination process should be regularly tested. For this a suitable broth of bile

17.3   Hundreds of millions of people have no piped sanitary water supply

salts and lactose is inoculated with water samples of known volume and incubated in flasks at 44°C. Any flasks becoming gaseous and acidic contain at least one *E. coli*. The presence of just one bacterium in 100 cm^3 of water is sufficient to declare the source of the water sample impure.

The United Nations water decade

In 1981 the International Water Supply and Sanitation Decade was launched with the goal of providing 'clean water for all'. At the end of ten years it must be admitted that the task still remains largely uncompleted. The proportion of the world's population with good water sources is slowly increasing, but there are still hundreds of millions of people with no piped sanitary water supply or adequate sewage disposal system. The scientific technology to improve this situation exists; sadly it is Third World poverty, not ignorance, which still condemns so many to die.

Additives and contaminants

The European Community defines water quality in terms of 66 parameters that should be met; 6 of these are microbiological and 13 concern levels of toxic substances. For each of these a **maximum**

admissible concentration, known as **EC MAC**, is the upper safe limit.

Fluorine (EC MAC 1.5 ppm) occurs naturally in water which has been in contact with calcareous rock. Fluorine is commonly added to water at levels of 0.1 ppm to reduce dental caries. However, the precise level is critical: 1.3 ppm may cause bone fusion diseases. Fluoridation is definitely highly beneficial in reducing tooth decay in children, but mistakes in fluoridation (or addictive eating of fluoride toothpaste!) may be harmful.

Iron salts colour water brown. They are harmless, but the removal of the brown colour is considered cosmetically important to consumers. Iron salts may be oxidised and then removed with aluminium sulphate in treatment works.

Aluminium (EC MAC 0.2 ppm [200 micrograms dm^{-3}]) occurs naturally in acidic peaty water. Aluminium is readily excreted by healthy people, but there is a direct link between higher aluminium intake levels and the incidence of **Alzheimer's disease**. People on artificial kidney machines (renal dialysis) are more easily poisoned

17.4 The west of England and Wales has many water sources with dissolved aluminium levels exceeding EC limits of 200 micrograms per litre. More aluminium seems to mean a raised Alzheimer's disease incidence

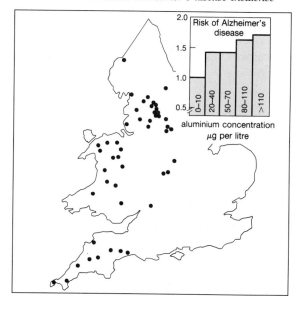

by aluminium in the dialysis saline than are people with functioning kidneys. For the former, levels above as little as 0.014 ppm (14 micrograms dm^{-3}) in the dialysis water increase the risk of brittle bones, anaemia and dementia. Present evidence suggests that levels over 0.110 ppm for the general public increase the incidence of Alzheimer's disease by one and a half times (see Figure 17.4). Alzheimer's disease is a degenerative brain condition not uncommon among the elderly. Aluminium accumulates in plaques in the brain. While the metal is certainly not the prime cause of Alzheimer's disease it is unquestionably related to it.

In an accident at a chemical treatment works at Camelford in the United Kingdom, in 1988, some 20 tonnes of 'clarifying' 8% aluminium sulphate went straight into the public water supply. As a result many people suffered nausea, diarrhoea and skin problems, and the hair of some blondes even turned green! More seriously, even after two years some people are still suffering adverse effects.

Lead (EC MAC 0.05 ppm) is a heavy-metal water contaminant that is toxic and is significantly more dangerous in soft-water areas. Here water is more acid and so dissolves the metal more easily from the rocks and from the insides of lead pipes. High lead levels cause brain damage and retard the development of intelligence in children, possibly even increasing their aggressive behaviour. There are still many domestic supplies in the north and west of Britain above the EC MAC for lead.

Nitrates (EC MAC 50 ppm) are added to crops in Britain at a rate of 1.6 million tonnes per annum, at an average dosage of 150 kg per ha. The nitrates cost farmers £500 million each year; they are more than paid for by increased crop yields. The vast majority of this nitrate is rapidly assimilated by crops, and only a minute amount is leached directly into ground water and run-off (contrary to popular belief!). However, much nitrate is leached in the autumn and winter from the crop residue, and this, not the fertiliser itself, is the problem. Nitrates in ground water are disconcertingly high and are rising steadily in lowland Britain (see Chapter 32).

Nitrates have been linked with two diseases.

Blue baby syndrome is a rare condition of unweaned infants exposed to high levels of nitrate, typically above 100 ppm in the water. Nitrites are formed from nitrates by pathogenic bacteria in the infant gut and absorbed into the blood. Nitrite occupies oxygen sites on haemoglobin molecules, leading to **methaemoglobinaemia**. This condition is not unlike carbon monoxide poisoning, but the child becomes a slaty-blue colour. There have been only 14 cases in 37 years, in the UK, and only one fatality (in 1950). The last case was in 1972. Every case was associated with microbially contaminated well-water at or above 100 ppm of nitrate, and not once with chlorinated supplies. Taken in comparison with other causes of infant mortality in Britain this disease is quite insignificant, though this is not so in southern Europe.

The second concern over nitrates is **cancer**. Nitrites formed by anaerobic bacteria in the gut from nitrates may combine with amines to form nitrosomines, and these are known to be **carcinogenic** (cancer forming). However, stomach cancer levels in the United Kingdom have been falling steadily even as **nitrate levels** have been rising. The lowest incidence is in East Anglia where the nitrate levels are highest! A recent study conducted by Sir Richard Doll – who established the link between smoking and lung cancer – investigated the health of nitrate-fertiliser factory workers. These people had inhaled and excreted high levels of nitrate for many years, and yet there was no indication of higher than normal association with any cancer. Nitrate levels in many fresh vegetable juices are well above 100 ppm. These are not considered hazardous. 'There is no evidence that nitrates induce cancer in humans' (EC Technical Report (1988) No. 27).

Pesticides, herbicides and industrial solvents

If one is looking for an enemy in water today it is more likely to be chemicals whose action is so powerful that they are active at levels where they are barely detectable. The EC MAC for any one pesticide is 0.1 micrograms dm^{-3} (0.0001 ppm); for all pesticides together it is five times this figure. Many **agrochemicals** are hard to test for. Many do not break down naturally, or even degrade microbially; they must therefore accumulate, and as they are soluble they must eventually leach into water supplies. The carboxyacid- and phenylurea-based herbicides, widely used in agriculture, are now present in all ground water in trace amounts; in England simazine, atrazine and 2,4,5-T locally exceed EC MAC levels. **Organic solvents** such as trichloroethylene (used in dry cleaning, paints and varnishes) are occasionally spilled as a result of industrial accidents or road collisions. Trichloroethylene is found in one-third of British ground-water supplies. Trichloromethane (chloroform) (EC MAC 0.1 ppm) is found in drinking water where the water source has a high organic content. This pollutant is undoubtedly a trace by-product of chlorination.

Bottled water

Despite the high levels of purity achieved in our household water supplies many people feel safer, or prefer, drinking bottled water. Most continental Europeans on average drink more than 50 litres of bottled water a year – the British so far drink only 3 litres! Bottled water costs one thousand times as much as tap water and does not reach every criterion of 'purity'. It is certainly bacterially 'clean' at the time of bottling; otherwise it would contravene the **Natural Mineral Water** legislation (1985). However, once opened it may not be completely harmless. In the absence of added chlorine any bacteria that enter the bottle may breed, especially if there is any organic matter (such as a few human skin cells) in the water. In 1988 the University Hospital of Wales conducted a survey on 29 different bottled mineral waters. Of these, 11 had bacterial contaminants – amongst them 17 strains of Gram-positive cocci, including some which were potentially pathogenic. However, no *E. coli* (faecal) contamination was recorded.

Most mineral-water drinkers express the view that the product is rich in important minerals for health, is excitingly fizzy and free of nitrates. It should, additionally, be acidic enough to kill bacteria! Perrier is one firm that has built its reputation on such purity; certainly the chemical content of its mineral water is health-giving and its formation is geologically unique. At the Perrier plant water comes from three different sources into a subterranean lake. Rain falling on the Vistrenque plain provides the first contribution. Here Perrier own the farmland and agrochemicals are not allowed. The rain-water percolates through deep layers of silica sand and gravel, emerging filtered, clean and acidic. Other water percolates in from the Nimes limestone, rich in calcareous rock minerals such as calcium, magnesium and carbonate. This neutralises the water. Then, from a deeper aquifer that has been heated by the earth's molten rock, a hot mineral water comes up through limestone beds and joins the other waters below ground. This third water source contains much (acid) carbon dioxide under pressure, causing the emergent spring to bubble dramatically at a constant 15°C.

Perrier's analytical laboratory would be the envy of most water companies. Four photospectrometers take 40 samples of water an hour from the 60 cubic metres of water which are produced per hour. The tiniest trace of pollutants is detected. In a recent incident naturally formed benzene appeared, but this was quickly removed with special charcoal filters. All this is not without cost – hardly 'clean water for all' but certainly 'pure water' for some.

Further reading

Benenson, A.S. (1981) *The Control of the Communicable Diseases of Man*. American Public Health Association, New York.

Taylor, D. (1989) *Human Physical Health*. Cambridge University Press.

Turk, D.C. *et al.* (1983) *Medical Microbiology*. Hodder & Stoughton.

UNEP (1987) *Safeguarding the World's Water; Environment Brief No. 6*. United Nations Environment Programme, Nairobi.

Also, much valuable information is available from your local water company.

Thought questions

1 What are your criteria for water being considered 'clean'?

2 Suppose you are founding a settlement on a desert island. How would you site your pit latrine and protect your well which is your only source of water?

3 The following volumes of drinking water from the same supply are given the test for *E. coli* contamination. The results of each test are given.

10 cm³	negative	80 cm³	negative
20 cm³	negative	160 cm³	positive
40 cm³	positive	320 cm³	positive

Why is the critical volume for a positive result rather uncertain? What is the approximate number of *E. coli* in a litre? Is the water safe to drink?

Things to do

Using old plastic mineral-water or soft-drinks bottles (of one uniform type) construct a tall column of five inverted and interconnected bottles. To connect them cut the bottoms off four of the bottles and stack them up so that the neck of one fits into the opened bottom of the one below. Put a fine nylon gauze in the lowest to contain the sand, and then fill the column with fine sand as you build it up. Tape the joints strongly and support the whole column vertically. It will be heavy. Leave the topmost water bottle open so that substances can be poured in. Have a free bottle, without a neck, upright at the bottom of the column to catch the water that comes out.

Test the filter with a water suspension of humus-rich garden soil. Mix about 50 g of active soil in a litre of water. Using a serial dilution technique, assess its bacterial population (likely to be millions per cm³). Pour the litre of soil water through the filter and, when the water emerges, test the filtrate for bacteria again.

How efficient is this first physical filter?

Add half a litre of freshly made soil water daily. Does the filtrate become more or less microbially contaminated? Does it become clearer? If its quality improves, make a hypothesis to explain why. How could you test that hypothesis?

WARNING. Do not drink the product of this filter even if it looks crystal clear!

18
A Doctor's Duties

Medical practitioners of all sorts are commonly referred to as 'doctors'. Some are in **general practice** (like your own GP). Some are attached to hospitals, where they may be learning a **speciality** either in training or as a consultant, dealing with particular kinds of disease or disorder. Others, such as a specialist school doctor, are in community medicine. All have a basic bachelor of medicine qualification. A few have done a research doctorate.

All are given the title 'Doctor' except those who become surgeons. By tradition the latter are referred to as 'Mr', and increasingly today as 'Mrs' or 'Miss'.

In this chapter 'Doctor D.', who is a specialist, explains what it is like to carry out medical consultation and describes how doctors see themselves and think about their work. Both 'Doctor D' and his patients 'Sean' and 'Emma' have been given fictitious names to protect their confidentiality.

The consultation

When a patient comes to see me I always hope he or she will feel reassured after the visit, even if I have not been able to find a quick solution to the medical problem the patient has brought. Everything that goes on in my consulting room is confidential to the two of us; if I am going to ask other doctors to help I will refer my patient only if he or she gives permission. I am always conscious of my professional calling to put the interests of my patient first. It would be no good if doctors viewed their patients only as a means to make money. This is one of the benefits of the National Health Service. Doctors are paid by the number of patients on their list, not by how many times those patients need their help. Each doctor in general practice normally has about two thousand patients.

Being healthy is not just a question of being free from disease or disorders. **Health** is a positive state of complete physical, mental and social well-being. So as soon as a patient comes into my surgery I am interested in him or her as a person, and in learning a little of the background to the patient's life. Age, occupation, and family and personal history are important. Knowing how the patient feels and whether he or she is happy or worried about life in general is often significant in helping me to decide what may lie behind the patient's problem.

Generally when a patient comes in he or she tells me quickly about the problem. Manifestations of illness are called **symptoms**. If the patient has been referred to me by another doctor, because of my speciality, I will have a letter of introduction. In a general practice the doctor has the patient's medical notes to hand, because knowing about past history is often the key to sound diagnosis. The term **diagnosis** is used both when describing the process of assessing the symptoms and signs presented by the patient and when identifying the disease or disorder that exists. In a real sense diagnosis is both a science and an art.

When a patient comes to see me I usually recognise initially that he or she is worried. This stress must be appreciated in itself and may be related to the problem. Patients who are referred to consultants often feel that they are very ill and will need much reassurance at the start, whatever the problem. Therefore I often emphasise to my patients that there is a difference between a **disease** and a **disorder**. Most commonly the problem is not a disease like an infection, ulcer or cancer; much more probably there is some disorder of function. This may be due to psychological factors, or to environmental influences such as smoking, diet or lifestyle. Even lack of sleep and recreation can easily make people ill. It is tempting to think sometimes that a patient's symptoms are only in the mind. But they are usually not imagined; they are very real. The patient therefore comes to the doctor expecting help for the relief of a real state of disorder or disease. However trivial it may seem to be to me, there is a real cry for help. I therefore have got to do my best.

As soon as a patient enters the surgery or I visit him or her at home, I note their general appearance, demeanour and behaviour. Complexion, voice, attitude, irritability, state of physical development and nutrition are all of key importance. What I observe forms the basis for the thought processes in my mind that then follow. I suppose that much of my thinking is guided by experience and training. However, when I have talked to a patient for a minute or two I quite quickly have in my mind a number of ideas – you could call them hypotheses if you like – that might explain the symptoms. What I then have to do is to look for any physical abnormalities by examining the patient.

Taking clothes off in front of the doctor can be rather embarrassing for a patient. The doctor knows that, and will not mind. Obviously I must not be embarrassed myself, and certainly I could not do the job if I was. My patients would not trust me if they imagined that I was being unprofessional in my behaviour towards them. This is therefore not a problem generally, but if for example a male doctor needs to examine a Muslim woman (who has never undressed herself before anyone but her intimate family) there may be a cultural difficulty. In such circumstances it is common for a male doctor to arrange for a female nurse or assistant to be present.

During a **physical examination**, knowledge of anatomy is important. My knowledge of the body and its workings allows me to recognise abnormalities such as heart murmurs, unusual swellings, or diseases of the joints. Doctors also quickly learn to look out for particular disabilities, signs of disorder

or manifestations of disease. Talking to the patient all the time during an examination reassures him or her, and allows a more complete picture to emerge. After an examination is over, I generally have a clearer idea of my diagnosis.

Clinical investigations, which go beyond a straightforward examination of the patient, are often important in achieving a diagnosis. Abnormalities of the blood or urine are looked for and swabs (sterile cotton wool samples) may be taken to try and find suspected pathogens (disease-causing organisms); these are then cultured and are identified a day or two later in a pathology laboratory. Reports on clinical tests are sent back to me very quickly. The patient may need to be prepared for these tests and for the results. If, suppose, I want to take a blood sample, it is often important to reassure the patient and let him or her know how much it can tell me about their condition. Clinical analysis of a blood sample in the haematological laboratory of a hospital will show whether the blood has any abnormalities. Different levels of specific antibodies or counts of particular cell types in the the blood may be very valuable in confirming or guiding my diagnosis. If I am intending to test blood for a disease such as HIV (see Chapter 21) I would always seek the **patient's permission** first. The results of such a test, if positive, might have important implications for his or her whole future from other aspects such as life insurance policies.

In cases of serious illness a large number of clinical tests may be necessary. These include **X-rays** and **scans** which can detect structural abnormalities not recognised in an external examination. By using **endoscopy**, flexible instruments permit views of the deepest recesses of the body. Some investigations are hazardous in themselves, in which case the patient is warned and given a chance to talk it over.

Following on from all this is the final diagnosis. It is very straightforward for most visits to a GP. However, it is not always easy for a doctor to break bad news gently to a patient when the diagnosis is serious. These days most patients welcome a frank statement on the cause of their condition (this is

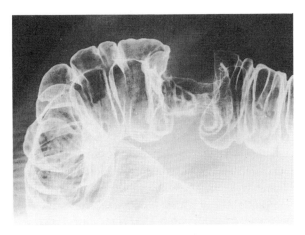

18.1 A colonic obstruction revealed by an X-ray

called the **aetiology**) and on the outlook for the condition after treatment (this is the **prognosis**). It is rarely in the best interests of the patient for the doctor to hide the truth. Reassurance should always accompany a prescribed treatment, whether the patient is worried about something minor or whether, at the other extreme, he or she is found to be very ill.

Two case studies

To show how a doctor thinks, and uses his or her biological and medical knowledge, I shall take two real-life examples from my work. The first is a very common one and the second much rarer and rather more serious.

Sean

Sean is 16. As soon as he enters my surgery I know he is nervous, so I welcome him and ask him about his family, for I have seen him, his parents and his sister in my surgery before. I do not have many notes on Sean in his file; he has not been ill often. When he has relaxed a little I look at his notes and ask him about a sports injury he had some months ago. By this time I have noticed that he has moderately bad acne on his face and I have guessed that it, and its effects on his social life, may

be the worry. When he tells me of the problem, it is.

Straight away I tell Sean that nine out of ten teenagers have trouble with spots, but they are only a justifiable worry if they are severe. I add that I can give him some good advice. We soon move to an examination. Sean takes off his shirt. I do not need to see more of him than that, for infected sebum (oil) glands are concentrated on the face, chest, shoulders and back only. I can tell from Sean's physique that he is growing fast at the moment; he is tall but his skeleton has not filled out with the muscle that he will have later on. This rapid growth is due to a large increase in testosterone hormone released from the testes. One of the effects of testosterone (and of progesterone in girls) is to increase sebum production. I can see several sebum glands that are blocked and swollen. The blockage has led to the oxidation of pigment, resulting in the familiar 'black heads'. Raised red patches have formed behind many of these, in the central hollow of which millions of follicle bacteria are growing and being fought off by his immune system. The pus which the spots contain is the result of the battle that has been going on. Some of the older pustules have healed and have formed ugly cysts and scars.

I can see that Sean needs two kinds of help. First, he needs good advice on cleansing and management of the condition; and second, he needs help to enable him to recognise the potentially worse damage that may be done to his self-esteem. He clearly feels 'ugly and out of it'. I can remember the same feeling when I was in my teens.

Once Sean has got dressed I invite him to sit down. I emphasise how common the problem is, that it will soon pass, and that doctors now know that the cause is to do with upset hormonal levels probably with a hereditary component as well. I can recall his father's face as showing a few signs of such scarring. I mention this. I tell him that diet is important; plenty of protein and fresh fruit and vegetables may help, but no research shows that particular foods such as chocolate are to blame, However, I do encourage him to experiment with his diet, because individual differences do occur. I then prescribe for him a cleansing gel which contains an antibiotic. I have read recently that this was found to be very effective in some trials. I decide not to give him tetracycline antibiotic pills as well because I am aware that there are side-effects in many cases. I give him some advice about washing with a good, gentle soap twice a day. Hot water opens pores and cold water causes them to close again; it is therefore worth washing first in hot water and then in cold. Because the condition is worsened by hot and humid weather, I warn him that the problem might worsen when he goes on holiday to Greece.

However, my most important message is about the stress and the impact on his self-image that the condition may produce. I tell him that being too self-conscious about it will do much more harm to his personality than the condition itself. Worrying about it could even make it worse! I hope that he is convinced of this. Accepting the trouble positively and dealing with it sensibly is the best he can do. Sean smiles weakly . . . yes, life is hard . . . but there are worse problems that come to my surgery every day. I encourage him to come back again.

Emma

Emma walks into my gastro-enterology clinic at the hospital – in part, I have specialised in this particular area of medicine, concerned with alimentary canal (gut) function. She has been referred directly by her GP who was shocked at the state she is in. Her doctor has guessed rightly that it is a problem either to do with food intake or with food uptake after she has eaten. This is made clear in a letter. The GP also states that for a long time Emma's parents have not thought there was anything much the matter; she was considered to be just 'rather sickly' and a 'late developer'.

As soon as Emma comes into my consulting room I know that she is potentially very ill. The notes I have received say she is 16 years old but she could pass for twelve. She is pale, almost white, and her skin seems transparent. She has almost no breast development and she looks very thin indeed. Immediately two possible diagnoses come to my

mind: either she is not eating enough, or she is suffering from some gut disease that is preventing food digestion or absorption, for if she had been absorbing and assimilating food normally she would be bound to look more healthy. If a girl is a natural late developer she certainly should not have the symptoms of looking so starved.

Talking to Emma, I quite soon know that she is not starving herself. *Anorexia nervosa*, a form of self-starvation, would have been a more probable diagnosis, for this illness is quite common in her age-group. Many young people, especially girls, may starve themselves of food deliberately, even if not admittedly, for what are essentially psychological reasons (see Chapter 20). Emma, however, seems not to want to eat much because she cannot eat much. She complains of chronic diarrhoea (the term chronic refers to any long-lasting problem, whereas a short and critical attack is described as acute).

This sets me thinking about conditions that cause obstruction to the processes of digestion and absorption. Coeliac disease comes to mind. This is an allergy to the (gluten) proteins in wheat and other cereal grains. It means that any intake of bread, pasta, cake, pastry or other wheat-flour product causes an allergic reaction of the gut lining to gluten, and hence absorption fails. In Emma's case, however, this and other allergies are subsequently ruled out by clinical tests.

When I examine Emma I find that she has both retarded physical growth and retarded sexual development. She is not developing properly, her breasts are child-like, and she has hardly any pubic hair. She is not having menstrual periods. It is clear to me that her pituitary gland or ovaries are retarding puberty, probably as a result of malnutrition. She does not have the nutrient resources for her teenage growth-spurt.

Subsequently clinical tests reveal that she has an obstruction in her digestive tract, just below her stomach in the duodenum. Her food can barely pass into the intestine. A decision is taken to perform a simple operation to clear the obstruction. Emma is quite happy with this after we have discussed it thoroughly together, though she is naturally very apprehensive. She has been wondering and worrying about her development. In the end she approached the operation with a very positive attitude. Feeling positive in such a situation can sometimes do much more than drugs.

In the operation the obstruction is by-passed. Emma is now eating well; she is putting on weight and is growing to physical maturity. Her sexual development will catch up fully and she now has a better prospect for a healthy life.

More of medical practice and medicine

People often ask me whether the medical profession is changing. In some ways it is still conservative and even male-dominated, but this is now much less so, for 50% of medical-school entrants are young women. Practising medicine is very hard work, it is certainly stressful and doctors suffer not infrequently from psycho-neurotic conditions themselves: when you know so much about diseases you can easily imagine that you have the worst condition yourself. Medical students often think they are ill when they are not, and the same may even be true of students studying biology at school. It is worth remembering that even doctors 'go to the doctor's! A problem shared is a problem halved.

Keeping up with one's speciality is important. I read the medical press, medical journals and specialist journals as well. Sometimes there is a conference to attend – occasionally in a faraway and exciting place. It is a good profession to be in.

Treatments are always changing too, but not as much as some people might expect. Old friends like aspirin and penicillin are still vitally important. New treatments appear daily and are often tested against existing treatments in a **double-blind trial**. In such a trial neither I nor my patients know whether they are receiving the new or the existing drug; all we know is that their treatment is known to be effective in some positive way. The pharmacy holds a code for the two drugs under trial; it and the surgery record what is prescribed. The codes for the drugs are held centrally by research clinicians, and eventually the long-term results of the two treat-

ments are compared. This type of double-blind trialling is essential for there are so many other factors, besides administered drugs, that can help people to recover from problems such as heart attacks.

Sometimes **conventional medical science** has no clear solution to a disease. Quite often careful biochemical, pathological and genetic studies suggest a cure, but in other cases there seems little that drugs and surgery can do. This should not surprise us; we still know very little about the human body. It is not merely a machine, although various mechanical faults can be put right. The human body has a rational mind and a powerful will and emotions. These have a strong effect on our well-being. I therefore have no hesitation, as a medical practitioner, in suggesting to a patient that some **alternative medicine** may well help him or her if I have not been able to do very much. This attitude is not unscientific, it is just that science at present is unable to explain how seemingly 'unscientific' treatments like faith healing, homeopathy or acupuncture work in practice to effect a cure. Such treatments sometimes work wonders, though we do not know why.

Further reading

MacQueen, I.A.G. (1987) *Family Health Medical Encyclopaedia*. Collins.
McCoy, K. and Wibbelsman, C. (1989) *The Teenage Body Book*. Judy Piatkus Ltd, London.
Richards, P. (1990) *Learning Medicine*. British Medical Association, BMA House, Tavistock Square, London WC1H 9JP. (Leaflets on *Becoming a Doctor, Medical Schools and Entrance Requirements* are also available from the BMA.)

Thought questions

1 How should people decide whether to go and see a doctor if they feel ill?

2 Your grandparents once had to pay to see a doctor. What are the advantages and disadvantages of a free National Health Service?

3 Why does smiling make you feel better?

19
How Children Grow Up Happy

What do children need to develop successfully into adults? Obviously they require a considerable amount of physical care. Indeed, humans are dependent on their parents for longer than any other species. For several years after birth a child cannot even obtain its own food. Physical care involves giving a child food, protection from danger and disease, and much help in simple tasks. However, there is much more to bringing up a child than merely providing physical care. A baby not only grows physically but also grows in **personality**. Personality is difficult to measure. It is partly the product of genetic inheritance, but is mostly the result of accumulated experiences that, in subtle ways, affect the ways our brains develop. The human brain is immensely complex, but happiness is something it can give to its possessor! In this chapter we will look at other factors besides physical care which enable successful child development.

Mothers

Perhaps the first answer to spring to mind when asking 'What do children need in addition to physical care?' is 'A mother' – someone to love them, hold them and to provide comfort when things go wrong. But just how important is a mother? Obviously we cannot do controlled experiments on people. It would be unacceptable to take a sample of twenty newborn children, remove half of them from their mothers and then see several years later how these children compare with the ones who stayed with their mothers. However, experiments of this kind have been done with monkeys.

The American biologist Harry Harlow investigated how rhesus monkeys grew up when separated from their mothers. He removed eight rhesus monkeys from their mothers immediately after birth. Each was then placed in a separate cage containing two 'model' mothers. These models were identical except that one of them was covered with towelling cloth as shown in Figure 19.1. Harlow found that the young rhesus monkeys spent most of the time holding on to the model covered with the towelling cloth. The naked wire model was almost totally ignored.

Harlow found that even when he attached the feeding bottle to the naked model the young rhesus monkeys would spend almost all their time on the other model, only going to the naked model for their feeds. In other words, the young rhesus monkeys were attracted to the models covered with towelling irrespective of whether or not these models were their source of food. This indicates the importance of close, appropriate contact.

After a few months, Harlow put the same eight monkeys into a large compound with several normal monkeys of the same age. The normal monkeys had been reared by their mothers and had been allowed to play with other monkeys of their own age. Harlow found that the orphaned monkeys reared in solitary confinement were unable to behave normally. They appeared frightened and refused to play. When they subsequently reached adulthood their sexual behaviour was abnormal. The males were unable to mate and those females that did rear young proved to be hopeless mothers. Clearly, the contact a young rhesus monkey has with its mother is crucial to its successful development.

19.1   Harlow's young rhesus monkey with a choice of 'model' mothers (see text)

In a later experiment Harlow again removed young rhesus monkeys from their mothers at birth. As before, the monkeys were reared in solitary confinement with naked and clothed models. However, this time the young monkeys were allowed 20 minutes each day to play with each other. When this group of monkeys was subsequently put in a large enclosure with monkeys of the same age who had been reared by their mothers and allowed to play with other monkeys of their own age, the orphaned monkeys fared much better than those in Harlow's original experiment. The second group of orphaned monkeys joined in the play. When they matured into adults they were all able to mate and rear young. Evidently 20 minutes of play a day with other orphaned monkeys had at least partly compensated for the absence of their mothers.

So much for young rhesus monkeys. Is such work relevant to humans? In 1948 the United Nations decided to make a study of the needs of homeless children. They approached Dr John Bowlby, an expert in child development, and his report *Maternal Care and Mental Health* was published in 1951.

Bowlby studied children who had been separated from their mothers for some reason. He looked at children whose mothers were in hospital or in prison, and he looked at children in residential nurseries and in orphanages. Bowlby believed that previous researchers had underestimated the **bond** between young children and their mothers. He argued that children formed an **attachment** with one person which was very difficult to transfer. Bowlby cites the case of a nursery run in Hampstead, London during the Second World War. The two people running it, Mrs Burlingham and Miss Freud, were experienced in their jobs and 'made every effort to make the change from home to nursery easy for the child'. However, in one of their monthly reports Burlingham and Freud wrote:

> ... we have found that *very little can be done to prevent regression* [i.e. return to more infantile behaviour] *where children between one and a half and two and a half are concerned.* Infants of that age can withstand sudden changes and separations of a day's length without any visible effect. Whenever it is more than that they tend to lose their emotional ties, revert in their instincts and regress in their behaviour.

Bowlby believed that even for children as old as eight, a fortnight's separation from their mothers could have serious long-term consequences. Bowlby showed how young children who had been separated from their mothers for a few weeks or months would often tearfully accuse their mothers on reunion 'Why did you leave me, Mummy?' Bowlby wrote:

> Thence forward for many weeks or months he never allows his mother out of his sight, he is babyish, anxious, and easily angered. Wisely handled, these troubles may gradually fade away, though once again the real possibility of unseen psychic scars must not be forgotten which may become active and give rise to emotional illness in later life. That this is a real danger is made clear by observation of sudden panics in children who have apparently recovered emotional balance,

when confronted with someone whom they associate with the separation experience. If the babyish anxious behaviour on return home is unsympathetically handled, vicious circles in the child's relation to his mother develop, bad behaviour being met by rebuffs and punishments, which in their turn call forth more babyishness, more demands, more tempers. In this way develops the unstable neurotic personality, unable to come to terms with himself or the world, unable especially to make loving and loyal relationships with other people.

A number of people have criticised Bowlby's work. In particular, he conducted his research at a time when only women were thought capable of 'mothering'. Although he defined a mother as the person who has principal care of a child, the role of fathers was hardly considered. Work done after Bowlby's shows that children who are separated from their parents are less likely to suffer as a consequence if their home environment is relaxed and comfortable. Some people have concluded from Bowlby's work that mothers with young children should not go out to work and leave their children with childminders. This is an unfair extrapolation from Bowlby's conclusions. Bowlby was concerned with young children separated from their mothers for periods of at least several days. There is absolutely no evidence that childminding is bad for children. Of course, as many mothers know, paying for your child or children to go to a childminder is expensive and it may not be possible to find a good one.

Thanks in part to Bowlby's work, many hospitals and some prisons now have facilities which enable mothers to spend more time with their children. However, there is more to growing up happy than physical care and having a good mother or father.

Socialisation

The process by which people learn to be members of society is called **socialisation**. Primary socialisation occurs during the first few years of life and within the immediate family. Secondary socialisation refers to the learning which takes

place as people learn to fit in with others at school or at work. Secondary socialisation therefore continues into adulthood.

For children to grow up successfully, they need to learn how to get on with other people and how to fit into society. **Play**, such as that seen in Figure 19.2, serves a number of functions. One of these enables children to become used to getting on with others and to learn from them. Children play in different ways as they get older. Play can help children to learn about the world they live in. Through play children can learn that if you knock a tower of bricks over, the tower falls down but the bricks remains bricks; if they mix blue and yellow paints together they turn green; if they do not let others have their turn they will not play with them; and that most games have rules which have to be kept.

School plays a particularly important role in secondary socialisation. In 1964 John Holt, an American teacher, wrote an important book called *How Children Fail*. In it he argued that almost everyone who goes to school fails to develop more than a tiny part of the tremendous capacity for learning, understanding and creating with which they are born. Holt maintained that we only make full use of this capacity during the first three or so years of our life. In later childhood, schools fail children because the activities children are given to do are usually very trivial and dull. One problem is

19.2 Children at play learn about the world they live in

simply that school classes usually contain between twenty and thirty children. Most teachers do not believe that children want to learn. Consequently, they do not let their pupils behave as individuals, managing their own learning at their own pace. Rather, they tell their pupils what to do, treating the whole class as if it consists of children of pretty much the same ability, none of whom really wants to learn. All this does is to bore half the class, for whom the lesson is going too slowly, and frighten the other half who cannot understand what is going on.

Teachers find it difficult to realise how frightening a school may be for some children. John Holt recounts how he once asked a class the question 'What goes through your mind when the teacher asks you a question and you don't know the answer?'

> It was a bombshell. Instantly a paralysed silence fell on the room. Everyone stared at me with what I have learned to recognize as a tense expression. Finally Ben, who is bolder than most, broke the tension, and also answered my question, by saying in a loud voice, 'Gulp!'.
>
> He spoke for everyone. They all began to clamour, and all said the same thing, that when the teacher asked them a question and they didn't know the answer they were scared half to death. I was flabbergasted...

John Holt then goes on to describe an incident that once happened to him during a flute lesson.

> The lesson was in the late afternoon. I had had a difficult and discouraging day in class, followed by a tense and unpleasant committee meeting. I was late in leaving, was delayed by heavy traffic, and arrived late for my lesson, with no chance to warm up. My teacher had also had a trying day and was not his usual patient self. He was exasperated that I had made so little progress since the previous lesson, and began, as exasperated teachers do, to try by brute will power to force me to play the assigned passage as fast as he thought I should be able to play it.
>
> The pace was much too fast; I began to make mistakes. I wanted to stop, but, cowed by his determination, hesitated to make the suggestion. A feeling of physical pressure built up in my head. If felt as if something inside were trying to burst it

open but also as if something outside were pressing it in. Some kind of noise, other than my miserable playing, was in my ears. Suddenly I became totally note-blind. The written music before me lost all meaning. *All* meaning. It is hard to describe what I felt ... The sensations were indescribably frightening and unpleasant. After a second or two, I put down my flute and turned away from the music. My music teacher sensed that I had been driven over the edge of something, and after a short rest, we went on at a more relaxed pace. But suppose I had been a child. Suppose I had not been free, or felt free, to turn away? Suppose my teacher had felt that it would be good for my character to force the pace harder than ever?

Blue for boys: pink for girls

Every culture treats boys and girls differently. In our western society most people tend to admire 'feminine' qualities in girls such as kindness, thoughtfulness and gentleness. Boys are admired for being independent, brave, enthusiastic and assertive. In her book *Just Like a Girl: How Girls Learn to be Women*, Sue Sharpe looks at the way in which our culture tends to control women.

Boys and girls are still presented differently in many children's books. Girls are more likely in the illustrations to be pictured with their mothers and to be smiling sweetly. Boys are more likely to be active, making things and controlling situations. During the last ten years, the major children's publishers have responded to public pressure and these stereotyped representations of the sexes, though still to be found, are less obvious.

At school, girls do better than boys on average in most subjects at GCSE level. Despite this, more boys than girls stay on to do A levels. The percentage of girls who go on to university is even smaller. When they do go into paid employment, women tend to earn about two-thirds of what men do.

It is largely a matter of opinion as to whether the different way in which our society treats girls and boys is bad. Some people argue that the situation is getting better for women. More women go on to higher education than ever before, and more women have an independent income. On the other hand, society apparently makes impossible demands on women. The perfect woman seems to be in her mid-thirties. She has a stimulating, creative job and two young, healthy, clean children. However, she still does all the cooking, and manages to be stunningly attractive and well dressed. Perhaps it is not surprising that more women than men suffer from depression, and that one in six women receives psychiatric treatment at some time during her life.

Child abuse

In 1896 a young Austrian doctor delivered a lecture in which he argued that children were often seduced by their parents. The young doctor was called Sigmund Freud, and the lecture was not well received. As Freud wrote to a friend: 'the donkeys gave it an icy reception'.

Freud invented the technique of **psychoanalysis**. His method was to allow his patients to relax

19.3   Sigmund Freud

and then talk about their childhood and their dreams. Psychiatrists today are still divided about the validity of Freud's conclusions, but there is no doubt his theories have changed the way we think about ourselves.

The National Society for the Prevention of Cruelty to Children recognises four main categories of child abuse.

- **Physical abuse**. This is where parents physically hurt, injure or even kill a child. It may involve hitting, shaking, squeezing, burning or biting. Excessive force may be used in feeding or when changing a nappy.
- **Sexual abuse**. This happens when girls or boys are sexually abused by adults. It may involve fondling, masturbation, exposing of the child to pornography or sexual intercourse.
- **Neglect**. Neglect happens when parents fail to meet the basic physical needs of their children. The child may not receive enough food, clothes, warmth or medical care.
- **Emotional abuse**. Constant lack of love and affection, or threats and verbal attacks, can lead to a child losing self-esteem and becoming nervous and withdrawn.

No one knows if child abuse is increasing, though more cases are certainly coming to light. The incidence of child abuse is still unknown; some surveys suggest that one in ten girls is sexually abused. We still do not know much about why some people abuse children. It is often difficult to identify cases of child sexual abuse, though new techniques are being developed, including the analysis of drawings such as that reproduced in Figure 19.4.

The effects of child sexual abuse are still not adequately known. Child sexual abuse is not a simple phenomenon. At one end of the scale is the child who is assaulted by a stranger on a single occasion. At the other extreme are children who have been victims of incest several times a week for many years. The psychological after-effects of a single assault are similar to those observed in adults following rape. The child shows symptoms of acute anxiety, with nightmares and fears of another

19.4   A child's portrayal of her sexual abuse

attack. Guilt feelings are common, and a feeling of helplessness may prevail. Boys abused by men may fear that they will now become homosexuals.

The effects of long-term abuse are variable. The most common reactions are neurotic disorders or a deterioration in the child's behaviour. Pre-school children may develop temper tantrums. Older children may be unable to concentrate, and usually do less well at school. Often they may be depressed and feel guilty. They may begin to lie and steal, or become aggressive with their friends. It is known that adolescent girls who have been sexually abused over a long period of time are more likely to become pregnant, to turn to prostitution or to become anorexic.

Finally, even in the absence of any help it is probable that many abused children make a relatively complete recovery. Nowadays **therapy** is available for people who have been abused. A GP can confidentially refer someone who wants help to a specialised therapist.

Further reading

Bowlby, J. (1965) *Child Care and the Growth of Love* Second edn, Penguin.

Holt, J. (1969) *How Children Fail*. Penguin.

Sharpe, S. (1976) *Just Like a Girl: How Girls Learn to be Women*. Penguin.

Sylva, K. and Lunt, I. (1982) *Child Development: A First Course*. Basil Blackwell.

Thought questions

1   How could schools be better organised so as to enable pupils to learn more without getting bored or frightened?

2   Do you think mothers should have full-time jobs before their children go to school?

3   Some people feel that people guilty of child sexual abuse should be sent to prison. Others argue that if they are closely related to the victim, this only serves to break up the family and make the victim of the abuse feel even more guilty. What do you think?

Things to do

1. Try looking at children's books, newspapers and advertisements to see how girls and women are portrayed differently from boys and men.
2. Look at children playing. Can you describe the different sorts of play they engage in? How do children of different ages differ in their play?
3. Animal behaviour study techniques may be used to observe human behavioural interactions. An example of this is observation and recording of parent-child interactions. You can do this just by sitting on a bench in a park in the summer and recording what you see. For example, hand-holding behaviour may be observed between two adults, between two parents with children, between parents and children of different ages. How long are hands held for? When are hands held? Which parental hand is used most frequently for holding? When infants are carried, which arm takes most weight? If one child is carried and one held by the hand, which hand is used most commonly for which? Such studies may be quietly made without disturbing the subjects, and objective behavioural results obtained. Obviously very large samples are needed for any certainty to emerge but hypotheses may be statistically tested.

20

You Are What You Eat:
A Review of Human Nutrition

> 'Let us neither call diet a frivolous knowledge nor a curious science; but let us embrace it as the leader to perfect health, which, as the wise man saith, is above gold, and a sound body above all riches.'
> *From "Health's Improvement" by Thomas Muffett, 1655.*

From our infancy we grow in size by eating material from our environment. We either absorb the material directly, or hydrolyse it into smaller units first. We then sift, rearrange and resynthesise molecules, using them for growth. Others are burnt in respiration or thrown away through excretion. Powerful internal and external environmental forces also influence our development, but we are what we eat; even if we have become what we are with just a small fraction of our food.

Diet

The term 'diet' (from the Greek *diaetia*) was originally used to describe an individual's lifestyle and hence way of eating. The term should not be used for simply not eating. A person may depart from his or her normal diet in order to adjust their metabolism. Thus an athlete eats pasta as a special diet to build up glycogen before long exertion; a pregnant woman eats more protein, calcium and iron-rich foods as a supplement to feed her growing foetus; and a man may eat fish twice a week to change the composition of his blood lipids and so avoid coronary heart disease. These are diets that are altered to balance food intake with the body's needs. Similarly, avoiding all foods containing sugar

and fat in order to reduce body fat is another modification of diet. Daily alterations of food intake affect our energy reserves, growth, health and body composition. They illustrate the dynamic nature of balancing diet and lifestyle.

Nutrients

Human nutrition is a vast science with applications in medicine, health care and food technology. Many food scientists are closely involved in the chemical analysis of the food we buy and eat. Their work involves **qualitative analysis**, analysing food by the classes and sub-classes into which all foods may be divided, and **quantitative analysis**, assessing the amounts of each food class in a given food. The major nutrients are:
- **Carbohydrates**: sugars, starch, fibre (non-starch polysaccharides)
- **Proteins**: composed of amino acids
- **Fats**: steroids, neutral fats or phospholipids
- **Vitamins**: complex organic molecules fulfilling co-enzyme functions
- **Minerals**: simple inorganic salts
- **Water.**

This classical list disguises the fact that some substances in food fall under more than one class (for example, glycolipids are both carbohydrate and fat). Also, other important molecules (not listed here as nutrients) may be synthesised afresh in each organism: for example, the component nucleotides of DNA and RNA are not apparently necessary in the diet. Furthermore **dietary fibre** is essential not because we need it for energy or body building, but because the unassimilated fibre is a vehicle for conveying food through the gut and transporting away our waste products in faeces. Eating sufficient fibre greatly reduces the incidence of many diseases (see Chapter 22).

What are humans made of?

The composition of the human body reflects our diet, and in many ways is similar to that of other mammals. Barely half a dozen human bodies have been analysed completely for chemical composition – and not many of them were fit young people. (This lack of analysis is surprising when compared to the innumerable analyses which have been carried out on the food we eat.) Remarkably, results from bodies which have been analysed are very constant in certain respects but highly variable in a few others. For example, **fat** comprises a minimum of 4% of the body by mass in a starving person, and can be as high as 70% in someone who is very obese. The body of an average 19-year-old male contains 15% fat, whilst an average 19-year-old female contains 23%. Of our body fat, the lipids in membranes and nervous tissue comprise no more than 6% of total body mass, the remaining fat being largely stored under the skin.

The percentage of body mass that is **water** varies inversely with the amount of fat; the mean is 60%. If all the body fat is subtracted from the total body mass, the proportion of water in the remainder is very close to 72% for all individuals. More than half of this water is present in cell cytoplasm, which comprises about 80% water. Surprisingly there is only 1.5% carbohydrate in the fat-free body; much of it is glycogen, and there is barely a teaspoonful of glucose in circulation in the blood at one time. On average, proteins account for 17% of

total body mass, much of it being muscle and connective tissue.

By mass, the three principal **chemical elements** in the body are oxygen, carbon and hydrogen. Nitrogen, occurring mostly in proteins and nucleic acids, comprises 3.4%. In descending order of abundance (by mass per kilogram of body weight) the minerals and trace elements of the human body are: calcium (22g), phosphorus (12g), potassium (2.7g), sulphur (2.0g), sodium (1.8g), chlorine (1.4g), magnesium (0.47g), iron (74mg), zinc (28mg), copper (1.7mg), manganese (0.2mg), chromium (0.1mg), selenium (0.1mg), iodine (0.05mg) and cobalt (0.021mg). There are also traces of fluorine, molybdenum, vanadium, arsenic, nickel and silicon. All 25 of these elements are known to have a specific function in metabolism. For example, tiny amounts of trace elements are essential for specific enzymes to function. Each of us also contains traces of the elements boron, lithium, tin, aluminium, lead, mercury and cadmium. These last elements have no known nutrient function and may well be unexcreted contaminants of our food.

What should humans eat?

We are brought up to like particular foods. During the twentieth century the science of nutrition has grown and we are now offered much advice on the subject. We are also surrounded by tempting advertisements for food and have access to a great variety of different diets. It all looks good – but what is the best diet?

All archaeological evidence indicates that *Homo sapiens* and our predecessor species *Homo erectus* were primarily **vegetarians** during the past million years, but from well before this time they were also **hunters.** Our nearest animal relatives the chimpanzees are occasional meat-eaters in the wild.

Up until the origins of farming, our **hunter-gatherer ancestors** depended mainly upon roots, fruits and nuts for their food. The largest single dietary item of the present-day Kalahari Bushmen is the *mongongo* nut *Ricinodendron rautenenii*. This is a good source of protein, and the oil it contains is rich in polyunsaturated fats. Bushmen also eat much small-animal meat and a small amount of meat from large game. The meat in their diet has virtually no fat, unlike the meat of our domestic animals. Bushmen have very low blood cholesterol levels and on this diet they are never obese (although they become very fat on a diet of milk and cattle meat). Bushmen eat almost no sugar and have no tooth decay. They eat little salt and have very low blood pressure; in middle age their blood pressure levels fall rather than rise, and despite a harsh lifestyle spent constantly out of doors, their life expectancy is almost the same as that of people in Britain. We cannot all become Bushmen, or indeed live like them, but we can examine our traditional diets and question whether they are suitable for the lifestyles that we follow today.

The British Government has a standing Committee on the Medical Aspects of Food Policy (COMA) which every ten years produces a report of Dietary Reference values for food energy and nutrients for groups of people in the United Kingdom. The 1991 Report details the estimated average requirement for 35 nutrients and spells out levels at which deficiency will occur, or levels at which excessive intake may cause harm. This chapter just looks at some less known aspects of protein and fat nutrition. It concludes with a brief look at problems of obesity and eating disorder.

Proteins

We do not need to eat meat to be well nourished, but we need good sources of protein; not all proteins are of equal nutritional value. Proteins are required for making enzymes, many structural components and cell secretions. They are made from 20 different amino acids. The body can make some of these itself but in humans there are 8 that cannot be synthesised at all, and these are therefore essential in the diet. The amount of each of the 8 **essential amino acids** varies in different protein foods. Some foods have a greater value than others. Animal proteins such as eggs and milk are rich in essential amino acids. Eggs and milk have, after all,

evolved by natural selection for rearing whole animals – chicks and calves respectively. Table 20.1 shows the biological quality of different proteins relative to the spectrum of essential amino acids required in the human diet.

The advent of ion exchange chromatography for the separation of amino acids has led to the development of the fully automated **amino acid analyser** which rapidly produces a qualitative and quantitative print-out for any protein material under test. This allows critical assessment of the value of a food protein for human nutrition.

Many plant proteins are less valuable than animal proteins as sources of essential amino acids. Cereals, for example, are short of lysine. For this reason plant breeders have concentrated on breeding varieties of 'high-lysine' maize (corn) for use in poorer Third World communities where maize is the principal food source. However, an essential amino acid which occurs in inadequate amounts in one plant species may occur in excess in another. Hence with the right combination of plant food a **vegetarian diet** can easily meet all the body's protein needs e.g. a cereal with peas or potatoes. For nutritionists working in very poor human communities, or in famine relief, a knowledge of good protein sources is important for countering malnutrition. **Kwashiorkor** (infant protein malnutrition) is usually due to malnutrition of infants

Table 20.1 The biological quality of different proteins for growth varies with their amino acid composition. (Ideal quality =100)

Food	Quality	Deficiency
Egg	94	None
Milk	90	Methionine and cystine
Pork	79	Methionine and cystine
Beef	76	Methionine and cystine
Whole rice	75	Lysine
Soya	75	Methionine and cystine
Whole wheat	67	Lysine
Potato	67	Methionine and cystine
Oats	66	Lysine
Maize	60	Lysine
Peanuts	56	Methionine
Peas	48	Methionine and cystine

through ignorance rather than lack of available protein sources. Foods such as beans and peas have high protein concentrations, although they are not always as digestible as cereals are.

Adults need only 50g of protein per day for maintenance, but growing children need much more, and of higher quality. Most people in affluent societies obtain more than enough protein. Eating a certain amount of protein, however, does not guarantee that it will be assimilated. Proteins that are denatured by cooking are not so easily broken down by digestive enzymes. Raw meat is therefore more completely digested than cooked meat, but being tougher it takes much longer to digest unless it is well divided up. **Cooking** may effectively destroy the amino acids as building blocks for future protein: for example, dibasic amino acids such as lysine combine with reducing sugars in the cooking process to produce the dark brown pigments of meat and bread crusts; these are not absorbed by the gut (see chapter 8).

Fats

No food class is more controversial than fats, nor indeed more complex. What percentage of the general public knows a mono-unsaturated fat from a polyunsaturated fat? Yet information about their relative proportions is paraded in advertisements and on tubs of margarine. Some people may even be led to believe that certain fats are practically poisonous, and wish that their bodies contained no cholesterol at all. Their cells would literally fall apart if this were so.

The structure and variety of fats

Fats are solid at room temperature and oils are runny; both are lipids, but their fluidity depends on whether the fatty acid tail is kinked rather than straight. Both are **neutral fats** formed from **glycerol** and **fatty acids**. Most fats consist of three fatty acid chains condensed on to a single glycerol residue. Much of our dietary fat is digested by lipase; the fatty acid and glycerol products are absorbed and transported to the liver. **Cholesterol** is a steroid fat, vital in membranes and in hormone synthesis. It is intimately involved in the transport of triglycerides and has a regular turnover in the body, being formed, destroyed and then excreted in bile.

The fatty acids are susceptible to many different alterations, each sort having its own characteristic form. When you eat an animal you take in the modifications to the fatty acids that that animal made to the fats in its own food. Thus if you feed a pig on fishmeal the fats it contains are partly

20.1 Fatty acids vary in their saturation. Stearic acid is fully saturated, having no double bonds. Oleic acid is a mono-unsaturated fatty acid, whilst the essential fatty acids are polyunsaturated. Our metabolism cannot add double bonds to the methyl end of a saturated fat. Polyunsaturates are therefore essential to health

derived from fish, and the fish fatty acids are derived from some crustacean fatty acids. In turn, the crustacean fatty acids are derived from protozoa and algae in the ocean. Synthesis and modification occur all along the food chain.

Fatty acids are carbon-to-carbon chains, commonly with two hydrogen atoms joined to each carbon atom along the chain. At one end of the chain is a **methyl group** (CH$_3$) and at the other a **carboxyl group** (COOH); the latter end is condensed to glycerol in a fat (see Figure 20.1). Long chains have as many as 24 carbon atoms, and short chains as few as 10. If all the bonds between the carbon atoms are saturated (i.e. single bonds, not double) then the fatty acid is described as **saturated** and is straight. Stearic acid, common in the fat of herbivores, is an example. It has a chain of 18 fully saturated carbon atoms with no double bonds. It is therefore described as 18:0. Oleic acid, found in olive oil, is the same length but has one unsaturated link; it is therefore described as 18:1, and is a **mono-unsaturated** fatty acid. When double bonds form, as in oleic acid, the fatty acid chain becomes kinked and the fats formed are more fluid. Oils, which are runny, have a high unsaturated fatty acid component.

Our cells have a **fluid mosaic** membrane structure. To make membranes fluid under varied conditions the body needs highly unsaturated fatty acids to incorporate into phospholipids. How are we to obtain the right ones in our diet? Look back at Figure 20.1.

The drawing of the linoleic acid structure shows that our bodies can only make limited modifications to the fatty acid tails. In the fatty acid chain the carbon atoms are numbered from the methyl end. In unsaturated fats double bonds are commonly found at one or more of the third, sixth and ninth positions. Plants can make these bonds easily but animals cannot insert double bonds at the tail end. This means that fatty acids such as linoleic (18:2) and linolenic acid (18:3) cannot be synthesised by humans and must be obtained from the diet. They are therefore described as **essential fatty acids (EFAs)** and come to us in the food chain from plants. Both linoleic and linolenic acid are **polyunsaturated fatty acids,** having more than one double bond. It seems that the typical western diet is most deficient in the long-chain fatty acids with 20–24 links; some of these have up to six double bonds. For example, we know that arachidonic acid (20:4) is an EFA important in humans for synthesising local hormones called **prostaglandins.** The EFAs eicosapentaenoic acid (20:5) and docosahexaenoic acid (22.6) are found in fish oil; our bodies cannot make them. Thus, many **polyunsaturated fatty acids (PUFAs)** seem to be

20.2 Space filling models of a saturated, mono-unsaturated and two polyunsaturated fatty acid

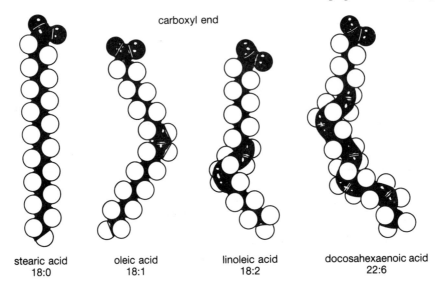

carboxyl end

| stearic acid | oleic acid | linoleic acid | docosahexaenoic acid |
| 18:0 | 18:1 | 18:2 | 22:6 |

important in the human diet in ways that have not been recognised until recently.

Changing fat diets

Have we been eating too much hard animal fat? Coronary heart disease and atherosclerosis (the development of fatty plaque on the inside of arteries) are two common diseases which we now know are made worse by fat **malnutrition** (malnutrition is bad feeding, not just lack of food). Raised blood levels of triglycerides and cholesterol are significantly associated with these diseases.

What changes might be advised to a typical western diet? Certainly wealthy people everywhere tend to eat proportionally more fats and oils than the very poor. However, there are differences between cultures. Consumption of olive oil in Mediterranean countries never produced the high blood-fat levels that we have seen in the communities of northern Europe where **butter** and **lard** are eaten. Furthermore, the eating of some oily fish such as herrings (including kippers) has declined in Britain during this century. Could such differences partially explain the rise in coronary heart disease?

Perhaps the first change for the better in our fat diets was the invention of **margarine**, by Mège-Mourie in 1869. This was achieved by the hydrogenation of oils at 200°C. When butter was expensive and few people could afford as much of it as they would have liked, margarine became popular. Today it is made mostly from **vegetable oils** of maize (corn), soya, sunflower, groundnut, palm and oil-seed rape. Each of these oils has a relatively high polyunsaturated fatty acid content (see Table 20.2).

One of the nutritional mistakes made with the early margarines was the over-conversion of unsaturated runny vegetable oils into more solid saturated fats. It was not known that this destroyed large amounts of valuable linoleic EFA. Because of this the early solid margarine butter-substitutes lost some of their nutritional value.

There is a link between **blood-fat levels**, particularly cholesterol, and **heart disease**. Cholesterol is an important fluidiser of membranes. However, excessive cholesterol carried in the blood may contribute to **atherosclerosis**, where plaques

form in the arteries and lead to coronary heart disease.

In 1954 E.H. Ahrens discovered that a diet high in saturated fats raised the blood cholesterol level. In 1962 it was shown by C. Hornstra that raising the concentration of PUFAs in the diet had the opposite effect, lowering blood cholesterol levels. Saturated fatty acids raised the cholesterol level by twice as much as PUFAs were able to lower it. Mono-unsaturates (such as oleic acid in olive oil) were shown to be neutral in their effect. This quite rightly identified **animal fats** as the culprits, resulting in a review of animal-fat consumption and an investigation of the composition of margarines.

Attempts were made successfully to increase PUFAs in the margarine by hydrogenating the oils less, and by adding emulsifiers and stiffeners to the margarine to make an otherwise oily substance smoother in texture. Vitamins are now added, as is colouring to give a more butter-like appearance.*

In 1985 H.O. Bang and J. Dyerburg reported on a ten-year medical study of nutrition and disease in

---

* Some hard margarines contain many unsaturated fat isomers in the trans- rather than the natural cis-form, as a result of hydrogenation. These 'unsaturated fats' seem to act as saturated fats in the body, a fact often concealed in product labelling.

Table 20.2 Percentage fat composition of vegetable oils and lard (animal fat)

	Saturated fats	Mono-unsaturated fats	Poly-unsaturated fats
Vegetable oils			
Coconut	89	9	2
Corn	14	31	55
Cotton seed	28	20	52
Groundnut (peanut)	15	55	30
Oil-seed rape	7	56	37
Olive	14	74	12
Palm	45	46	9
Sunflower	12	31	57
Walnut	14	23	63
Animal fat			
Lard	39	47	14

Eskimos in Greenland, Eskimos in Denmark and Danes in Denmark. The results were striking. Eskimos in Greenland with a high fish and sea-mammal (seal and whale-meat) diet had much less coronary heart disease. This was not due to genetic factors: the Eskimos on a Danish diet acted as a control group in the investigation, and their results were very similar to those of the Danes. Marine oils are high in **long-chain PUFAs** (20:4, 22:5 and 22:6). Other dietary studies on volunteers have shown that regular twice-weekly fish consumption lowers blood cholesterol levels and the levels of the lipoproteins which transport fat. Moreover, studies in Cardiff and Sheffield have recently shown that the probability of second heart attacks is reduced by about 30% in those heart-attack patients switched to an oily-fish diet. It may be that fish-oil PUFAs are more important than we originally realised. They appear to help in the improved synthesis of cell membranes and in the synthesis of prostaglan-

din hormones. They probably also help to prevent thrombosis by making blood platelets less 'sticky' and so less easily ruptured, reducing the likelihood of clots in the blood.

How much fat?

So what fats should we eat, and how much? Adults should not let fat exceed 30% of their energy intake (the mean at present in Britain is 40%), unless they are working very hard physically or using fat to keep warm in a very cold climate. At the other extreme fat should not comprise less than 20% of the energy intake. Less than 15% of the energy intake should come from saturated fats. Vegetable oils which are high in PUFAs should be eaten in preference to animal fats or hydrogenated vegetable fat margarines. Cold-water fish oils are very valuable in lowering blood fat and cholesterol.

What about 'cholesterol-free foods'? Eating cholesterol itself seems to be less important in raising plasma levels of cholesterol than eating high levels of saturated fat. It is the saturated fats that induce the liver both to produce more cholesterol and to inhibit steps in PUFA metabolism. Only foods such as egg yolk have high enough levels of cholesterol to affect plasma concentrations (see Table 20.3).

20.3 Fatty fish like mackerel lower blood cholesterol levels and make thrombosis less likely

Fatties and thinnies

There are hereditary differences between people that are very significant in nutrition. You are what you eat, but you also are what you are, genetically. One person in 200 has familial **hypercholestero-laemia,** in which a dominant gene raises the blood cholesterol level four times higher than normal. This increases the risk of coronary heart disease and strict dietary control is essential.

Obesity and **leanness** are of much greater general concern. Strong genetic factors are again involved here, but disentangling them from people's behavioural characteristics is difficult. Many lean people have high metabolic rates, release more heat, do not feel the cold very much and eat a high-energy diet. People who are 20% or more above the mean mass for their height are defined as

	Total fat/g per 100g	Saturated Fatty Acids (total)/g per 100g	Mono-unsaturated Fatty Acids (total)/g per 100g	Poly-unsaturated Fatty Acids (total)/g per 100g	Longchain Polyunsaturated Fatty Acids (total)/g per 100g	Cholesterol /mg per 100g
Plaice	1.9	0.3	0.5	0.5	0.2	70
Trout (rainbow)	3.4	0.6	1.0	1.2	0.5	57
Salmon (Atlantic)	12.0	3.0	4.6	3.1	1.2	70
Herring (Atlantic)	18.5	3.7	9.3	3.3	1.6	60
Mackerel (Atlantic)	16.3	4.0	6.3	4.1	2.5	80
Beef	21.1	8.9	10.0	0.8	0.2	85
Lamb	18.7	9.1	7.1	0.9	0.2	71
Pork	24.2	9.6	10.8	1.9	0.5	67
Eggs	10.9	3.4	4.3	1.2	0.3	1602
Chicken	7.3	2.4	3.3	1.1	0.1	90
Milk	3.8	2.3	1.2	0.1	-	14
Cheese (average)	33.1	21.1	9.0	0.9	-	105
Double cream	48.2	28.8	15.4	1.3	-	137
Butter	81.7	49.0	26.1	2.3	-	230
Hard margarine	81.6	40.1	23.9	13.0	-	285
Dairy fat spread	73.4	28.1	29.9	11.3	-	105
Low fat spread	40.5	11.2	17.6	9.9	-	6

Table 20.3 Fat composition of foods by fat classes

obese. It is common to find obese people with high food intakes. Some clearly overeat largely for psychological reasons, often because of mild depression. However, there are many other obese people with below average food intakes and low metabolic rates, who easily feel the cold, and who readily put on weight. Obese people take little exercise, but their greatly increased mass means that they need to expend more energy to move a shorter distance. Much of their extra weight is in the form of muscle to carry their weight! Most fat cells form when we are young.

Much obesity could be avoided if children learn to eat sensibly.

Anorexia and bulimia

Not eating normally may be as common a problem as obesity, particularly for young women. The term **anorexia** is used to describe any reduced desire to eat and may accompany illness; but **anorexia nervosa** is a specific psychological condition in which the reduction of body weight becomes

obsessive. Anorexia nervosa sufferers suppress or ignore hunger signals, they often have an inflated view of their emaciated body shape, and their self-starvation can become a serious medical problem. It is most common in intelligent girls in the higher social classes, starting when they are between 14 and 18 years of age. The idealised or romantic slim female figure, reinforced by vivid images in media and advertisements, may initiate a pattern of avoiding food. However, underlying the anorexic's desire to be slim there is a deeper insecurity in personality, often rooted in precarious family relationships. It is not an easy condition to treat, or one to manage if you suffer from it. Anorexic girls seem to find security in avoiding the onset of the development of the adult female body shape. After considerable weight loss menstrual periods stop, as the physical resources to support them are inadequate. The brain is seemingly stimulated by the fasting, and furious or perfectionist efforts may be made in school work. Recovery takes a long time. If the illness is prolonged a young woman's future fertility may even be at risk.

Bulimia nervosa is a related disorder, often occurring later in adolescence, in which there is an irresistible urge to overeat. The desire for food is met by avid eating, but is followed by self-induced vomiting to prevent weight gain. As with anorexia this behaviour results from a psychological condition, the recognition and treatment of which may easily return the person to normal health.

Most people eat well and should not worry about their diet. It is important to eat a good variety of foods, to eat when you are hungry, to maintain your ideal body weight, to avoid sugar and salt and to eat plenty of fibre. In the end, eating is much more than a nutritional matter alone: it should be an enjoyable social activity, for which our friends and families gather. This is equally important for our health; for though we are what we eat, we are judged by what we are.

Further reading

Anon. (1984) *Diet and Cardiovascular Disease, Committee on the Medical Aspects of Food Policy.* DHSS COMA Report on Health and Social Subjects no.28, HMSO.
Bingham, S. (1987) *Food and Nutrition.* Dent.
Panel on Dietary Reference Values of the Committee on Medical Aspects of Food Policy. (1991) *Dietary reference values for food energy and nutrients for the United Kingdom.* London. HMSO.
Saynor, R. and Eastwood, M.A. (1986) *Human Nutrition and Dietetics.* Longman.
Taylor, D. (1989) *Human Physical Health.* Cambridge University Press.

Thought questions

1 Are there any arguments against vegetarianism?

2 How could the system of labelling foods containing fat be improved for the benefit of the consumer?

Things to do

Write down a list of all the good features of your present diet. Write a second list of all its poor features. Then set yourself **three** targets for improving your diet. Write them in your diary one week ahead, one month ahead and one year ahead. Check in the future to see whether you have been successful in changing your lifestyle.

21
AIDS, HIV and the Search for a Cure

In 1981 a number of American doctors began to find uncommon diseases in otherwise healthy males in their twenties and thirties. One of these diseases was a very rare form of pneumonia caused by *Pneumocystis carinii*, a unicellular organism. Another disease which was being detected more often was Kaposi's sarcoma, a rare form of skin cancer. As more and more cases of these diseases were found it became clear that something was causing otherwise healthy people to suffer from a collapse of their **immune system.** With their bodies unable to defend themselves against diseases, these people were prone to **opportunistic infections.** In 1982 the condition was given a name: **AIDS (Acquired Immune Deficiency Syndrome).**

The difference between AIDS and HIV

A flurry of medical research soon established that AIDS was caused by a virus, now known as **HIV (Human Immunodeficiency Virus).** However, as tests for the virus were developed it became clear that most people infected with HIV did not show any of the symptoms of AIDS. The distinction between HIV and AIDS is an important one. HIV causes AIDS in the sense that AIDS only develops in people infected with HIV: people who are not infected with HIV cannot develop AIDS. However, most people infected with HIV are perfectly healthy and do not have AIDS. To understand how this can be, one has to know something of the structure and biology of HIV.

The structure and biology of HIV

The human immunodeficiency virus is an unusual virus in a number of respects. First, although like all viruses it consists of nucleic acid and protein, its nucleic acid is RNA, not DNA. The structure of HIV is shown in Figure 21.1. At the centre of the virus is the RNA with an enzyme, **reverse transcriptase,** which helps the virus to multiply. Around the RNA and reverse transcriptase is a core

consisting of protein molecules given the uninspiring name 'p24'. p stands for protein, and 24 refers to the size of the protein. Around the p24 core is a coating of smaller p18 proteins. Outside these is the viral envelope, consisting of a lipid bilayer which comes from the human cell where the virus was made. The lipid bilayer contains characteristic **glycoproteins** which are proteins with sugar residues attached. The lipid bilayer also holds so-called HLA antigens, again derived from the human cell in which the virus was made.

HIV belongs to a group of viruses called **retroviruses.** Retroviruses all contain RNA as their genetic material. When HIV attacks a human cell, it first binds to the cell surface. This is where the glycoproteins in the viral envelope come in. They recognise and bind to molecules of CD4. CD4 is a glycoprotein found on the outer membrane of some human cells. One of the most abundant group of cells to have CD4 molecules is a group of **white blood cells** called **T-helper cells**.

Once HIV has bound to the surface of a CD4-bearing cell its viral envelope fuses with the cell membrane, causing the inner part of the virus to enter the cell as illustrated in Figure 21.2. When in the cell, the viral RNA begins to behave as a special sort of **messenger RNA (mRNA).** Instead

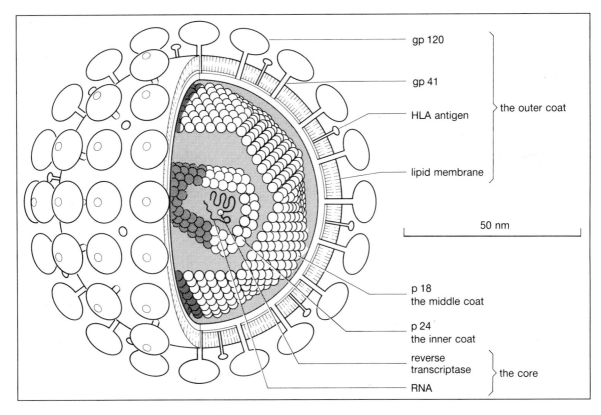

21.1 A model of the diagram of the virus. This figure tries to indicate the three-dimensional nature of the virus, while revealing its internal structure. In reality, the p24 core surrounds the RNA and reverse transcriptase molecules and is in turn surrounded by the p18 layer. In turn, this is surrounded by the viral envelope consisting of a lipid membrane with HLA antigens and the glycoproteins gp120 and gp41

of making protein, however, its function is to make a complementary strand of DNA. To do this it uses the reverse transcriptase enzyme from the virus and nucleotides from the host cell. The single-stranded DNA thus formed then makes a complementary strand of DNA, with the result that double-stranded viral DNA is formed.

It might be thought that HIV would simply make many copies of itself and then leave the human cell. However, this does not happen. Instead the double-stranded viral DNA inserts itself into the DNA of the host cell nucleus. Here it can lie dormant for months or years, comprising the

latent phase of the infection. The latent phase is the reason why people infected with HIV may remain healthy for many years. Indeed, it is still not known whether everyone infected with HIV will progress to AIDS, or whether some people will never develop the disease. It looks as though about 75% of people infected with HIV do develop some of the symptoms of AIDS within about eight to ten years, but we do not know whether there are some people with HIV who will never develop AIDS.

Once the viral DNA does start to make RNA copies of itself, these RNA molecules are soon read by the machinery of the host cell to make viral proteins in the same way in which mRNA translates into proteins on ribosomes. The viral proteins with the single-stranded RNA spontaneously aggregate into new viruses at the surface of the cell. Soon dozens of new viruses bud out of the cell, as indicated in Figure 21.3, and the cell subsequently dies. These new viruses may end up in any of the body's fluids, including blood, semen, vaginal secretions, saliva, tears and breast milk. However,

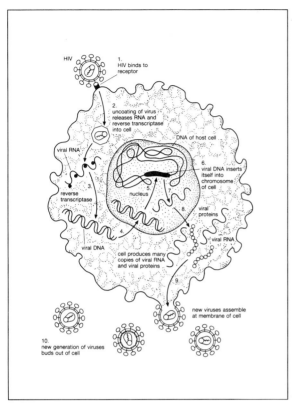

21.2 The life cycle of the human immunodeficiency virus. The time lag between stages 6 and 7 may be many years

the only ways that HIV can be passed from one person to another are via blood, semen, vaginal secretions and breast milk.

Why is HIV so serious?

The above account of the biology of HIV explains how the virus can infect certain human cells and multiply in them, but it does not explain why HIV is so dangerous. There seem to be four features of HIV which make it particularly serious. First, by integrating itself into our DNA, HIV can effectively hide from our **immune system** (see Chapter 16). Second, HIV strikes right at the heart of our cellular defence system. T-helper cells are in the front line of attack against invading micro-organisms. In essence they help control our immune system by regulating the activities of many of the

other components of our defence system. For instance, in the absence of T-helper cells, B-cells (which with T-cells make up our lymphocytes) effectively go out of control and release their antibodies at inappropriate times. (It must be admitted that immunologists still do not understand why HIV has such a dramatic effect on the overall activity of the T-helper cells. For one thing, it looks as though only a small minority of T-helper cells ever become infected with HIV.) A third problem with HIV is that it has an exceptionally high **mutation rate,** making it very difficult for our bodies to produce antibodies to overcome the virus. Fourth, precisely because HIV can hide inside the body's cells, it can be carried to the central nervous system. This is why about one-third of patients with AIDS have **neurological problems.** Such problems range from forgetfulness, loss of concentration and slowness of thought to severe dementia. Once HIV is established in the central nervous

21.3 A transmission electron micrograph of a number of HIV particles budding off from the surface of an infected T-helper cell

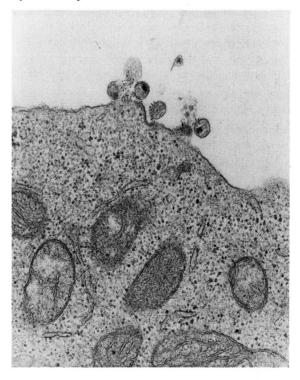

system it is almost inaccessible to drugs because of the so-called **blood-brain barrier.** This is a natural anatomical defence mechanism which prevents almost any foreign substance in the blood, including a drug, from entering the central nervous system.

Curing AIDS

The first drug to be approved for use in treating patients with AIDS was a **nucleoside analogue** called 3'-azido-2',3'-dideoxythymidine, which thankfully also goes under the commercial name of **zidovudine.** Its structure is shown in Figure 21.4, along with the structure of the naturally occurring nucleoside **thymidine**. The important thing to notice about zidovudine is the presence of N_3 on one of the carbon atoms where thymidine has an OH group. The significance of these three nitrogen atoms can be seen in Figure 21.5. When a molecule of zidovudine is incorporated into a growing DNA chain, no further nucleotides can be added. This is because the presence of the nitrogen atoms prevents the addition of the next nucleotide. Zidovudine therefore prevents complete chains of viral DNA being made from the virus's RNA.

Zidovudine is marketed worldwide by the firm Burroughs Wellcome, and slows down the rate at which AIDS progresses. However, it must be emphasised that zidovudine is not a cure for AIDS. At the moment AIDS remains incurable. Most people die within two years of developing AIDS, whatever the treatment they receive. One problem with zidovudine is that it often suppresses the production of blood cells by the patient's bone marrow, leading to severe anaemia. Patients taking zidovudine also report feeling sick, having aching muscles and suffering from severe headaches. Zidovudine is expensive: a year's treatment works out at about £6000.

A further problem with zidovudine is that in most patients, reduced viral sensitivity to the drug is found after a few months of treatment. In some cases, viral sensitivity to zidovudine may decrease by a factor of over a hundred. What seems to happen is that there is selection within the patient

21.4 The structure of zidovudine, an anti-AIDS drug, (a) compared with the naturally occurring nucleoside thymidine (b)

for strains of HIV that are less sensitive to zidovudine. This is precisely analagous to the way in which many bacteria have evolved resistance to penicillin.

As one might expect, a tremendous amount of research is currently being carried out to try to find other drugs effective against HIV and AIDS. A number of other nucleoside analogues are under investigation. For instance, 3'-fluoro-3'-deoxythymidine, or FLT for short, is being investi-

to 5′ end
of DNA (a)

$$O = P - O - CH_2 \quad \text{adenine}$$

$$O = P - O - CH_2 \quad \text{guanine}$$

OH

to 5′ end
of DNA (b)

$$O = P - O - CH_2 \quad \text{adenine}$$

$$O = P - O - CH_2 \quad \text{guanine}$$

$$O = P - O - CH_2 \quad \text{thymine}$$

N_3

21.5 (a) shows a strand of DNA which has had guanine added as the last base, and adenine as the penultimate base. (b) shows how, if a molecule of zidovudine is added, the DNA chain can no longer grow because nucleotides cannot now be added

gated. Where zidovudine has three nitrogen atoms, FLT has an atom of fluorine. Tests show that, like zidovudine, FLT has an adverse effect on bone marrow. However, it seems as though it may be

about five times more powerful than zidovudine, giving rise to the hope that it will be effective in smaller doses and will therefore have fewer side-effects.

Drugs with other modes of action are also being investigated. One hopeful candidate is **dextran sulphate.** Laboratory studies indicate that dextran sulphate can prevent HIV from binding to T-cells. Clinical trials are in their early stages, but there is some evidence to suggest that dextran sulphate may help. Some drugs which initially looked promising have proved ineffective. For instance, a trial to investigate the effectiveness of a drug called **ampligen** came to a premature halt when interim analysis provided no evidence that it worked.

Traditionally, new medical drugs take about a decade to develop. During this time, careful **long-term studies** are carried out on the effectiveness of the drug and on its side-effects, if any, on humans and other mammals. In the case of anti-AIDS drugs, however, pharmaceutical companies are spending far less time on the development phase, under the authorisation of many governments. In one sense this is good, since it decreases the time from initial research to final marketing. However, a potential disadvantage is that new anti-AIDS drugs could be used widely and only subsequently be found to have serious side-effects.

A further problem with the testing of anti-AIDS drugs is to find suitable controls. New medical drugs are tested by means of a **double blind trial.** In this system, patients are randomly assigned to one of two groups. One group receives the drug under investigation. The other group receives only a **placebo,** a neutral substance known to have no effect. Neither the patient nor the doctor knows to which group the patient has been allocated. Not surprisingly, however, many people with AIDS are not prepared to take the risk of being assigned to a control group. They want to be treated with the best drugs currently known, even if those drugs have not been fully investigated. A major American trial to investigate whether zidovudine prevents people infected with HIV but with no symptoms of AIDS from later developing AIDS is facing consider-able problems. Within the first year, approximately

157

30% of the 1900 participants dropped out. Almost all of them were on the placebo. Presumably they had somehow found this out, possibly from the absence of any of the anticipated side-effects of zidovudine. Some of those who dropped out subsequently re-entered the trial under a different name. It was clear that the major factor motivating many people to enter the trial was the possibility of obtaining free zidovudine.

Researchers have begun to look at why some people develop AIDS only months after being infected with HIV, while others may be completely healthy ten years after HIV infection. Genetic differences have been found to influence the risk of progressing from HIV infection to AIDS. It is known, for instance, that possession of certain alleles at the loci responsible for the major histocompatibility complex increases the chance of developing AIDS. Another factor which is almost certainly important is general health. It is possible that infection with other sexually transmitted diseases may increase the risk of AIDS developing. Other research suggests that stress increases the risk of HIV infection developing into AIDS.

It is worth emphasising that even though AIDS cannot currently be cured, most of the opportunistic infections characteristic of patients with AIDS can be successfully treated. People with AIDS often recommend eating well, not getting too tired, keeping fit without getting exhausted and remaining busy as ways of keeping as healthy as possible.

Vaccines against HIV

Immunisation is a powerful and effective way of controlling many human diseases (see also Chapter 16). Smallpox has been eliminated throughout the world thanks to vaccination, and many diseases such as measles, poliomyelitis, whooping cough and diphtheria are now far less prevalent in countries with active immunisation programmes than they once used to be. Unfortunately, there are a number of reasons why the development of a vaccine against HIV is proving extremely difficult.

In **vaccination**, a small dose of the disease-causing organism is deliberately given to the person being vaccinated or immunised. The dose must satisfy two conditions. First, it must have been treated in some way so that the risk of it causing the disease in question is minimal. Typically, this means either that an attenuated, or weak, form of the micro-organism is given, or else that the organism has been killed or has had its genetic material destroyed so that it cannot reproduce. Second, the vaccination dose must be capable of stimulating an antibody response sufficient to ensure that, for at least a few years, the immune system of the person who has been immunised can respond sufficiently quickly to destroy any organisms entering the body which might otherwise cause that disease.

One problem with HIV is that it mutates very rapidly. It may therefore be almost impossible to develop a single vaccine against it. This is similar to the situation with influenza strains. Vaccination against one strain may not be effective against other strains. Another problem with HIV is that any vaccination will have to stimulate a very rapid attack by the body against the virus. If HIV succeeds in inserting itself into a person's DNA, immunisation has failed.

A further problem with HIV is that humans are the only species which can contract AIDS. Most of us may think that this is a good thing. However, it does mean that it is difficult to test quickly whether the vaccines actually work. Unfortunately, practically the only animals which can be infected with HIV are chimpanzees, yet the chimpanzee is already a rare species. Many people also question the ethics of keeping these animals in laboratory cages and deliberately infecting them with HIV. Some scientists are trying to breed genetically engineered mice which can become infected with HIV and develop AIDS-like symptoms.

Most of the research into possible vaccines centres around the observation that to enter a T-helper cell, the gp120 molecule on the surface of the virus has to fit receptors on the surface of the T-helper cells as shown in Figure 21.6. One possibility would be to stimulate the immune system to produce antibodies against these gp120 molecules. Unfortunately the viral gene responsible for making

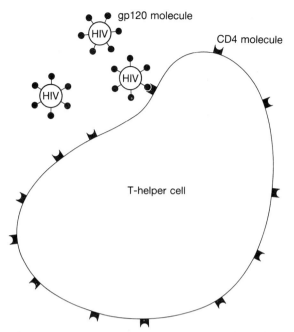

gp120 molecule

CD4 molecule

HIV

HIV

HIV

T-helper cell

21.6 HIV is able to attack T-helper cells because its surface glycoproteins can recognise and bind to CD4 molecules on the surface of T-cells. HIV can also infect macrophages and immature monocytes which also have CD4 molecules on their surfaces. Some cells, including immature cells in the bone marrow known as stem cells, can also become infected with HIV, even though they don't appear to bear any CD4 molecules.

gp120 and gp41, known as **env**, has a high mutation rate. A second problem is that HIV is now known to be able to attack cells that lack the CD4 molecule which is recognised by gp120.

Conclusions

It is still not known whether a successful vaccine against HIV will ever be developed, or whether a cure for AIDS will be found. For the foreseeable future, the solution to the problems of HIV and AIDS is likely to lie in the avoidance of infection.

Further reading

Adler, M.W. (1987) (ed.) *ABC of AIDS.* British Medical Journal.
Connor, S. and Kingman, S. (1989) *The Search for the Virus.* Penguin Books.
Herve, J. (1988) (ed.) *Love in a Cold Climate. AIDS: Some Pastoral and Theological Perspectives.* CLA.

Thought questions

1 Why is it proving so difficult to develop a cure for AIDS?

2 Should animals be used in the development of vaccines against HIV?

3 Do you feel some people have only themselves to blame for becoming infected with HIV?

Things to do

HIV, AIDS, attitudes and education
The control and elimination of HIV will be made much easier by controlling and influencing human behaviour than by any drug cure. The knowledge and attitudes of young people are important in this. Within a school or college it is well worth conducting an initial survey, having an AIDS education programme for all students, and then doing another survey to evaluate the education programme's success. Such an investigation will reveal where there is ignorance, and help to improve the education that is given. It should be organised by staff and students together; if this is something you can do, talk to your teachers about it.

22
Cancer

Many of us find the thought of developing cancer very frightening, if we think about it at all. However, most people know very little about the subject. In recent years huge advances have been made in our understanding of cancer. Many new treatments are now available, so that a number of cancers that were once life-threatening can now be successfully treated.

What is cancer?

There are hundreds of different types of cancer. They all have one aspect in common: they are due to breakdowns in the control of cell division. Consider, for example, what normally happens as food passes through the alimentary canal. Inevitably cells lining the digestive tract are rubbed off by the passage of the food. Cell division gives rise to new cells which replace the ones that are lost. The same process happens if we cut our skin: new cells are produced to cover over the cut. Normally, once the wound has been covered no more cells are produced.

Imagine, though, what happens when excessive cell growth and division occur. Instead of producing the correct number of cells it needs, the body produces too many. The result is a **tumour**. A tumour is a mass of cancerous cells. There are two sorts of tumours. **Benign tumours** remain in one place. **Malignant tumours** on the other hand spread throughout the body, often via blood vessels and the lymphatic system as shown in Figure 22.1. Malignant tumours tend to grow more rapidly than benign tumours and invade neighbouring tissue.

It is clear that malignant tumours are the more serious type. They can cause cancers throughout the body, which makes treatment more difficult. Benign tumours may also be serious for they starve nearby non-cancerous cells. They do this by diverting amino acids, sugars and other vital substrates carried in blood from the normal cells to themselves. Benign tumours may also grow to such a size that they cause problems by pressing on nearby nerves or blood vessels.

What causes cancer?

All cancers are the result of **mutations** in the DNA of a cell. The great majority of cell mutations do not give rise to cancers. However, some mutations damage the cell's ability to control its growth

22.1 A single cancerous cell (a). This divides more than normal cells do and gives rise to a tumour (b). The tumour may invade the surrounding tissue and be carried to other parts of the body via blood vessels or the lymphatic system (c)

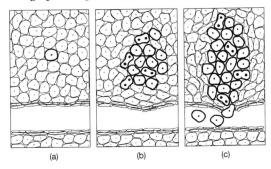

(a)　　　　(b)　　　　(c)

and multiplication. When this is the case the cell may start to grow and divide more than a normal cell. Soon the descendants of this single cell form a mass of cancerous cells.

Most cancers occur more commonly in older people. This is simply because the older we get, the more chance there is of a cancer-causing mutation. Natural DNA-repair mechanisms become less efficient the older we become. Nowadays life expectancies are greater than they used to be in many countries. As people live longer, and as serious infectious diseases become less common, more people develop cancer. In the United Kingdom about one in three of us will develop cancer at some time. About 70% of new cancer cases occur in people over the age of 60.

Certain chemicals are an important cause of many cancers. This was first realised in 1775 when a surgeon in London, Percival Pott, noticed a very high incidence of cancer of the scrotum in chimney sweeps. In Denmark, subsequent legislation required chimney sweeps to wear protective clothing and wash more frequently; as a result, fewer sweeps developed scrotal cancer. A chemical that may induce cancer is described as **carcinogenic**.

In Britain today the chemicals causing most cancers are those in cigarettes. Smoking is Britain's largest avoidable cause of disease and premature death. Almost a third of all the deaths in Britain from cancer are a direct result of cigarette-smoking. Smoking kills about 35 000 people each year through lung cancer, and approximately twice that number die as a result of coronary heart disease. Smoking also results in bronchitis, emphysema and cancers of the mouth, throat, oesophagus, bladder and pancreas. Cigarette smoke contains a suspension of millions of tiny particles which are breathed into the lungs. The most important substances in cigarette smoke are nicotine, tar and carbon monoxide. Nicotine causes the addiction to cigarettes, tar causes cancers, and carbon monoxide causes heart disease. The relationship between the number of cigarettes a person smokes and his or her chance of getting lung cancer is approximately linear. On average each cigarette shortens a smoker's life by five or six minutes. There is no safe number of

cigarettes which can be smoked. However, if smokers give up smoking the probability of developing lung cancer gradually falls, as demonstrated in Figure 22.2. It is also possible for non-smokers to develop lung cancer induced by breathing in another person's cigarette smoke. This is known as **passive smoking**. Living with someone who smokes makes a non-smoker about 30% more likely to develop lung cancer than if neither person smoked.

Hundreds of different chemicals are known to cause cancers. Some of these **carcinogens** are found in our food. There is good evidence that up to 30% of all the cases of cancer in Britain are due to what we eat. For a start, cancers of the liver, mouth, throat and oesophagus are all more common in heavy drinkers. Cancers of the breast and cancer of the bowel are most common in countries like the United Kingdom, where people eat a relatively high proportion of fat, as shown in Figure 22.3. It is difficult to know for certain why this is. There is absolutely no evidence that switching to a

22.2 Smokers are approximately 14 times more likely to die from lung cancer than are non-smokers. However, a smoker's chance of dying from lung cancer lessens from the time he or she gives up smoking. After 15 years of non-smoking, his or her chance of dying from lung cancer is the same as that of someone who has never smoked

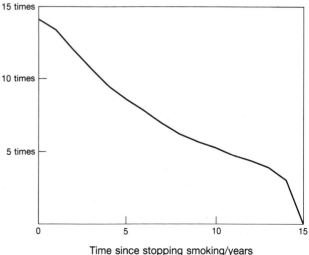

Time since stopping smoking/years

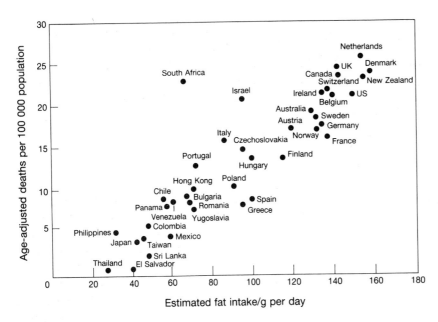

22.3 Across different countries there is a strong correlation between fat intake and mortality among women from breast cancer. However, this does not prove that eating fat causes breast cancer. International breast cancer rates also correlate closely with industrialisation, Gross Domestic Product and average adult female height. There is no evidence that switching to a low-fat diet reduces a woman's chance of developing breast cancer

low-fat diet reduces a woman's chance of developing breast cancer. In countries where people eat a large amount of fat, they also tend to eat little **fibre**. There is good evidence that if most of us ate more fibre we would be less likely to develop cancer of the bowel. A higher fibre intake also makes it more difficult to become overweight and reduces the risk of constipation. Fruits, vegetables and wholemeal breads all have a high fibre content. The fibre in fruits and vegetables is thought to be especially beneficial (see Chapter 20).

Different types of **radiation** can cause cancers. Exposure to too much sunlight can lead to skin cancer, especially if sunburn results. Medical X-rays, though very useful in diagnosis, carry with them a small risk. That is why pregnant women tend not to be given X-rays: developing foetuses are particularly sensitive to X-rays. Nuclear power-stations inevitably produce nuclear radiation, just as coal mines produce coal dust. There is some evidence of a higher incidence of leukaemia in children growing up near nuclear power-stations, though this is still not known for certain. However, the probability of dying of cancer through the peaceful use of radiation is thousands of times less than the chance of dying in a car accident.

Some cancers are caused by viruses. This is the case with cervical cancer, which is associated with the presence of **human papilloma viruses (HPVs)**. Certain strains of these HPVs are sometimes passed on during sexual intercourse. Thus the more sexual partners a woman has, the greater the risk of her developing cervical cancer. The risk is also influenced by the sexual history of her partner(s).

A number of cancers have a **hereditary component**. A person with a first-degree relative (parent, brother, sister or child) who has cancer of the colon is approximately three times as likely to develop it too. A hereditary component is found in a number of diseases besides cancers.

Treating cancer

Cancer is difficult to treat because the cancerous cells are very similar to the normal healthy cells of the body. The body is not being invaded by foreign organisms; cancer is caused by small mistakes in the genetic material of otherwise normal human cells. The most direct form of treatment is surgery. Other forms of treatment rely on the fact that cancerous cells do behave differently from normal cells.

Surgery is widely used in the treatment of cancer and is carried out in almost half of all cancer cases. It is particularly appropriate if the

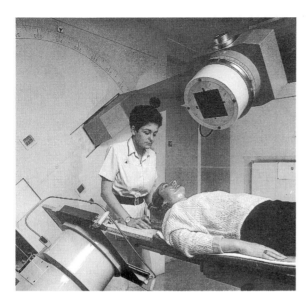

22.4 A radiographer positions the head of a cancer patient prior to focusing a beam of radiation at a tumour

tumour is still localised. Obviously, if cancerous cells have spread to many other parts of the body there is less chance that surgery will prove successful. As with all treatments for cancer, the earlier a diagnosis is made, the greater the chance that surgery will prove successful. In addition, the operation will be smaller. For instance, breast cancer used only to be treated by **radical mastectomy**. Not only was the entire affected breast removed, but also the accompanying lymph nodes up to the armpit. The development of new diagnostic and surgical techniques means that nowadays surgery can still be successful, while removing much less tissue.

Radiotherapy is the use of high-energy rays to kill cancer cells. The underlying principle is that DNA is sensitive to radiation; this is especially so during the **S phase** of the **cell cycle** when the protective **histone proteins** that usually shield the DNA temporarily leave it, allowing the DNA to replicate. However, normal cells are also sensitive to radiation. This problem is alleviated by placing the patient on a table around which a beam of radiation can be rotated as indicated in Figure 22.4. The path the radiation takes is carefully calculated to ensure that the tumour is at the centre of rotation.

Various types of radiation are used in radiotherapy. **X-rays** are perhaps the most common; **gamma rays** from cobalt and caesium are also used widely. **Electrons** from linear accelerators may be more suitable than X-rays and gamma rays for certain sorts of radiotherapy. **Neutron beams** are also being developed. It is worth stressing that after receiving radiotherapy, the person is not radioactive.

Many chemical substances can be used to treat cancers. This is what is meant by **chemotherapy**. Chemotherapeutic drugs work by attacking cells either when they are synthesising DNA or while they are dividing. One great advantage of chemotherapy over surgery or radiotherapy is that it can work even when the cancer has spread from its primary site to other parts of the body. The larger a tumour is, the slower its cells tend to divide. This means that chemotherapy is more effective with small tumours. Chemotherapy is often most effective if two or three different drugs can be used in combination. It seems as though some cancers can overcome the effect of a single chemotherapeutic drug. Another reason for using several drugs in combination is that each may operate in a different way. Together they will provide the greatest opportunity of getting rid of the cancer.

Nowadays surgery, radiotherapy and chemotherapy are often used in conjunction with one another to treat cancers. Often such an approach is more effective than using just one type of treatment on its own. Another approach which is sometimes useful is **hormone therapy**. Early this century a Scottish doctor called George Beatson found that the flow of milk in sheep is at least partly controlled by the activities of the ovaries. The ovaries of sheep produce hormones which are carried round the body and affect the mammary glands. Soon after Beatson discovered this, he was called upon to treat two women who both had very advanced breast cancer. At that time such a condition was almost always fatal. Beatson operated to remove their ovaries in the hope that by severing the hormonal link between the ovaries and the breasts, he might arrest the growth of the tumour. Amazingly, his experiment was a partial success: in one of the two patients the tumour grew smaller and almost disappeared.

Nowadays hormone therapy is used to help treat a number of cancers. For example, the drug tamoxifen can be used in the treatment of breast cancer. It blocks the action of oestrogen, which may otherwise cause a tumour to grow.

The future of cancer

It is extremely unlikely that a 'cure' will ever be found for cancer. As we have discussed, there are many different types of cancer with many different causes. Nevertheless, major advances in the understanding and treatment of cancer are occurring, and there are good reasons to expect fewer people to die of it.

Fewer people overall are smoking, as you can see from Figure 22.5, though there are some indications that more teenage girls are smoking now than in the past. Provided fewer people smoke, the incidence of lung cancer which is still largely incurable should decline. People do seem to be becoming more health conscious, particularly with regard to what they eat. If people eat more fibre, this should reduce the incidence of cancers of the colon and rectum. On the negative side, it is important to bear in mind that any major disaster at a nuclear power-station or the use of nuclear weapons could lead to an

increase in the number of cancer cases, possibly on a large scale.

New treatments are being developed for cancers, and great advances have already been made in the treatment of certain types. Testicular cancer used to be fatal in most cases; now over 90% of cases can be cured. In the late 1950s, only 2% of patients with acute lymphoblastic leukaemia (a childhood cancer of immature blood cells) were alive five years after diagnosis. By the early 1980s, the figure had risen to 47%.

The aim of **immunotherapy** is to strengthen the body's own immune system, allowing it to combat cancer cells more effectively. One approach being investigated is to remove part of a tumour, kill the cells by irradiation, and then inject them into the patient's bloodstream. The cancer cells, though dead, should still carry on their surfaces antigens characteristic of the cancer, allowing the body's **lymphocytes** to produce antibodies against the antigens.

22.6   This child lived 50 kilometres from Chernobyl, yet the measured radiation levels were so high that the population was evacuated

22.5   The decline of cigarette smoking in Britain

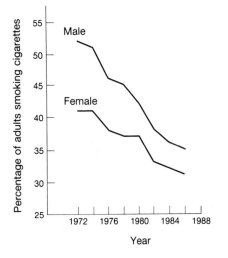

Advances are being made in radiotherapy. New ways are being found to increase the sensitivity of cancer cells to radiation. For instance, it is known that large tumours become starved of oxygen which reduces their sensitivity to radiation. As a result, artificial blood substitutes are being investigated to try and increase the oxygen supply to tumours before radiotherapy. Other approaches under investigation include neutron therapy and new techniques involving neon and argon ions.

There is every likelihood that significant advances in chemotherapy and immunotherapy will continue to be made. One very promising line of attack involves the use of so-called 'magic bullets': these consist of a toxic drug attached to an antibody specific to cancer cells. A different approach involves the use of **monoclonal antibodies** to stimulate the body's white blood cells into greater activity (see also Chapter 16).

Another promising area involves the use of **recombinant DNA technology** to synthesise chemicals such as interferon and interleukin which help to combat infection and which are released by certain cells. Interferon has already proved useful in the treatment of hairy cell leukaemia and Kaposi's sarcoma. It is hoped that interleukin 2 can stimulate lymphocyte activity, though early trials have given mixed results.

Finally, major advances in molecular biology mean that more is now understood about the molecular basis of cancer. It is too early to predict whether such knowledge will lead to significant reductions in the number of cancers. However, during the last hundred years an understanding of the biology of infectious organisms has led in many countries to huge reductions in the incidence of infectious diseases. So perhaps the fear of cancer may yet become a thing of the past.

Further reading

Sikora, K. and Smedley, H. (1988) *Cancer*. Heinemann Medical Student Reviews
Williams, C. (1988) *Cancer*. Family Doctor Publications.
Young, P. and Dudley, H.A.F. (1986) *Guide to Cancer*. Churchill Livingstone.

Useful organisations

BACUP (British Association of Cancer United Patients), 121–123 Charterhouse Street, London EC1M 6AA. Tel. 071 608 1661. Produces an excellent series of booklets on all the major cancers. Also provides free confidential information and professional advice and support to cancer patients, their families and friends.
Health Education Authority, 78 New Oxford Street, London WC1A 1AH. Tel. 071 637 1881. Produces a large number of helpful leaflets including one entitled *So You Want To Stop Smoking*.
Women's National Cancer Control Campaign, 1 South Audley Street, London W1Y 5DQ. Tel. 071 499 7532/7534. Produces some excellent leaflets, such as *Everyone's Doing the Breast Test!* and *Everyone's Having the Smear Test!* Also runs several mobile clinics and organises screening for women in local shopping centres and at their place of work.

Thought questions

1 If we all knew more about cancer, would we alter our behaviour to reduce the risks?

2 Should more be taught about cancer in schools?

3 What could the government do to reduce deaths from cancer?

'Europe against Cancer' is a campaign to encourage people to take action to reduce the number of deaths from cancer in Europe by 15%. Countries in the European Community are publicising a ten-point code based on current knowledge and early detection.
- Smokers, stop as quickly as possible!
- Go easy on the alcohol
- Avoid being overweight
- Take care in the sun
- Observe the Health and Safety regulations at work
- Cut down on fatty foods
- Eat plenty of fresh fruit and vegetables and other foods containing fibre
- See your doctor if there is any unexplained change in your normal health which lasts for more than two weeks
- Women, have a regular cervical smear test
- Women, examine your breasts monthly

23
Transplantation Today

Patients suffering from life-threatening diseases of organs or tissues may be treated with drugs or by surgical removal of the affected part. However, certain organs such as the heart, liver and kidneys are vital to life and their functions must be maintained if a patient is to live. This may sometimes be achieved through **transplantation**. It involves the replacement of the diseased or damaged organs or tissues with healthy ones. Although transplants are often rejected by the body, the rejection may be overcome. In attempting to solve the problem of rejection our understanding of the immune system has increased. Complex ethical issues surround the future of 'spare part surgery'.

Types of transplants

Transplants can be of several types, depending on the relationship between the donor and the recipient:

- **autograft** – a transplant from one part to another of the same body
- **isograft** – a transplant between identical twins, i.e. genetically identical
- **allograft** – a transplant between non-genetically identical individuals of the same species
- **xenograft** – a transplant between individuals of different species.

Autografting has long been successfully practised. In one of the oldest surgical texts known, the Indian Susruta, the creation of false noses by autografting is clearly described. The demand for such transplants was due to the laws of the time, which prescribed cutting off the nose as a punishment for adultery!

The use of dead bodies as donors for allografts was also established very early. A fifteenth-century painting, attributed to Girolamo da Cremona, depicts the legend of Saint Cosmas and Saint Damian (Figure 23.1). The saints transplanted a leg from a man who had recently died to a sleeping patient from whom they had removed a cancerous leg. According to legend, the transplant was a complete success.

It was not until 1954, however, that the successful transplantation of an organ from one person to another became a reality. Much of the success of this operation may be attributed to the fact that it was an isograft, the donor of the healthy kidney being the identical twin of the sick patient. As such, he was genetically identical to his twin brother.

Isografts are not often possible. Most transplant surgery apart from skin grafts involves allografts. It

23.1 Reproduction of part of a painting, attributed to Givolamo da Cremona, of Saint Cosma and Saint Damian who has just completed the successful transplant of a leg from a dead donor to a sleeping patient

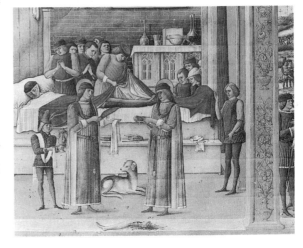

became apparent during early work in the 1920s that although transplanted kidneys were initially fully functional, they soon failed and were destroyed over a period of days or weeks. It was subsequently found that the **rejection** of the grafted organ was caused by the immune response of the recipient.

Rejection

Unless the implanted tissue or organ is obtained from a genetically identical individual, it will be recognised as 'non-self' by the recipient's body and will elicit an immune response (see Chapter 16). Rejection has been shown to be caused mainly by **cell-mediated immunity**, in other words by T-cells. Rejection may be immediate or, if it occurs at all, it may begin one to two weeks after the operation. Signs of rejection are fever in the patient and swelling of the graft which soon fails to function.

On the surface of all human cells there are molecules which are recognised by other individuals as foreign antigens. Antibodies are produced against them. The occurrence of these antigens makes the avoidance of rejection a complex and difficult process. Two systems of cell recognition are important. There are the antigens of the **ABO blood-group system** and the **human leucocyte antigens** (HLAs), which are found on lymphocytes and other tissues. The HLAs, which comprise a group of several hundred antigenic proteins, are coded for by the Major Histocompatibility Complex. This is a group of genes, each with multiple alleles, which is present on chromosome 6. There are two major HLA groups. The first has three series, HLA-A, HLA-B and HLA-C, which are expressed on the surface of all cells of the body. The second group, which is expressed on B-lymphocytes but also occurs on some T-lymphocytes and other cells, consists of the HLA-D and HLA-DR series.

The more closely related two people are, the more similar are their genotypes and the likelihood of their possessing similar antigens. Prior to transplantation every attempt is made to 'match' as closely as possible the tissue type of the donor with that of the recipient. Usually the HLA-A and HLA-B antigens are used in tissue typing but the DR antigens may also be included to improve the assessment of tissue compatibility.

Unless an identical twin or possibly a sibling is used, only partial matching and hence partial avoidance of rejection is possible. If transplantation is to be successful rejection must be minimised.

Prevention of rejection

Two main methods are used to prevent or reduce rejection: tissue matching and immunosuppression.

Tissue matching is carried out both for blood-group and histocompatibility antigens. A patient can receive a transplant only from a donor with a compatible blood group. Otherwise, transplantation will result in an immediate rejection of the graft due to agglutination of the blood. For tissue antigens, as close a match as possible is required.

Immunosuppression involves an enforced reduction in the activity of the immune system. Early attempts at immunosuppression caused the collapse of the patient's defences against disease. The challenge to the transplant surgeon has always been how to suppress tissue rejection without destroying the body's capacity to defend itself. There are five methods of immunosuppression, described below.

Total body irradiation

This was an early form of immunosuppression which involved exposing the whole body to X-rays. A sufficient dose destroyed the immune system, so preventing the possibility of rejection. However, it also resulted in damage to the bone marrow and the gastro-intestinal tract, leading to an unacceptable death rate.

Irradiation of bone marrow and lymphoid tissues

This is a more localised X-ray treatment which inhibits production of blood cells. The reduced numbers of leucocytes results in a slower rejection, although serious side-effects including severe anaemia and cancer often result.

Chemical immunosuppression

Chemical immunosuppression employs drugs which inhibit the production of lymphocytes. Since the 1950s, the most widely used drugs have been **azothioprine** and the steroid hormone **prednisolene**. Although effective at low doses in limiting rejection by reducing the activity of the immune response, these drugs render the patient highly susceptible to all infections. They may also cause side-effects. The formation of tumours and damage to the skeleton and skin is not uncommon in patients treated with these drugs.

During the mid 1970s a new drug, **cyclosporine**, was developed from a fungal peptide. It has a lower toxicity to the patient than the earlier drugs had. Also, it acts selectively in preventing rejection without greatly reducing the patient's overall resistance to infection. Cyclosporine can, however, cause nephrotoxicity (poisoning of the kidney tissue) but this is reversible if the drug dosage is reduced.

Suppression of T-cell activity

Two main techniques have been developed which specifically suppress the T-lymphocytes responsible for the cell-mediated rejection process, while the antibody-producing B-cells remain almost fully functional. Consequently, rejection is controlled while resistance to general infection is maintained.

Anti-lymphocyte immunoglobulin (ALG)

Using the immune system of another mammal such as a horse, the injection of human T-lymphocytes may be used to raise anti-T-cell antibodies, known as **anti-lymphocyte immunoglobulin (ALG)** (see Figure 23.3). The antibodies are collected and purified, and then injected into a transplant patient. In combination with drugs, ALG is effective in preventing rejection even where the donor and recipient are unrelated.

Drawbacks with ALG are that it can destroy platelets because of shared platelet and lymphocyte antigens (this will harm the patient's blood-clotting mechanism). Also, patients treated with ALG remain susceptible to viral infections in which protection depends on cell-mediated immunity.

Monoclonal antibodies (see Chapter 16)

Orthoclone OKT-3 is a **monoclonal antibody** which destroys T-cells by reacting specifically with the OKT-3 antigen found on the surface of all T-cells. The antibody has proved to be more effective than drugs in preventing kidney rejection, and less likely to cause side-effects or permanent damage to the patient. Reversible side-effects such as nausea, fever, chills and chest pains have, however, been reported.

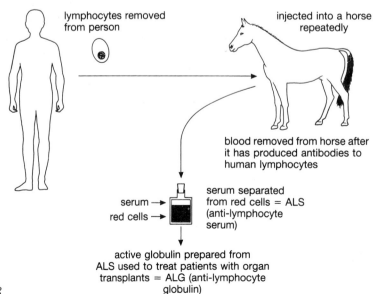

lymphocytes removed from person

injected into a horse repeatedly

blood removed from horse after it has produced antibodies to human lymphocytes

serum →
red cells →

serum separated from red cells = ALS (anti-lymphocyte serum)

active globulin prepared from ALS used to treat patients with organ transplants = ALG (anti-lymphocyte globulin)

23.2 The methods used to produce anti-lymphocyte globulin (ALG)

None of the above methods of immunosuppression is without risk. However, they represent a vital component of the transplantation procedure.

Replacement of tissues

Tissues, rather than whole organs, may be replaced. The most important of these are blood, skin, bone marrow, the cornea of the eye, pancreatic tissue and nervous tissue.

Blood

Transplants of the liquid tissue, blood, are routine operations. Successful transfusions depend on the compatibility of the blood groups of the donor and recipient, as shown in Table 23.1. The different **blood groups** are determined genetically. They depend on the presence or absence of the antigenic mucopolysaccharides A and B (known as agglutinogens) on the surface of red blood cells. A person with blood group A possesses only antigen A; similarly, only antigen B is present on the erythrocytes of a group B person. Some people possess both A and B antigens (group AB), and others have neither of them (group O). In addition, there are in the blood plasma antibodies (agglutinins) against the antigen which is not expressed on the erythrocyte membrane. It follows, then, that a person with one antigen type can accept blood either from a donor with the same antigen type, or from a donor of group O who has no antigens. A person with both antigen A and antigen B can accept blood from a donor of any of the other groups (universal recipient). A person of group O with no antigens can donate blood to people of all blood groups (universal donor). However, due to the presence in the plasma of both anti-A and anti-B antibodies, he or she can accept blood only from another person with no antigens.

Prior to any transplant operation, the recipient's serum is tested for antibodies against the red blood cell antigens from the donor to ensure compatibility.

Skin

Skin grafting is a standard procedure for the treatment of burns and for cosmetic surgery. As an autograft, it is generally successful. In cases of severe burns, allografts from donors may be used. They are useful only as a temporary measure as, even with immunosuppressive treatment, vigorous rejection of skin allografts usually occurs. Nevertheless, the short-term protective barrier created by the allografts greatly helps the patient to resist infection.

Skin may be taken from corpses shortly after death and stored in liquid nitrogen until needed.

With the recent major advances in the development of skin substitutes, the techniques of skin allografting may soon become redundant.

Bone marrow

Bone marrow transplantation may be carried out in patients with **leukaemia** or severe **anaemia**. The donor must possess histocompatibility antigens which are identical to those of the patient. Consequently, either an identical twin or a sibling is used. As shown in Figure 23.3, there is a one-in-four chance that two siblings will have inherited

Group	Erythrocyte membrane antigens	Plasma antibodies	Accepts blood from group	Can donate blood to group
O	none	anti-A, B	O	A,B,AB,O
A	A	anti-B	A,O	A,AB
B	B	anti-A	B,O	B,AB
AB	AB	none	A,B,AB,O	AB

Table 23.1

169

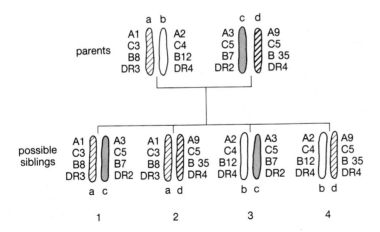

23.3 Each of the children, 1 to 4, has a half chance of receiving one of the two parental pairs of chromosomes, a or b and c or d respectively. There is therefore a probability that one in four siblings will be HLA identical

identical HLA alleles from their parents (providing there is no crossing over).

Bone marrow transplantation has the unique and often fatal complication of **graft-versus-host disease (GVHD)**. This occurs due to the presence of lymphocytes in the transplanted marrow which recognise the patient as foreign and so mount an immune response against him or her. Even in patients who have successful transplants, GVHD occurs to some extent. Once established, GVHD is difficult to treat and, of the patients who suffer from severe symptoms, over 70% die. However, the use of cyclosporine or the pre-treatment of the marrow transplant with OKT-3 to destroy mature T-lymphocytes will lessen the risk of GVHD.

Cornea

Since the 1950s, corneal transplantation has been routinely performed to restore sight. There is no need for tissue typing or for immunosuppression because rejection will not occur unless the graft becomes vascularised, that is, tiny blood vessels form.

Corneas may be obtained from dead people of any age.

Pancreatic islet cells

In patients suffering from **diabetes mellitus**, the islets of Langerhans, which are groups of cells found throughout the pancreas, fail to secrete

sufficient insulin. Without insulin replacement therapy, high levels of blood sugar build up and result ultimately in metabolic failure, coma and death. Even with therapy, diabetics have a decreased life expectancy and may suffer heart disease, blindness, kidney failure and disorders of the nervous system.

The ability to transplant the whole pancreas is one of the most recent advances in transplantation surgery. At present, the survival rate for the operation is about 45% in the first year. In 1989, isolated insulin-secreting cells were successfully transplanted into two diabetic patients. Cells placed in the peritoneum, the membrane lining the abdominal cavity, proceeded to secrete insulin. The transplantation of isolated cells rather than the whole pancreas has several advantages: it involves simple surgery; less immunosuppression is required and no matching of tissues is necessary. Also, since islet cells can be frozen and stored indefinitely, it is no longer necessary to carry out a transplant operation within hours of an organ becoming available. To date, there is a 50% survival rate for transplanted islet cells after one year.

Nervous tissue

Recently, the potential for treating sufferers from Parkinson's disease by using embryonic nerve cells taken from the brains of aborted foetuses has been demonstrated. **Parkinson's disease** is a degenerative disease of the brain which is characterised by rigid muscles, trembling hands and an inability to perform voluntary movements. The main cause is the death of cranial nerve cells which produce the neurotransmitter dopamine. When foetal nerve cells are grafted into the brain of a patient there is surprisingly little immune response and no tissue rejection. The cells divide rapidly and produce dopamine. Several months after a transplant, patients are found to have regained considerable movement. This form of foetal tissue transplant treatment for Parkinson's disease is highly controversial for obvious reasons.

Replacement of organs

Apart from kidney transplants where the donor may be living, organs for transplantation are obtained from people (including foetuses) who have recently died. In such cases the donor must be an individual who is 'brain dead': that is, the brain has been irreversibly destroyed. This may be as a result of a tumour or of an accident involving trauma or haemorrhage to the brain. The tissues of such a brain-dead person may be kept biologically alive on a life-support machine (maintaining ventilation and blood flow). In such cases organs are removed from

brain-dead donors without delay. They are then perfused (washed through) with specialised solutions at low temperature (4⁰C) and then stored, surrounded by crushed ice.

Kidneys

Each year in the United Kingdom alone, some 2500 people develop chronic kidney disease. For these people a **kidney transplant** is a viable alternative to death through renal failure or to a regime of **dialysis** which is both disruptive to the patient's life and costly. Dialysis, which must be carried out every few days, involves the circulation of the blood from the body through a machine for filtration of unwanted waste materials. The cleaned blood then returns to the body. In the United Kingdom it costs more than £15 000 to provide dialysis for one patient for a year.

About 1500 kidney transplants are carried out in Britain each year, although there are 3000–4000 people awaiting operations. The failed kidney is usually left in place and the donated organ is implanted in the lower abdomen near the groin. The renal blood supply of the donor kidney is attached (anastamosed) to the recipient's iliac

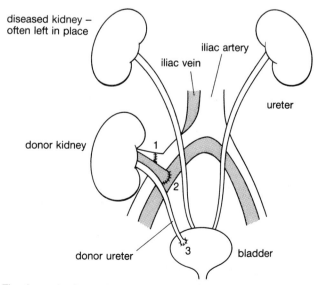

23.4 A donor kidney is transplanted into the lower abdomen with an iliac blood supply

The donor renal vessels are attached to the iliac vessels of the recipient at (1) and (2); the ureter draining urine is implanted into the bladder (3).

artery and vein, and the ureter is connected to the top of the recipient's bladder (Figure 23.4).

The survival rate for kidney transplants is high – over 90% after one year for transplantation between HLA-identical patients, and about 70% using a kidney from an HLA-matched corpse. Some recipients of kidney grafts are now alive and fully rehabilitated 20 years after the operation. There are several reasons for this success rate. First, although it must be carried out within 24–28 hours of obtaining the donor kidney, the transplant operation is relatively straightforward, mainly because the kidney has a simple vascular supply. Second, by using the proper functioning of the ureter as an indicator, the success of the operation can be established within minutes and subsequently monitored. Also, the kidney is a paired organ and it is perfectly possible for a healthy person to survive with only one kidney. This permits close tissue-matching and consequently a reduced likelihood of rejection. However, should rejection occur, a patient can be sustained in a relatively stable condition by dialysis until another kidney becomes available for transplant.

Liver

Liver transplantation was pioneered in the United States and was first carried out in England during 1968 by Sir Roy Calne in Cambridge. The operation is used in cases of progressive and otherwise fatal liver disease for patients of any age up to 65. The main considerations prior to transplantation are blood-group compatibility and, especially in the case of young patients, the size of the available organ.

Liver transplant operations will probably never be as widely performed as kidney transplants for several reasons. First, the liver has a complicated blood supply and consequently the transplant operation is technically very demanding. Removal of the diseased liver is difficult, and when the donor organ is in place the inferior and superior vena cavae, the hepatic artery and hepatic portal vein must be reconnected. A major problem is the connection of the biliary tract, which runs from the donor gall bladder to the recipient's small intestine (Figure 23.5). An added complication is that patients with liver disease suffer from poor blood clotting and so have a tendency to bleed heavily. Despite these problems, with the use of immuno-suppressive drugs which are vital to prevent rejection, the predicted survival rate for one year for all patients is over 75% and as high as 80% for young patients. Some people have lived as long as 12 years following successful liver transplants. Recently, surgeons in Australia transplanted part of a woman's liver into her one-year-old son. This is

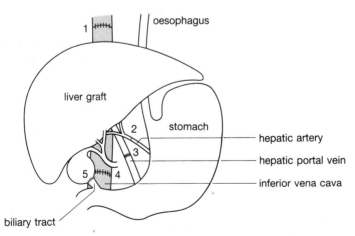

Connections made between recipient's vessels and donor liver:
1. inferior vena cava above liver; 2. hepatic artery; 3. portal vein;
4. inferior vena cava below liver; 5. gall bladder of donor to biliary tract of recipient.

23.5 A donor liver is transplanted into the upper abdomen, replacing the diseased liver. Five different points of connection are required

the first report of a liver transplant involving a living donor, and the prognosis for both mother and child is good.

Heart and heart-lung

The first **heart transplant** operation was carried out in South Africa by Christian Barnard during 1967. Although the patient did not survive, the operation attracted much attention, possibly due to the universal sentiment that the heart is the very seat of life.

Heart transplantation began in the United Kingdom in 1979. Patients are considered for the operation if they are aged between 1 and 60, have severe cardiac failure, no longer respond to medical treatment and have a life expectancy of only 6–12 months. Matching is carried out for blood group and chest size. The operation, which lasts 3–5 hours, involves relatively simple surgery. Much of the recipient's atria, vena cavae and pulmonary veins are left in place and the donor heart is connected to these (Figure 23.6). During the operation the patient's blood is circulated and oxygenated artificially.

Following transplant surgery rejection is a major problem and can be monitored only by observing small samples of heart tissue under the microscope. These samples are obtained by inserting a fine tube directly into the heart.

All heart transplant patients must take immuno-suppressive drugs to prevent rejection, although these often cause kidney damage and high blood pressure. A common post-operative problem is that of atherosclerosis in the coronary arteries, so anticoagulant and antithrombotic drugs must also be taken. However, there is no doubt that a heart transplant increases life expectancy and improves the quality of life for patients. Over 80% of patients lead independent lives within a year of the operation, and more than half are still alive after five years.

For patients suffering from cardiac failure and lung disease, a heart-lung transplant operation may be carried out. Survival rates for this operation are around 75% for one year.

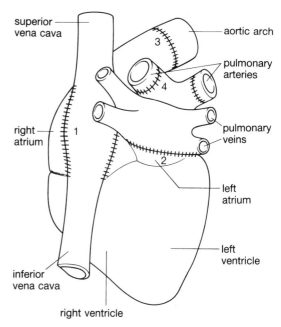

Connections made between the donor heart and the recipient's vessels: 1. right atrium; 2. left atrium; 3. aorta; 4. pulmonary arteries.

23.6 A donor heart is sutured (stitched) to the recipients major arteries and veins (from Hobson's Science Support (1988))

Transplantation in perspective

Despite the major medical advances in transplantation surgery, many **social and moral implications** of these procedures remain unresolved. They are discussed below.

Transplant surgery does not attempt to address the underlying causes of tissue and organ disease. It aims for cure rather than prevention. Would money be better spent on primary research into the diseases?

The cost of transplant operations is relatively high: a heart transplant, for example, costs about £13 000 for the first six months and £2000–£3000 each year after that to cover check-ups and drug therapy. Are potential transplant patients more deserving of treatment than patients suffering from diabetes or multiple sclerosis? On the other hand, the cost can sometimes be argued to be low. The alternative to a kidney transplant patient is death or dialysis. Currently, £15 000 per patient per year is being spent on dialysis; each kidney transplant costs about £20 000. Kidney transplantion costs are therefore balanced out in little over a year after the operation.

On what basis ought the selection of organ recipients to be made? In the United Kingdom the policy is to choose on the grounds of suitability of blood group and, if necessary, tissue type of the patient without regard to status, sex, race or creed. However, renal patients who are diabetic, older than 65 or who have medical complications other than kidney failure are not considered for transplant surgery. This is not the case in the United States, where all kidney patients are given an equal chance of a transplant. In the United States and in Holland there is a computerised register of potential recipients which includes tissue-typing information. These systems provide the potential for rapid selection of recipients, and regional or international exchange of donated organs. Obviously the resources available have a direct bearing on the numbers of transplant operations performed.

It is very difficult to assess whether the degree of rehabilitation of patients justifies the expense of transplantation. An important factor is that the failure rate of transplant operations is high and this can be extremely psychologically damaging for everyone involved. If successful, the operation certainly extends a patient's life, but the ability of liver transplant patients, for example, to achieve a satisfactory quality of life has been questioned. Can a value be placed on quality of life?

A major procedural difficulty is obtaining sufficient organs to be transplanted. In the case of potential living donors, great care must be taken to exclude any moral or social pressure to donate. In Europe only 9% of transplanted kidneys are from related donors, this perhaps reflecting an unwillingness to put pressure on relatives and also recognising that there is undoubtedly a risk to the donor.

The removal of organs from a brain-dead donor is considered by many people to be an ethical procedure, provided that the individual in his or her lifetime would not have wished otherwise. Some unease has been expressed over the definition of brain death, though there is a very rigorous code of practice to be applied in every case. Medical staff must obtain permission from next-of-kin before removing organs and this must be handled very sensitively.

Fifteen states in the United States have enacted 'required request' laws by which hospital staff are legally obliged to ask relatives of all dead patients who are potential donors for permission to remove organs. The numbers of organs donated in these states increased immediately the laws came into effect. Most European countries allow doctors to remove organs from a dead patient unless that individual had specified otherwise (an 'opting out' system); in the United Kingdom however, a **donor card system** operates which means that written consent to become a donor must be given. Consequently, organs often go to waste after the death of people who failed during their lifetime to give consent.

The sale or purchase of organs is a controversial issue. In Britain, people caught trading in organs face fines of up to £2000 or a prison sentence. However, there is no national register of organ removals from live donors and so it is almost impossible to identify payments for human organs. Some people believe that trade in organs ought to be permissible. First, it would increase the supply of organs; and second, it would help the donor to provide financially for his or her family. However, it is likely to be the poor and the powerless, such as the Turks who sold their kidneys to a London hospital in 1989, who put themselves at risk. The legal perspective is that the sale of an organ is an act of such desperation that voluntary consent is impossible.

With improved control of rejection, xenografts (between, for example, other mammals and humans) could become a reality. If it became possible to transplant organs between species, many of the present ethical concerns would be resolved. We routinely slaughter animals for food, so would it be any less acceptable to use animals' organs for the treatment of humans?

Further reading

Anon. (1988) *Transplants for the Body. Biology Now!* Hobsons Science Support.

Calne, R. (1970) *A Gift of Life.* MTP

Also, for general information on immunology:

Roberts, M.B.V (1986) *Biology, a Functional Approach.* Nelson.

Green, N.P.O., Stout, G.W. and Taylor, D.J. (1990) *Biological Science.*

Thought questions

1 Explain why immunosuppressant antibodies can only be used once or twice in a patient before they become ineffective.

2 Is transplantation really justified? How far should doctors go in time and expense to save human life?

Things to do

Do you carry a kidney donor card? If not, think about doing so – you can get a card from your doctor or health centre. You should be at least 18 years old to do this. In the event of your death someone else could have a much better life.

24
Cystic Fibrosis: The European Disease

Cystic fibrosis is the most common genetic disease in the United Kingdom. It affects a total of about 6000 people, and approximately 1 in every 2000 babies born suffers from the disease. Fifty years ago 80% of babies born with cystic fibrosis died before their first birthday. Nowadays this is no longer the case in the United Kingdom, though at present few survive beyond their twenties. However, a tremendous amount of research into the disease has been carried out over the last 10–15 years, and although a cure is not in sight there is every reason to expect that the next ten years will see major advances in the understanding and treatment of the condition.

What is cystic fibrosis?

Cystic fibrosis is a condition with a variety of symptoms. People with the disease have severe breathing problems and suffer from lung infections; their digestion is poor; they may develop diabetes; and their sweat glands produce abnormally salty sweat. Studying the pattern of inheritance of the trait in families, using so-called **pedigree analysis**, all the evidence implies that the condition is caused by a single recessive allele. People with the condition have two copies of the allele and are therefore nearly always the children of two **carriers** (heterozygous individuals).

So if cystic fibrosis is caused by a single faulty allele, rather than being a **polygenic** trait determined by the interaction of several genes, how come it has such a variety of effects? Most of the symptoms of the disease can be traced back to a single consequence of the faulty allele – the excessive production of abnormally thick and sticky mucus. In the lungs this thick mucus clogs up the delicate alveoli and smaller bronchioles. As a result breathing is difficult and the person is far more prone to lung infections and high blood pressure in the pulmonary arteries. In the pancreas the large amounts of sticky mucus block the exit for the pancreatic digestive enzymes produced there. Not surprisingly, a consequence of this is poor digestion as the enzymes fail to reach the small intestine. A further consequence is that the enzymes accumulate in the pancreas and may start to attack the pancreas itself. As a result the pancreas is literally eaten away, and the islets of Langerhans are destroyed. As these groups of cells produce insulin which helps regulate the blood sugar levels, diabetes can follow as the production of insulin ceases.

It is clear that several of the effects of cystic fibrosis stem from the excessive production of thick mucus. But what is the cause of the abnormally salty sweat produced by people with the disease? Recent research suggests that cystic fibrosis is caused by a failure in the regulation of a protein that forms an **ion channel** in the membrane of certain epithelial cells. The normal function of this channel is to control the passage of chloride ions. However, in people with cystic fibrosis the channel cannot be activated correctly. This disrupts the transport of chloride ions and water across the epithelium. As a result the epithelial cells that line the sweat ducts excrete too many negatively charged chloride ions; positively charged sodium ions follow to restore electroneutrality and the result is abnormally salty sweat. However, for epithelial cells that produce mucus the consequences are more severe and result in the production of extremely thick (non-watery) mucus. The net result is that the cystic fibrosis allele has several **phenotypic effects,** for which reason it is said to show **pleiotropy**.

Treatment of cystic fibrosis

As you can see from Figure 24.1, there has been a dramatic increase in the average life expectancy of people with cystic fibrosis. As recently as 1970 most people with the disease died before they reached five. Now many are living into their twenties. This improvement is due to developments in the diagnosis and management of cystic fibrosis. It is particularly apparent among patients who attend specialist centres providing expert care. People with cystic fibrosis in social classes I and II (non-manual occupations) tend to live several years longer than those who come from working-class families. This may reflect difficulties in getting to specialist centres which are few and far between: it helps to have a car. The class difference in survival may also be caused by such factors as parental smoking and poorer housing both of which are more common in working-class families.

High-quality **physiotherapy**, as illustrated in

24.1 Average (median) age of death for people in England and Wales with cystic fibrosis plotted against the year of their death

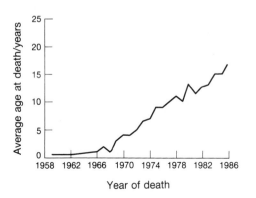

Figure 24.2, can help to reduce the effects of mucus accumulation in the lungs and significantly increases life expectancy. Treatments for chest infections include taking **antibiotics** and using **bronchodilators** that relax the muscles in the bronchi and make breathing easier. The problems caused by poor digestion can be alleviated by eating a high-protein and high-calorie diet. The reduced supply of enzymes from the pancreas can be compensated for by swallowing capsules that contain pancreatic digestive enzymes. The enzymes are released after the capsules have passed through the stomach, allowing at least some digestion to take place in the small intestine. Vitamin supplements should be given routinely. Gallstones may be a problem, but can be treated relatively easily. Diabetes can be treated by insulin injections. Finally, it should be remembered that even with the best available medical treatment, patients with cystic fibrosis rarely live longer than 35 years. It is perhaps surprising that psychological problems such as depression are not reported more often than they are. Careful counselling and the use of support networks among fellow patients help.

A rather more dramatic treatment for cystic fibrosis is a heart-lung transplant. Here the new lung tissue, coming from the donor, lacks the two copies of the cystic fibrosis allele and so makes normal bronchial mucus. As discussed in Chapter 23, the success rate of these operations has increased greatly in recent years. It is unlikely that heart-lung transplants will ever be given to more than a minority of people with cystic fibrosis. It is possible, though, that recent advances in molecular biology may help patients. This prospect has been helped by the recent discovery of the gene responsible for cystic fibrosis.

Finding the gene for cystic fibrosis

'This is one of the most significant discoveries in the history of human genetics.' Thus the chief geneticist at the Hospital for Sick Children in Toronto described the announcement on 24 August 1989 that his colleagues had cloned the gene responsible for cystic fibrosis. How did they do

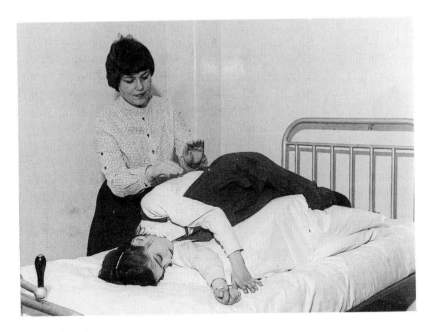

24.2 Physiotherapy plays an important part in the management of cystic fibrosis. Heavy clapping on the back helps to dislodge the viscous mucus in the lungs, while breathing exercises increase the flow of air into the lungs

it? The interesting thing is that Lap-Chee Tsui and Jack Riordan at the hospital in Toronto and Francis Collins at the University in Michigan managed it without even knowing what protein the gene makes! This is the opposite of what happened, for instance, in work on various genetic blood disorders such as sickle-cell anaemia. There, investigators first worked out what the faults in the proteins were and then, many years later, located the genes responsible.

The strategy used by the researchers trying to pinpoint the gene for cystic fibrosis involved the use of **genetic markers**. This requires finding some natural variation either in a piece of DNA or in a protein linked to the cystic fibrosis gene. Such **linkage** is demonstrated when pedigree analyses show that the genetic marker and the cystic fibrosis gene fail to segregate independently. In 1985 researchers at the University of Copenhagen found that a polymorphism in the gene that makes a protein called paraoxonose was linked to the cystic fibrosis gene, so that the two genes occur on the same chromosome. Soon afterwards other researchers succeeded in showing that the gene for paraoxonose is located on chromosome 7.

Evidently the gene for cystic fibrosis also occurs on chromosome 7, as it is linked to the gene for paraoxonose. But precisely where is it located? Using the latest techniques of molecular genetics, Tsui, Riordan and Collins finally succeeded in pinpointing its exact position. The main approach they used was one called **chromosome walking**. This involves cutting up human DNA using restriction endonucleases (see Chapter 9). The sequences of these fragments can then be investigated.

Tsui, Riordan and Collins could concentrate on fragments close to the gene for paraoxonose. Eventually they found what they were looking for: a gene close to the gene for paraoxonose whose nucleotide sequence matched that of a gene known to be active in sweat glands. The gene turned out, as expected, to code for a membrane protein which has been called the **cystic fibrosis transmembrane conductance regulator** or **CFTR** for short. The protein proved to be very large and was present only in small quantities which no doubt explains why cell physiologists had not already isolated and identified it. Sixty-eight per cent of cases of cystic fibrosis seem to be caused by the loss of one amino acid about one-third of the way along the molecule. Apparently the loss of this amino acid disrupts a key binding site for ATP, which is probably required for the normal functioning of CTFR.

How will the identification of the gene for cystic fibrosis help? Now that the primary sequence of the protein it makes is known, it should not be long before its tertiary structure has been worked out by X-ray crystallography. Once that has been done it will be much easier for pharmacologists to design drugs to correct the fault in the membrane transport. This will be a significant breakthrough as the drugs currently used in the treatment of cystic fibrosis can only treat the secondary infections that result from the accumulation of the large amounts of sticky mucus. A drug that reduced the production of the mucus might make a huge difference. Producing and testing new drugs takes a long time, though, and the **Cystic Fibrosis Research Trust** estimates that it will be five to ten years before one is on the market.

Another possibility for the treatment of cystic fibrosis, now that the gene has been identified, would almost amount to a cure. Groups in Edinburgh and at St Mary's in London are working on ways to insert a normal gene into the lung cells themselves. Such **gene therapy** is probably many years from realisation. If it ever comes about, then humans themselves will have been 'genetically engineered'.

Gene therapy, and even the advent of designer drugs for cystic fibrosis, lie in the future. A more immediate consequence of the localisation of the gene for cystic fibrosis is that it facilitates the accuracy with which screening and genetic counselling can be done.

Screening and genetic counselling

Most children born with cystic fibrosis are born to couples who did not realise that they were carriers for the faulty allele. Now that the allele has been identified, it is relatively easy to tell whether or not someone is heterozygous at that locus. Such a test became available at the end of 1989, and in June 1990 a large-scale **genetic screening programme** started in Britain. The study involves participants either giving a tiny sample of blood obtained by a finger-prick, or washing the mouth out so that loose cells can be collected. In both cases the DNA from the cells is extracted, multiplied up and examined for the presence of the faulty allele.

It is hoped that up to 20 000 people will be tested in the trial, which is the first large-scale

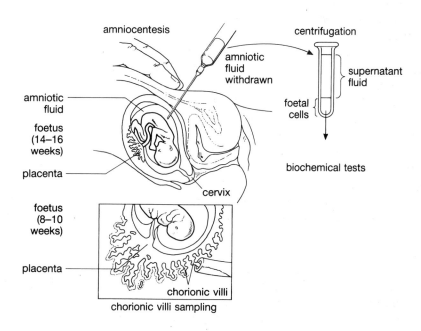

24.3 Amniocentesis and chorionic villus sampling compared

genetic screening programme ever carried out in Britain. Screening is being done in Edinburgh, London and Cardiff where people attending certain GP surgeries and antenatal clinics will be offered the test. However, although a positive result means that the person definitely is a carrier, a negative result only means that the person is about 80% certain not to be a carrier. The reason for this is that although most cases of cystic fibrosis are due to the mutation identified by Tsui and his colleagues, about 30% of cases are due to other mutations in the same gene.

It is interesting to compare this screening with the testing for HIV. Many people, and organisations such as the Terrence Higgins Trust, generally do not recommend testing for HIV on the grounds that nothing much is gained by taking the test, while a positive result if it becomes known may lead to discrimination: at work, from one's insurance company or even from family and friends. Being known to be a carrier of the cystic fibrosis allele does not appear to lead to any discrimination, however. The point of knowing whether one is a carrier is that if one is and one has a child, there is about a 1% chance that he or she will have cystic fibrosis.

Suppose a couple know that they are both heterozygous for the cystic fibrosis allele. What can genetic counselling offer? It is clear that there is a one-in-four chance that any child they have will suffer from cystic fibrosis. Until recently the only technique available to determine whether or not the baby would have cystic fibrosis was **amniocentesis**. In amniocentesis, analysis of cells from a foetus around 16–18 weeks post-conception allows affected individuals to be identified with about 95% certainty. In the unfortunate event of a foetus being found to be homozygous for the cystic fibrosis allele, the parents, or mother on her own, can choose whether to terminate the pregnancy, that is, have an abortion. Most mothers choose to do so.

More recently a technique known as **chorionic villus sampling** has been developed as outlined in Figure 24.3. It has two great advantages over amniocentesis. It can be carried out between 8 and 12 weeks post-conception and for the identification

of cystic fibrosis it is more reliable, being about 99% accurate. The procedure involves taking a sample from the villi of the chorion. These cells are foetal, not maternal, in origin. Once the cells have been collected their DNA is analysed to see if the foetus is homozygous for the faulty allele. The one disadvantage of this technique is that the frequency of spontaneous miscarriage after its use is slightly higher (by about 2%) than it would have been had the procedure not been carried out. The comparative figure for amniocentesis is about 0.5%.

Why is cystic fibrosis so common?

Given that about 1 in 2000 babies born to white people in Europe and the United States have cystic fibrosis, and given that cystic fibrosis is due to a recessive allele, you should be able to work out from the Hardy-Weinberg equation that between 1 in 20 and 1 in 25 whites carry the recessive allele. (If you are not familiar with Hardy-Weinberg calculations of the frequencies of alleles in populations, you can find description of the method in standard biology text books.) This is a remarkably high proportion compared to many other hereditary disorders such as Huntington's chorea or pheynlketonuria. What is the reason? The honest answer is that we still do not know for certain. One theory is that the condition shows **heterozygous advantage**. Although homozygous recessive sufferers are manifestly unfit in the Darwinian sense of having fewer children, perhaps heterozygous carriers are fitter than people who are homozygous for the normal dominant allele. This would mean that heterozygote carriers have more children than average, as indicated below.

Genotype	Phenotype	Darwinian fitness
Homozygous recessive	Sufferer from cystic fibrosis	Very low
Heterozygous	Normal	Slightly above average
Homozygous dominant	Normal	Average

This idea may seem far-fetched, but remember sickle-cell anaemia. This too is a very serious, often fatal condition caused by a recessive allele, yet in some parts of Africa it occurs in 1 in 40 people. The reason is that heterozygotes are more resistant to malaria than people homozygous for the normal allele. It has been suggested that people heterozygous for the cystic fibrosis allele may be more resistant to diarrhoea. Diarrhoea kills millions of people worldwide every year through dehydration (see Chapter 17). There is some evidence that people heterozygous for the cystic fibrosis allele lose less fluid when suffering from diarrhoea, because one of the effects of the allele is to decrease the loss of water from cells. It should be realised, though, that this theory is highly speculative. In particular it fails to explain why cystic fibrosis is very rare in non-whites.

Further reading

Bray, P. (1989) *Cystic Fibrosis – A Guide for Parents and Sufferers.* Souvenir Press / Human Horizon Series.
Davies, K. (1989) *The Search for the Cystic Fibrosis Gene.* New Scientist 21 October 1989, 54–58.

Further information

Cystic Fibrosis Research Trust, Alexandra House, 5 Blyth Road, Bromley, Kent BR1 3RS.

Thought questions

1 Explain how pedigree analysis can distinguish between the following types of inheritance: autosomal dominant; autosomal recessive; X-linked recessive.

2 If a person is known to be a carrier for the cystic fibrosis allele, why is there a 1% chance that a child born to that person will have cystic fibrosis?

3 If it eventually became possible to alter the genetic make-up of people so that they did not suffer from cystic fibrosis, would you approve unreservedly?

Things to do

Attitudes to genetic screening.
People can now be tested to see if they are carriers of sickle-cell anaemia; the first general population screening for the cystic fibrosis carrier status is currently under way. What are ordinary people's attitudes to the tests and to the diseases? Is it best to know or not to know? These are important questions for the future and current attitudes can be assessed objectively by a survey. See if you can conduct such a survey as part of your course. Make sure that the wording of the survey is carefully checked by your teacher before you begin.

25

Woodland Conservation

Trees have evolved to be tall because of competition between plants for light. Many species of tree grow to 20 or 30 m in height, and some to over 100 m. Due to their great size, trees take a long time to reach maturity. It is because trees take many years from germination to reproduction that woodland conservation is important. If a wood is cut down it takes a long time before it **regenerates**. Forest is the **climax vegetation** in many parts of the world.

This chapter will concentrate on woodland conservation in Britain. It is worth remembering, though, that huge areas of tropical rainforest are being cut down every year. Tragically, very little is gained from this. Although valuable wood is sometimes extracted, indigenous people are removed from their homes, huge areas of land are laid bare and countless species are lost for ever. Some people argue that all species have a right to life. In addition, even those who do not take that view agree that among the plant species we are losing through the destruction of tropical rainforests are many which could have yielded valuable products such as drugs for our use.

History of woodland in Britain

About 10 000 years ago (8000 BC) there were almost no trees in Britain. This was because the last glaciation was still retreating northwards. As our climate warmed and the ice retreated, trees were able to recolonise Britain, starting from the south and east.

The best evidence we have for the order in which trees recolonised Britain comes from **pollen analysis**. Despite the fact that pollen lives for only a short time, its outer wall, made from the complex lipid **sporopollenin**, is remarkably resistant to decay. As trees produce large amounts of pollen, identification of the pollen they have released since the last ice age, combined with **radiocarbon dating**, allows a botanist to determine which trees existed where and when.

Ten thousand years ago Britain was joined to the mainland of Europe by dry land: the sea-level was lower because so much water was frozen and trapped on land in glaciers. The first species of tree to spread from the continent was birch. About 7500 years ago pine invaded, followed by hazel, elm, oak and alder in that order. Lime invaded around 5500 BC, and hornbeam even later.

Until about 3000 BC almost the whole of Britain was covered with virgin forest, so called because it was almost entirely unaffected by human activity.

Throughout Great Britain and Ireland there was a sudden decrease in the amount of elm pollen from about 3100 to 2900 BC. This is known as the **Elm Decline**. It is associated with a sudden increase in farm weeds such as plantains and stinging nettles. Often there is also archaeological evidence of early **Neolithic** settlement. It is possible that in a land where there was as yet little grass, cattle may have been fed on leafy elm shoots obtained from trees on a short cutting cycle. This practice may have prevented the trees from flowering and producing pollen.

Thus widespread human influence on forests in Britain may have begun around 5000 years ago. Figure 25.1 shows the types of forest that existed in Britain before then.

During the Bronze Age (1700–500 BC) human

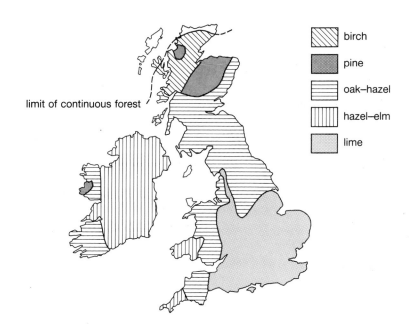

birch

pine

oak–hazel

hazel–elm

lime

limit of continuous forest

25.1 Regional variation in woodland in about 4500 BC showing the dominant tree species in the virgin forest of the British Isles. Derived from the work of John Birks and others

clearance of woodland continued and extended into higher ground. At the same time the climate became wetter and blanket bogs began to develop in parts of Scotland and Ireland, at the expense of the remaining forest. By about 400 BC iron tools and heavy ploughs were being used. These made agriculture possible even on heavy clay soils, and this led to the destruction of more woodland.

The Romans developed England and Wales into one of the chief agricultural and corn-exporting lands of the classical world. This development went hand-in-hand with disturbances to more of the virgin forest. Oliver Rackham has suggested that the last virgin forest in southern Britain may have been the Forest of Dean in Wales, in about 1150 AD. Even in Scotland no virgin forest remains today. (Strictly, the difference between a forest and a wood is that a forest is land outside human settlement and under Forest Law. Woods may be almost any size.)

This brief survey of the history of woodland in Britain should have made it clear that whatever is meant by woodland conservation in Britain, it cannot mean protecting existing woods in the hope of preserving virgin forest. We are too late for that. We could of course try to recreate a woodland which resembled primeval forest.

Why is woodland management necessary?

Given that all the woods in Britain have either been managed by humans, influenced by human activity or even planted by us, what would happen if they were simply left alone? In almost every instance the answer is that they would change over the years. Often they would become less **species-rich**. Frequently they would look less attractive. Successful **woodland management** requires clear management aims and is usually helped by a knowledge of the history of a particular wood.

Woods that have been planted need to be looked after; in particular the trees typically need to be thinned. **Thinning** is the practice of removing some of the young trees from a stand, so allowing the remaining trees to become larger and stronger. Without thinning, very little light penetrates so that even the trees suffer, while almost no ground flora may survive.

Many woods have had whole trees, stems and branches removed from them over the centuries, even if this is often no longer the case. Large trees may have been felled for the building of houses or ships. Branches or young stems may have been removed for fencing, fuel and other purposes.

183

Figure 25.2a shows part of Hayley Wood in Cambridgeshire just after **coppicing**. This traditional technique of woodland management involves cutting shrubs down almost to ground level. After about 6–15 years sufficient regrowth has occurred for coppicing to be worthwhile again. Figure 25.2b shows the same area of Hayley Wood five years after coppicing. We know from written documents that throughout medieval times many woods were coppiced regularly. One interesting consequence of coppicing is that more light penetrates to ground-level, often resulting in spectacular displays of bluebells, wood anemones and other flowers.

Woodland management can help to preserve the conditions necessary for rare species. The black hairstreak butterfly shown in Figure 25.3 is almost totally confined to ancient coppiced woodland. However, it is important that the coppice is not cut too frequently as its larvae feed on blackthorn (*Prunus spinosa*) which must have at least twenty years' growth.

A further reason why it may be necessary to manage woodland is to ensure regeneration of the wood. Excessive browsing may prevent young seedlings from growing into adult trees. Such browsing may be by domestic stock such as sheep or cattle but is often by introduced herbivores. Fallow deer, grey squirrels and rabbits, for example, often prevent regeneration.

25.2a Part of Hayley Wood in Cambridgeshire immediately after coppicing. Shrubs of hazel and ash have been cut down. The tall trees, known as 'standards', are ash and oak

25.2b The same part of Hayley Wood seven years later. The hazel coppice is now 2–3 m high and the ground vegetation is beginning to become shaded out

Ecological principles underlying woodland management

Successful woodland management reflects basic ecological principles. Some of these are outlined below.

Mineral recycling

To permit **mineral recycling** any temptation to 'tidy up' the wood too much must be resisted. Dead plant and animal matter is broken down by a variety of soil organisms, resulting in a gradual release of minerals. Resisting the temptation to tidy

25.3 Black hairstreak butterfly

up too much will have other advantages. Fallen branches will provide valuable sites for invertebrates and fungi. Dead standing trees can provide nesting sites for woodpeckers. On the other hand, if a wood has suffered from mineral enrichment, for instance due to fertiliser drift, removal of some organic matter may increase the number of species in the wood.

Climax vegetation and diversity of species

It is important to recognise that the presence of **climax vegetation** does not result in maximum **diversity** of species in the area. To maximise the number of species in a wood, which may be a management aim, a variety of habitats should be created. Glades through the wood can serve as paths for visitors and allow sunlight to enter, benefiting smaller plants, many invertebrates and many birds. If an old pond exists but has been filled up over the years with dead leaves and other plant matter, it may be worth dredging it and clearing trees to the south of the pond, thus allowing the colonisation of species restricted to open water.

Management objectives

It is important to have clearly defined management objectives. In many cases choices have to be made between different management options; for example, selling timber or the shooting rights generates income but they have implications for the ecology of the wood, which may or may not benefit depending on the circumstances. It may be necessary to decide whether access to the wood should be open or restricted. If non-native species have previously been introduced, should these be removed?

Regeneration

If regeneration is being prevented by large herbivore browsing, fencing may be required, though at 1990 prices the cheapest fencing costs £150 for 100 m. Waiting for regeneration may require patience A combination of many factors may be necessary for successful regeneration including several years of favourable weather to provide suitable conditions for the production of large quantities of seed and their subsequent germination. Even undisturbed woods often have trees all of the same age in parts of the wood, suggesting that the right conditions for regeneration may be rare.

Catastrophes

It is important to realise that a catastrophe is not a disaster. Trees may live for hundreds of years and woods may require occasional **natural catastrophes** such as fire or severe wind damage for regeneration. Particularly for very large woods, this may be the best way to ensure their long-term survival.

Afforestation

One hundred years ago only 5% of Britain was wooded. Although the area of woodland composed of native trees continues to shrink – we have lost almost half of it in the last 40 years – 8% of Britain is now wooded. This increase is mostly due to the planting of conifers in upland northern and western Britain where heathland, acid grassland, blanket bogs and valley mires have been afforested on a very large scale.

The percentage of woodland in Britain is small when compared to many other countries. In France 24% of the country is woodland, while in west Germany the figure is 28%. In Britain 92% of the demand for wood and wood products is supplied from abroad.

Almost without exception the plantations have been even-aged **monocultures** (one species) or two-species mixtures of conifers. When moorland is afforested, sheep and deer are excluded by fences, the soil is often ploughed and fertilised, and drainage is improved. For about 10 to 15 years the growing saplings have little effect on the vegetation, but as the conifer canopy closes, little light reaches the ground and the ground vegetation virtually disappears. Few species survive vegetatively under evergreen conifer plantations. However, seeds persist for many years in the soil in a dormant state, constituting what is known as the **seed bank**. Because of these dormant seeds, once the trees are harvested something like the previous vegetation type may develop again, though it is usually lower in species diversity. It should be pointed out that some attractive and rare plants may colonise conifer plantations including the delicate orchid creeping lady's tresses (*Goodyera repens*).

Under afforestation there may also be major changes in the animal species found in the area. Table 25.1 shows that conifer plantations contain fewer bird species than native woods. However, some species might not have been found in the habitat that existed before the trees were planted. So selective planting of conifers may increase the overall diversity of birds and other animals in an area. Some of our rare carnivores, such as the wildcat and pine marten, are now becoming more common in Scotland and northern England as a result of afforestation. At least in the early years after their establishment, conifer plantations allow hen harriers and short-eared owls to breed, as the birds feast on the large numbers of voles (Figure 25.4). On the other hand, species restricted to moorland, such as the beautiful merlin, our smallest bird of prey, naturally decrease in abundance as moorland is lost.

Many foresters see themselves as conservationists. It is true that the afforestation of some areas, such as the remarkable Flow Country in Scotland,

Table 25.1

Origin of stand	PLANTATION				SEMI-NATURAL				
Species	Sitka spruce	Norway spruce	Sitka spruce	Japanese larch	Scots pine		Scots pine/birch		Mixed*
Planting year	1927	1938	1953	1946	1926 c.1935		regeneration from 1945		?
Date of survey	1973	1973	1975	1973	1975	1925	1974	1974	1974
Siskin	9		5						
Crossbill	9		9				11		
Crested tit					4				
Goldcrest	136	132	172	99	22	34	39	21	70
Coal tit	20	46	41	47	35	57	45	8	70
Chaffinch	102	101	96	82	26	88	45	124	302
Wren	57	52	25	116	44	92	71	146	186
Robin	5	16	53	47	22	29	79	92	140
Dunnock				9		4		4	
Tree creeper	9	11		17		13	5	8	47
Blackbird							16	17	47
Willow warbler				17		23	105	292	279
Long-tailed tit				17			11	4	23
Song thrush							5	17	23
Blue tit							16	25	186
Redstart									23
Garden warbler							5	8	
Spotted flycatcher							5		12
Spotted woodpecker							5		12
Total species in plot	9	6	8	8	6	8	15	18	17
Pairs per km²	351	598	411	444	151	340	463	825	1593

*A mainly broadleaved stand (birch, oak, ash, sycamore) with scattered spruce and pines

25.4 *The short-eared owl nests on heather moorland and feeds its young on voles. These owls can survive in the young stages of afforestation, but once open ground is lost they lose their habitat*

is an ecological disaster which has caused irreversible damage to delicate ecosystems of international importance. However, recent (1988) changes in legislation afford some hope that damaging afforestation may be reduced in extent. Certainly afforestation on moorland can produce a valuable crop, generate jobs and even increase the wildlife interest of an area. It can only be hoped that future schemes will be designed more carefully allowing the creation of woods with more natural shapes and including a variety of paths and walks for the visitor.

Once the destruction of the tropical rainforests has finally slackened, as it eventually must if only because there is little left, the economic value of broadleaved trees may increase sharply. A far-sighted landowner who plants broadleaves now may benefit in 50–100 years' time.

Further reading

Brooks, A. (ed) (1980) *Woodlands: A Practical Conservation Handbook*. British Trust for Conservation Volunteers.
Peterken, G.F. (1981) *Woodland Conservation and Management*. Chapman & Hall.
Rackham, O. (1976) *Trees and Woodland in the British Landscape*. J.M. Dent & Sons.

Thought questions

1 If none of the woodland in Britain is virgin forest, why does it need conserving?

2 Should Britain aim to be self-sufficient in the production of timber?

3 Is there a wood near you that needs conserving?

Things to do

1. If you are interested in finding out about the ecology of your local woods or in helping with their conservation, get in touch with the staff of your local Trust for Nature Conservation. If you do not know how to contact them you can find out from the Royal Society for Nature Conservation, The Green, Witham Park, Lincoln LN5 7JR. Tel: 0522 544400.

2. If you like walking in woods, getting to know an area well and looking at old maps, see Oliver Rackham's classic book *Hayley Wood: Its History and Ecology* (1975), Cambridgeshire Wildlife Trust Ltd, for an example of how careful research can tell a tremendous amount about the management and natural history of a wood. A great deal of work in this field needs to be done throughout Britain.

26
Acid Rain

Acid rain is a serious environmental threat. It is not, however, a new phenomenon; as early as 1851 Robert Angus Smith, Britain's first air pollution officer, coined the term to describe the polluted and acidic rain which was falling on Manchester. Smith made the link between **atmospheric pollution** and damage to stone, iron and to vegetation: 'When the air has so much acid that two or three grains are found in a gallon of the rainwater ... there is no hope for a vegetation such as we have in the northern parts of the country.'

Acid rain becomes a global issue

In Smith's day acid rain was largely a local phenomenon, the areas most affected being those surrounding growing industrial towns and cities such as Manchester, Edinburgh ('Auld Reekie') and Stoke-on-Trent ('Smoke-on-Stench'). The main cause of the pollution was the burning of the fossil fuel coal, but severe damage to vegetation also occurred as a result of certain industrial processes. For example, the manufacture of soda by the Le Blanc process in and around the town of St Helens led to the release of a vast amount of hydrogen chloride into the atmosphere. This killed large areas of local vegetation.

The effects of industrial pollution became more widespread with the introduction of tall chimney stacks in power-stations. Although the chimneys decreased pollution near the power-stations, they resulted in the deposition of pollutants hundreds (or even thousands) of kilometres away. In Britain the predominantly westerly winds now export much of our air pollution as acid rain to Scandinavia and West Germany. It was during the 1960s that Scandinavian scientists first began to link air pollution from Britain and mainland Europe with the acidification and the loss of fish in the lakes and rivers in Norway. Likewise, extensive environmental studies implicate acid rain originating in the United States in the damage caused to Canadian lakes and trees. 'Environment Canada' estimate that as much as 3.7 million tonnes of airborne sulphur flowed into Canada from the United States in 1980. Airborne pollutants do not respect political bounda-

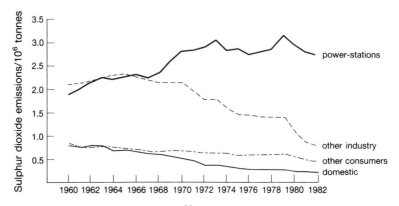

26.1 The sources of British sulphur dioxide emission since 1960

ries! In recent years acid rain has become an emotive political and environmental issue, often causing poor relations between purported polluter and the polluted.

What is acid rain?

Rain is naturally quite acidic (pH 5.0–5.6). This is due mainly to dissolved atmospheric **carbon dioxide** which forms carbonic acid. Naturally emitted **sulphur dioxide** (for example from sulphur springs, volcanoes, sea spray and microbial activity) and **oxides of nitrogen** (for example from lightning and microbial and volcanic activity) also dissolve to make rainwater acid. It is thought that in addition, organic acids account for between 5 and 20% of the acidity in the upper atmosphere.

In the industrialised regions of central Europe, however, rain is far more acidic (pH 4.1 on average). Even in Portugal, on the western fringes of the continent, the rainwater has an average pH of 4.9. The increased acidity is due to the presence in the atmosphere of extra sulphur dioxide (SO_2), nitric oxide (NO) and nitrogen dioxide (NO_2) in particular. Nowadays, these acidic gases are present in concen-

trations which are much higher than they would be naturally. As they can damage the environment these substances are known as **pollutants**.

By definition the release of pollutants into the air is due to the activities of humans. The term 'anthropogenic' has been used to separate pollutants with a human origin from natural emissions. Principally it is the burning of fossil fuels such as coal and oil in power-stations that produces sulphur dioxide, various oxides of nitrogen and hydrochloric acid. In addition, the exhaust fumes from motor vehicles contain nitrogen dioxide, nitric oxide, various hydrocarbons and carbon monoxide. The manufacture of the fertiliser ammonium nitrate also results in significant release of nitrogen oxides, which often give rise to local pollution.

'**Acid rain**' is the term given to a variety of processes all of which involve the deposition of these acidic gases from the atmosphere. Sulphur dioxide and the oxides of nitrogen are regarded as **primary air pollutants** as they are emitted directly into the atmosphere. It is important to consider what happens to these pollutants once they are in the air, and what effects they have when they are deposited.

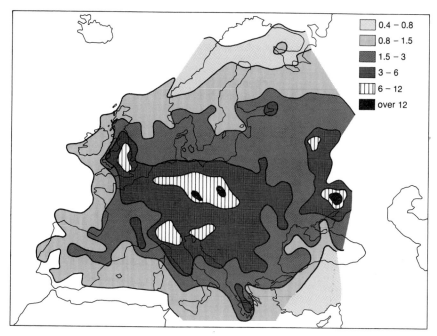

26.2 Sulphur fallout over Europe (gm m^{-2} yr^{-1})

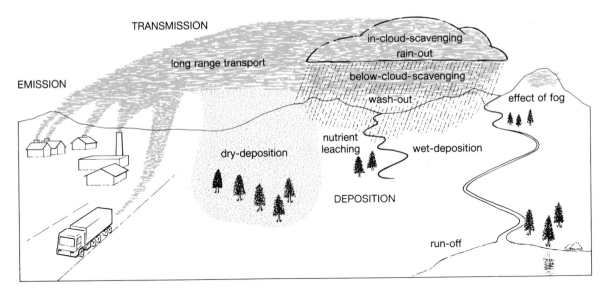

TRANSMISSION

long range transport

in-cloud-scavenging
rain-out

below-cloud-scavenging

wash-out

effect of fog

EMISSION

nutrient
leaching

dry-deposition

wet-deposition

DEPOSITION

run-off

26.3 Emission, transport and deposition of atmospheric pollution (from Wellburn, A. (1988) Air Pollution and Acid Rain, *Longman)*

The reactions of sulphur dioxide

The amount of **sulphur dioxide (SO$_2$)** emitted by human activities exceeds natural emissions by a factor of nearly five. Most of this is due to the burning of coal. In the United Kingdom before the **Clean Air Acts** of 1956 it was estimated that 6 million tonnes of sulphur dioxide were released each year from this source into the atmosphere.

Several processes of deposition of sulphur dioxide occur without the immediate presence of water. **Sulphur trioxide (SO$_3$)** is formed, for example, through the reaction of sulphur dioxide with monatomic oxygen (O). This later reacts with water to form **sulphuric acid (H$_2$SO$_4$)** which dissociate into hydrogen (H$^+$) and bisulphate (HSO$_4^-$) ions:

$$SO_3 + H_2O \rightleftharpoons H_2SO_4 \rightleftharpoons H^+ + HSO_4^-$$

Another source of sulphuric acid is the hydrogen sulphide (H$_2$S) produced by various industries such as the wood pulp industry. The hydrogen sulphide molecule oxidises in the atmosphere to sulphuric acid:

$$H_2S + 2O_2 \rightleftharpoons H_2SO_4$$

When dissolved in cloud water, many oxidising agents such as ozone (O$_3$) and hydrogen peroxide (H$_2$O$_2$) readily oxidise bisulphate ions resulting in still more acidity:

$$H_2O_2 + H_2SO_4 \rightleftharpoons HSO_4^- + H_2O$$
$$H_2SO_4^- \rightleftharpoons H^+ + SO_4^-$$

Finally, sulphur dioxide readily dissolves in water to form **sulphurous acid (H$_2$SO$_3$)**; this dissociates into hydrogen (H$^+$) and bisulphite (HSO$_3^-$) ions:

$$SO_2 + H_2O \rightleftharpoons H_2SO_3 \rightleftharpoons H^+ + HSO_3^-$$

The reactions of nitrogen oxides

The presence and composition of nitrogen oxides in the atmosphere is complicated; they may undergo a multitude of reactions which are influenced by factors such as temperature, light and level of their dilution.

Nitric oxide (NO) is formed by the high-temperature combination of oxygen and nitrogen as occurs in the furnace of power plants or in the internal combustion engine:

$$N_2 + O_2 \rightleftharpoons 2NO$$

The subsequent rapid cooling of the exhaust gases encourages the formation of nitrogen dioxide (NO$_2$) and dinitrogen tetroxide (N$_2$O$_4$):

$$2NO + O_2 \rightleftharpoons 2NO_2 \rightleftharpoons N_2O_4$$

Alternatively, once in the atmosphere, nitric oxide may be oxidised to **nitrogen dioxide (NO$_2$)** mainly by reaction with ozone:

$$NO + O_3 \rightleftharpoons NO_2 + O_2$$

Nitrogen dioxide may then undergo a variety of reactions:

- Absorbs light and splits to form nitric oxide and atomic oxygen:

$$NO_2 + light \rightleftharpoons NO + O$$

- Reacts in bright sunlight with free radicals such as OH$^-$ to produce **nitrous acid (HNO$_2$)**. This is essentially a warm summer reaction:

$$NO_2 + OH \rightleftharpoons HNO_2$$

- Reacts very rapidly in the gas phase with nitric oxide and water:

$$NO_2 + NO + H_2O \rightleftharpoons 2HNO_2$$

- Reacts with ozone to produce **nitric acid (HNO$_3$)**. This series of reactions occurs in cooler conditions, both in the gas phase and as soon as dinitrogen pentoxide (N$_2$O$_5$) comes into contact with water:

$$NO_2 + O_3 \rightleftharpoons NO_3 + O_2$$
$$NO_3 + NO_2 \rightleftharpoons N_2O_5$$
$$N_2O_5 + H_2O \rightleftharpoons 2HNO_3 \rightleftharpoons 2H^+ + 2NO_3^-$$

The reaction of nitrogen dioxide with free radicals may also result in the formation of a variety of organic nitrogen compounds such as **phenoxyacetic nitrate (PAN)**. These compounds are regarded as **secondary air pollutants** because they are not emitted directly into the atmosphere but instead result from the reactions of primary air pollutants with natural compounds found in the atmosphere.

Dispersion and transport

Pollutants may be released at ground level (for example by traffic) or from high chimney stacks. The altitude reached by these pollutants, the distance travelled and the speed of dispersion depend on factors such as climate, weather and local topography.

For example, when the atmosphere is stable, emissions from a chimney stack may travel a considerable distance as a coherent plume. On hot days, convection currents may cause pollutants to rise to considerable heights before lateral dispersion occurs, this being dependent on the direction and strength of winds. Emissions from low chimneys may be trapped in valleys; high ground may cause downdraughts. Both of these topographical factors can cause intense local concentration of pollutants.

Deposition

Deposition of air pollutants may be either 'dry' or 'wet'.

Dry deposition

The acidic gases may be deposited directly on surfaces: for example, lakes, soils, buildings and trees. This form of deposition is a slow, continuous process and it predominates in the regions closest to emission sources.

Wet deposition

Tiny airborne particles (diameter 0.1–2.0 μm) act as nuclei for water condensation; these wet particles then increase in size and merge to form droplets. Pollutants such as sulphur dioxide may be incorporated during this process of cloud formation. The droplets may contain high concentrations of pollutants, up to five times the concentration found in rain. Below the cloud, falling droplets (or snowflakes) may also take up pollutants by impaction or interception. In this way, acidic gases may be deposited as rain, hail, sleet or snow. Fog or mist aerosols may deposit pollutants by hitting (wet impaction) or by condensing (occult deposition) on a surface.

Wet deposition is a rapid process with most of the pollutants being deposited during intermittent periods of precipitation. This process is important, for example, in upland regions which characteristically have cloud cover for long periods of time.

The effects of acid rain

Acid rain causes changes in **physical systems** such as soil, rivers and lakes and consequently affects **the biological systems** of microbial, plant and animal life. Also of concern is the deterioration it causes to metal, glass and stone. Increasing evidence indicates that the accelerated decay of ancient buildings is due to acid deposition.

Effects on soils and water

Acid deposition transfers sulphates (SO_4^-) and nitrates (NO_3^-) to the soil and causes an increase in acidity (H^+ ions). The enhanced acidity results in the **leaching** of nutrient ions such as potassium, magnesium and calcium with a consequent drop in soil fertility. It also accelerates weathering processes, causing **mobilisation of metals**, notably aluminium, in the soil. **Aluminium** is usually found in an insoluble form bound to the soil but can be split from its complex compounds by hydrogen ions (H^+) from acid rain.

Many soils have buffering systems which resist changes in soil acidity. For instance, soil containing many calcium ions (Ca^{2+}) are able to buffer against acidity by exchanging ions:

$$\text{soil-Ca} + 2H^+ \rightleftharpoons \text{soil-2H} + Ca^{2+}$$

However, some soils such as those in areas of hard granite rocks are thin and acidic. They contain few exchangeable cations (positively charged ions) and are incapable of buffering against the increase in hydrogen ions due to acid rain.

It was in areas with such soils, for example in southern Scandinavia, that the **acidification** of freshwater lakes and rivers was noted during the 1960s and 1970s when fish were dying or failing to reproduce. The **brown trout** *(Salmo trutta)* and **salmon** *(Salmo salar)* have since disappeared from thousands of lakes in Scotland, Scandinavia (Figure 26.4), Canada and parts of the eastern United States. Investigations into the history of certain Scottish lakes by analysis of fossilised diatoms (algae) have been made. **Diatoms** are very sensitive to acidity and it was revealed that marked population changes occurred in the lakes at a time corresponding to the industrial revolution (Figure 26.5). Acidification of these watercourses was not due to long-term weathering of the surrounding rocks. Atmospheric pollution appears to be the most likely cause.

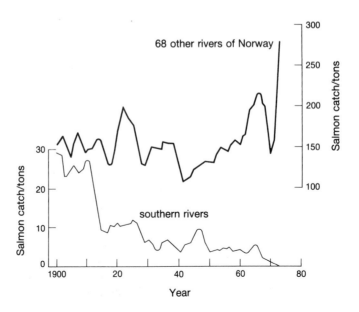

26.4 Salmon catches in the rivers of Norway 1900-73

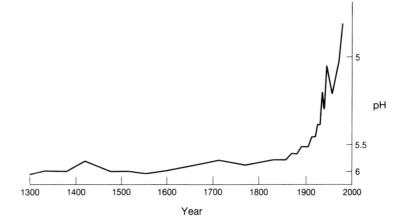

26.5 The reconstructed history of acidity in Round Loch, Galloway, as revealed by diatom analysis

Effects on animals

Fish

Pronounced seasonal variations in water acidity may occur. The period of snowmelt is often associated with high acidity and a consequent increase in the level of aluminium ions released from the soil-rock system.

Very few fish are found in water with a pH less than 4.5. However, it is the aluminium ions, mainly Al $(OH)^{2+}$ rather than the hydrogen ions directly, which appear to be the main toxic agent. These ions promote the loss of essential sodium ions (Na^+) from the gills of the fish; they cause coagulation of mucus on gill surfaces and can interfere with metabolic processes such as respiration. Also, adequate uptake of calcium for **calcification** of the skeleton is prevented.

Invertebrates and birds

As the pH of acidic waters falls below 5.4, a decline in populations of invertebrates such as mayflies, freshwater shrimps, snails, limpets and beetle larvae occurs. Algae and moss proliferate, whilst the exoskeleton of the crayfish softens and the animal becomes infested with parasites.

High dietary levels of aluminium have been found to cause the dipper *Cinclus cinclus* to lay eggs with thin shells. These eggs are more prone to damage and consequently there has been a reduction in dipper numbers.

Humans

The increase in aluminium concentration in water due to acid rain can also affect people. High concentrations of aluminium in drinking water (1000–2000 ppm) have been linked to incidences of osteomalacia (bone softening), **Alzheimer's disease** (a form of premature senility) and dementia (see also Chapter 32). In certain parts of Scandinavia aluminium is routinely removed from water destined for use in kidney dialysis or baby feeds.

The direct effect of acid rain on people became apparent during the London **smog** of December 1952, when about four thousand people died. Dissolved sulphur dioxide formed tiny, highly acidic particles which combined with smoke to cause severe irritation of the bronchial tubes. It has been estimated that the pH of the smog was about 1.6 – more acid than lemon juice.

Effects on plants

Although damage to plants is frequently observed, the extent to which this is due to specific acidic pollutants is uncertain. **Lichens** are extremely sensitive to sulphur dioxide and they have disappeared from regions with high levels of sulphur deposition. Lichens have often been used as **biological indicators** of the long-term presence of high levels of atmospheric pollution, although there are many other environmental factors which may limit the growth of lichens.

A major concern about acid rain is that it may be causing *Waldschaden*, that is **forest decline**, in Europe and North America. Signs of the decline were first observed in the Alps during the mid 1970s and soon after in West Germany. Coniferous species such as silver fir (*Abies* Spp.) and Norway spruce *(Picea abies)* began to show yellowing of needles and needle drop (Figure 26.6). Deciduous broadleaved tree species are also becoming increasingly affected.

The marked decline of trees which is observed at the edges of forests and at high altitudes may be due to the combined effects of acid mists and **ozone**, possibly enhanced by climatic factors. Although when high in the atmosphere ozone plays a protective role, at ground level the gas enters plants through stomata and damages cell membranes. Ozone has also been found to cause a reduction in the amount of resin produced by the pine *Pinus ponderosa*. This has important consequences for the pine trees as resin is produced as a defence against attack by insects and other pathogens.

The high concentrations of sulphur dioxide which were once released in industrial towns caused visible damage to local vegetation by direct contact. Striking changes in vegetation have been recorded in areas such as the Peak District of Britain which are possibly a consequence of acid rain. Plants such as bog myrtle (*Myrica gale*) and various bog mosses (*Sphagnum* spp.) which were present prior to the industrial revolution have since disappeared. Although mixtures of sulphur dioxide and oxides of nitrogen have been shown to reduce the growth of plants considerably, the occurrence of injury to foliage and the death of plants as a direct consequence of acid rain alone is controversial. There are so many variables involved that it is hard to prove.

To date, more than 150 possible theories about causes of forest decline have been put forward. Most likely of these, on present evidence, is that acid causes damage to trees by soil processes. For example, essential ions such **magnesium (Mg^{2+})**, required for synthesis of chlorophyll, are leached from tree leaves and from the soil. Also, aluminium is mobilised, causing the death of fine roots and their associated mycorrhizal fungi. Consequently nutrient uptake and the growth of trees are adversely affected.

In mountain regions the amount of nitrate in the soil is a major limiting factor for plant growth. The deposition of nitrate in acid rain permits growth to be prolonged into autumn, the trees

26.6 The remains of spruce trees devastated by acid rain in the Karkonoski National Park, in south-west Poland. The acid precipitation came largely from neighbouring Czechoslovakia and reached at one time a record low of pH 1.7

consequently being susceptible to frost damage.

Low levels of individual air pollutants may be harmless on their own, but in combination they appear to have severe **synergistic effects** on plants. Sulphur dioxide, for instance, is much more damaging to plants when mixed with nitrogen dioxide or ozone than when occurring alone. It is possible that the **interaction of pollutants** may reduce a plant's ability to tolerate environmental stresses such as low temperatures, drought, wind and winter desiccation. Various factors complicate this situation and make it difficult to carry out controlled experiments into the effects of acid rain on plants. For instance, genetic differences exist between plants in their susceptibility to pollution. Also, the soils in which they grow have varying buffering capacities.

Although many people believe that acid rain is responsible for the decline of the forests, the scientific evidence so far remains inconclusive.

Tackling acid rain

The chemistry of acid rain is complex. Research must be continued in order to obtain a full understanding of the problem so that it can be tackled efficiently and effectively.

A reduction in the amount of polluting sulphur dioxide and oxides of nitrogen from power-stations (Table 26.1) and motor vehicles is vital. Nearly every developed country has introduced legislation to control or limit emissions of atmospheric pollution. International agreements exist concerning air quality standards, but policies must be adopted to ensure that these are met. Monitoring, inspections and enforcement of standards must be rigorous.

Emissions of sulphur dioxide from power-stations can be reduced using the appropriate technology and combustion processes. Sulphur may be removed from fuels before or during combustion. The process of flue gas **desulphurisation** removes sulphur before emissions reach the atmosphere. The process has been fully implemented in the United States, Japan and Germany, but the fitting of British power-stations has only just begun.

The recent development of **fluidised-bed combustion** involves the burning of solid or liquid fuel at relatively low temperatures. Calcium carbonate (limestone) particles can be added to the burning fuel to trap the sulphur in calcium sulphates. This reduces sulphur dioxide emissions by up to 90%.

The low temperature of combustion also reduces the emissions of oxides of nitrogen. Such a reduction may also be achieved by a new German process, 'NO$_x$OUT', which involves the use of a blend of chemicals containing nitrogen.

The fitting of **catalytic converters** to the exhaust systems of motor vehicles removes a proportion of the nitric oxide, hydrocarbons and carbon monoxide from the exhaust fumes. The converters are fitted as standard in cars in the United States and Japan.

The introduction of **lean-burn engines** which burn fuel more efficiently would lead to a reduction both in the emission of nitric oxide and in fuel consumption. However, the total number of cars in use continues to rise rapidly.

The outlook is rather gloomy. Attempts are being made to neutralise the acid in soils and

Type of power plant	Maximum thermal efficiency/%	Emissions		
		CO	SO$_2$	NO$_x$
Oil-fired	35–37	trace	high	considerable
Natural gas-fired	35–37	trace	low	very high
Conventional coal-fired	35–40	low	high	considerable
Gas turbine	18–28	high	very high	very high
Fluidised bed	50–70	trace	low	low

Table 26.1

waters through the spreading of vast amounts of powdered limestone. However, this short-term and costly measure may be at best ineffective and at worst damaging to the environment. It has been established that limestone dissolves much more slowly in an acidic solution than was previously thought. Also, when it does eventually dissolve, the limestone may upset further the ecological balance of many ecosystems. Even if air pollution were to be halted completely, the accumulated sulphate and acid would persist in soils and the acidified waters would retain their toxic aluminium, perhaps for decades.

Further reading

Lee, J. (1988) Acid Rain. *Biological Science Review 1*, pp.15–18.

Pearce, R. (1987) *Acid Rain*. Penguin Books.

Thought questions

Britain's energy-generating coal-fired power-stations are the largest single source of pollution within the European Community, producing about 4 million tonnes of sulphur dioxide annually.

1 Can you suggest why so much sulphur dioxide is produced?

2 Why do you think the new technology available to reduce sulphur dioxide emissions has so far not been fully applied in Britain?

Things to do

Investigations of acid rain.

1. Construct a large rain-gauge using a plastic mineral-water bottle. Cut off the conical neck in such a position that if inverted into the rest of the bottle it will make a funnel. Make daily recordings of any rain, its pH, the prevailing wind and the type of precipitation (rain, hail, sleet or snow). Keep the rainwater in a larger container for investigation 2.

2. Alongside the rain-gauge construct microcommunity ecosystems in pots. Each one should have the same plant species, for example rye grass, oak or pine seedlings, but with differing soil types, for example loam, clay, quartz sand, chalky soil, moss peat, fen peat. (The more replicates there are the better.) Place a funnel-trap system beneath each pot for catching the water and record the pH of the water percolating **through** the soils. If they become very dry, keep them equally watered with the rainwater already collected. What conclusions can you draw about when precipitation is most acid, where the acid comes from, what effect if any it has on the plants, and what the influence of the soil is on the ground water?

As an alternative investigation plant out a number of plants of one species in vermiculite in pots. Supply the plants with water containing adequate nutrients from below by capillarity. Using sulphuric acid in a dilution series, made up with the culture water, assay the tolerance of each species grown hydroponically to acid water.

Simple chemical experiments concerned with acid rain are described in an article by J.M. Hadfield, *School Science Review 69*, pp.755–58 (1988).

27

Global Greenhouse? Watching the Carbon Cycle

This chapter is concerned with the carbon cycle: how it works, how we influence and exploit it and why we may be in for trouble if we upset its balance. Humans are now making vast changes to the biosphere, clearing rainforests and draining swamps. We burn non-renewable fossil fuels that were formed by living organisms millions of years ago. Carbon dioxide levels are increasing in the atmosphere as it interacts with the biosphere. There may already be an enhanced atmospheric **greenhouse effect**, which will have consequences for climatic and vegetational change, and may lead to rising sea-levels. Today we face an immediate and important challenge to our way of living and the management of our global ecosystem. In this challenge there is a role for plant ecologists.

Carbon

The element carbon is central to life. In chemistry, complex carbon compounds are described as 'organic' for this reason. Because of the carbon atom's four-valency structure and **covalent bonding**, carbon compounds can be assembled in countless ways. With other atoms they make the chain-like, branched and ringed forms of the many biochemicals that make up living organisms. The chemical energy bonding organic molecules together also makes them rich **energy** stores: for example, firewood and petroleum. The primary source of the energy in most biochemicals is sunshine. Light is captured by chlorophyll in the process of **photosynthesis** to produce chemical energy (ATP) and reducing potential. Inside the chloroplasts of green plants carbon dioxide is chemically reduced by means of the electrons captured in that light reaction. The product is sugar, but much of this is converted into complex structural carbohydrates used to build plants; some will be passed on to animals and a minute fraction may eventually become transformed into peat, coal, oil or natural gas.

The carbon cycle

Figure 27.1 is a diagram of the carbon cycle. It includes much data on the amounts of carbon around the cycle and their rates of flow. The units are in thousand millions of metric tonnes (10^9 tonnes). The quantities in the boxes are the amounts of global carbon in each compartment. The numbers beside the arrows are the thousand millions of tonnes that change each year from one compartment to another.

Two food chains are shown in the diagram, one for terrestrial ecosystems and one for marine ones. Carbon is taken directly from the atmosphere into the green leaves of land plants and indirectly, through water, by such other plants as algae. This photosynthetic generation of biomass is called **primary production**. Although there are only about 350 parts per million (ppm) of carbon dioxide in the air (0.035%) the atmosphere is so deep (150 km) and so extensive around the earth that there are about 730 thousand million tonnes of carbon up in the air, almost all in the form of carbon dioxide. One sixth of this, 120 thousand million tonnes, is captured each year by plants in photosynthesis.

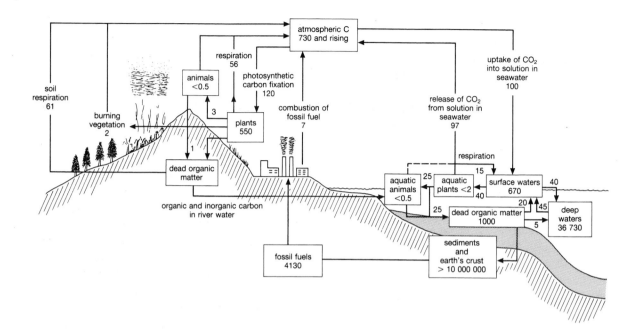

27.1 The Carbon cycle, showing the approximate total mass of the element carbon which is contained in each part of the system and the annual flow rates between compartments. Units are billions (10^9) of tonnes

Carbon dioxide dissolves in rainwater quite readily, and also dissolves in the surface waters of the sea, so about one seventh of it is taken into the oceans each year. A small fraction of this is used in photosynthesis. Although 71% of the planet is covered in water the oceans only account for 33% of the primary production. It seems that algal growth in the seas is extremely limited by nutrient deficiencies so that, from a photosynthetic point of view, the oceans are rather like deserts, not through want of water but through want of nitrates and phosphates. Carbon dioxide is also returned to the atmosphere from the sea, for in some places deep water, rich in carbon dioxide, rises to the surface.

Fossil fuels and the origin of carbon sinks

Reserves of **fossil fuels** are a result of the remains of plants and animals sedimented long ago. Along with limestone sediments they are the **sinks** of the carbon cycle. The huge **coal forests** of the **Carboniferous** period 300 million years ago were formed from tree-ferns that grew in swampy conditions. It took about 20 million years to produce the coal measures of Europe in what must have been a tropical swamp forest. The number of sites where such fossilisation can proceed today is very small and coal is therefore regarded as a **non-renewable resource**.

The formation of oil and natural gas (methane) is not as clearly understood; it seems that they are the products of aquatic ecosystems in which large amounts of organic matter were deposited out of the reach of oxygen. At great depths anaerobic respiration proceeded, eliminating nitrogen and sulphur. The remaining hydrocarbons formed **oil** and **natural gas**. Natural gas is liquified under the immense pressure of the earth's crust. To some extent this hydrocarbon formation is still continuing on the ocean bed (see Figure 27.1).

The photosynthetic origin of the energy in sedimented fossil fuels is often forgotten, and the present use of this resource is upsetting the atmospheric balance of carbon dioxide. Seven thousand million (7×10^9) tonnes of carbon are being discharged into the air annually by the burning of fossil fuels. As every nation tries, understandably, to reach the standards of living of the wealthiest, the rate of increase in use is currently rising exponentially at 4.3% per annum. China, one of the poorest countries, has the largest reserves of coal. The rate of increase cannot be expected to slow down quickly.

The rise in carbon dioxide levels

One of the world's remotest places is the top of an extinct volcano on **Mauna Loa atoll** in the Hawaiian Islands of the Pacific Ocean. Atmospheric carbon dioxide levels have been recorded there

27.2 The rise in atmospheric carbon dioxide levels

(a)

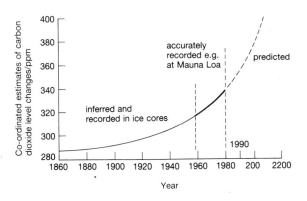

(b)

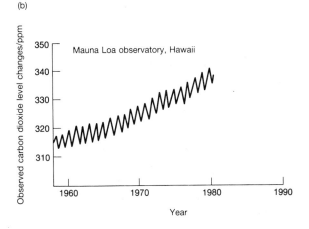

every month since 1957. Figure 27.2 shows the annual fluctuation, the steady increase from year to year and the incrementally increasing rate. The figures speak for themselves.

It has recently been discovered that ice formed from snow on the earth's ice-caps contains air from the time of its formation. Drilled out **ice-cores** have provided a wonderful data bank on atmospheric changes back into history and prehistory. During the ice ages, the levels of carbon dioxide were 200 ppm during the glaciations and 280 ppm between them. Levels did not rise above this higher figure until the industrial revolution (1750). By 1900 the level had risen to 300 ppm. Today (1991) it is 353 ppm and rising by about 1.4 ppm per annum. Of the 7000 million tonnes of extra carbon entering the atmosphere as a result of fossil fuel combustion, about 3000 million tonnes remains in the atmosphere. The rest is being absorbed by the oceans.

The case for an increased greenhouse effect

The earth has a mean surface temperature of about 15°C, although the temperature on its surfaces varies from -60°C to 80°C. The planet is in a **heat balance**. Radiated light energy from the sun warms up the surface of the earth; consequently infrared (heat) energy is radiated from the earth's surface into space, so cooling it down. If the earth had no atmosphere around it, its surface would be some 33°C colder on average. This is because the gases in the atmosphere absorb infrared radiation. **Short-wave radiation** such as sunlight can pass through them but the **longer wave length radiation** cannot so easily get out again. As with the glass in a gardener's greenhouse which lets in light but holds back infrared radiation, the earth's atmosphere warms up. This is known as the **greenhouse effect**. The power of the greenhouse effect is well illustrated by our near neighbour, the planet Venus. Venus is a little nearer the sun than we are and if it lacked an atmosphere it would be expected to have a mean surface temperature of 37°C. However, its atmosphere comprises 96% carbon dioxide. When a recent space probe landed it found a surface temperature of 482°C!

The **greenhouse gases** which absorb infrared radiation are water vapour, carbon dioxide, ozone, methane, nitrous oxide and the freons or chlorofluorocarbons (CFCs). Water vapour is by far the most important and abundant greenhouse gas; it is well known, for example, that cloud cover reduces both heating by day and cooling by night. Ten per cent of the greenhouse effect is attributed to carbon dioxide. Given that carbon dioxide is only present in the atmosphere at about 0.03%, it is quite powerful in its effect. Most computer models suggest that if the pre-industrial levels of carbon dioxide double, the mean surface temperature would rise by between 1°C and 5°C. The increase in temperature around the world would not be uniform, it being probably greater at higher latitudes. This might mean changed weather patterns, ice-cap melting and sea-level rises. Despite much observation, there is relatively little evidence that these changes are occurring, and they might not even be related to the carbon dioxide increase at all. Long-term weather cycles do occur naturally.

Ozone and **CFCs** are much less important as greenhouse gases, but it should be noted that the first is being destroyed by the second, causing a thinning of the ozone layer. The problem of ozone depletion is a separate issue, but nothing in environmental science is entirely independent of other influences; as we shall see, an increase in ultraviolet light, coming through an ozone hole, might damage the capacity of algae to photosynthesise. **Methane** is present in the atmosphere at a concentration of only 0.00017% or 1.7 ppm. It is increasing and like carbon dioxide it is a major greenhouse gas with a biological origin (methane is discussed further below).

How will plants respond to raised carbon dioxide levels?

Horticultural greenhouse growers have known for a long time that raising carbon dioxide levels increases the **growth** of cucumbers and tomato plants. It is interesting to see how plants have responded to the 25% increase which has occurred over the last 300 years: from 280 ppm in 1700 to

a value greater than 350 ppm now.

A typical land plant has a dilemma – how to encourage carbon dioxide to diffuse into the leaf without allowing too much water vapour to diffuse out. It is a choice between feeding well by photosynthesis and drying up, or not feeding quite so well and maintaining adequate water in the tissues. Millions of years ago the first land plants hit upon a partial solution – having dilating guard cells around numerous holes in the leaf. By opening during the day, while there is sunlight, the **stomata** allow carbon dioxide to enter; they shut by night so that the plant reduces its water loss. Many plants under water-stress vary this pattern. Some, like maize, close their stomata in the afternoon. Experimental studies have shown that when plants are grown at levels of carbon dioxide lower than the level in the atmosphere they increase the number of stomata per unit area **(stomatal density)**. However, when grown at levels above the atmosphere level the stomatal density decreases. It is as if the stomatal density is controlled very largely by the prevailing levels of the gas.

Ian Woodward of Cambridge University wondered therefore if the stomatal density had changed in the last two hundred years. In the University Herbarium there are specimens of leaves collected over the past 230 years. Sure enough, on the leaves of eight British tree species the density of stomata has been decreasing since the industrial revolution. The sycamore tree *Acer pseudoplatanus* was found to show this effect well. Woodward decided to do an experiment. When sycamore seedlings were grown in an atmosphere typical of 300 years ago, with 280 ppm carbon dioxide, the plants grew well and had greater stomatal densities. A **control group** with 'normal' (350 ppm CO_2) was used for comparison. However, the lower level carbon dioxide plants, with more holes in their leaves, experienced much more **water stress** than the control plants. It is therefore possible that our modern trees are slightly more drought-tolerant than they used to be. Certainly sycamores, which are tolerant of sulphur dioxide pollution, grow very fast in urban environments with higher levels of carbon dioxide. It is probable that many plants are

Initial atmosphere in which plants were grown/ppm CO_2	Experimental atmosphere /ppm CO_2	Carbon dioxide uptake/mol CO_2 per m^2	Total daily transpiration /mol H_2O per m^2	Water use efficiency 10^{-3} mol CO_2 per mol H_2O
330	330	0.87	351	2.48
330	800	1.78	288	6.18
800	330	1.03	494	2.08
800	800	1.71	363	4.71

(from Jones (1985) in Salisbury, F. b. and Ross C. W. Plant Physiology, Wadsworth)

Table 27.1 The effect of carbon dioxide enrichment on the carbon dioxide uptake rate, transpiration rate and hence water use efficiency of soya beans

growing a little faster than they used to.

Table 27.1 shows the results of an experiment with soya beans. The plants were divided into four groups. Two were initially grown at 330 ppm and two at 800 ppm carbon dioxide. The latter groups developed fewer stomata. Then half the plants were left in their original atmospheres, but the others were moved, so that some of the plants grown at 330 ppm were placed in 800 ppm carbon dioxide while some of the plants initially grown at 800 ppm were placed in 330 ppm carbon dioxide. Measurements were then made of carbon dioxide uptake and of transpiration rates. The third and fourth columns show carbon dioxide uptake and transpiration rates whilst the fifth shows carbon dioxide uptake per unit of water transpired. What conclusions can be drawn from these data about the behaviour of plants in a carbon-dioxide-rich world?

Such patterns of behaviour have started crop scientists thinking about the future. There is good reason to believe that **C3 plants** (typical of temperate regions) will grow a little faster and be more **water use efficient**. However, **C4 plants** such as maize and sugar cane, that have already evolved a superior carbon dioxide harvesting machinery in the leaf, do not seem to grow appreciably faster if carbon dioxide levels are doubled. We might therefore see a changed emphasis on the type of crops in different regions. Computer-controlled experiments are planned at Harvard University on the growth rates of forests enriched with carbon dioxide. The International Rice Research Institute in

the Philippines is planning similar experiments with carbon-dioxide-enriched rice plots. If some of the world's plants grow faster the effects of the increased carbon dioxide levels may be lessened a little.

Forests and the carbon balance

There are approximately 1200 thousand million tonnes of living **plant biomass** on land (see Figure 27.1 for tonnes of carbon and Table 27.2 for tonnes of dry matter). This total figure is less than it used to be, for the loss of forests has been considerable. As forests are still being cut down, it will go on decreasing for some years to come. There is a **net primary production** by photosynthesis of about 133 million tonnes each year. Forests and woodland account for 79% of the world's plant biomass on land and for about 38% of the primary production. Crops, however, only account for 12% of the world's primary production. Grasslands are very productive, but their turnover is high. If we are seeking 'a sink' for excess carbon dioxide on land, the forests and woodlands are the best candidates. After all, a hectare of rainforest can take up nearly 100 kilograms of carbon dioxide a day.

You might well wonder how anybody is able to produce the values quoted in Figure 27.1 and Table 27.2 in the first place. How can anyone possibly know what is happening on such a large scale? **Forest ecologists** have been working for many years to obtain the answers, both in temperate countries and particularly in the tropics. An understanding of forest ecologists' research methods will show how some of these figures are derived.

Sometimes the forest ecologist will take a small

plot of forest for a **profile transect**, studying it in great detail by recording the species, girths, heights, distribution, canopy crown areas, spacing, health and reproduction of the trees. This work may involve felling large trees to do calculations on their shape and dimensions. As a result of such work it has been found, for example, that in a forest the spacing between trees is proportional to their diameter. Such studies give a good idea of **forest structure** but it is too exhaustive (and exhausting!) an approach to repeat many times. For this reason the forest ecologist will have small numbers of **long-term plots**, many of which may have been studied for more than fifty years. Obviously anyone entering these plots must tread carefully. Studies here give a good idea of recruitment from new seedlings, rates of growth, and rates of death (mortality). Then, working more widely, numerous **sample plots** can be examined and counts made of tree species' frequency and size. One-third of the basal area multiplied by the height of a tree gives a good idea of timber volume ($\frac{\pi r^2 h}{3}$), whilst height alone may correlate with soil fertility. On a wider scale, the forest cover of these plots may be related to **aerial photographs**, giving some idea of the extent of forest resources. These in turn may be related to **satellite imagery**, which today provides us with rapidly gathered data on the extent of global deforestation and other large-scale environmental change.

Sadly forests, particularly tropical rainforests, are being lost at a great rate. (Cutting down forests is nothing new, for Britain was deforested in prehistoric times: see Chapter 25.) Worldwide, there were 25 million km² of **closed canopy forest** in 1980; estimates suggest that this will be reduced to about 22 million km² by 2000 and 18 million km² by 2020. This rate of disappearance does not look as alarming as some estimates of depletion suggest. There has been, rightly, a worldwide outrage where some concentrated local effect has led to enormous losses. It is also true that free enterprise in pursuit of tropical hardwood has caused the devastation of the finest rainforests. The proportion of Thailand's land surface covered by forest fell from 58% to 33% between 1960 and 1985.

There are many reasons for wanting to save forests. With respect to the greenhouse effect, it is clear that burning them produces much carbon dioxide and cutting them down considerably reduces the biosphere's capacity to lower carbon dioxide levels through photosynthesis. To understand the rainforest crisis, four different land-use patterns need to be seen.

- **Deforestation** is the loss of forest to other land uses such as peasant agriculture and cattle ranching. This is the greatest loss by far.
- **Afforestation** is the return of tree cover to the area by planting trees for timber or firewood, but this may not be with native species.
- **Regeneration** is where logging is managed sustainably and the forest structure is allowed to redevelop fully before the next logging cycle.
- **Reservation** is where the forest is conserved as an intact ecosystem and as a means of safeguarding its genetic diversity.

From the viewpoint of acting as a **carbon dioxide sink**, these options are listed in increasing order of value. The first involves the greatest carbon release from burning and the most permanent loss of carbon from the standing crop of world vegetation. It is by far the most destructive and

27.3 Tropical rainforest ecologists making plant collections

needs to be arrested as fast as possible. Regeneration provides the best solution for Third World countries seeking sustainable development.

Wetlands and limits to aquatic productivity

In the 1960s and 1970s the International Biological Programme was set up to find out more about the workings of the **global ecosystem**. One of the discoveries was that coastal **wetlands** are highly productive. Environments such as estuarine marshes, saltmarshes, mudflats and mangrove swamps have primary productivity levels equal to or greater than those of rainforests (see Table 27.2). The reasons for this high productivity are that in shallow coastal waters there is an influx of minerals and dead organic matter from rivers, decay rates are high, carbon dioxide is abundant and so photosynthesis is rapid. Similar research has

focused on **coral reefs** where there is an influx of nutrients from animal life from the sea on one side, and from coastal fringing mangrove swamps on the other, as well as extensive nutrient recycling within the reef ecosystem. Ecologists looking at these aquatic ecosystems have realised their great potential for removing carbon dioxide from circulation. Reefs are very ancient ecosystems and have always been capable of literally 'sinking' vast amounts of carbon as calcium carbonate in coral. One current worry is that high ultraviolet levels have been 'bleaching' corals, killing the polyps at the surface. If sea-levels rise slowly due to the global warming the fastest coral growth should just about keep up!

Too many paddies and cows?

Methane is a greenhouse gas. Although present at only 1.7 ppm in the atmosphere, molecule for molecule it has a much greater effect than carbon

Table 27.2 Terrestrial primary production and biomass

Ecosystems	Mean net primary productivity* /g per m^2 per yr #	Total net world production /10^9 tonnes	Total world plant biomass 10^9 tonnes
Tropical rainforest	2300	23.0	420
Tropical seasonal forest	1600	7.2	112
Temperate forest and woodland	1450	11.4	210
Coniferous forest	1083	9.8	235
Tropical grassland	1725	39.3	145
Temperate grassland	800	9.7	20.2
Tundra	101	2.1	13.0
Semi-desert	150	3.0	16.5
Tropical swamps (freshwater)	4000	6.0	22.5
Mangrove swamps (tropical marine)	1000	0.3	9.0
Temperate swamps (freshwater)	2500	1.2	3.7
Cultivated land	1250	15.0	6.6
Other		5.0	30
	Global mean 850	Total 133	Total 1244

divide by 100 for tonnes per ha   *Net primary production is the increase in organic production after losses to respiration. Gross production, the dry mass amount actually photosynthesised, is higher by a factor of between 1.3 (for crops and grass) and 2.4 (for tropical rainforest). Biomass is approximately 44% carbon. (from Atjay 1979, in Kimmins, J. P. (1987) Forest Ecology, Macmillan)

dioxide as a greenhouse gas, and it is increasing at a much faster rate from a lower base level. Where is it coming from?

Methane is a fossil fuel trapped in the earth's crust above petroleum deposits. It leaks from all coal and petroleum operations in small amounts, but as it is explosive its release is controlled or harnessed to **natural gas** production as much as possible. Some of the increase in its atmospheric release can be attributed to forest burning. However, well over half of the release is thought to be due to a sudden increase in microbial activity. Methane is one of the principal **anaerobic decay** products excreted by bacteria feeding on dead organic matter (methane is also called **marsh gas** because it bubbles up from boggy pools in swamps and marshes). Although the extent of bogs and marshland has been much reduced in recent times, land under water has grown enormously with the increase in **paddy rice farming**. During the establishment phase of the rice crop the soil is flooded and much methane is produced. **Paddy fields** have increased almost in proportion to the increase in the world population. In Britain large amounts of methane are produced from landfill sites.

In addition, methane is generated in, and expelled from, the bacterial ferments in the alimentary tracts of mammals. Ruminants like cattle are the biggest producers for they employ **anaerobic fermentation** of ingested food in the rumen; methane is consequently burped up during rumination.

The **ice-core record** for methane is clear. It has varied from between 0.35 ppm in the atmosphere during cold ice ages, and up to 0.65 ppm in warmer interglacial periods. Its present level is 1.7 ppm, almost three times higher than any prehistoric level.

The methane increase means that carbon dioxide is not the only concern in global warming: 0.6 billion tonnes of methane are entering the atmosphere each year. The capacity of the atmosphere to oxidise it all is reduced by about 30% by the presence of another pollutant, **carbon monoxide**. This is principally a product of burning fossil

fuels, especially in motor cars. A further concern over global warming is the frozen waterlogged tundra of North America and Asia. If this frozen ground warms up without drainage it will add substantially to worldwide methane production.

People have a fondness for 'gloom and doom' scenarios. If the climate does alter dramatically and sea-levels rise, it will happen relatively slowly. However, on an evolutionary time scale, it would probably be very fast. Good plant management to meet the consequences will require a sound understanding of ecology.

Further reading

Kimmins, J.P. (1987) *Forest Ecology*. Macmillan.
Wright, D.E. (1990) *The Greenhouse Effect – Causes and Consequences*. Hodder & Stoughton.
Bolin, B. *et al.* (1986) *The Greenhouse Effect, Climate Change and Ecosystems*. John Wiley & Sons.

Thought questions

1 What three conclusions can you draw from the Mauna Loa data (Figure 27.2)?

2 One suggestion for reducing the greenhouse effect has been to transport all the high-nutrient sewage from rich countries to the surface waters of the tropical oceans. Were this to be done huge blooms of algae would occur and massive sedimentation of organic matter would follow. Is this a solution?

3 What is the 'Gaia hypothesis'? How might the planet correct the present carbon dioxide disequilibrium even if the human species does not alter its behaviour?

4 Forests can only move slowly across a continent. If the Mediterranean climate shifted north to Britain and the British climate shifted to northern Norway in just a hundred years, how could we help plants and animals to move too?

28

Are We Making Deserts?
The Ecology of the African Drylands

During the 1980s a severe crisis affected the continent of Africa. Thirty countries were struck by famine or severe food shortage. From 1983 to 1985 our TV screens showed the terrifying images of starving children with wasted bodies, wizened features and helpless stares. In the worst affected areas, millions of people were in trouble because the rains repeatedly failed. Wells dried up. There was no forage for livestock and no crops. Seed failed to germinate; any remaining grain was eaten in desperation. Farmers sold their sheep, their goats and then their cattle and donkeys to buy grain. Next they sold their last cows, which by that time were failing to give milk; then they sold their ploughs and the oxen that they had used for ploughing. Finally they sold their homes. People wandered, ate only roots and leaves and, if they were strong enough to reach a distribution centre, might finally have found famine relief. Hundreds of thousands died.

To what extent is this an ecological problem? Are people making deserts by over-populating, over-grazing and mismanaging the ecosystem? Or are famines due to political problems, natural cycles of climate or some other cause? We need to know the answers to such questions because famines may well happen again. Biologists have carried out a great deal of research on the plant and animal communities of tropical drylands. How relevant is their work to the human problem?

The physical environment of the drylands

Ecologists need to understand the physical environment they are studying and be able to analyse its components. In the drylands of tropical Africa there is a complex interplay between the patterns of rainfall and the solar radiation, winds and soils. In more than half the continent the rainfall is unreliable and is less than 1000 mm per annum. Passing from the wetter to the drier areas, as mean annual rainfall decreases the relative reliability of the rains also declines: where it is most arid rainfall is least predictable. When rain occurs it often comes in intense rainstorms. When looking at the ecology of the drylands it is important to have some understanding of these factors and to distinguish between such terms as aridity, drought, degradation and desertification.

There is clearly a strong correlation between rainfall and vegetation types on the African continent, much of which is semi-arid or desert (see Figure 28.1). **Aridity**, which is lack of moisture, is common within large continental masses distant from the sea, in regions where there are offshore cold currents, or beneath frequent high-pressure anticyclonic systems. Annual rainfall over the past century in the Sahelian region (south of the Sahara Desert) shows great fluctuations (see Figure 28.3), with possible long-term cycles but no certain long-term downward trend. Indeed the wetter 1950s decade allowed pastoral people to move into desert areas from which they have been driven out again in the droughts of the 1960s and 1980s. Nevertheless, very dry years have become more common and there have been some changes in the seasonal patterns of rainfall. Recent crop failures in Nigeria have been due to mid-season droughts in August,

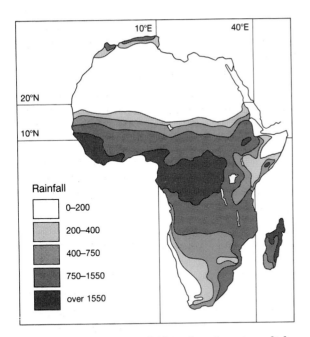

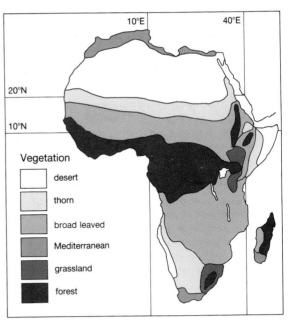

28.1 On the continent of Africa there is a strong link between the type of vegetation and the annual rainfall

and those in Ethiopia due to lack of spring rains. Changes in precipitation patterns may be as important for plant growth as changes in the mean amount falling. Where land degradation has occurred (loss of soil and plant cover) rainwater may be rapidly lost in run-off and not absorbed

slowly by the soil. This means that the same amount of rain is used less effectively by plants.

Drought is an unexpected failure of the rain. Droughts therefore cause losses of crops, forage and grazing; they are not just unexpected dry seasons. Farmers whose soil has been over-cultivated and has therefore lost much of its retentive capacity for water may experience crop failure and hence food shortage without a reduction in total rainfall.

28.2 Fluctuations in the central Sahelian rainfall between 1900 and 1990. The level datum zero line shows the mean 90 year rainfall for all locations, for which records exist, between 10° and 15° latitude North and the 10° and 40° longitude East. The graph line shows the extent of mean increase or decrease in each year above and below this mean

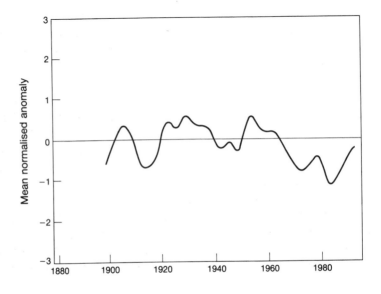

206

Similarly an area overstocked with cattle and from which too much vegetation has been removed during the dry season may experience a 'drought' even though the preceding rainfall was not abnormally low. Drought may therefore reveal an ecological imbalance and not be the cause of it.

Degradation of land is a term applied to phenomena such as the **erosion of soil** by water or wind. Arid lands suffer from water erosion because of the intensity of storms and lack of vegetation cover. On bare land heavy rain may not penetrate the soil sufficiently quickly to be absorbed. Sheets of water may run down gentle slopes and gather to form streams; these in turn may create gullies as some of the topsoil is carried away with the water. On the credit side, soil eroded in one location commonly accumulates at a lower level, transferring fertility and resources for plant growth. In arid areas these wet, deeper valley soils, which are the products of degradation elsewhere, provide dry-season fodder for herds and flocks.

Wind erosion is dramatic. Light, dry topsoil easily blows away and drifting sand makes it hard for plants to survive. Sand dunes in the desert, like those of the seashore, may be colonised by vegetation. Some dunes are valuable to grazing animals because they quickly absorb rainfall. The water percolates down out of reach of the sun's evaporative power, so conserving it for deep-rooted plants. Huge vegetated areas of the sub-Sahara are composed of such well-colonised dunes. The topsoil of the dune is richer in fine particles and organic matter than the sandy soil deeper down. This makes the environment very fragile if ever the wind can cause a 'blow out' of the surface.

Irrigation of drylands with slightly salty water causes a problem. As the water evaporates salt accumulates at the soil surface. This **salinisation** is a major form of degradation in irrigated lowland areas.

Any land surface that has been degraded will experience a decline in the productivity of its plant community, be it crop plants or natural vegetation, and will probably not have the capacity to return to its former state. Soils can reform, but if they are continuously degraded their capacity to recover is

diminished. A **desert** is defined as a land surface without plants. **Desertification** is therefore a term best confined to describing the loss of vegetation from the land surface. Acute de-vegetation only affects small areas of semi-arid lands at any one time and it may be short-lived. Nevertheless, when a sand dune does march over an oasis and smothers the deep-rooted green plants it is dramatic. Where major drought occurs at desert fringes the advance of the desert may appear to occur very fast indeed and, if it is your home, it will be extremely frightening.

Monitoring climatic and vegetational change

Many environmental changes today are monitored by satellite. Surface temperatures may be recorded and the various wavelengths of reflected radiation analysed. Rainfall and cloud cover can be monitored. Such **remote-sensing ecological surveys** of areas in Africa are carried out routinely at ground stations, for example at Swindon in Britain. Monitored changes may lead to the formulation of hypotheses to explain them. Some of the hypotheses may be complex.

Changes in patterns of Sahelian rainfall are due in part to remote events, like sun-spot cycles or the cold El Niño current in the Pacific Ocean. Other causes are closer at hand. The deforestation in West Africa may increase aridity further north-east, for much of the rain within a continent forms from water transpired by the plants of that region.

Albedo is a term used to describe the reflection of solar radiation from the earth's surface. It is the highest in areas with little vegetation, and can be accurately measured. Many studies since 1975 have found no significant change in surface reflectivity of the Sahel. However, such changes could contribute to long-term change in the following way. It has been suggested that if solar reflection was increased then the atmosphere would absorb less energy and the lower atmosphere would be more stable. Less turbulence would mean less rain. Dust clouds in the desert also prevent the cooling necessary to induce precipitation. Drier soils have a higher albedo, leading to a positive feedback effect; drought, in other words, may breed more droughts.

Even if no albedo change seems to be taking place, it is important to have ecologists on the ground looking at the vegetation. In central Sudan where pastures are losing palatable plants for livestock there is invasion by unpalatable shrubby species such as *Acacia mellifera*. As a result the herd animals have much less to eat, yet the reflectant albedo for the area is unchanged and the vegetational index (green cover) is greater. Again, removal of grasses in East Africa by over-grazing leads to less competition for water in the soils when the rains do come. As a result the bushes grow more quickly; biomass and green cover increase but productivity for the pastoral people declines. Satellites are a help in recording overall trends but it is important for the **field ecologist** to be on the ground recording vegetation and talking to the farmers who know their environment well.

The distinctiveness of dryland vegetation

In tropical dryland soils water is often too scarce to allow much soil formation. Surface salt is not easily washed away by the low rainfall. There is no rapid growth of plants to ensure good ground cover or to build up a rich humus from the plant material that dies back. The topsoil tends to be very thin and to contain the highest concentration of nutrients, which are rapidly recycled when the rains eventually come. Dryland plants themselves are thinly spread, and often very unevenly distributed across an area. Grazing animals may therefore need to walk long distances to gain enough food.

However, in a few places where there is good, deep soil and water, the high temperatures and bright sunlight ensure very high biological productivity. Where crops are irrigated in the desert they grow wonderfully – the desert oasis is proverbial. Dryland vegetation therefore exhibits a **pulse-response** to rain. Seeds germinate, grow fast and flower soon; shrubs burst into leaf in a matter of hours. Very quickly there is far more food than the

primary consumer (herbivores) can handle. Human communities are poised to exploit the rains with crops such as millet, which will be grown and harvested in weeks rather than months. Livestock that have been kept during the dry season in the least arid areas are now moved to the most arid ones to graze the first flush of new grass. Because farming of crops is so hazardous and because some pest problems are great (for example locusts, grain weevils and quelea birds) the more arid an area is, the more dependent the human community becomes on pastoral herding. Wherever the rainfall in Africa is less than 500 mm per annum, the erratic rains discourage crop-farming. In such unstable environments large herds of cattle, sheep, goats, donkeys and camels are kept by **nomadic pastoralists**. It is these people who have been unfairly accused of worsening the droughts and extending the deserts.

Optimising plant production

To understand the predicament of human communities living close to the edge of deserts one needs to understand the biology of **grazing** and **browsing**. Grazing, the eating of plants such as grass close to the ground, is distinguished from browsing where animals eat the green parts of bushes and trees. Plants that are eaten by herbivorous mammals have evolved with them for many thousands of years. The reason that pastoral people are able to live in the drylands at all relates to their symbiosis with the herbivores and the herbivores' co-evolved relationship with the **forage plants** (plants eaten as food by herbivores).

The biological productivity of forage plants, such as grasses, which are adapted to grazing, is well studied. Figure 28.3 shows how the size of a grazed plant relates to how fast it can produce plant material for a herbivore. If grazed down so that it has few leaves, it clearly cannot photosynthesise much and its rate of growth (productivity) will be low. If on the other hand it is under-grazed it becomes bigger, needs more water and minerals, and may grow less fast. Between these two ex-

28.3 The relationship between a grazed plant biomass and the absolute rate of increase in that plant's biomass if it is grazed. Grazed plants grow fastest if eaten off at an optimum level

tremes lies an optimum. In the drylands, well-grazed plants lying close to the ground may in fact be most productive to herbivores. They may also be better able to withstand drought. Productive but low-vegetated plant communities conserve soil moisture well and are not threatened by increasing over-grazing until they are either heavily trampled or they lose their reservoir of seeds which are waiting to germinate.

Carrying capacity – optimising animal production

The idea of grazing forage plants to an optimum level is familiar to farmers in Britain; the grazing intensity should be best for the production of forage and for the animals produced from it. A particular area can permanently carry only so much stock. This idea of **carrying capacity** is familiar to biologists. There is a limit to the number of animals an environment can carry for a sustained period of time. Studies of sheep stocking rates in Britain show that as the stocking rate increases beyond a certain point the live-weight gain per sheep de-clines. The gain in live weight per hectare of the whole flock of sheep increases initially with in-creased stocking. As the stocking rate increases

further, the gain in live weight declines sharply as competition between sheep for the available food destroys the pasture. This enables a determination of the optimum stock rate which maximises the use of the grass. Figure 28.4 shows, with respect to the animal and not the plant, the meaning of **over-grazing** and **under-grazing**.

Rangeland biologists have made very signifi-cant contributions to our understanding of the densities of herbivores that an environment can carry. Studies of how much each herbivore eats in relation to body mass and age have led to precise means of calculating stocking rates. The standard tropical livestock unit is a 250 kg animal, equiva-lent to eight sheep or goats. Such figures allow a rancher to mix animals of different sorts and ages on a known area of range and be confident that they will be fed adequately by the carrying capacity of the land without over- or under-grazing for a prolonged period of time.

Figure 28.4 gives an optimum of 40 sheep per hectare (British data) for a closely grazed summer pasture. Here there would have been a high rainfall and long hours of sunshine. In African drylands, however, stocking rates are expressed in hectares per sheep not sheep per hectare! Are such ideas of carrying capacity appropriate to African drylands where rainfall is so unpredictable? Table 28.1

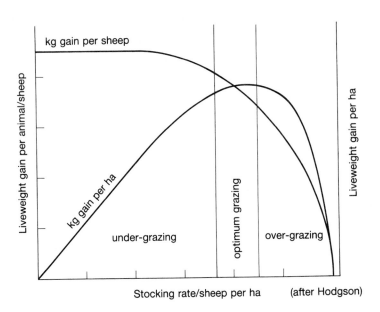

28.4 The relationship between the density of animals grazing an area (stocking rate) and how much each animal gains, in contrast to how much all the animals may gain on that area. If grass production is constant there is a stocking density with an optimum return to the owner of the animals

shows the relationship between rainfall, cattle stocking rate, weight gain per animal per day and live-weight gain per hectare per annum. The data are based on an attempt to define **optimum stocking rates** on unfertilised native grassland in Africa. The pasture varies from rich savannah grassland with a fair rainfall at one extreme to semi-desert at the other.

The striking feature of the data in Table 28.1 is the variation in animal productivity with the mean annual rainfall. Without water the drylands are seemingly unproductive. However, it is striking that the daily growth rate of individual animals is seemingly so constant (at about 0.12 kg per day for a 250 kg animal) over this vast range of conditions, and that it is so high in the driest areas.

Is dryland animal production different?

Some important studies have been made on livestock feeding on dry or heavily grazed pastures. Animals need a dry matter intake of 2.5 to 3.0% of their body weight per day to survive. Only 30–40% of the available forage may be digestible. Not surprisingly, livestock on poor pasture spend more hours feeding per day, take more bites of forage material altogether and take less dry matter per bite than animals on rich pasture. Cattle will eat the uppermost leaves only if there is plenty of forage, but as the available pasture declines, they will eat

Table 28.1 The relationship between rainfall, cattle stocking rates and productivity

Location	Rainfall mm of rain per year	Stocking rate 250 kg steers per ha	Productivity kg per animal per day	Productivity kg per ha per year
Serere, Uganda, East Africa	1400	5.0	0.14	255
Ibadan, Nigeria, West Africa	1200	3.2	0.12	140
Ankole, Uganda, East Africa	1000	1.2	0.12	52
Maasailand, Kenya, East Africa	710	0.31	0.09	10
Samburu, Kenya, East Africa	500	0.26	0.08	8
Southern Niger, Niger, West Africa	450	0.22	0.09	7
Kordofan, Sudan, NE Africa	350	0.08	0.17	5

(based on P. C. Whiteman et. al. (1980) Tropical Pasture Science, *Oxford University Press)*

28.5 Fulbe herders in Niger, with sheep and cattle during a period of drought

more leaf and stem and finally eat very little of each plant at all, seeming impatient to move on to the next where the amount of available leaf might be greater. It is wrong to regard all herbivores as unselective lawnmowers: some of them are very selective, not merely choosing leaves but selecting older or younger leaves, stem tops, flowers or seed heads. This is particularly true of sheep and goats which have smaller mouths. There is also much browsing of bushes and trees. As grazing pressure increases on rangelands there is a tendency for the perennial and then annual grasses to decline in ground cover, and for the bushes to increase. Herb cover and bush cover are negatively correlated. The animals herded by pastoralists have adapted to this and are to some extent responsible for creating and maintaining the diversity (see Table 28.2).

Such studies are fundamentally important, not least in demonstrating that in the drylands animals can grow well if the stocking density is low

Table 28.2 Percentage annual diet composition for cattle, sheep and goats in semi-arid Mali

Food source	Cattle	Sheep	Goats
Residues from rainy season crops	43	7	2
Herbaceous grazing (grass etc.)	53	59	11
Browse from trees and bushes	4	34	87

(IUCN (1986) The Sahel Report, IUCN, Gland)

enough. Indeed, individual animal **growth rates** may be very high, especially in the semi-arid zones after good rains.

Monitoring the vegetation change due to livestock

Range ecologists classify plants into three classes by their successional behaviour under heavy grazing or browsing – 'increasers', 'decreasers' and 'invaders'. **Increasers** are plants that expand their frequency or ground cover under grazing or browsing. Some of these may well be surviving and increasing because the animals avoid them. Others will provide good grazing, be well eaten, and respond by growing better. **Decreasers** decline in frequency, or ground cover, as pressure increases. Unfortunately some of these may be nutritious grasses. **Invaders** are absent from normal grassland but invade over-grazed areas. They are the **indicator species** of over-grazing. In Ankole in East Africa, *Brachiaria decumbens* is an increaser in cattle-grazed grasslands and is important in raising the carrying capacity of heavily grazed pasture as it provides excellent forage. By contrast, *Cenchrus biflorus* in the semi-arid Sudan is a highly palatable grass but declines under heavy grazing. Unpalatable and poisonous invaders are a major problem in certain areas. Some ecologists argue that unpalatable plants such as *Acacia mellifera* allow the soil to recuperate by lowering the carrying capacity and increasing the vegetation cover. Perhaps later the more palatable species will return. To the perceptive ecologist the relative abundance of such species makes them important environmental indicators.

Have ecologists anything to contribute?

Our earliest attempts to understand the grazing ecology of the African drylands were too simplistic and were based on the ideas of carrying capacity from temperate, high-rainfall environments. Many **ranching schemes** in Africa have failed for this reason or are unsustainable. Range ecologists are therefore now viewing the way that nomadic pastoralists manage their grazing with acute interest.

First, it seems important to realise that over the past 6000 years the pastoralists have gradually displaced the original wild animals and human hunter-gatherers. At one time the herbivorous **wild animals** filled every conceivable grazing and browsing **niche** in the food chain. The pastoralist's livestock are evolving into these patterns and have been subjected to intense selection pressure at each drought. Livestock clearly utilise plants differently. Cattle are efficient grassland grazers, but do not graze as close to the ground as sheep. Goats, by reaching up to and climbing up trees, eat back much woody vegetation. Their plant preferences may complement those of sheep and by their behaviour they keep mixed flocks, containing sheep, on the move. Goats have the greatest stamina in droughts and reproduce fastest at the end of a drought when other stock will take longer to recover. If one-third of the numbers of a herd are lost in a drought, goats recover to previous levels in one and a half years, whilst cattle take four years. In very dry areas pastoralists keep the more desert-adapted camels and donkeys in addition but many fewer cattle.

Nomadic herding is a skilled practice. The pulse of plant production after rain produces much food that waits for the herds to come to it. Herd movements over very large distances therefore commonly take place.

If animals were to be confined to a fenced ranch, the carrying capacity would need to be set very low indeed to allow for drought years. Also production levels would be too low to support the human population, though exporting saleable beef from well-grown animals would be easier.

In contrast to any settled ranching scheme the pastoral system is **opportunistic**. Very large herds build up in good years. Although individual animals may not grow fast all the time, there is a much higher production of food from a unit area of land than is possible with ranching. Pastoralists feed on milk rather than meat to a large extent. Daily yields of milk from wandering herds are very good indicators of the quality of food ingested by the animals. Confined animals may not have the necessary food choices to do so well.

The **human population** is undoubtedly growing in many of the drylands, at a rate of about 1% per annum, and over-grazing may well be causing degradation from which it is hard for the land to recover. Human population growth is due, in some part, to medical and veterinary services that did not exist before. However, these services are extremely rudimentary and **population growth rates** are not nearly as high as in less arid areas (2–3%), where there has been inexorable population growth (half the population of Africa will be urban-dwelling by 2000). Nomads seem to adjust their meat and milk supply to their needs as well as they can. They have many social customs and land-ownership systems which limit population growth rates. Sadly it is these sorts of bio-sociological controls that have increasingly broken down under political pressure, outside influences and even offers of help. Not least of these have been aid programmes involving the sinking of numerous wells to obtain deep ground-water sources. Watering points have become surrounded by huge treeless over-grazed circles.

Drylands have been managed successfully by people for thousands of years and, until recently, wildlife and pastoralists were in good balance. This is why Africa still has so many wild animal species. To be of any help ecologists need to learn their science in the field, by painstaking investigation. So far, in the African drylands they have discovered something of how species interact and why it is that traditional management systems are successful, against the odds. Are we making deserts? Only time will answer that question.

Further reading

Cloudsley-Thomson, J.L. (1984) *Sahara Desert.* Pergamon.
IUCN (1986) *The Sahel Report.* International Union for the Conservation of Nature and Natural Resources, Gland, Switzerland.
Whiteman, P.C. (1980) *Tropical Pasture Science.* Oxford University Press.

Thought questions

1 What methods of ecological analysis would you use to study natural vegetation in a semi-desert area?

2 Look at the data in Table 28.2. Plot a graph of total animal productivity (kg per ha per year) against rainfall (mm per year). What does the line of best fit tell you about rain and the growth of cattle in tropical environments?

29

Pandas, Polar Bears and Zoos

Zoos arouse great passion and controversy. Some people argue that the keeping of any animal in captivity is wrong and that zoos should therefore be banned. Others maintain that zoos can play a vital role in education, conservation and research.

Whatever side is right, there is no doubt that the good modern zoo is a very different institution from its counterpart 40 years ago. In this chapter we will look at whether zoos do have a role to play in the modern world.

Zoos as entertainment

It may seem odd to start with the notion that zoos should provide **entertainment**. Yet if zoos do not provide what people want to see, people will not go to them. As the great majority of zoos rely entirely on the money that people pay at the turnstiles, this means that no zoo can afford to ignore the wishes of the public. In 1982 the English Tourist Board carried out a major survey into why people visit zoos and found that the main reason is so that families can enjoy a day out. In other words, zoos must attract and entertain. People will not pay to go to a zoo simply because of all the good work it does in conservation, education and research.

What most people want from zoos nowadays is to have good views of impressive and exotic animals looking healthy in a high standard of accommodation. Now, this actually fits quite well with the other objectives that zoos have – **conservation**, **education** and **research**. These necessarily require keeping animals, often rare ones, in good conditions. However, there are some problems. The public's perception of what makes a good zoo enclosure may not always be the same as an animal's. For instance, many visitors prefer to see an animal moving around. Yet such movement may be the awful stereotyped and repetitive tread one sometimes sees in big cats such as leopards (Figure 29.1) A better enclosure for such an animal

is one which allows it to move fast a few times a day, and spend much of the rest of the day resting. This means having a very large enclosure, which may be prohibitively expensive, and also means that most of the time visitors do not have a very good view of the animals.

Increasingly, people want more from a zoo than being able to see healthy and impressive animals. They want, for example, good quality, inexpensive food, clean toilets and somewhere to sit down. Over half the visitors to zoos are children, yet many zoos pay almost no attention to their needs and expectations. However, some zoo owners are beginning to realise that providing what the public wants is a

29.1 A caged leopard will repeatedly walk the same pathway exactly

good way of generating income, to the disapproval of some more conservative zoo owners. When the Paradise Park in Cornwall built a 3000ft² amusement arcade, some traditional zoo managers were extremely scathing. But the money raised from space-invader machines, shops, a cafe, a pub, a restaurant and an on-site brewery helped the zoo to build extensive breeding facilities for the park's 40 endangered species of birds.

Conservation and zoos

There was a time when the only reason zoos bred animals was to attract customers who liked seeing young elephants, lion cubs or whatever. Then public opinion began to react against the continued capture of zoo specimens from the wild. Obtaining animals from the wild frequently involves disturbance to natural environments. Also, in order to capture some species such as chimpanzees, it is often necessary to kill other animals of the same species as they try to protect one another. In addition it is very expensive if a zoo has to keep on replenishing its stocks from distant countries.

As zoos began to breed more of their animals, some far-sighted zoo owners realised that through breeding, zoos could make a major contribution to species conservation. One of the earliest zoo owners with this attitude was Gerald Durrell, founder of the

29.2 The golden lion tamarin (see text)

Jersey Wildlife Trust. With a few other like-minded people Durrell organised the first **World Conference on the Breeding of Endangered Species**, held in 1972 on Jersey. The conference produced a six-point declaration, delivered at the end of the meeting by its chairman Sir Peter Scott.

- The breeding of endangered species and subspecies of animals in captivity is likely to be crucial to the survival of many forms. It must therefore be used as a method of preventing extinction, alongside the maintenance of the wild stock in their natural habitat.
- The techniques must be learned, improved, extended and published.
- All who keep endangered species have a responsibility to carry out breeding programmes and for this purpose to co-operate both with other zoos or collections and with conservationists in returning them to the wild.
- Such programmes will reduce the demands being made currently on wild populations and may serve to reinforce them, or if they have disappeared in the wild, to re-establish them.
- Even if reintroduction proves to be impossible, maintaining a captive population is obviously preferable to the irrevocable alternative of extinction.
- Wherever possible breeding programmes should be encouraged and supported in habitats or regions natural to the endangered species. One important reason for this is the education of the indigenous human population, who otherwise may not completely understand the significance, the requirements or the future of the animals, upon which they themselves will depend.

Since 1972 zoos have increasingly seen **conservation** as one of their major priorities. Almost every zoo, however small, has at least one **captive breeding programme**. One of the more successful captive breeding programmes has involved the rescue from near-extinction of the golden lion tamarin.

Captive breeding of the golden lion tamarin

In the wild the golden lion tamarin *Leontopithecus rosalia*, shown in Figure 29.2, is restricted to low-altitude forests in coastal parts of the state of Rio de Janeiro in Brazil. Unfortunately this area is easily cleared for agriculture and pasture land. Another problem for the tamarin is that during the 1960s and 1970s thousands were exported as pets or to zoos. Finally, the animal is considered a local delicacy and is possibly still killed for its meat.

By the early 1980s the species was represented in the wild by only two populations. By the mid 1980s the tamarin had become extinct in one of these, mainly because of the erection of large numbers of beachfront houses. However, tamarins were still found in the other, the Poço d'Anta Biological Reserve, set up in 1974 mainly for the protection of the tamarin. Even this reserve was in danger, though. It was traversed by a railway line and a road, a dam was being completed which would flood some of it, and poaching was rife.

Fortunately Dr Devra Kleiman of the National Zoo in Washington has co-ordinated an internationally run captive breeding programme. From a zoo population of 70 in 1977, numbers reached over 500 by 1988. By then the success of the zoo programme had been such that it had become possible to reintroduce some of the zoo-bred tamarins back into the wild in the Poço d'Anta Reserve. As so often happens in these situations there was initially considerable mortality. However, the reintroductions have proved successful: it is known that the tamarins have succeeded in re-establishing themselves and are breeding. As a result the population of the reserve has increased from about 75–100 animals in the mid 1980s to 450 by 1990. Despite this, the importance of zoos continuing to keep and breed the species was emphasised early in 1990 when an unseasonal fire destroyed 30% of the reserve.

Zoos and the problems of inbreeding

With the growth of captive breeding programmes, zoos have become more sensitive to the problems of **inbreeding**. Inbreeding occurs when offspring result from parents which are themselves closely related, for example a brother and sister. Some species inbreed naturally in the wild. In such cases inbreeding in zoos poses few problems. However, many species show strict **outbreeding** in nature; parents are at most only distantly related to each other. Dr Katherine Ralls has shown that, in such cases, inbreeding in zoos is associated with reduced offspring viability. The reasons for this are well known to geneticists. Inbreeding greatly increases the chances of an individual inheriting the same deleterious recessive allele from both parents. For instance, each of us carries on average four **lethal recessives** – alleles which, if homozygous, would kill us. On average humans inherit two of these from one parent and two from the other. Now consider a child born as a result of a sexual relationship between a brother and sister. There is a high risk that the child will inherit two copies of the same recessive lethal – one from each parent. Thankfully there is not a large amount of data on which to test this theory in humans. However, data that do exist agree with the predictions of geneticists. Children born as a result of **incest** very often die soon after birth or suffer considerable physical or mental handicaps.

One example of how zoos are ensuring that they avoid the problems of inbreeding and maintain the **genetic diversity** of their animals is provided by Rothschild's mynah, a very handsome bird also known as the Bali starling. Rothschild's mynah is the only vertebrate that is **endemic** to Bali, that is, native to the island and occurring nowhere else in the wild. A survey carried out in 1984 revealed the presence of only 200 birds on the island. By 1987 the population had fallen to around 55. However, there are at least 500 Rothschild's mynahs in captivity. Unfortunately they do not breed very well in captivity. An examination of the breeding records of zoos revealed that over half of all the captive birds were descended from only five individuals. Just five birds were responsible for over half of all the birds. This is far too few for genetic comfort. Most population geneticists reckon that a population of around five hundred is adequate to avoid inbreeding and conserve genetic variation, provided all the individuals contribute to each generation. A further problem was revealed by DNA fingerprinting (see Chapter 13): most of the birds that have contributed to the captive population are themselves closely related. Dr Georgina Mace at the Institute of Zoology in London Zoo now sorts out by computer the best possible matings to avoid inbreeding and ensure that as many birds as possible contribute to the next generation, so that few alleles are lost from the genetic pool. In 1988, for instance, Mace advised Harewood Bird Garden in Yorkshire to swap its male mynahs with others in Bristol and Paignton zoos; Guernsey Zoo to swap with Jersey Zoo; Edinburgh Zoo to receive some birds from Lotherton Hall Bird Gardens in Leeds and send some to London Zoo; and so on. Early indications are that these re-paired birds produce more surviving offspring.

Education and zoos

Captive breeding sounds very exciting, but Norman Myers, a protagonist of rainforest conservation, has pointed out that when you look at the economics of it all, zoos will never be able to save more than a handful of species endangered in the wild. At 1990 prices it costs a zoo at least £500 per individual for the annual maintenance (space, food, heating, veterinary care, etc.) of an 'average' mammal or bird. Suppose that the zoos of the world were to keep 2000 species of mammals or birds, each with a population size of 500 individuals, for just 20 years. The total cost works out at over £10 thousand million, over half of what it cost the United States to put a man on the moon.

The conclusion to be drawn from Myers' analysis is that while zoos may play a direct role in the conservation of some species, they cannot hope to conserve more than a fraction of the world's endangered animals. After all, there are probably around twenty to thirty million species of organisms in existence today. However, zoos may be able to play an important but less direct role in conser-

vation through **education**. The number of people who go to zoos should not be underestimated. Each year Europe's zoos receive approximately 100 million visitors – a lot of people.

If zoos are to play a major role in education, it is important that they play to their strengths. In the 1980s many zoos used cheaply duplicated worksheets that could be given by teachers to school children. These often contained such riveting questions as: 'From which part of the world do lions come?' 'What do lions eat? and 'What is the hair around the head of a male lion called?' Now there is nothing intrinsically wrong with such questions, but they are far from ideal. The problem is twofold. First they are not very exciting; and second, they can be answered without having to go anywhere near a zoo. It is important, instead of this, for zoos to make the most of what they have. Zoos are not natural places, and therefore you will never be able to see a lion hunting as you might on a television documentary. However, what a zoo can offer is a real live lion. If zoos have to produce worksheets, they would do better to ask the sorts of questions that can best be answered in a zoo: 'Can you hear a lion when it walks?'; 'Can you move as quietly as that?'; 'What do lions smell like?' and 'How does it feel when a lion looks straight at you?'.

A good zoo should inspire its visitors into believing that it is worth fighting to preserve nature.

Some zoos have established excellent working relationships with local schools. For example, Drusillas, a small zoo in Sussex, has a carefully thought-out work experience scheme in which children trail staff including the zoo director himself, the curator, the assistant curator, animal keepers, the shop manager, a gardener and some of the secretarial staff. This gives the child a much better idea of the workings of the zoo and is often more fun than just meandering around the zoo rather aimlessly for an hour in a group of 20. The scheme seems to have been a great success. The pupils learnt a great deal by talking with and listening to the staff, while some staff found the children's help quite useful.

Research and zoos

A zoo cannot avoid doing **scientific research**. London Zoo, for instance, houses over 8000 animals of more than 900 species, and over 1000 animals are born there each year. By the time a zoo has worked out how to feed its animals, keep them healthy and allowed them to reproduce it has done a tremendous amount of applied research. To take just one example, most large zoos carry out many investigations into reproductive physiology. Almost everything we know about the reproduction of the giant panda comes from zoo studies: the research has involved determining oestrous cycles, pregnancy testing by analysing hormone levels in the urine, assessing the fertility of males by microscopic analysis of semen, and investigating the possibilities of artificial insemination.

Is it right to have zoos?

The only way in which zoos can fundamentally be justified is if they help animals through conservation, education, research and the promotion of public awareness done in the zoos. The animals that they help must include both the animals they house and, looking further afield, the animals conserved in the wild. If zoos really take this rule to heart, it may mean some important changes in the animals they keep.

29.3 A polar bear in its Arctic environment

Take the polar bear shown in Figure 29.3, for instance. In 1986 a pressure group called Zoo Check reported that more than half the polar bears in Britain are 'psychotic'. They pass their days in endless pacing and swaying movements; sometimes they even mutilate themselves. Stefan Omrod of the Royal Society for the Prevention of Cruelty to Animals studied zoo designs both in Europe and in the United States. He concluded that no zoo can provide enough space and stimulation to keep these magnificent animals mentally healthy. The reason is that in their native habitat polar bears roam over thousands of square kilometres. They find zoos small and boring. Tacoma Zoo in Washington State is generally reckoned to have the finest polar bear enclosure in the world, situated on a pine-covered hillside and containing a stream and lake. Even there, though, the polar bears show characteristic and repetitive pacing, rocking and head-swaying movements never observed in the wild. It must be concluded that there are really no convincing conservation, educational or research arguments to justify keeping polar bears in zoos. In particular, polar bears are in no danger of becoming extinct.

In contrast to the polar bear, the golden lion tamarin is an example of an animal that was in danger of going extinct, but now looks as though it has been rescued by zoos. Between these two extremes there are less clear-cut examples, such as the giant panda.

The giant panda is in danger of going extinct. No one knows precisely how many there are, but the number is probably fewer than a thousand. Several factors conspire to threaten pandas. First, they reproduce extremely slowly. Females are sexually receptive only once a year and for only about half of their 20 years of life. Although two or even three young are born at once, no more than one has ever been known to survive. Once mated, a female panda is not usually receptive again for two years. All in all, panda populations do not exactly bounce back from times of adversity. An additional problem is that once every 10–30 years their staple food plant bamboo fails completely in huge areas. This is because plants of bamboo species die as soon as they have finished flowering, though the plants may be many years old before they flower. However, when they do flower, they do so synchronously across huge areas. As a result, every now and again many pandas die of starvation. Despite being the symbol of the **World Wide Fund for Nature (WWF)**, panda skins can still fetch $200 000 in Japan. Even though nine people have recently been given life sentences in China for killing pandas and trading their skins, the killing continues. In 1988 in Sichuan province, Chinese police discovered more than 140 panda pelts, due to be smuggled abroad.

In the face of these dangers to the panda, captive breeding may be the only option. Unfortunately it is extremely difficult to breed pandas. In 1989 there were 15 pandas in zoos outside China: 5 in Mexico, 4 in Japan, 4 in Europe and 2 in the United States. These zoos have a good record of working together, pooling the results of their research and loaning their pandas to one another to try to encourage breeding. One zoo with an encouraging breeding record is Chapultepec Zoo in Mexico. The current plan is to collect semen from the European males and fly it to Mexico to try artificial insemination when either of the two females there becomes receptive.

Whether or not zoos succeed in rescuing the giant panda from extinction, the years ahead are likely to see significant improvements in the way zoos operate, the conditions in which they keep their animals, the education they provide and the research they carry out. Zoos depend on the public and so, ultimately, their fate will depend on whether they are seen by the public to be doing a good job and to be worth paying money to go and visit. However, zoos must never be regarded as an alternative to the conservation of endangered species and their environments in the wild. Rather, they should help spur people on to make the financial commitments and display the political will needed to enable sustained advances in conservation to be made.

Further reading

Universities Federation for Animal Welfare (1988) *Why Zoos?* UFAW, 8 Hamilton Close, South Mimms, Potters Bar, EN6 3QD.
Tudge, C. (1988) Breeding by Numbers. *New Scientist*, 1 September 1988, pp. 68–71.
Durrell, G. (1976) *Catch Me a Colobus*. Penguin; first published in 1972 by Collins.

Thought questions

1 If you were going to set up a zoo, what criteria would you use to decide upon your choice of animals?

2 Why do you think most zoos allow almost no close contact between the animals and visitors?

3 How do you imagine that genetic fingerprinting could help in the setting up of a captive breeding programme (see Chapter 13)?

Things to do

You should get permission from the zoo's owners before undertaking these or any related projects.

1. Find an animal species kept by two or three zoos within travelling distance of where you live. Work out an objective way of comparing their living conditions (size of enclosure, frequency of feeding, variety in their daily routine, etc.) and see if this correlates with their behaviour in any way.

2. Prepare a questionnaire and conduct a survey to examine the reasons why visitors go to a particular zoo.

3. If you live near to a zoo, visit regularly so that you can research an animal's behaviour. This could be related to its daily cycle of activities. Repetitive walking, body-swaying and head-swinging are often observed. When are these behaviours indulged in? Are they due to such factors as boredom, over confinement, or the stress of human observers being near at hand? How could you discover the latter without you yourself being a factor in determining the animal's behaviour? Write up your report for the zoo.

30
Botanic Gardens and Gene Banks

Just as zoological gardens carry out work in conservation, research and education and yet have to provide entertainment, the same is true for the world's 1400 **botanic gardens** and **arboreta** (botanical gardens specifically for trees; singular aboretum). Unlike zoos, botanic gardens do not have to raise a large proportion of their funding from the public, mainly because, to be honest, not enough people would pay to go into a botanic garden. Thus they may give the appearance of not being much affected by commercial considerations and the modern world. Nothing could be further from the truth. Behind the leisurely façade that they seem to display, and which makes them such peaceful places to walk through and relax in, many of today's botanic gardens are run with the cost-effectiveness and purpose of any business and are in the front line of both pure and applied botanical research. It is probably also fair to say that while zoos have only recently become heavily involved in conservation, botanic gardens have played an important role in this area for many years.

The changing role of the botanic garden

It is not that easy to define a botanic garden. When does a botanic garden become a park or ordinary garden? The International Union for the Conservation of Nature and Natural Resources (IUCN) states that botanic gardens have plant collections that are managed in a scientific way and have a particular purpose other than simply pleasure or amenity. To the visitor, perhaps the best single criterion is that the plants in a botanic garden are generally labelled with their scientific names. Frequently the label also displays other information, such as the origin of the plant or date of its planting.

The earliest botanic gardens were created in China, in prehistoric Mexico and in the Arab world. Unfortunately we still do not know a great deal about them. In the West the first botanic gardens were medicinal gardens whose main function was to grow plants of medicinal value such as herbs, for the training of medical students. The first of these gardens was founded at Pisa in 1543. Others soon followed at Padua, Florence, Bologna and Zurich. The first in Britain was at Oxford, and was established in 1621 (see Figure 30.1).

Botanic gardens soon diversified and the focus of research shifted to taxonomic studies. In the eighteenth and nineteenth centuries European plant collectors explored the world, bringing back huge quantities of both living and dead material. This all had to be identified, or described if new to science. The living material needed to be carefully grown, often in large glasshouses that could mimic the warm, moist climate of the tropics. The dead material had to be catalogued and stored. As a result, botanic gardens soon became

30.1   *The Oxford Botanic Garden*

associated with herbaria, glasshouses, libraries and laboratories.

Nowadays there are many different types of botanic garden. Although the great botanic gardens still resemble those of the nineteenth century in layout and essential purpose, today there are also many smaller specialist botanic gardens. For instance, India and some European countries have a number of agrobotanic gardens specialising in the cultivation of and research into agricultural and horticultural plants; in Britain the national horticultural collection of vegetables is at Wellesbourne in Warwickshire. There are also several specialist orchid gardens. These focus on the cultivation and propagation of orchids and may generate much of their income from the sale of orchids. One of the largest is the Wheeler Orchid Collection and Species Bank at Bell State University, Indiana which has 3000 orchid species in cultivation including several which are believed to be extinct in the wild.

The IUCN Botanic Gardens Conservation Strategy

What should be the functions of botanic gardens nowadays? During the 1980s, the IUCN gave a great deal of consideration to the role of botanic gardens and formulated an **IUCN Botanic Gardens Conservation Strategy**. The aim was to encourage a far greater involvement by botanic gardens in international plant conservation. The IUCN believes that the major role of botanic gardens will be to contribute to the preservation of **plant genetic diversity** and to help ensure the **sustainable utilisation** of **plant species** and **ecosystems** in which they occur.

This work is very urgent: it is generally agreed that approximately one-quarter of the world's 250 000 species of plants are in danger of extinction within the next 30 years. It is also a source of great concern that only 20 plant species provide over 85% of the world's food, yet even these few species are suffering a decline in their genetic diversity. Finally, many plants have never been examined for their possible commercial exploitation; indeed countless thousands remain totally unknown

to science. It should also be remembered that the world's botanic gardens receive about 100 million visitors a year, which means that they should be able to achieve a tremendous amount of education.

The Royal Botanic Gardens, Kew

For an example of what a modern botanic garden does in the fields of **conservation** and **research**, we can look at the Royal Botanic Gardens at Kew. The difference between what a zoo can hope to achieve in conservation and what a botanic garden can is clear from the fact that while London Zoo houses 900 species of animals, Kew boasts over 50 000 species of plants! Plants are, of course, cheaper to feed and easier to house than animals.

Most usefully, their seeds can often be kept for long periods of time. Kew's **seed bank** grew from the need to deal more effectively with the huge number of requests it receives each year from other botanic gardens for plants. Until the advent of the seed bank, the seeds would be collected afresh each year. The seed bank became possible when botanists gained a better understanding of plant **quiescence** (the condition of a seed unable to germinate only because the external conditions required for growth are not present) and **dormancy** (the condition of a seed when it fails to germinate because of its internal state, even though external conditions such as temperature and moisture are suitable). It soon became possible to hold seeds under tolerably good storage conditions for several years. Nowadays, for most plants careful reduction of the moisture content under conditions of low temperature followed by freezing will preserve seed for many years, probably often for as long as 200 years.

In the 1970s Kew's policy began to shift away from the collection of seed from its own garden to the collection of seed from the wild, the aim being to ensure that it holds seed obtained from a variety of individuals with truly wild genotypes. This policy shift has helped to ensure that the great plant-collecting trips of the eighteenth and nineteenth centuries have continued, albeit in twentieth-century guise. Botanists from Kew collect seeds and other plant specimens from all over the world, in places as far away and exotic-sounding as the Tortoise Islands in the Indian Ocean, the Wakhan Corridor in Afghanistan, the Yunnan Mountains of China and the Solomon Islands in the Pacific Ocean.

Initially the Kew seed bank set out with the ambitious target of holding seed of all the world's plant species. However, some species, including a large number that occur in tropical rainforests, have seeds that are large and fleshy and are impossible to store for long periods of time with present-day technology. Increasingly it is felt that *in situ* conservation is the only real solution both for these plants and for the animals, fungi and other organisms associated with them. Seed collecting in the dry tropics, such as the savannahs of Africa, is much easier and more productive.

Planning a seed-collecting trip takes at least as long as planning any other expedition. Permissions have to be obtained; gone are the days when foreign collectors could collect what they liked. Nowadays for permission to be given, the benefit to the country from which the seed is being obtained must be apparent. Usually this means leaving a representative sample of seeds or duplicate pressed specimens, suitably identified, in the country of origin. Conservation considerations are paramount. The generally accepted rule is never to collect more than 20% of the available seed.

Once collected, the seed must often be dried. Sun-drying has to be avoided because, although rapid, the temperature it induces may reduce the longevity of seed intended for long-term storage. The best drying agents to use depend on the types of seed and the weather. They vary from silica gel to dried rice.

Gene banks

For purely historical reasons, the term **gene bank** is usually confined to the storage of crop plants. It is nearly always seeds that are stored, as in the case of non-crop plants. The importance of gene banks cannot be overestimated. The genetic uniformity among most of our food plants is frighten-ing. So far, we have managed to avoid complete disaster through the use of huge amounts of pesticides. However, as pesticide resistance becomes ever more common, there always lurks the possibility that one year the entire wheat, maize or potato harvest of a country may be wiped out. As more and more countries tend to grow the same crop varieties, the crisis could well be international in scope.

Such a scenario may seem alarmist, but there is good evidence that genetic uniformity was one of the major contributing factors to the devastating Irish potato famine of the late 1840s. The famine resulted in the starvation of over a million people and the emigration to the United States of about one and a half million – and that from a population of only nine million people. Unlike their counterparts in the Andes, where the potato was domesticated over 8000 years ago and where numerous varieties of potato are grown, the Irish grew potatoes descended from only a few clones introduced from England and mainland Europe. These in turn were the result of just two samples of potatoes brought from South America to Spain in 1570 and to England around 1590. In the Irish potato famine potato blight, caused by the protoctist *Phytophthora infestans*, spread like wildfire. In the Andes, the mixture of different natural varieties provided some protection against the disease. (Such naturally occurring varieties are generally called **landraces**.)

It is even possible that the genetic uniformity of crop plants may have played a part in the collapse of the Mayan civilisation in Mexico. In Mexico increases in the human population led to the intensification of agriculture from around AD 500. The traditional pattern of slash-and-burn farming gave-way to extensive terracing of slopes and reclamation of formerly untilled swamp land for agriculture. Maize became the dominant food and year-in, year-out production may have facilitated the build-up of pests. Successive outbreaks of maize mosaic virus transmitted by corn leafhoppers probably led to a collapse in maize production and may well have contributed to the demise of the Mayas and their conquest by the Toltecs in about AD 900.

The importance of conserving wild relatives of crop plants

In 1977 Rafael Guzmán, seen in Figure 30.2, was a botany student at the University of Guadalajara in Mexico. That year he discovered a wild relative of maize (corn) new to science – *Zea diploperennis*. Seeds of the new species were sent to some 500 institutions for investigation. One of them, the Ohio Agricultural Research and Development Centre, found that the plants were immune to, or tolerant of, seven of the nine tropical viral diseases of corn. For three of these diseases *Zea diploperennis* is the only source of viral immunity. This may prove to be of great value as some of the viruses cause commercially important diseases. The species may also provide genes for greater stalk and root strength, for multiple ears and for tolerance to poorly drained soil. These attributes are not expected to be integrated into commercial corn until the late 1990s, but Guzmán's discovery illustrates the potential importance of conserving the wild relatives of crop plants.

A good example of a plant where the potential of wild relatives has already been exploited quite thoroughly is the tomato. It is true to say that without its wild relatives, the modern tomato would not exist. Extensive hybridisation over many years has incorporated several of the valuable features displayed by the many different native species of tomato, as indicated in Figure 30.3.

30.2 Rafael Guzman standing beside the wild relative of maize that he discovered

Conventional plant breeding has dangerously narrowed the **genetic base** of crop plants. When the Plant Breeding Institute in Cambridge was privatised in June 1987 and became Plant Breeding International, the president of the IUCN, Professor Swaminathan, urged the rich countries of the world to recognise that it was many of the poorest peasant farmers who were keeping primitive crop varieties in existence. He asked the assembled plant breeders whether, when the value of these genetic resources was recognised, the peasant farmers would be rewarded for conserving vital genetic variation.

Field gene banks

Some important crop plants produce seed only rarely or produce seed that can only be kept for a few weeks or months in a seed bank. In such cases, one possibility is to maintain a **field gene bank**. This involves growing the plants year after year, generation after generation. The disadvantages of the system are obviously the space required and amount of work, and hence expense, involved. At least it means that adult specimens are available for experimental purposes. Species that have to be kept in field gene banks include cocoa, rubber, coconut, mango, cassava and yam.

Tissue culture

Tissue culture is now widely used in the horticultural industry. Its use in maintaining genetic diversity is relatively new. However, clones of cassava, sweet potato, potato and coffee can now be stored as test-tube plantlets for several years. The basic principles of tissue culture are outlined in Figure 30.4. The first step is to obtain a plant known to be free from pathogens. It is then cut up into smaller pieces and grown either on agar or in a liquid medium. The resulting plants can be potted up and brought to maturity.

As the usual use of tissue culture is to speed up the propagation of plants, it is somewhat ironic that the approach has been modified to allow the long-term storage of small volumes of plant tissue. Slow

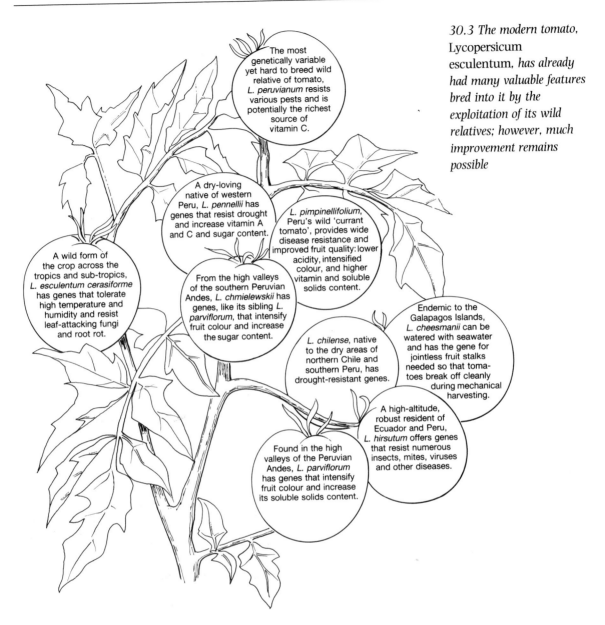

The most genetically variable yet hard to breed wild relative of tomato, *L. peruvianum* resists various pests and is potentially the richest source of vitamin C.

A dry-loving native of western Peru, *L. pennellii* has genes that resist drought and increase vitamin A and C and sugar content.

L. pimpinellifolium, Peru's wild 'currant tomato', provides wide disease resistance and improved fruit quality: lower acidity, intensified colour, and higher vitamin and soluble solids content.

A wild form of the crop across the tropics and sub-tropics, *L. esculentum cerasiforme* has genes that tolerate high temperature and humidity and resist leaf-attacking fungi and root rot.

From the high valleys of the southern Peruvian Andes, *L. chmielewskii* has genes, like its sibling *L. parviflorum*, that intensify fruit colour and increase the sugar content.

Endemic to the Galapagos Islands, *L. cheesmanii* can be watered with seawater and has the gene for jointless fruit stalks needed so that tomatoes break off cleanly during mechanical harvesting.

L. chilense, native to the dry areas of northern Chile and southern Peru, has drought-resistant genes.

A high-altitude, robust resident of Ecuador and Peru, *L. hirsutum* offers genes that resist numerous insects, mites, viruses and other diseases.

Found in the high valleys of the Peruvian Andes, *L. parviflorum* has genes that intensify fruit colour and increase its soluble solids content.

30.3 The modern tomato, Lycopersicum esculentum, *has already had many valuable features bred into it by the exploitation of its wild relatives; however, much improvement remains possible*

growth storage usually involves keeping the cultures at temperatures of 5–15°C (compared to the 23–25°C typical of tissue culture). Slow growth storage is also helped by inducing osmotic stress in the growing medium, supplying nutrients in suboptimal amounts, employing growth retardants and reducing the light intensity.

Research is also progressing on the possibility of **cryopreservation**. This would involve keeping tissues at temperatures of around -196°C, the boiling point of nitrogen. Animal sperm can be kept in this way for years, but it is more difficult to keep clumps of cells alive for long period of time.

Whatever the future of cryopreservation, it is clear that botanic gardens and gene banks have a vital role to play in the years ahead. It must always be remembered, however, that the preservation of whole ecosystems is the ideal solution, and not the maintenance of plants in seed or gene banks, or the keeping of animals in zoos.

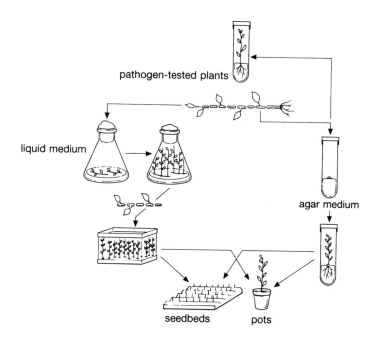

30.4 The fundamentals of plant tissue culture. Plants known to be free of pathogens are cut up and grown under appropriate conditions, either in a liquid medium or on agar. Once the resulting plantlets have rooted and grown sufficiently, they can be potted up

Further reading

Bramwell, D., Hamann, O., Heywood, V. and Synge, H. (1987) *Botanic Gardens and the World Conservation Strategy.* Academic Press.

Hepper, F.N. (ed.) (1989) *Plant Hunting for Kew.* Her Majesty's Stationery Office.

Plucknett, D.L., Smith, N.J.H., Williams, J.T. and Anishetty, N.M. (1987) *Gene Banks and the World's Food.* Princeton University Press.

Thought questions

1 Do you think botanic gardens should be paid for by governments or subject to market forces?

2 Why do you think most modern crops are so genetically uniform?

Things to do

Apple varieties.

1. Apple trees are grown by vegetative propagation. There are a great many different varieties but some are very rarely marketed. Carry out a survey of the apple varieties available in your local shops, markets, greengrocers and supermarkets.

2. Does your school have a conservation area? Why not establish an orchard of all the different apple varieties you can obtain? The trees should be formally labelled with permanent notices and the orchard layout mapped so that tree identity is not lost. Subsequent generations of students will be grateful to you and their appreciation of apple diversity will ensure the conservation of these trees!

31

Where There's Muck There's Money

In an average year over eighty million tonnes of waste is produced in the United Kingdom alone. It includes sewage, domestic refuse and a diversity of waste substances from industry and agriculture. This may be anything from carbohydrate-rich solutions, toxic organic compounds and heavy metals to strong acids and alkalis. The natural degradation of organic waste substances is carried out by microbial communities (decomposers) which use the substances as a source of energy or nutrients. However, in the absence of any microbe able to degrade them, many other waste compounds become persistent and highly toxic pollutants. This chapter is concerned with the biology of waste management.

What can be done with waste?

The waste produced by society requires **disposal**. Most attractive to the producer is the process of disposal which involves least trouble and expense. An obvious solution is to dump the waste in holes in the ground and cover it with soil: this is known as **landfill**. Alternatively, waste may be poured down drains or discharged untreated into a river or the sea. However, as people become increasingly concerned about the detrimental effects of waste on the environment, there is pressure for greater care to be taken. Also, government legislation in many developed countries requires waste to be disposed of in a defined and acceptable manner. Breaches of the law may result in fines being levied or other action being taken. The implementation of such legislation costs money, however, and although desirable, safe disposal may not be regarded as economically viable in the developing nations.

The nature of sewage

Sewage may be described as water-borne waste. It comprises both domestic waste water from sinks, baths and toilets, including human urine and faeces, and industrial waste water from factories, hospitals, power plants and many other sources.

Sewage contains a vast amount of water and a diversity of organic and inorganic matter such as detergents, pharmaceuticals, petroleum-based oil, heavy metals and pesticides. It also contains large numbers of microbes such as *Escherichia coli*, bacteria which are present in the faeces of human and other animals. Present too are viruses, protozoa and nematode and helminth parasitic worms. Many of the microbes are pathogenic (disease-causing).

It is important that sewage is treated before being discharged for several reasons. First, the large number of **suspended solids** in untreated sewage has the effect of increasing the turbidity of water bodies. This reduces the amount of light which can penetrate the water and so limits photosynthetic activity. Consequently, the amount of oxygen produced by bottom-rooted water plants and suspended phytoplankton is reduced. This limits the oxygen available to fish.

Second, the **organic matter** in sewage is a major pollutant. It provides a rich source of nutrients for microbes which multiply rapidly as they convert some of the organic compounds into microbial biomass. The majority of the compounds are oxidised by the microbes to carbon dioxide and water through respiration. This also requires much oxygen. The greater the number of microbes, the greater the demand for oxygen (see **biochemical**

oxygen demand below). Consequently, the larger the quantity of raw sewage which is discharged into water, the more likely it is that oxygen will be depleted and that aerobic organisms such as fish will die. Quite apart from its inherent unpleasantness near the discharge point, **untreated sewage** may also spread disease because of the pathogenic organisms it contains (see also Chapters 17 and 32).

Biochemical Oxygen Demand (BOD)

BOD is expressed as the amount of oxygen in milligrams taken up by one litre of a sample of effluent over a period of five days. For untreated sewage, this is typically around 200–300 milligrams per litre. BOD is used as a measure of the degradable organic material present in sewage; as they digest this material, aerobic microbes use up oxygen in the process of respiration.

Systems of sewage treatment are therefore designed to kill pathogenic bacteria and to degrade organic matter and other pollutants. They rely on the natural activities of both aerobic and anaerobic microbes, harnessing and controlling these activities so that they proceed at optimal rates.

The treatment of sewage

Every day in England and Wales alone, around fifteen million cubic metres of sewage are treated and subsequently released into watercourses. Sewage treatment processes vary in detail but all involve several distinct stages.

Preliminary treatment

Sewage flows from sewers into the treatment plant through a series of steel screening bars which remove large solids and debris such as wood, cans, plastic containers and condoms. The retained material is either incinerated or sent to landfill sites.

The sewage then flows slowly through a chamber to allow particles such as sand, grit, gravel and

31.1 A flow diagram of a modern sewage treatment works

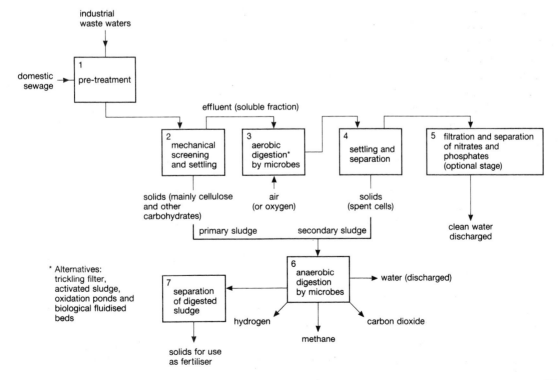

small pieces of glass and metal to settle out. These particles are either transported to landfill sites or used in road construction.

Primary treatment

Sewage is next directed into large circular **primary sedimentation tanks** where it remains for about two hours. During this time, the organic solids settle to form a **sludge** at the bottom of the tank. This settling process is aided by flocculating agents such as ferric chloride, which cause the solids to clump and to settle more readily. Once separated, the solid sewage sludge fraction and the soluble and suspended matter effluent undergo different treatments. The sludge is digested quite slowly by **anaerobic microbes** (see below) whilst the soluble and suspended matter effluent is subjected to rapid **aerobic digestion**.

There are several types of **primary aerobic treatment processes** currently in use. These are described below.

Trickling filter system
In a **trickling filter system**, the effluent from the primary sedimentation tanks is sprinkled from rotating distributors and trickles down through a filter bed. The moving sprinklers are easily seen in a treatment works. The large circular beds have

traditionally been filled with gravel or coke or, more recently, with plastic blocks. These inert materials provide a large surface area on which a diversity of microbes (mainly bacteria) settle to form a film. Although the microbes are predominantly aerobic, the inner layers of the film are probably anaerobic.

As the water filters through the bed, oxygen is absorbed from the air and the microbial film on the solids digests the organic compounds in the liquid. The major chemical reactions occurring on the filters result in the production of carbon dioxide, nitrates, sulphates and phosphates.

The effluent from trickling filter beds contains fine suspended matter (mainly microbial cells) called **humus sludge** which is washed off the filter material and allowed to settle. Humus sludge is removed at intervals for disposal or anaerobic digestion and the now clear effluent is discharged with or without further treatment (Figure 31.1 Stage 5).

A potential problem with trickling filter beds, particularly for people living downwind of a sewage plant, is that they produce unpleasant smells. Sulphate-reducing bacteria are present in the filters; they are obligate anaerobes and generate hydrogen sulphide ('bad egg' gas). However, if properly operated, little smell should be produced from filter beds.

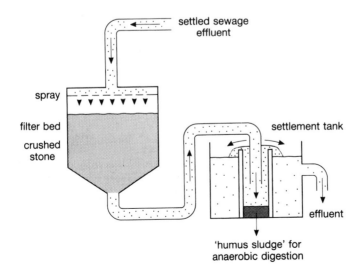

spray

filter bed
crushed stone

settled sewage effluent

settlement tank

effluent

'humus sludge' for anaerobic digestion

31.2 A trickling filter system

Besides their microbial flora of bacteria and fungi, trickling filter beds contain a large fauna. The detritivore nematodes, annelids and beetle and fly larvae form the start of a food chain later exploited by birds such as starlings and swallows.

With the introduction of lightweight plastic blocks instead of coke or gravel, filter beds can now be taller with consequent savings in space. These filters also allow better ventilation and a more even flow of liquid.

Activated sludge processes

Activated sludge systems are currently widely used for the primary treatment of sewage and have the advantage of being more compact than trickling filters. Both systems may be found running in parallel in one sewage works.

31.3 The activated sludge process

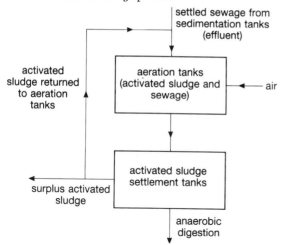

31.4 The biological fluidised bed system

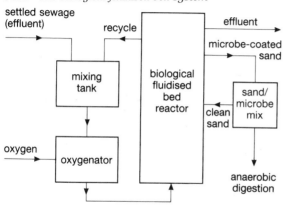

The effluent from primary sedimentation tanks is fed into large tanks and actively aerated. The microbial population is therefore kept in suspension rather than forming a film, but the overall microbiology and chemistry of the process are similar to that in trickling filter systems. Due to the turbulent conditions in the aeration tank fewer complex organisms are found than in filter beds, though nematode worms persist.

The **aeration tank** is followed by a **settlement tank** where the sludge settles leaving a clear supernatant liquid for disposal. Some of the sludge, which is rich in sewage-digesting microbes, is fed back into the aeration tanks while the remainder is removed for disposal or anaerobic digestion.

Oxidation ponds

This is a more primitive and lower-cost system that requires a large area of land and a warm, sunny climate. Consequently, although cheap to construct and easy to maintain, oxidation ponds are not appropriate for sewage treatment in the United Kingdom.

Untreated or settled sewage enters large, shallow basins (ponds), 1–2m deep, where aerobic microbes digest the organic matter. The oxygen required for this aerobic degradation comes from the photosynthetic activity of large algal populations (such as *Euglena* and *Chlamydomonas*) present in the ponds. The algae benefit from the carbon dioxide and minerals released from the sewage by the activity of the aerobic bacteria.

Biological fluidised beds

In **biological fluidised beds** the aerobic microbes grow on particles of fine sand which are kept in suspension in reactors (i.e. 'fluidised') by the rapid inflow of oxygenated settled sewage. The sand provides a vast surface area for the growth of microbes and consequently a very high rate of digestion per unit volume occurs. Clean effluent is discharged and, once separated from the sand, the waste sludge is removed for anaerobic digestion. Essentially this combines elements of the two processes above.

Fluidised beds are relatively new and, although highly efficient, it is unlikely that they will become widely used at least in the near future because of the initial capital cost.

The liquid effluent from the primary treatment process has a low BOD and is virtually free of suspended solids and so is often discharged directly. Sometimes, however, it undergoes further processing such as filtration to remove any fine suspended solids which may remain. Ideally, chemicals such as nitrates and phosphates should also be removed before discharge. These cause ecological problems in that they stimulate the growth of algal blooms. A recently developed technique involves passing the effluent through beds of sand containing immobilised denitrifying bacteria. These microbes denitrify the dissolved nitrates, stripping them of oxygen to release harmless nitrogen gas.

The solid material from the primary treatment (primary sludge) and usually that resulting from the aerobic digestion process (secondary sludge, mainly microbial biomass) is subjected to further microbial digestion, this time by anaerobic microbes.

Secondary anaerobic treatment

Sludge is fed into heated enclosed tanks from which air is excluded. A wide range of **anaerobic microbes** hydrolyse the organic matter and convert it to organic acids, alcohols, ketones, hydrogen and carbon dioxide. **Methanogenic bacteria** generate methane gas (CH_4). In many installations the methane produced is piped off to heat the anaerobic digestion tanks and is also used to generate the electricity required to power the rest of the sewage works.

During the slow anaerobic digestion of the sludge, about 90% of the organic matter is converted into gases and water. Only a small proportion of the substrate is converted into new biomass which then has to be disposed of. This is of great economic significance; in the United Kingdom the cost of sludge disposal is about £20–100 per tonne.

Anaerobic digestion also improves the odour of

the sludge and, through heat and acidity, reduces the concentration of pathogens present.

The final sludge is dried and then disposed of in the following ways:

- spread on agricultural lands as a fertiliser and soil conditioner
- dumped in landfill sites and mixed with rubbish
- dumped at sea (the most common option in Britain, which is to be discontinued by the end of this century)
- incinerated (the most expensive procedure).

Disposal of the sludge does, however, constitute an environmental problem because it often still contains organic matter and toxic heavy metals (see also Chapter 32).

Industrial wastes

Certain types of industrial waste waters, for example from the food and fermentation industries, are very rich in organic matter and are effectively 'strong sewage'. These may be treated on site in digestion facilities similar to a sewage treatment plant or else discharged into sewers. Various biological treatment systems are used to treat industrial effluent.

Many types of industrial waste, however, pose more difficult problems of disposal as they may be highly acidic or alkaline, or contain high concentrations of metals or organic compounds. Such wastes are toxic to the microbes in a sewage works and so require pre-treatment. This may involve simple chemical methods such as neutralisation of the wastes using a calculated amount of acid or alkali.

Heavy metals such as lead, copper, zinc and plutonium are usually removed at source, often by expensive chemical methods. Microbes cannot be used as the materials are highly toxic to these organisms as well as to humans.

Certain **toxic wastes**, for example phenols, can be 'biodegraded' (broken down) by microbes. However, for many compounds there are no microbes with the capacity to metabolise them;

some organic molecules, such as the polychlorinated biphenyls (PCBs) or others used in many pesticides and herbicides, are highly toxic to microbes and are serious pollutants.

Agricultural wastes

A consequence of the intensive rearing of livestock is the production of a vast quantity of waste that is not only very smelly but is also a formidable pollutant. In The Netherlands, for example, there is a growing mountain of pig and chicken manure. Of the 94 million tonnes produced annually, only 50 million tonnes of it can safely be absorbed by the land as fertiliser. As wet manure is spread on fields, acrid ammonia rises in clouds and proceeds to destroy the natural vegetation. The excess nitrogen weakens plant cell walls and results in shallow tree root systems since the roots have no need to penetrate the soil deeply for nutrients.

31.5 A pig slurry digester

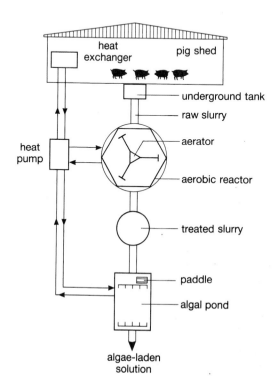

Another problem is the accumulation in ground water of nitrates and phosphates which are natural components of manure. This is due in part to the dumping of manure.

Heavy metals are used as additives in animal feed. For example, **cadmium** is added to make pigs retain water and put on weight quickly. This metal, and other feed additives such as **copper** and **zinc**, are excreted by the animals. When manure is spread on fields, the metals are highly polluting and tend to concentrate in the topsoil where they kill earthworms.

A process which is based on the same principle as oxidation ponds has recently been developed to treat pig manure (see Figure 31.5), although to date only a pilot plant has been built. The slurry is pumped into an aerobic reactor where bacteria digest the organic matter to produce heat, carbon dioxide and various nutrients. The heat is used to heat the pig house and the carbon dioxide is released into the air. The now odourless slurry is allowed to settle and then trickles into a system of open channels containing algae. As they photosynthesise, the algae metabolise the remaining nutrients. After about five days the remaining solution is almost pure water with suspended algal cells. The latter may be used to feed invertebrates and fish (see below).

31.6 The production of animal feed from sludge

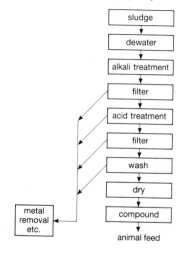

Feedstock	Microbial species involved	Products
Potato-processing waste	*Endomycopsis* and *Candida*	Single cell protein
Pulp-mill waste	*Paecilomyces*	Single cell protein (Pekilo protein)
High-carbohydrate food industry wastes, sewage sludge, agricultural wastes, municipal refuse	Bacteria degrading cellulose and organic acids, methanogens	Methane and sludge for fertiliser or animal feed
Sugar-cane waste	Yeast strains	Ethanol
Whey from milk processing	Yeast strains	Ethanol

From: Slater and Somerville (1979) Microbial Aspects of Waste Treatment, in Microbial Technology: Current State, Future Prospects, Symposium No. 29 of Society for General Microbiology.

Table 31.1 *Some examples of proposed and operating microbial effluent treatments coupled to product formation*

Putting waste to work

There is a growing awareness that waste can be a very valuable commodity if it is recycled rather than being dumped. **Recycling** may involve the transformation of waste into useful matter or the extraction from waste of useful materials.

Various industrial processes use industrial waste waters as a feedstock for microbial species (Table 31.1). For example, starch-rich effluent from the potato industry is used as a medium for the aerobic growth of two yeast strains. One strain, *Endomycopsis*, hydrolyses the starch to glucose on which the other, *Candida*, grows. The mass of microbial cells produced represents high-quality **single-cell protein** (SCP) which is used as animal feed.

Similarly, the algae resulting from the treatment of pig slurry are a valuable by-product. They may be used to feed rotifers, a type of zooplankton, which are used as feed on many fish farms.

Ethanol is another valuable product which is

31.7 *A 7m³ methane (biogas) production plant*

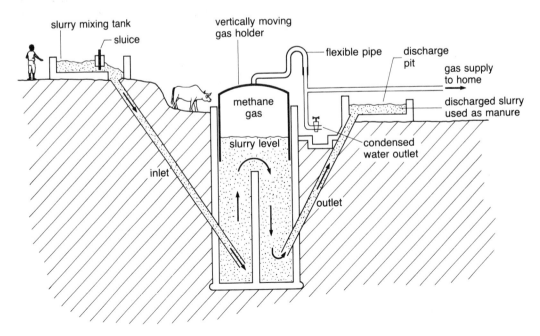

derived from industrial waste. It is produced when yeasts metabolise wastes from the dairy industry and from sugar cane. In Brazil, as early as the 1930s ethanol was being used in place of petrol as a fuel; Brazil currently obtains about 28% of its total energy from home-grown sugar cane.

As stated above, the standard anaerobic digestion of wastes produces a residue which may be used as a fertiliser or as animal feed. Obviously, the removal of any heavy metals remaining in the sludge and rigorous screening for the presence of pathogens would be important.

Another product generated from the anaerobic

31.8 The exploitation of landfill gas

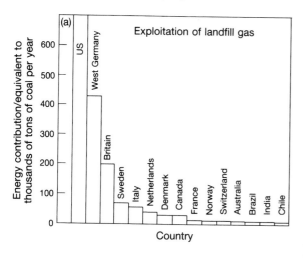

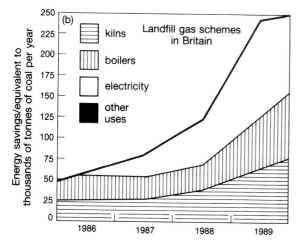

digestion of organic matter is methane – **biogas**. The raw materials used specifically for the production of biogas include agricultural and industrial wastes and also domestic refuse in landfill sites. Digesters range from small pits to large digesters which resemble industrial reactors.

Small-scale **biogas generation technology** was developed in China from 1958 onwards and today there are over seven million family-scale digesters there (Figure 31.7). Plant, human and animal wastes are fed into the digester and the methane produced may be used in lamps and stoves, as fuel for machinery and to generate electricity. A typical 10 000-litre domestic digester normally supplies enough gas to cook three meals and boil 15 litres of water daily for a family of five. However, problems with these digesters are that they are unpleasant to feed and, more important, they are functional only in the warmer months of the year.

In Europe, agricultural waste is the most usual substrate from which methane is derived. The generation of biogas in a sewage works, for example, is secondary to the disposal of waste; any cash or energy returns from the gas basically offset the cost of waste treatment. The United States leads the world in exploiting landfill gas though the use of this form of energy is growing in other countries. There are now six British schemes which variously use landfill gas to fire kilns, furnaces or boilers, to generate electricity or, once the gas is cleaned, to produce a higher-grade fuel. It is estimated that if waste were deposited in suitable sites, some 800 million cubic metres of biogas worth about £42 million could be extracted per year. Methane is produced naturally in landfill sites. Untapped, it is not only wasted but is also a possible hazard as the gas can travel long distances underground, enter buildings and cause explosions. It also adds to the enhancement of the 'greenhouse effect'.

Much research into the recycling of waste is still needed. However, it is clear that there is considerable potential for advancement in this area. As the world's population continues to increase, so too will the volume of waste produced and with it, the potential to make money from muck!

Further reading

Pearson, H. (1989) Muck an' Brass, the Sewage Story. *Biological Science Review*, March.

Richards, H. (1989) All Gas and Garbage. *New Scientist*, June.

Thought questions

1 In developing countries, why is sewage treatment sometimes difficult and the risk of faecal-spread epidemics often high?

2 What wastes do you produce from your home that you could recycle? How would you operate, at home, if all sewage disposal and refuse collection were to cease?

3 How could you convince someone, disgusted by rubbish and sewage, that through creative waste management on a large scale they could turn 'muck into money'?

Things to do

1. In the lab, build a tall compost column from a series of four or five plastic mineral water bottles. (These should have their bases cut off and be inverted and fitted into a stack, each unit being taped to the next.) They should have a collecting bottle at the bottom and holes punched through the sides to allow aerobic respiration. The top of the column may be left open. Any dead plant material from the lab and such biodegradable oddments as apple cores and orange peel may be added at the top. What happens as the organic matter rots? What are the agents of decomposition? When you have collected enough brown juice at the bottom, dilute it and recycle it as a nutrient solution for potted plants.

2. Design and build a small biogas generator. Warning: methane is an explosive gas so consider safety aspects carefully. Once you have sufficient methane to produce a flame, use the heat produced to accelerate the fermentation process. How could you scale up your model? How would you design a pig unit (see Chapter 3) so that the waste manure could be used in heating the houses? How could you utilise the post-fermentation slurry on the farm to increase food yields for the pigs?

32

Monitoring Water Pollution

'Pollution' is a word, often uttered with exaspera-tion or despair, to describe some less than lovely blot on what might otherwise have been a better environment. Nowhere is pollution more obvious than in water, which we would hope to see clear, clean and oxygenated. Too often it is found murky, anoxic and foul-smelling or even oily, poisoned and lifeless. Although distaste for pollution is splendid

sentiment, the solution to preventing it is essentially rooted in the application of science.

This chapter describes the nature of water pollution and water pollutants and covers some of the ways in which they may be monitored. It tells how our developing awareness of pollution prob-lems helps us to undo damage already caused.

Pollution and pollutants – some terms and concepts defined

The word 'pollution' is derived from the Latin word *prolutum*, which describes the act of 'washing forth' one's dirty water, and worse, into a river. At low human population densities and with adequate dilution the problem of what to do with human waste was easy. The trouble is that the size of our communities has changed and the nature of what we throw out has altered.

Pollution is defined as any human act of adding to the environment some substance which is harmful to other humans or to the environment itself. This definition sensibly rules out natural phenomena like volcanic eruptions that may harm the environment but have no human agency. It also identifies the cause of pollution as **pollutant substances**. It is usual to extend the definition of the pollutant, as a material substance, to include the **energy pollutants** such as damaging radiations, heat and sound.

The definition of a pollutant requires that harm is caused, so that two other features of pollutants are immediately perceived as important: the pollut-ant's **persistence** and its **dilution**. Many pollut-ants are only considered to be polluting because they are concentrated in one place at one time. In this case rapid **dispersal** may be effective in

diluting the pollutant and so reducing the harm. **Degradation**, or breaking down of the pollutant to form something less harmful, may equally well solve the problem. In the case of pollution by heat, acids and alkalis, dilution removes the harm as the heat or ions are dispersed. Cyanide, which is highly toxic, dissociates rapidly in sea-water when very dilute and so becomes quite harmless. Organic wastes such as faeces may degrade biologically under microbial action. However, many pollutants do not degrade and although diluted may become reconcentrated again in the bodies of organisms which are not able to excrete them. This is known as **bioaccumulation**. If passed up the food chain in ever greater concentrations, these pollutants produce their toxic effects in high-order carnivores: a phenomenon known as **bioamplification**.

Figure 32.1 illustrates a now classic story of pollution. Clear Lake in California is a large area of fresh water used for recreation. In 1949, 1954 and 1957 there were plagues of non-biting midges that irritated visitors. Consequently, in 1949 a chlorin-ated hydrocarbon DDD was first sprayed on the water at a dose of 1 kg per ha. The midges were killed, but when the treatment was repeated in 1954, western grebes died and by 1960 the original population of 1000 pairs of breeding birds had been reduced to 30 non-breeding adults. In 1957 it was discovered what the cause was. The

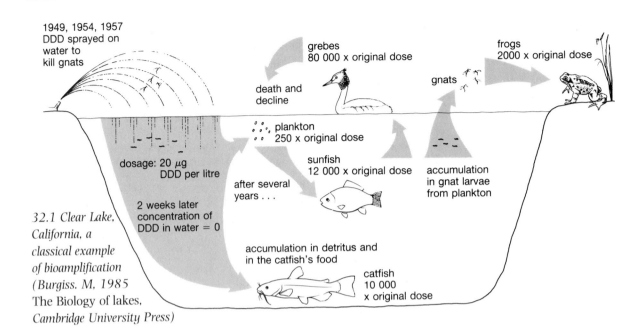

1949, 1954, 1957
DDD sprayed on
water to
kill gnats

grebes
80 000 x original dose

frogs
2000 x original dose

death and
decline

gnats

plankton
250 x original dose

dosage: 20 µg
DDD per litre

sunfish
12 000 x original dose

after several
years . . .

accumulation
in gnat larvae
from plankton

2 weeks later
concentration of
DDD in water = 0

accumulation in detritus and
in the catfish's food

catfish
10 000
x original dose

*32.1 Clear Lake,
California, a
classical example
of bioamplification
(Burgiss. M, 1985
The Biology of lakes,
Cambridge University Press)*

fish were heavily contaminated and the grebes had up to 1600 parts per million (ppm) of DDD in their body fat. It is events such as this, soon after the first use of a chlorinated hydrocarbon pesticide, that have taught us so much.

Ecotoxicology

The Clear Lake story introduces the subject of **ecotoxicology**, the study of environmental poison-ing. Once an environmental contaminant which is released by human actions causes any harm it is by definition a **pollutant**. At a particular level in the body it may have a poisonous effect, in which case it is said to be a **toxic contaminant**. At a higher level if it kills it is a **lethal contaminant**. Figure 32.2 shows the relationship between environmental levels of pollutant in the sea for several important marine pollutants, and the levels known to be lethal to a range of organisms. Note the logarithmic scale.

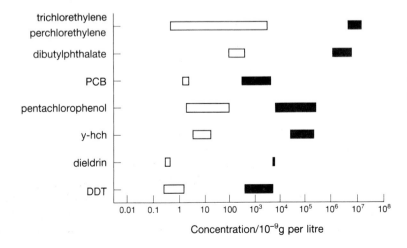

trichlorethylene
perchlorethylene

dibutylphthalate

PCB

pentachlorophenol

y-hch

dieldrin

DDT

0.01   0.1   1   10   100 10^3 10^4 10^5 10^6 10^7 10^8

Concentration/10^{-9}g per litre

*32.2. A comparison
between the known levels of
concentration of some toxic
organic chemicals in sea-
water (unshaded) with
levels known to produce
lethal effects in laboratory
animal experiments (shaded)
(from Clarke, R. B. (1989)
Marine Pollution, Oxford
Science Publications)*

How is the lethality of pollutants discovered in the environment? It is not a pleasant business, but it is sometimes necessary to do so. There are known levels of water pollutants at which half a population of organisms exposed to the pollutant for a particular time will die. The **lethal concentration 50%**, written as LC_{50}, is commonly expressed in parts per billion (parts per thousand million) of water. Thus for **mercury poisoning**, the rainbow trout *Salmo gairdneri* has an LC_{50} of 903 ppb (μg per dm^3) over 24 hours, which is reduced to 66 ppb over 48 hours and 42 ppb over 96 hours. Such data are only obtained by careful experiments on fish, many of which die as a result. Once done well the experiments do not need to be repeated unnecessarily, and data once obtained can sometimes define levels of pollutant that have been released into the environment. In this case, trout can clearly survive a short-term high exposure to mercury poisoning of up to 1 ppm in the water, but they must escape to levels 20 times more dilute if they are to have a chance of escape. Experimental conditions for LC tests are standardised. Trout will survive less well if the water is warmer or less oxygenated. Because pollutants are often well dispersed in water the 96-hour figure is more often quoted as the realistic level that the organisms will need to endure. Like us, many organisms do not detect some pollutants; indeed, some fish are seemingly attracted to them and swim up the concentration gradient.

An environmental pollutant may become a body contaminant present at levels out of all proportion to its external concentration. This is often what makes pollutants so toxic; molecules may be attracted to fats or bind with proteins. Water fleas, *Daphina magna*, have an LC_{50} of 1.5 ppb for the pollutant arochlor over a period of three weeks. When exposed to 1.1 parts per *billion* of the pollutant, a sub-lethal exposure in which they survive, they are found to have a contaminant level of 52.8 parts per *million* after four days – that is a 48 000-fold increase in concentration. Arochlor is a PCB, one of the most toxic pollutants. It is easy to see why water fleas that are so contaminated (bioaccumulation) are able to produce such a rise

in tissue levels in higher-order carnivores (bioamplification).

The most toxic and non-degradable pollutants have to end up somewhere. Given time they sediment and go into the rocks of the earth's crust. Pollutants tend to decline slowly with an **exponential decay**. The time taken for a quantity to disappear is called its **half-life**.

The principal water pollutants

There is an enormous variety of forms of water pollution. Classifying them is difficult, but perhaps the easiest approach is to classify the water pollutants according to their origins. Classification by origin focuses on their sources and ways of reducing their harmful influence.

Organic matter

Organic matter is the best known form of water pollution, be it farm slurry or untreated sewage. It causes the water to be turbid, so stopping light from reaching algae and bottom-weed. Photosynthesis is therefore depressed. Organic matter releases nutrients as a result of decay. Later this may cause algal blooms. Because of microbial breakdown, organic matter uses up oxygen in the water, creating a large **biochemical oxygen demand** (BOD) (see Chapter 31).

Nutrients

Nutrients such as **nitrates** and **phosphates** are released from organic matter; they also arise from inorganic fertiliser. Agrochemical fertilisers are rarely added directly to water, but some do leach from the soil as the soluble minerals are carried down into the water-table. Later when the crops have been harvested, the minerals are released from the soil into the ground water. Such nutrient enrichment is known as **eutrophication**.

Detergents

Detergents are a source of **phosphates**. They lose

their frothiness by microbial **biodegradation**, but unless arrested in the sludge of a sewage works the phosphates will pass on into watercourses and so out to sea. Phosphate pollution promotes algal growth at the expense of other plants in fresh water. Both in fresh water and at sea algae grow in large blooms, some forms of which may be highly toxic (see Chapter 31).

Pesticides

Pesticides, that is, insecticides, fungicides and herbicides, pass into water from agricultural land. The organo-mercurial fungicides are highly toxic to other forms of life and accumulate in the environment. The **chlorinated hydrocarbons** DDD, DDT, lindane, aldrin and dieldrin are all persistent and subject to ecoamplification. Some triazine herbicides, commonly used to kill weeds around buildings and on railway tracks, last a long time. When they enter rivers they may not only kill bottom-weed but may also harm crops if the river water is used for irrigation. The **chlorophenoxy acids** 2,4-D and 2,4,5-T are very rapidly biodegraded if there are bacteria in the water. Glyphosate ('Roundup') has a half-life of two months. **Organophosphorus**

insecticides are short-lived as they degrade rapidly in the soil, but as water pollutants they may seriously deplete populations of crustaceans such as water-fleas which would otherwise keep down the algae.

Industrial wastes

Industrial wastes include hot water, solid suspensions, organic wastes, heavy metals and organic chemicals.

Hot water is a pollutant because it raises the temperature of water, so increasing metabolic activity and microbial and algal growth; it also depresses dissolved oxygen levels. In hot water, therefore, fish have to pass more water over their gills to obtain enough oxygen, and so may take in more toxins if these have been produced by algae. In lowland waters, fish deaths occur in hot summers if there is mild eutrophication.

Suspended solids, of material such as china clay or mineral washings, form turbid conditions in rivers and estuaries. Later some of these will sediment out and may be contaminated with toxic substances like heavy metals. Sugar-beet factories, cheese-making factories and tanneries produce high-

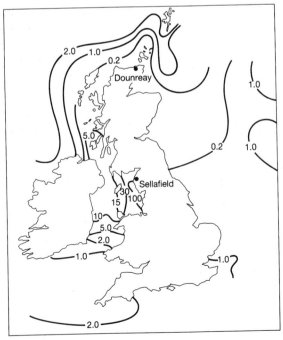

32.3 *The relative concentration of Caesium*[137] *(pCi per dm³) around the British Isles in 1973 revealed the pollutant's source as Sellafield (Windscale). Levels of this pollutant fall rapidly because of dispersion in coastal currents but only slowly through radioactive decay*

organic-matter wastes that raise BOD.

Heavy metals, in order of decreasing toxicity, are mercury, copper, cadmium, zinc, nickel and chromium. Several are important trace elements for living organisms, but all at high levels cause damage to enzyme systems. **Tributyl tin (TBT)** has been used as an anti-fouling paint for the bottoms of boats. Around boating marinas, as a result, there is often great damage to shellfish by tin poisoning.

Industrial organic chemicals include not only those released from factories but also those resulting from the breakdown of manufactured products. **Polychlorinated biphenyls (PCBs)** are used as insulators in transformers and capacitors and are also found in many plasticising substances, paints and varnishes. They are fat-soluble, completely non-degradable and are bio-amplified in aquatic food chains. PCBs cause sterility and death in mammals such as dolphins whose very survival is perhaps now threatened by these chemicals. Alternatives are urgently needed. **Oil pollution** comes from industrial spills, roads, tanker wreckages and collisions at sea. The problem is often local, although devastating to sea birds and fish, and harmful to recreation and tourism.

Radionuclides are generally a local pollution problem. Leaks from the nuclear power plant at Sellafield (formerly Windscale) have been sufficient to make the Irish Sea the most radioactive sea in the world (Figure 32.3). Caesium[137] has a half-life of 33 years.

Faecal contaminants arise from **sewage**, in which *Escherichia coli* is most abundant. Marine outfalls of raw sewage are still found in many coastal areas. For the minimal bathing water standard, European Community (EC) regulations set a maximum of 2000 coliforms per 100 cm^3 and a mean of less than 100 per 100 cm^3. Fortunately summer ultraviolet light, which kills bacteria, makes most beaches safer.

Assessment of environmental quality

Environmental scientists faced with making any assessment of environmental quality need to have a good understanding of the ecosystem they are assessing as well as a knowledge of the pollutants. Water-pollution monitoring focuses on everything from the gross picture that a body of water presents, through detailed assessments of specific water-quality tests, to a finer focusing on the impact of specific pollutants on specific organisms. There is often important fieldwork, and much laboratory work on collected samples. All assessments need to be viewed in relation to long-term trends; it may be months or years before a pattern emerges. In the United Kingdom, under the 1989 Water Act, the National Rivers Authority has been given statutory duties and responsibilities for all surface waters, rivers, estuaries, and the sea to a distance of three miles from the shore.

Chemical monitoring

BOD is one of the principal water-quality assessments regularly performed. It measures the amount of organic matter and microbial decomposition of that organic matter in the water, but expresses it in terms of the impact that this pollution has on a river. Sewage and slurry from farms place a demand on the river's supplies of oxygen. If the demand for oxygen for microbial decomposition is high then the river may not be able to support its fish. The BOD test is carried out by taking a litre sample and measuring the dissolved oxygen concentration (mg dm^{-3}). It is then incubated in the dark at 20°C for five days and the dissolved oxygen concentration measured again. The difference between the two figures is the BOD (mg per dm^{-3}). If the sample is highly polluted it is necessary to dilute it down with oxygenated water, and then multiply the result by the dilution factor. Some typical BOD figures are given below.

	BOD mg per dm^{-3}
Upland stream	1
Lowland stream	3
Large lowland river	5
Treated sewage	20
Crude sewage	300
Pig slurry	30 000
Silage liquor	60 000

It is clear that organic agricultural effluents are very dangerous to aquatic life.

Freshwater biologists are now much helped by the high-tech machinery in water-analysis laboratories. This has replaced long and tedious titrations. **Automatic analysers** can give a printout within minutes on the amounts of forty or more set substances. **Nitrate monitoring** is now very important because it has become clear that nitrates in groundwater are affecting water supplies (see Chapter 17). It is possible to test for nitrates with a nitrate meter, using colorimetric test strips. Typically nitrate levels are low (less than 10 ppm) in the summer months when plants assimilate them very rapidly. Leaching occurs principally during autumn and winter in lowland Britain. At that time nitrate levels may become very high (greater than 50 ppm) and exceed EC permitted drinking-water levels. Figure 32.4 shows this seasonal fluctuation and indicates the enormous value of long-term records in assessing trends. Strong growth of weed occurs in the spring in response to these nitrates and this causes some decrease in aquatic species diversity.

Biological monitoring

Water analysts are only able to take samples intermittently so the chemical analysis only shows what was there when the sample was taken. It is easy to miss the critical polluting event, especially if a deliberate polluter knows when you do the analysis! Organisms, however, are there all the time and may act as pollution watch-dogs.

Biological monitoring is an indirect analysis of water quality based on the species found in the water; by their variety, abundance, condition or content, the organisms that live in the water inform the biologist about long-term water quality.

In open water, measurement of the **algal population** can be used to assess eutrophication. Using a spectrophotometer, the fluorescence of chlorophyll *a* in a sample under a blue light may be correlated with the algal biomass. This assessment may be automated and even fitted to a boat to make assessments on a longitudinal river transect.

Microscopic counts of species in the algal community give a bio-assay of the quantitative and qualitative nature of the water nutrient levels and pH. Different species prefer different conditions. Looking at the balance between **algae** and **bottom-weed** in a river is a rapid means of assessing relative **nitrate** and **phosphate pollution**. The bottom-weed species (like *Potamogeton*) grow well in water with high nitrate and low phosphate concentrations. If phosphate levels increase the surfaces of the weed become increasingly encrusted with algae (such as *Cladophora*), and the weed may disappear altogether because of competition, leaving a thick blanket of the alga. Recent research at Durham

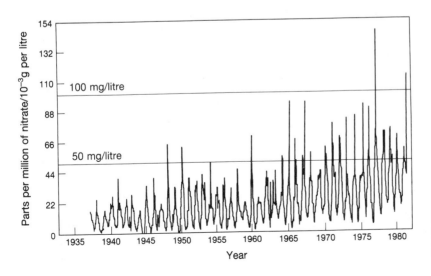

32. 4 Nitrate levels in the River Stour at Langham, Essex

University has established that algae, mosses and liverworts are very reliable indicators of the extent of **heavy metal pollution** in fresh water. There is a strong positive correlation between zinc concentrations in the plants and in the water, the plant bioaccumulation being one thousand times greater than the water concentration.

The use of certain **macro-invertebrates** (aquatic arthropods, annelids and molluscs) for bioassays is well known. The **Trent Biotic Index** was the first set of tables produced for assessing water quality based on the presence of species in particular groups. As a result of pond-netting and some careful examination, a stretch of water may be indexed to a quality scale ranging from 1 to 10. The following animals are listed in rough order of the decreasing index of water quality – stoneflies (Plecoptera), mayflies (Ephemeroptera), caddis flies (Trichoptera), water louse (*Gammarus*) the water slater (*Asellus*), sludge worms (*Tubificidiae*), midge larvae (*Chironomidae*) and the rat-tailed maggot (*Eristalis*). This series is specific to general levels of pollution, and is not an assay of one pollutant.

British rivers are now fully surveyed every five years. In the 1990 river survey the **RIVPAC System** (River Invertebrate Prediction Classification System) was used. This enables a comparison to be made between what is actually found and the species that would be expected for an unpolluted stretch of river typical of that locality. Analysis of the results gives an indication of the intensity and duration of the pollution. **Acid rain**, causing river acidity to fall to pH 4.5, produces a dramatic

32.5 A range of macro-invertebrates from fresh to organically polluted waters (from Hynes, H.B.N. (1971) The Biology of Polluted Waters, Liverpool University Press)

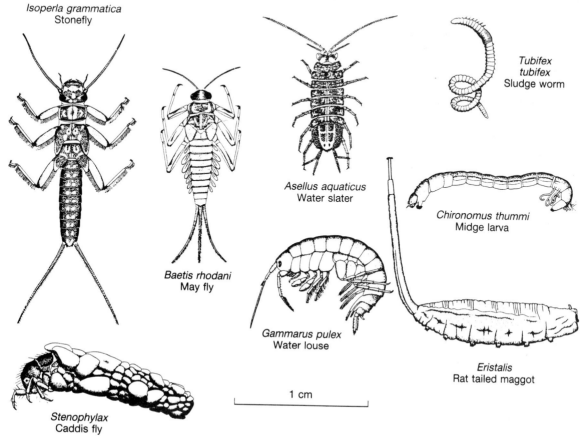

Isoperla grammatica
Stonefly

Baetis rhodani
May fly

Asellus aquaticus
Water slater

Gammarus pulex
Water louse

Stenophylax
Caddis fly

Tubifex tubifex
Sludge worm

Chironomus thummi
Midge larva

Eristalis
Rat tailed maggot

1 cm

change in the abundance and variety of invertebrates and fish (see also Chapter 26).

North West Water now employ 'moss bags' to monitor intermittent discharges from industrial outfalls. A significantly greater concentration of a heavy metal pollutant in a downstream moss bag compared with one upstream provides hard evidence that pollutants have been released. Faced with a fish kill from an unknown source, Phil Harding of North West Water took numerous samples of the aquatic moss *Rhynchstegium riparioides*. This enabled him to discover a crack in a pipe carrying lead-rich effluent from a factory.

Organisms experiencing pollution go through a sequence of changes when exposed to pollutants either for increasing lengths of time or at increasing concentrations. Initially they may be able to compensate for the pollutant, but gradually they experience physiological breakdown or suffer from diseases before they die. Keeping an eye open for these effects is an important part of biological monitoring. Many pollution incidents have first been observed by local naturalists, bird-watchers and people out fishing.

A tale of two rivers – the Mersey and the Thames Estuaries

In 1984 the **Royal Commission on Environmental Pollution** reported:

'of the estuarine black spots, the Mersey stands out as the worst example. The estuary currently receives untreated domestic sewage, industrial effluent and surface run-off from the Liverpool and Wirral conurbations. With a population of 1.5 million this constitutes the largest urban area in the U.K. with untreated discharges. There are 50 outfalls in the lower part of the estuary alone, and substantial loads from river discharges upstream as well as from the Manchester Ship Canal and the River Weaver. The result is that the banks of the estuary are polluted with offensive solids and the water suffers a serious oxygen deficiency, which can cause smell, and, together with persistent and toxic industrial effluents, markedly restricts the ability of the estuary to support life.'

It is not surprising that such an indictment led to some improvements. The Mersey drains the heart of the industrial Midlands, which have produced pollutant waste since the industrial revolution. Liverpool has inherited not only a backlog of pollutants but also some outdated attitudes towards the sea as a place where waste can be dumped. Implementation of the 'polluter pays principle', in the present climate of public opinion about pollution, should help to redeem a past history of public under-funding and industrial vandalism.

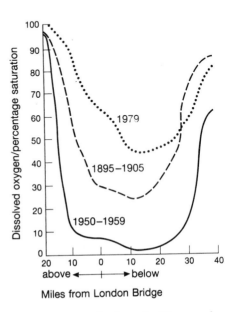

32.6 Dissolved oxygen levels in the Thames, above and below Tower Bridge

The local water company and the National Rivers Authority have made much progress since 1984, even though the estuary is still receiving about 100 million gallons of untreated sewage and trade effluent. There has been a welcome fall in the estuary water BOD from 45 to 5 mg per dm^3 and a gratifying rise in dissolved oxygen levels. However, there is still much amiss, for there has been a long and accepted tradition in the local industries of discharging toxic pollutants either directly into the estuary or through industrial discharges into the main sewerage system. Both forms of disposal are governed by guidelines on pollutant concentrations and rates of emission, but there have been bad breaches of both.

In 1979 bird-watchers noticed large numbers of waders, gulls and wildfowl sick and dying in the estuary from a sudden incident of what turned out to be lead poisoning. The discharge was traced to an outfall pipe from a chemical works producing **tetra-ethyl lead** (anti-knocking agent in leaded petrol). In 1984, 7×10^5 m^3 per day were still being discharged from this factory outfall into the Manchester Ship Canal. Since then, one of the local chemical works (Shell UK) has invested, with the local water company, in improvements to the sewage works. Much toxic waste from the chemical industries is now channelled through the sewage works, but this still causes problems. Efficient biodegradation at microbial level may not be possible due to the high levels of heavy metal toxins coming in. At the end, the whole treatment process is still dependent on sludge-dumping into the sea (see also Chapter 31).

In 1985 the local rate of dumping of **mercury**, the most toxic heavy metal, was as follows:

32.7 Recording fresh water invertebrates is a part of pollution monitoring.

	Mercury kg per day
Treated and untreated sewage into estuary	0.2–0.5
Mersey River discharge into estuary	0.5
Sewage sludge disposal in bay	1.1
Industrial discharge into estuary	3.8
Dredgings disposal in bay	6.6

Analysis of dredgings indicates that the mercury pollution problem used to be worse; nevertheless the Marine Pollution Monitoring Management Group described this as 'arguably the most important pollution problem in the Irish Sea'. The Liverpool Bay fish and mussels are at the toxicity threshold for mercury, having a content just below 0.3 ppm. It would be foolish to eat them very often, if at all. Fish exposed to mercury develop sores on their skin and their gills degenerate. These symptoms, together with fin rot, tumours and ulcerated lesions, are more prevalent in the fish of this region of the Irish Sea than elsewhere around Britain. The United Kingdom is still dumping sewage sludge into the North Sea, despite much protest, and intends to continue the practice well into the future also on the west coast from Liverpool Bay. Coping with sewage sludge is a huge problem and is not yet sustainably managed.

The extent to which British rivers have been cleaned up in recent years is often not appreciated. Forty years ago the **River Thames** was foul-smelling and had little life in it. Strenuous efforts were made to curtail sewage and increase dissolved oxygen levels. Slowly the dissolved oxygen levels have been raised from 10% saturation to 39%. This has been just enough to make it possible for marine-freshwater migrants such as salmon (*Salmo salar*) to re-enter the river for the first time since 1820 (see Figure 32.6).

Thames Water have a purpose-built laboratory launch that is used for field analyses and the investigation of pollution incidents. In order to cope with the very varied aquatic environments, many different investigative techniques are employed, including sampling for invertebrates with hand nets, trawling with a beam trawl, sediment grabbing, inter-tidal surveying for animals living on the river-bed, and collection of fish from specially devised screens that cover the inlets of the cooling inflows at power-stations. In the Thames valley the numbers of mute swans is increasing again as a result of the ban on lead fishing weights. On the mud of the Thames Estuary large numbers of wading birds have returned. It is not all bad news.

Further reading

Clark, R.B. (1989) *Marine Pollution*. Oxford Science Publications.
Freedman, B. (1989) *Environmental Ecology*. Academic Press.
Hellawell, J.M. (1986) *Biological Indicators of Fresh Water Pollution and Environment Management*. Elsevier.

Thought questions

1 Distinguish between the following pairs:

pollution and pollutants
pollutants and contaminants
Sewage and sewerage
µg per dm^3 and micrograms per litre
2000 ppb and 2 ppm

2 Birds of prey that eat fish excrete bioaccumulated mercury by incorporating it into their feathers. Up to half the body mercury may be in the feather at any one time. Feathers are moulted regularly and the mercury is therefore effectively excreted. Feathers from sea eagles in a Swedish museum, collected before 1940 from the Baltic Sea, had a mean of 6.6 ppm mercury. By 1965 the mercury levels in sea eagle feathers had risen to 50 ppm and the birds began to die out. How would you set about investigating whether mercury was to blame for their local extinction?

3 Sewage may be dumped at sea, buried in landfill sites, incinerated or used as a fertiliser. None of these is without problems. Evaluate the choices and produce another solution for the disposal of sludge.

Things to do

Long-term studies of streams and rivers are very
valuable. Is there a stream near your home, school or
college that could be monitored? It is essential to map
the stream and then establish regular monitoring points.
These should be at bridges or places where it is easy to
gain access from the land. Using a plastic bottle on a
string, regular sampling from a bridge may be conducted. In the field, flow rates, water levels, dissolved
oxygen and temperature should be measured immediately, as should pH and nitrate levels with test strips or
meters. Back in the lab, sediment load and BOD can be
assessed later. Coupled with invertebrate 'bio-assays' a
check can be kept on the health of the water. National
Rivers Authority laboratories may be approached for
their own local data and they may even be interested in
yours if it is of quality. If you suspect that there is
unwarranted pollution the National Rivers Authority
may be able to run an analysis of your collected
samples.

Biology Topic Index

(How the chapters on applied biology topics relate to some classical areas of biological science)

Topic	Food & Food Production								Genes, Bugs & Cultures								Human Health & Hygiene								Our Environment							
	1	2	3	4	5	6	7	8	9	10	11	12	13	14	15	16	17	18	19	20	21	22	23	24	25	26	27	28	29	30	31	32
Artificial selection	•	•	•	•											•															•		
Bacteria		•						•	•	•	•	•			•		•									•					•	•
Behaviour			•	•		•	•											•	•										•			
Biochemistry		•	•	•				•	•					•	•				•	•			•									
Blood																						•	•		•							
Breathing					•									•	•	•						•										
Cells									•							•						•										
Chromosomes																	•								•	•	•	•	•	•		
Conservation																	•									•	•	•				
Cycles				•		•			•	•									•		•											
Diet				•	•							•								•			•									
Digestion							•						•							•												
Disease						•										•	•				•	•	•									
DNA and RNA									•				•	•		•				•										•	•	
Ecology	•	•				•											•								•	•	•	•			•	•
Ecological efficiency	•		•																													
Energy flow	•		•																								•				•	•
Environment	•	•	•			•											•								•	•	•	•			•	•
Enzymes								•	•	•	•	•		•	•					•									•	•		
Evolution	•		•																•		•											•
Excretion									•										•		•										•	
Fungi		•						•	•	•																						
Flowering plants	•	•					•							•	•											•	•		•			
Genes		•							•				•	•		•						•	•					•				
Genetics		•	•	•									•		•	•						•	•									
Growth	•		•	•		•			•									•	•		•				•	•						
Heart																			•													
Homeostasis				•																												
Hormones in animals			•	•														•														
Hormones in plants		•																			•											
Immunity													•								•		•									
Insects		•													•							•		•								
Mutation		•													•									•								
Natural selection		•																•	•													
Nervous system																	•	•		•												
Nutrition	•		•	•						•	•																					
Parasitism		•				•																										
Photosynthesis	•													•	•		•								•	•	•			•	•	
Pollution			•				•																		•	•				•	•	
Populations		•					•																					•				
Production	•	•	•	•			•				•			•	•																	
Respiration	•										•	•			•					•									•	•	•	
Species		•	•				•				•	•						•					•									
Tissues				•										•	•	•			•				•									
Transport																•					•											
Viruses		•										•				•	•									•		•			•	•
Water					•											•																

The best information on careers with biology

Students of biology would be well advised to study the Guide for School Leavers, produced in the Institute of Biology. It is entitled *Careers with Biology* and is regularly updated. Besides much useful information and an extensive bibliography on biological professions, it contains over one hundred addresses to which you may write for further career information and guidance. Copies of *Careers with Biology* may be obtained by writing directly to the Institute of Biology, 20 Queensberry Place, London SW7 2DZ. The Institute of Biology is the main professional body to which Biologists belong.

Biology Career Index

(How the applied biology chapters in this book relate to some of the careers which may follow an initial training in biology)

	Food & Food Production								Genes, Bugs & Cultures								Human Health & Hygiene								Our Environment							
	1	2	3	4	5	6	7	8	9	10	11	12	13	14	15	16	17	18	19	20	21	22	23	24	25	26	27	28	29	30	31	32
Agriculture	•	•	•	•						•	•			•															•		•	•
Animal ecology		•	•			•																						•		•		
Animal husbandry			•	•	•							•				•												•	•			
Apiculture							•																									
Brewing									•	•		•																				
Biotechnology		•						•	•	•	•	•	•	•		•	•						•								•	•
Child care																		•	•	•												
Conservation		•				•								•			•								•	•	•	•	•	•	•	•
Crop science	•	•												•													•			•		
Cytogenetics													•		•	•								•								
Dietetics			•					•			•	•	•				•	•		•				•								
Dentistry																•		•														
Dairy technology				•	•						•	•																				
Entomology		•					•																									
Environmental health								•			•	•				•	•									•						•
Epidemiology								•								•	•	•			•	•										
Farming	•	•	•	•	•							•		•														•	•		•	•
Fisheries						•														•											•	•
Food technology			•	•		•		•	•	•	•	•		•	•					•											•	
Forensic science														•		•																•
Forestry																									•	•	•					
Freshwater biology																	•														•	•
Genetic counselling													•					•						•								
Genetic engineering									•					•	•									•								
Haematology												•				•							•									
Health education								•			•					•	•	•		•	•	•	•	•								
Horticulture		•				•			•				•	•																•		
Immunology												•				•	•	•			•		•									
Industrial microbiology								•		•	•	•		•			•														•	•
Medical research									•					•	•	•	•	•		•	•	•	•								
Medicine												•				•	•	•		•	•	•	•								
Microbiology								•		•	•	•				•	•			•											•	•
Marine biology						•																										•
Nursing																	•	•			•	•	•									
Nutrition			•					•			•							•		•												
Pathology		•	•		•			•			•	•				•	•				•	•									
Pest control		•												•																		
Plant breeding	•	•							•					•													•			•		
Pharmacy												•						•			•	•	•									
Physiotherapy																		•						•								
Psychiatry																		•	•	•												
Psychiatric social work																			•													
Psychology																		•	•	•												
Public health								•			•	•					•	•		•		•	•		•		•				•	•
Radiology																		•				•										
Reproductive physiology				•	•		•															•							•			
Serology													•	•		•							•									
Social work																	•	•														
Surgery																		•					•									
Tissue culture									•			•		•	•	•							•							•		
Veterinary medicine			•	•	•							•	•			•							•						•			
Veterinary nursing			•	•	•																								•			
Waste management		•											•				•									•					•	•

247

Index

abscisic acid 3
acid rain 188 - 96, 241
adrenalin 27
afforestation 202
agrobacterium 104
AIDS 153 - 9
allergy 92
altruism 48
aluminium 129, 193
Alzheimer's disease 129, 193
amino acids 146
    essential 146
amniocentesis 95, 180
animal production 18 - 24
anorexia 136, 151
antibiotics 177
antibodies 30, 116, 117
antigens 116
aseptic conditions 110
atherosclerosis 149

B-cells 117
backcrossing 4
bacteria
    in cheese 83
    in food 56
    in milk 31
    in yoghurt 80
baking 93
beer 70 - 74
bees 47 - 53
bioaccumulation 235
bioamplification 235
biological control 15
biomass 5, 43, 201, 203
biosensors 90
biotechnology 29, 31, 105
birds 98, 186, 193, 293
blood
    clotting 90
    groups 116, 167, 169
    transfusion 169
BOD 227, 230, 237, 239

body composition 145
botanic garden 220
Bowlby, John 139
brassicas 101, 106
breeding 1
    animal 19, 22, 215
    plant 3, 4, 5, 13, 100, 101
bulimia 151
bumblebees 50

C3 plants 201
C4 plants 201
callus 102, 110, 111
cancer 124, 130, 160
carbon dioxide 189, 199
carcinogens 161
carrying capacity 209
case studies 135
catalysis 88
cell culture (see also tissue culture)
    67, 108, 109, 113
cheese 81
cheese making 82
chemotherapy 163
child abuse 142
children 138 - 43
chlorination 128
cholera 127
cholesterol 147
chorionic villus sampling 95, 180
chromosomal aberration 46
cloning 102, 103, 123
co-evolution 26
community 9
comunication in bees 49
conservation 215, 221
contaminants 236
conversion efficiency 23
cooking 59, 147
cows 25 - 32
crop rotation 11
curare 108
cystic fibrosis 176

desertification 207
diabetes 66, 170, 177
diagnosis 133
diet 144
disease
    of people 127, 133, 136, 176
    of plants 10, 126
disease resistance 13
diversity 185, 216
DNA 63, 64, 94
    fingerprinting 94, 96
    hybridisation 105
    recombinant 29, 67, 165
domestication 1, 18, 25
dormancy 221
drought 206
drug trials 137
drugs 107, 108, 113

ecological efficiency 19
ecology 205
economic production 19
ecosystem 205
education 217
electrophoresis
endangered species 214, 215
endonucleases 94
enzymes 87 - 93, 55, 87, 88
    replacement therapy 91
    specificity 87
essential fatty acids 148
ethics 23, 173
eutrophication 237

fats 22,79, 147, 150
fatty acids 147, 148
    essential 148
feedback 28
fermentation 56, 76, 204
fertility 19
fetoscopy 95
fish 39, 193, 244
fisheries 39

food policy 146
food webs 40
forensic plants 101, 106
fossil fuels 7, 8, 198
Freud, S. 142
fungi 9, 55, 83
fungicide 15

gender issues 141
gene 32, 99, 177
    bank 220, 222 - 3
    marker 178
    therapy 68, 179
    transfer 32, 104
general practice 33, 133
genetic
    disease 176
    engineering 63, 67, 105
    fingerprinting 94, 96, 97, 98
    probe 65
    screening 179
genotype 99
germ theory 128
glucose 50
greenhouse effect 199
growth 21, 23, 111
    hormone 23
    regulators 110

Harlow's monkeys 138
harvesting 5
HCG 123
health 133, 144, 152
heart 173
    disease 149
    transplant 173
heavy metal 46, 130, 230, 237,
    239, 243
herbicide 14, 130
heredity 162, 176
herring 38 - 45
heterozygous advantage 180
HIV 153 - 9
honey 50
hormones 23, 27, 135
human genome 68
hunting 45
husbandry 4, 11, 36
hybridisation 1

IAA 14, 102
immobilisation 89, 112
immune system 115, 155

immunisation 120, 121, 158
immunity 115, 116, 167
immunological memory 119
immunotherapy 165
inbreeding 216
insecticide 14, 238
IUCN 221

Kew Botanic Garden 221
kidney 166, 171, 174
    transplant 166, 171

lactation 20, 27
lactic acid 23
lactose 26, 30
LC$_{50}$ 237
leukaemia 169
lichen 193
liver transplant 172
lymphocytes (see also T-cells) 117,
    164
lysosomes 55

malnutrition 149
mammary gland 27
marker genes 105
    molecules 124
mastitis 31, 34
medicine 133, 137
    preventative 34
methaemoglobinaemia 130
methane 200, 203, 204, 232, 233
migration 41
milk 25 - 32
monitoring 240
monoclonal antibodies 115, 122,
    165, 168
monoculture 9, 185
mothering 138
mutation 46, 94, 160
    rate 155

nets 39, 45
niche 212
nitrates 60, 130, 237, 240
nitrogen fixation 106
    oxides of 190
nutrients 144

obesity 150
oestrous cycle 20
outbreeding 216
overfishing 43, 44

overgrazing 209
oxytocin 27
ozone 200

palatability 54
panda, giant 218
parasites 19
Parkinson's disease 170
parthenogenesis 48
Pasteur, L. 70
pasteurisation 57, 79
pathogens 9, 10, 20, 31, 127, 133,
    136, 176
PCB 46
penicillin 81
pest management 17
pesticides 14, 105, 130, 237 - 8
    persistence 15
    resistance 15
    toxicity 15
pests 10
phagocytres 115
pharmaceuticals 107
phenotype 99
pheromones 16, 48, 106
phosphates 237, 240
photosynthesis 6, 197
physiotherapy 177
pickling 61
pigs 18 - 24, 231
placebo 157
plant breeding 3, 100
    production 208
    products 113
plasmid 64, 104
play 140
poliomyelitis 127
pollen 50, 182
pollination 52, 53
pollutants 190 - 1, 192, 235
pollution 22, 46, 188 - 96, 235
polygenic inheritance 26, 176
polyploids 1
polyunsaturated fat 106, 148, 150
population 41, 212
    dynamics 42
potato 222
pregnancy 20
preservation 56
probes 65
production
    by animals 19, 210
    economic 6, 19

intensive 24
    primary 5, 6, 197, 201, 203
prolificacy 19
proteins 3, 20, 54, 79, 80, 83, 91, 146
proteolytic enzymes 91

quinine 108, 113

radiation 61, 162, 167
radiocarbon dating 182
radiotherapy 163
rainforest 187
recombinant DNA 67, 100, 121, 165
recycling 184, 232
reforestation 202
regeneration 202
    of woodland 185
rejection, tissue 124, 167
rennet 83
research 19, 34, 36, 218
resistance 15
restriction enzymes 63, 104
    endonucleases 94, 178
retrovirus 153
reverse transcriptase 65, 105, 153
rivers 242
RNA
    messenger 63, 153
    satellite 67

salt 60
seed protein 3, 105
    bank 186, 221
selection, artificial 4, 25, 101

sewage 226, 227, 239
sex hormones 27
skin, grafting 169
slurry 231
smoking 161
socialisation 140
soil 207
specificity, of enzymes 87
starch 54
sterilisation 57
stomata 200
straw 7, 8
substrate 87
sulphur dioxide 189
surgery 170 - 8, 162, 171
survivorship 42
symptoms 133

T-cells (lymphocytes) 117, 118, 119, 168
    helper cells 153
tanning 92
thermoregulation 22
tissue culture (*see also* cell culture) 101, 223, 225
tomato 224
totipotency 109
toxic wastes 46, 230
toxicity 237
toxin 56, 236
transformation 64, 105, 109, 114
transgenic animals 31, 68
transplantation 166 - 73

transplants 169, 173, 174
trial, double blind 137, 157
tumour 160
typhoid 127

vaccines 120, 121, 158
vacuum packing 59
vegetarianism 145
vegetation 207, 208
veterinary medicine 33 - 7
    nursing 37
    surgeon 33

virus 10, 20
vitamins 54, 80

waste 226
water 125, 145
weeds 10
wetlands 203
wheat 1, 105
wine 70, 74 - 7
woodland 182
WWF 219

X-rays 134

yeast 70
yield, crop 5
    maximum sustainable 44
yoghurt 27, 78

zidovudine 156
zoos 214